HUMAN RESOURCES 97/98

Seventh Edition

Editor

Dr. Fred H. Maidment
Park College

Dr. Fred Maidment is associate professor and department chair of the Department of Business Education at Park College. He received his bachelor's degree from New York University in 1970 and his master's degree from Bernard M. Baruch College of the City University of New York. In 1983 he received his doctorate from the University of South Carolina. His research interests include training and development in industry. He resides in Kansas City, Missouri, with his wife and children.

A Library of Information from the Public Press
Dushkin/McGraw-Hill
Sluice Dock, Guilford, Connecticut 06437

Visit us on the Internet—http://www.dushkin.com

The Annual Editions Series

ANNUAL EDITIONS is a series of over 65 volumes designed to provide the reader with convenient, low-cost access to a wide range of current, carefully selected articles from some of the most important magazines, newspapers, and journals published today. ANNUAL EDITIONS are updated on an annual basis through a continuous monitoring of over 300 periodical sources. All ANNUAL EDITIONS have a number of features that are designed to make them particularly useful, including topic guides, annotated tables of contents, unit overviews, and indexes. For the teacher using ANNUAL EDITIONS in the classroom, an Instructor's Resource Guide with test questions is available for each volume.

VOLUMES AVAILABLE

Abnormal Psychology
Adolescent Psychology
Africa
Aging
American Foreign Policy
American Government
American History, Pre-Civil War
American History, Post-Civil War
American Public Policy
Anthropology
Archaeology
Biopsychology
Business Ethics
Child Growth and Development
China
Comparative Politics
Computers in Education
Computers in Society
Criminal Justice
Criminology
Developing World
Deviant Behavior
Drugs, Society, and Behavior
Dying, Death, and Bereavement

Early Childhood Education
Economics
Educating Exceptional Children
Education
Educational Psychology
Environment
Geography
Global Issues
Health
Human Development
Human Resources
Human Sexuality
India and South Asia
International Business
Japan and the Pacific Rim
Latin America
Life Management
Macroeconomics
Management
Marketing
Marriage and Family
Mass Media
Microeconomics

Middle East and the
  Islamic World
Multicultural Education
Nutrition
Personal Growth and Behavior
Physical Anthropology
Psychology
Public Administration
Race and Ethnic Relations
Russia, the Eurasian Republics,
  and Central/Eastern Europe
Social Problems
Social Psychology
Sociology
State and Local Government
Urban Society
Western Civilization,
  Pre-Reformation
Western Civilization,
  Post-Reformation
Western Europe
World History, Pre-Modern
World History, Modern
World Politics

Cataloging in Publication Data
Main entry under title: Annual Editions: Human Resources. 1997/98.
    1. Manpower policy—Periodicals. 2. Human capital—Periodicals. I. Maidment, Fred, *comp.* II. Title: Human Resources.
ISBN 0–697–37291–X   331.11   91–641950

© 1997 by Dushkin/McGraw-Hill, Guilford, CT 06437, A Division of The McGraw-Hill Companies.

Copyright law prohibits the reproduction, storage, or transmission in any form by any means of any portion of this publication without the express written permission of Dushkin/McGraw-Hill, and of the copyright holder (if different) of the part of the publication to be reproduced. The Guidelines for Classroom Copying endorsed by Congress explicitly state that unauthorized copying may not be used to create, to replace, or to substitute for anthologies, compilations, or collective works.

Annual Editions® is a Registered Trademark of Dushkin/McGraw-Hill,
A Division of The McGraw-Hill Companies.

Seventh Edition

Cover image © 1996 PhotoDisc, Inc.

Printed in the United States of America   Printed on Recycled Paper

Editors/Advisory Board

Members of the Advisory Board are instrumental in the final selection of articles for each edition of ANNUAL EDITIONS. Their review of articles for content, level, currentness, and appropriateness provides critical direction to the editor and staff. We think that you will find their careful consideration well reflected in this volume.

EDITOR

Fred H. Maidment
Park College

ADVISORY BOARD

Lawrence S. Audler
University of New Orleans

Larry Brandt
Nova Southeastern University

John L. Daly
University of South Florida

Nur Gryskiewicz
University of North Carolina

Raymond L. Hilgert
Washington University

Marianne J. Koch
University of Oregon

Faten Moussa
State University of New York at Plattsburgh

Barbara C. Pendleton
Mars Hill College

Margaret A. Rechter
University of Pittsburgh

Joseph F. Salamone
State University of New York at Buffalo

Sheldon C. Snow
Pepperdine University

Rieann Spence-Gale
Northern Virginia Community College

Harold Strauss
University of Miami

Wesley H. Toler
University of Maryland University College

Albert A. Vicere
Pennsylvania State University

Richard J. Wagner
University of Wisconsin Whitewater

Ann C. Wendt
Wright State University

Staff

Ian A. Nielsen, Publisher

EDITORIAL STAFF

Roberta Monaco, Developmental Editor
Addie Raucci, Administrative Editor
Cheryl Greenleaf, Permissions Editor
Deanna Herrschaft, Permissions Assistant
Diane Barker, Proofreader
Lisa Holmes-Doebrick, Program Coordinator
Joseph Offredi, Photo Coordinator

PRODUCTION STAFF

Brenda S. Filley, Production Manager
Charles Vitelli, Designer
Shawn Callahan, Graphics
Lara M. Johnson, Graphics
Laura Levine, Graphics
Mike Campbell, Graphics
Juliana Arbo, Typesetting Supervisor
Jane Jaegersen, Typesetter
Marie Lazauskas, Word Processor
Kathleen D'Amico, Word Processor
Larry Killian, Copier Coordinator

To the Reader

In publishing ANNUAL EDITIONS we recognize the enormous role played by the magazines, newspapers, and journals of the *public press* in providing current, first-rate educational information in a broad spectrum of interest areas. Many of these articles are appropriate for students, researchers, and professionals seeking accurate, current material to help bridge the gap between principles and theories and the real world. These articles, however, become more useful for study when those of lasting value are carefully *collected, organized, indexed,* and *reproduced* in a *low-cost format,* which provides easy and permanent access when the material is needed. That is the role played by ANNUAL EDITIONS. Under the direction of each volume's *academic editor,* who is an expert in the subject area, and with the guidance of an *Advisory Board,* each year we seek to provide in each ANNUAL EDITION a current, well-balanced, carefully selected collection of the best of the public press for your study and enjoyment. We think that you will find this volume useful, and we hope that you will take a moment to let us know what you think.

The practice of human resource management is evolving into an exciting and highly diverse profession. Changes in the economic, social, and political forces in countries all over the world have made the study and practice of human resource management a key factor in the success of any organization.

Management must respond to these forces in many ways, not the least of which is the effort to keep current with the various developments in the field. The 50 articles that have been chosen for *Annual Editions: Human Resources 97/98* reflect an outstanding cross section of the current articles in the field. The volume addresses the various component parts of HRM (human resource management) from compensation, training, and discipline to international implications for the worker and the employer. Articles have been chosen from leading business magazines such as *Fortune* and journals such as *Human Resource Professional* to provide a wide sampling of the latest thinking in the field of human resources.

Annual Editions: Human Resources 97/98 contains a number of features designed to be useful for people interested in human resource management. These features include a *Topic Guide* to locate articles on specific subjects, as well as a *Table of Contents* with abstracts that summarize each article with bold italicized key ideas. The volume is organized into seven units, each dealing with specific interrelated topics in human resources. Every unit begins with an overview that provides background information for the articles in the section. This will enable the reader to place the selection in the context of the larger issues concerning human resources. Important topics are emphasized and challenge questions that address major themes are presented.

This is the seventh edition of *Annual Editions: Human Resources.* It is hoped that many more will follow addressing these important issues. We believe that the collection is the most complete and useful compilation of current material available to the human resource management student. We would like to have your response to this volume, for we are interested in your opinions and recommendations. Please take a few minutes to complete and return the postage-paid *Article Rating Form* at the back of the volume. Any book can be improved, and we need your help to continue to improve *Annual Editions: Human Resources.*

Fred Maidment
Editor

Contents

UNIT 1

Human Resource Management in Perspective

Eleven selections examine the current environment of human resource management with special emphasis on equal employment opportunity, affirmative action, the Americans with Disabilities Act, and sexual harassment.

To the Reader	iv
Topic Guide	2
Overview	4

A. THE ENVIRONMENT OF HUMAN RESOURCE MANAGEMENT

1. **Has Downsizing Gone Too Far?** *Challenge,* July/August 1996. — 6
   Whether you call it *downsizing, reengineering, or just plain firing,* American industry has been terminating waves of employees. Secretary of Labor Robert Reich has something to say about it in this comprehensive interview.

2. **Does Human Resource Management Make a Difference?** — 13
   Sheila Rothwell, *Manager Update,* Spring 1995.
   Today many *human resource departments are being reduced* in numbers of employees and often in terms of their importance in the organization as part of an overall downsizing trend. Sheila Rothwell has some ideas on this trend, the differences between human resources and personnel, and how to evaluate these functions.

3. **People and Their Organizations: Rethinking the Assumptions,** Marie A. McKendall and Stephen T. Margulis, *Business Horizons,* November/December 1995. — 19
   The old psychological *contract between workers and employers* is dead. But, say these two authors, that is not necessarily a bad thing. Marie McKendall and Stephen Margulis offer a new view of employee-organizational relationships.

B. HUMAN RESOURCES AND CORPORATE STRATEGY

4. **Wedding HR to Strategic Alliances,** Brenda Paik Sunoo, *Personnel Journal,* May 1995. — 27
   One of the fastest-growing ways to do business is *to establish strategic alliances with other firms.* U.S. companies have formed many of these alliances, but a large percentage of them have failed. Brenda Sunoo examines how human resources can mean the difference between success and failure.

5. **Do Your Human Resources Add Value?** Michael Donahue, *Management Accounting,* June 1996. — 32
   How do you evaluate your *human resources department*? This article describes a step-by-step process for creating an efficient, cost-effective service delivery operation.

C. EQUAL EMPLOYMENT OPPORTUNITY AND AFFIRMATIVE ACTION

6. **Moment of Truth for the Class of '70,** Caroline V. Clarke, *Black Enterprise,* August 1995. — 35
   The black Americans of the college class of 1970 were really the first to benefit in a major way from *affirmative action.* Caroline Clarke takes a look at where some of them are now and how they see their futures and their children's futures.

7. **Does Image Matter?** Jennifer J. Laabs, *Personnel Journal,* December 1995. — 43
   People should be evaluated on their performance, not their looks. Yet it is obvious that *appearance does play a role* in how people are perceived and in how much money they earn. Jennifer Laabs advises employers on how to avoid looks-based discrimination in hiring practices and personal appearance codes.

The concepts in bold italics are developed in the article. For further expansion please refer to the Topic Guide and the Index.

D. AMERICANS WITH DISABILITIES ACT

8. **The Americans with Disabilities Act and the Workplace: Management's Responsibilities in AIDS-Related Situations,** James D. Slack, *Public Administration Review,* July/August 1995. 51
People with HIV/AIDS are covered under the *Americans with Disabilities Act of 1990*. The dynamics of applying the act to this group of Americans are examined by James Slack.

9. **Get the Best from Employees with Learning Disabilities,** Gillian Flynn, *Personnel Journal,* January 1996. 57
There are many *learning-disabled people in the workforce,* and, as with many other disabled workers, they can do an outstanding job. How to help these employees maximize their performance is the subject of this article.

E. SEXUAL HARASSMENT

10. **Sexual Harassment: Reducing the Risks,** Sharon Nelton, *Nation's Business,* March 1995. 62
Sexual harassment has been on the front burner for human resources professionals ever since the testimony of Anita Hill during the Clarence Thomas Supreme Court nomination hearings. Sharon Nelton outlines what employers can do to keep the risks of being sued to a minimum.

11. **When Sexual Harassment Is a Foreign Affair,** Wendy Hardman and Jacqueline Heidelberg, *Personnel Journal,* April 1996. 65
Dealing with *sexual harassment* in a purely domestic setting is difficult enough, but when it involves people from different cultures, it becomes very complex.

UNIT 2

Meeting Human Resource Requirements

Seven articles discuss the dynamics of human resource job requirements, planning, selection, recruitment, and information systems.

Overview 70

A. JOB REQUIREMENTS

12. **Manage Work Better to Better Manage Human Resources: A Comparative Study of Two Approaches to Job Analysis,** James P. Clifford, *Public Personnel Management,* Spring 1996. 72
How you see something depends on your objectives and where you sit. This article reports a comparative study of two *approaches to job analysis* that yielded very different results.

13. **Family or Work? A Matter of Priorities,** Eugene H. Fram and Francena L. Miller, *USA Today Magazine (Society for the Advancement of Education),* May 1995. 78
Employees are starting to demand greater understanding on the part of their employers when it comes to *family issues*. This essay outlines some of the issues and solutions that have been raised and implemented in industry.

B. HUMAN RESOURCE PLANNING, SELECTION, AND RECRUITMENT

14. **How to Recruit Online,** Shannon Peters Talbott, *Recruitment Staffing Sourcebook,* Supplement to *Personnel Journal,* March 1996. 81
The newest way to look for *prospective employees is on the Internet.* Here are some do's and dont's on how to use this new tool.

The concepts in bold italics are developed in the article. For further expansion please refer to the Topic Guide and the Index.

15. **Unlock the Potential of Older Workers,** Charlene Marmer Solomon, *Personnel Journal,* October 1995. 84
    The workforce is aging, and employers are not going to be able to ignore their *older workers*. In fact, says Charlene Solomon, they are going to have to depend on them even more than they have in the past.

16. **Attracting the Right Employees—and Keeping Them,** Gillian Flynn, *Personnel Journal,* December 1994. 92
    Attracting good employees and keeping them is one of the most important things organizations can do, and it is one of the most difficult. It is the key to success for corporations, since it is people who do the jobs. This is a brief discussion of some of the practices that are currently being used to find and retain good employees.

C. **HUMAN RESOURCE INFORMATION SYSTEMS**

17. **Catch the Wave as HR Goes Online,** Samuel Greengard, *Personnel Journal,* July 1995. 96
    Cyberspace offers new opportunities in *networking, information* gathering, and recruiting. Samuel Greengard discusses how computer services are changing the way human resources is doing its job.

18. **Interactive Benefits Systems Save Time and Dollars for Employers, Employees,** Miriam Basch Scott, *Employee Benefit Plan Review,* February 1995. 104
    One of the most obvious ways that organizations can benefit from *computerized information systems* is in human resources. Miriam Scott looks at how interactive systems can be utilized to help employees and employers save time and money.

Overview 108

A. **MOTIVATING EMPLOYEES**

19. **The Top 20 Ways to Motivate Employees,** Shari Caudron, *Industry Week,* April 3, 1995. 110
    Organizations with motivated employees are going to be more effective and fun than organizations whose employees are not motivated. Shari Caudron presents 20 different *ways to motivate employees.*

20. **Empowerment: Myth or Reality,** Michèle Darling, *Vital Speeches of the Day,* May 15, 1996. 114
    What is meant by *"empowerment"* of employees and where is it going? This speech, delivered to the Human Resources Professionals Association of Ontario in February 1996, contains some thoughts on this issue.

B. **FACILITATING COMMUNICATION**

21. **Social IQ and MBAs,** Robert L. Dilenschneider, *Vital Speeches of the Day,* April 15, 1996. 118
    Communication is the key in most human endeavors. Yet, for some reason, most people simply are not very good at it. This speech, delivered by a veteran public relations executive at the Fordham University Graduate School of Business, offers cogent advice on watching for nonverbal cues from others and conveying one's own messages more effectively.

UNIT 3

Creating a Productive Work Environment

Six selections examine how to increase productivity in the workplace by motivating employees, developing effective communication channels, and providing good leadership and direction.

The concepts in bold italics are developed in the article. For further expansion please refer to the Topic Guide and the Index.

22. **Handling Communication Problems,** W. H. Weiss, *Supervision,* March 1994. — 122

Communication is one of the most difficult functions a manager can perform. W. H. Weiss has some practical suggestions on *how to communicate in organizations,* up, down, and across the chart.

C. LEADING AND DIRECTING

23. **Leadership: Seven Behaviors for Muddling Through,** James R. Houghton, *Vital Speeches of the Day,* July 1, 1996. — 125

How do leaders *transform organizations to meet the challenges* of the present, the future? James Houghton, the chairman and CEO of Corning Incorporated, shared his ideas on leading today's companies at the Senior Leadership/Corporate Transformation Conference in April 1996.

24. **Not Enough Generals Were Killed!** Peter Drucker, *Forbes ASAP,* April 8, 1996. — 129

Peter Drucker is considered one of the top two *management theorists* of the late twentieth century. Here he presents some of his thoughts on leadership.

UNIT 4

Developing Effective Human Resources

Six articles discuss how to develop human resources through employee training, career development, and performance appraisal.

Overview — 130

A. TRAINING EMPLOYEES

25. **Send Managers Back to School at the Local University,** Fred Maidment, *Human Resource Professional,* July/August 1995. — 132

In a *changing environment,* managers need training to help them cope. One source of such training and education is colleges and universities. But the buyer should beware, cautions Fred Maidment.

26. **New Skills Equal New Opportunities,** Gillian Flynn, *Personnel Journal,* June 1996. — 134

With all of the emphasis on reengineering, force reductions, and layoffs, isn't there *some way to save the jobs* of people who have worked for a company for years, perhaps decades? Chevron Corp. may have found an answer in an innovative mix-and-match strategy.

B. CAREER AND STAFF DEVELOPMENT

27. **Women in American Boardrooms: Through a Glass, Darkly,** *The Economist,* August 10, 1996. — 137

Are *women making progress* in entering the ranks of senior management? Yes, but the change is slow for many reasons, several of which are discussed in this article.

28. **Executive Women Confront Midlife Crisis,** Betsy Morris, *Fortune,* September 18, 1995. — 139

As women climb the ladder of corporate success, many of them will be experiencing burnout, dissatisfaction, and other forms of midlife crisis. Betsy Morris examines how some very successful female executives have handled these problems.

The concepts in bold italics are developed in the article. For further expansion please refer to the Topic Guide and the Index.

C. APPRAISING AND IMPROVING PERFORMANCE

29. **Improving Worker Performance,** Michael Barrier, *Nation's Business,* September 1996.
   There are many *ways to motivate employees* and to improve organizational performance. Michael Barrier outlines several of them in a readable question-and-answer format.   147

30. **Painless Performance Evaluations,** Mary Mavis, *Training and Development,* October 1994.
   Performance evaluation is one of the most difficult tasks a manager faces. Mary Mavis provides some useful clues on how to get the most out of this necessary managerial function.   150

Overview   154

A. MANAGING EMPLOYEE COMPENSATION

31. **Share the Pain to Share the Gain,** Jennifer J. Laabs, *Personnel Journal,* June 1996.
   When organizations hit hard times, how do they adjust? What are some of the steps that managers can take? Jennifer Laabs describes the techniques used by one corporation, including reductions in wages, work schedules, and raw materials.   156

32. **Nine Practical Suggestions for Streamlining Workers' Compensation Costs,** Charles L. Lorenz, *Compensation and Benefits Review,* May/June 1995.
   What can organizations do to reduce their *workers' compensation costs*? Charles Lorenz provides nine practical suggestions that can be implemented by organizations today.   160

B. INCENTIVE COMPENSATION

33. **Risky Business: The New Pay Game,** Steve Kerr, *Fortune,* July 22, 1996.
   This article describes GE's use of its *pay system to get people to work faster and smarter,* offering bonuses only to workers who achieve tough goals.   165

34. **The Long and Winding Road,** John D. McMillan and Steven Sabow, *Financial Executive,* March/April 1995.
   Executive compensation has come under fire over the past several years as it became obvious that the link between pay and performance for senior management has been, at best, tenuous. The response has been to strengthen that link, and new approaches are reported in this essay.   168

C. EXECUTIVE PAY

35. **And You Thought CEOs Were Overpaid,** John A. Byrne, *Business Week,* August 26, 1996.
   Over the past several years there has been great controversy over *the pay of CEOs.* While that controversy continues, the pay of outside directors is starting to draw fire. Is an outside director worth almost $200,000 per year? It seems some corporations believe they are.   173

36. **The Need for Greed,** *The Economist,* May 4, 1996.   175
   The methods by which *senior executives are compensated* are at least as important as how much they are compensated, as explained in this article.

UNIT 5

Implementing Compensation, Benefits, and Workplace Safety

Ten articles discuss employee compensation, incentive arrangements, executive pay, employee benefits, and safety and health considerations.

The concepts in bold italics are developed in the article. For further expansion please refer to the Topic Guide and the Index.

D. EMPLOYEE BENEFITS

37. **Balancing Work and Family Responsibilities: Flextime and Child Care in the Federal Government,** Marni Ezra and Melissa Deckman, *Public Administration Review,* March/April 1996.   176
    Do *family-friendly policies* make for a more satisfied workforce? The evidence is that they do and that on-site child care and flextime, in particular, help mothers to balance the demands of work and family.

E. SAFETY AND HEALTH

38. **Violence in the American Workplace: Challenges to the Public Employer,** Lloyd G. Nigro and William L. Waugh Jr., *Public Administration Review,* July/August 1996.   182
    Violence in the workplace is an increasing concern for American workers. How to prevent violent situations and deal with them when they do occur is the theme of this article.

39. **Workers Take Leave of Job Stress,** Christopher J. Bachler, *Personnel Journal,* January 1995.   190
    Sabbaticals, often thought of only as the province of academics, are now becoming more popular in industry, to help revitalize and renew workers.

40. **Surveys Document Wellness Initiatives, Link Health Risks to Higher Plan Costs,** Bernice Caldwell, *Employee Benefit Plan Review,* June 1995.   196
    Healthy workers generally mean less expensive and more productive workers. This may seem obvious, but many companies have doubted the cost effectiveness of *initiatives to improve their workers' health.* The evidence is in, and wellness initiatives do mean lower health costs.

UNIT 6

Fostering Employee/Management Relationships

Five selections examine the dynamics of labor relations, collective bargaining, contract administration, and disciplinary action.

Overview   198

A. DYNAMICS OF LABOR RELATIONS, COLLECTIVE BARGAINING, AND CONTRACT ADMINISTRATION

41. **Putting Collective Back into Bargaining,** Paul Grattet, *Public Management,* July 1995.   200
    Negotiating a contract is never easy, but there are ways to reach reasonable and effective agreements between labor and management.

B. DISCIPLINARY ACTION

42. **When the Fired Fight Back,** David Nye, *Across the Board,* June 1995.   204
    In an era of *downsizing,* many former employees are not going quietly. They are suing their former employers for a host of reasons. There are recommended ways to handle these situations, and David Nye presents some of them.

43. **Privacy,** Ellen Alderman and Caroline Kennedy, *Across the Board,* March 1996.   208
    How far can an employer go in looking into the personal lives of workers? Some recent court cases involving the *privacy of employees* suggest useful guidelines.

The concepts in bold italics are developed in the article. For further expansion please refer to the Topic Guide and the Index.

44. **Terminating Problem Employees,** Bettye Springer, *Public Management,* April 1996. — 211

There may come a time in every manager's life when he or she must *terminate a problem employee.* This article gives some tips on how to avoid litigation in such situations.

C. TEMPORARY AND PART-TIME EMPLOYEES

45. **Are Your Temps Doing Their Best?** Shari Caudron, *Personnel Journal,* November 1995. — 213

With more and more organizations using *temporary employees,* the question of how to motivate them to do a top job becomes more crucial. The answer—treat temps like regular employees.

UNIT 7

International Human Resource Management

Five articles discuss the increasing globalization of human resource management.

Overview — 216

46. **Jobs for Life: Why Japan Won't Give Them Up,** Eamonn Fingleton, *Fortune,* March 20, 1995. — 218

For several years, Westerners have been predicting the end of *lifelong employment in Japan,* yet it has not happened. Eamonn Fingleton discusses the system and why it is unlikely to end in the near future.

47. **Managing Human Resources in Mexico: A Cultural Understanding,** Randall S. Schuler, Susan E. Jackson, Ellen Jackofsky, and John W. Slocum Jr., *Business Horizons,* May/June 1996. — 221

Mexico and the United States are two different societies with two different cultures, especially as measured by adherence to four key workplace values. The authors show how different the two nations are in three of these key areas and discuss the implications for business management.

48. **Dealing with Diversity: The Coming Challenge to American Business,** Kenneth J. Doka, *Business Horizons,* May/June 1996. — 228

The American workforce has changed significantly and will continue to do so over the next several decades. Accordingly, corporations that encourage and nurture *diversity among their employees* are far better positioned in both differentiated domestic and global markets.

49. **Building a Global Workforce Starts with Recruitment,** Shannon Peters Talbott, *Recruitment Staffing Sourcebook,* Supplement to *Personnel Journal,* March 1996. — 233

Global corporations need global workforces, and building a workforce capable of working in a *global environment* begins with hiring employees who have the appropriate mindset.

50. **Put Your Ethics to a Global Test,** Charlene Marmer Solomon, *Personnel Journal,* January 1996. — 236

Western ethical conduct may frequently be at odds with accepted local practice in other societies, and walking this thin line can be difficult. Charlene Solomon offers tips for achieving the right balance between ethical fanaticism and ethical relativism.

Index — 241
Article Review Form — 244
Article Rating Form — 245

The concepts in bold italics are developed in the article. For further expansion please refer to the Topic Guide and the Index.

Topic Guide

This topic guide suggests how the selections in this book relate to topics of traditional concern to human resource management students and professionals. It is useful for locating articles that relate to each other for reading and research. The guide is arranged alphabetically according to topic. Articles may, of course, treat topics that do not appear in the topic guide. In turn, entries in the topic guide do not necessarily constitute a comprehensive listing of all the contents of each selection.

TOPIC AREA	TREATED IN	TOPIC AREA	TREATED IN
Benefits	3. People and Their Organizations 8. Americans with Disabilities Act 13. Family or Work? 16. Attracting the Right Employees 17. Catch the Wave as HR Goes Online 18. Interactive Benefits Systems 25. Send Managers Back to School 29. Improving Worker Performance 31. Share the Pain to Share the Gain 32. Nine Practical Suggestions 33. Risky Business: The New Pay Game 34. Long and Winding Road 35. And You Thought CEO's Were Overpaid 36. The Need for Greed 37. Balancing Work and Family Responsibilities 38. Violence in the American Workplace 39. Workers Take Leave of Job Stress 40. Surveys Document Wellness Initiatives 43. Privacy 46. Jobs for Life 47. Managing Human Resources in Mexico	Communication	2. Does Human Resource Management Make a Difference? 3. People and Their Organizations 4. Wedding HR to Strategic Alliances 7. Does Image Matter? 9. Get the Best from Employees 10. Sexual Harassment: Reducing the Risks 11. When Sexual Harassment Is a Foreign Affair 14. How to Recruit Online 17. Catch the Wave as HR Goes Online 18. Interactive Benefits Systems 19. Top 20 Ways to Motivate Employees 20. Empowerment 21. Social IQ and MBAs 22. Handling Communication Problems 23. Leadership 24. Not Enough Generals Were Killed! 27. Women in American Boardrooms 29. Improving Worker Performance 30. Painless Performance Evaluations 43. Privacy 44. Terminating Problem Employees 45. Are Your Temps Doing Their Best?
Blue-Collar Workforce	1. Has Downsizing Gone Too Far? 2. Does Human Resource Management Make a Difference? 3. People and Their Organizations 8. Americans with Disabilities Act 12. Manage Work Better 20. Empowerment 26. New Skills Equal New Opportunities 29. Improving Worker Performance 31. Share the Pain to Share the Gain 32. Nine Practical Suggestions 38. Violence in the American Workplace 41. Putting Collective Back into Bargaining 49. Building a Global Workforce	Day Care	13. Family Or Work? 18. Interactive Benefits Systems 27. Women in American Boardrooms 37. Balancing Work and Family Responsibilities 48. Dealing with Diversity
Career Development	1. Has Downsizing Gone Too Far? 2. Does Human Resource Management Make a Difference? 3. People and Their Organizations 6. Moment of Truth for the Class of '70 7. Does Image Matter? 9. Get the Best from Employees 12. Manage Work Better 13. Family or Work? 15. Unlock the Potential of Older Workers 16. Attracting the Right Employees 19. Top 20 Ways to Motivate Employees 20. Empowerment 21. Social IQ and MBAs 25. Send Managers Back to School 26. New Skills Equal New Opportunities 27. Women in American Boardrooms 28. Executive Women Confront Midlife Crisis 29. Improving Worker Performance 30. Painless Performance Evaluations 32. Nine Practical Suggestions 33. Risky Business: The New Pay Game 34. Long and Winding Road 37. Balancing Work and Family Responsibilities 39. Workers Take Leave of Job Stress 49. Building a Global Workforce	Education/Training	6. Moment of Truth for the Class of '70 7. Does Image Matter? 8. Americans with Disabilities Act 9. Get the Best from Employees 10. Sexual Harassment: Reducing the Risks 11. When Sexual Harassment Is a Foreign Affair 12. Manage Work Better 14. How to Recruit Online 15. Unlock the Potential of Older Workers 16. Attracting the Right Employees 17. Catch the Wave as HR Goes Online 18. Interactive Benefits Systems 20. Empowerment 21. Social IQ and MBAs 23. Leadership 24. Not Enough Generals Were Killed! 25. Send Managers Back to School 26. New Skills Equal New Opportunities 27. Women in American Boardrooms 29. Improving Worker Performance 49. Building a Global Workforce

TOPIC AREA	TREATED IN	TOPIC AREA	TREATED IN
Employee Stress	1. Has Downsizing Gone Too Far? 3. People and Their Organizations 9. Get the Best from Employees 10. Sexual Harassment: Reducing the Risks 11. When Sexual Harassment Is a Foreign Affair 12. Manage Work Better 13. Family or Work? 15. Unlock the Potential of Older Workers 16. Attracting the Right Employees 18. Interactive Benefits Systems 20. Empowerment 22. Handling Communication Problems 24. Not Enough Generals Were Killed! 27. Women in American Boardrooms 28. Executive Women Confront Midlife Crisis 29. Improving Worker Performance 31. Share the Pain to Share the Gain 32. Nine Practical Suggestions 33. Risky Business: The New Pay Game 35. And You Thought CEO's Were Overpaid 36. Need for Greed 37. Balancing Work and Family Responsibilities 38. Violence in the American Workplace 39. Workers Take Leave of Job Stress 40. Surveys Document Wellness Initiatives 43. Privacy	**Job Security (continued)** **Minorities in the Workforce**	43. Privacy 44. Terminating Problem Employees 45. Are Your Temps Doing Their Best? 46. Jobs for Life 5. Do Your Human Resources Add Value? 6. Moment of Truth for the Class of '70 7. Does Image Matter? 8. Americans with Disabilities Act 9. Get the Best from Employees 10. Sexual Harassment: Reducing the Risks 11. When Sexual Harassment Is a Foreign Affair 13. Family or Work? 16. Attracting the Right Employees 27. Women in American Boardrooms 28. Executive Women Confront Midlife Crisis 29. Improving Worker Performance 47. Managing Human Resources in Mexico 48. Dealing with Diversity 49. Building a Global Workforce
Health and Safety	2. Does Human Resource Management Make a Difference? 3. People and Their Organizations 8. Americans with Disabilities Act 9. Get the Best from Employees 10. Sexual Harassment: Reducing the Risks 11. When Sexual Harassment Is a Foreign Affair 13. Family or Work? 15. Unlock the Potential of Older Workers 18. Interactive Benefits Systems 28. Executive Women Confront Midlife Crisis 32. Nine Practical Suggestions 37. Balancing Work and Family Responsibilities 38. Violence in the Workplace 39. Workers Take Leave of Job Stress 40. Surveys Document Wellness Initiatives 43. Privacy 44. Terminating Problem Employees	**Relocation** **Substance Abuse** **Unions**	3. People and Their Organizations 13. Family or Work? 39. Workers Take Leave of Job Stress 49. Building a Global Workforce 8. Americans with Disabilities Act 38. Violence in the American Workplace 40. Surveys Document Wellness Initiatives 43. Privacy 44. Terminating Problem Employees 1. Has Downsizing Gone Too Far? 4. Wedding HR to Strategic Alliances 5. Do Your Human Resources Add Value? 12. Manage Work Better 18. Interactive Benefits Systems 20. Empowerment 22. Handling Communications Problems 26. New Skills Equal New Opportunities 31. Share the Pain to Share the Gain 32. Nine Practical Suggestions 33. Risky Business: The New Pay Game 41. Putting Collective Back into Bargaining 45. Are Your Temps Doing Their Best?
Job Security	1. Has Downsizing Gone Too Far? 3. People and Their Organizations 6. Moment of Truth for the Class of '70 7. Does Image Matter? 8. Americans with Disabilities Act 15. Unlock the Potential of Older Workers 16. Attracting the Right Employees 20. Empowerment 24. Not Enough Generals Were Killed! 25. Send Managers Back to School 26. New Skills Equal New Opportunities 27. Women in American Boardrooms 28. Executive Women Confront Midlife Crisis 29. Improving Worker Performance 30. Painless Performance Evaluations 31. Share the Pain to Share the Gain 33. Risky Business: The New Pay Game 35. And You Thought CEO's Were Overpaid 36. Need for Greed 37. Balancing Work and Family Responsibilities 38. Violence in the American Workplace 39. Workers Take Leave of Job Stress 41. Putting Collective Back into Bargaining 42. When the Fired Fight Back	**Women in the Workforce**	6. Moment of Truth for the Class of '70 7. Does Image Matter? 10. Sexual Harassment: Reducing the Risks 11. When Sexual Harassment Is a Foreign Affair 13. Family or Work? 16. Attracting the Right Employees 20. Empowerment 27. Women in American Boardrooms 28. Executive Women Confront Midlife Crisis 37. Balancing Work and Family Responsibilities 48. Dealing with Diversity 49. Building a Global Workforce

Human Resource Management in Perspective

- The Environment of Human Resource Management (Articles 1–3)
- Human Resources and Corporate Strategy (Articles 4 and 5)
- Equal Employment Opportunity and Affirmative Action (Articles 6 and 7)
- Americans with Disabilities Act (Articles 8 and 9)
- Sexual Harassment (Articles 10 and 11)

The only constant is change. Industrial society is dynamic, a great engine that has brought about many of the most significant changes in the history of the human race. Since the start of the Industrial Revolution in England, a little over 200 years ago, industrialized society has transformed Western civilization in a multitude of ways. Many great inventions of the last 200 years have significantly altered the way people live and the way they see the world.

At the time of the Declaration of Independence, the 13 colonies were an overwhelmingly agricultural society that clung to the Atlantic coast of North America. As the end of the twentieth century nears, the United States is a continental nation with the world's largest industrial base and perhaps the smallest percentage of farmers of any major industrialized country. These changes did not happen overnight, but were both the result and the cause of the technological innovations of the Industrial Revolution. The technological marvels of today, such as television, radio, computers, airplanes, and automobiles, did not exist until after the Industrial Revolution, and a disproportionate number of them did not exist until after 1900.

With technological changes have come changes in the ways people earn their living. When Thomas Jefferson authored the Declaration of Independence in 1776, he envisioned a nation of small, independent farmers, but that is not what later developed. Factories, mass production, and economies of scale have been the watchwords of industrial development. The development changed not only the economy, but also society. Most Americans are no longer independent farmers, but are, for the most part, wage earners, making their living working for someone else.

Changes in the American labor force include the increase in women and minorities working next to white males. The nature of most jobs has changed from those directly associated with production to those providing services in the white-collar economy. Many other changes are coming to the economy and society that will be reflected in the workforce. For the first time since the early days of the republic, international trade represents a significant part of the American economy, having increased greatly in the past 20 years. The economic reality is that the GM autoworker competes not only with Ford and Chrysler, but also with Toyota and Volkswagen.

The society, the economy, and the workforce have changed. Americans today live in a much different world than they did 200 years ago. It is a highly diverse, heterogeneous world, full of paradox. When people think of American industry, they tend to think of giant-sized companies like IBM and General Electric, but, in fact, most people work for small firms. The relative importance of the *Fortune 500* companies in terms of employment in the economy has been declining both in real and percentage terms. Small organizations are where the economic growth is today.

Change has brought not only a different society, but a more complex one. Numerous rules and regulations must be followed that did not exist 200 years ago. The human element in any organization has been critical to its success, and foreknowing what the human resource needs of the organization are going to be 1, 5, or even 10 years into the future is a key element for continuing success.

Individual decisions have also changed. In the first part of the twentieth century, it was common for a worker to spend his or her entire life with one organization, doing one particular job. Now the worker can expect to do many different jobs, probably with a number of different organizations in different industries. Mergers, technological change, and economic fluctuations all put a premium on individual adaptability in a changing work environment for individual economic survival.

The changes in industrial society have often come at a faster rate than most people were willing to either accept or adapt to. Many old customs and prejudices have been retained from prior times, and while progress has been made with regard to certain groups—no American employer today would dare to end an employment notice with the letters "NINA" (No Irish Need Apply), as was common at one time—for other groups, the progress has been slow at best. Women represent about half of Ameri-

UNIT 1

Increasingly, competition in world markets is becoming based on the skills and abilities of people, not machines. Indeed, among major competitors, virtually everyone has essentially the same equipment. The difference is often what the people in the organization do with the equipment.

Society, the workplace, and the way they are viewed have all undergone major changes. Frederick W. Taylor and Elton Mayo, early writers in management, held certain views about industry at the beginning of the century, while Peter Drucker, W. Edwards Deming, and others have different ideas now, at the end of the century. The American society and economy, as well as the very life of the average American worker, are different from what they were 200 or even 100 years ago, and both the workers and the organizations that employ them must respond to those changes.

Looking Ahead: Challenge Questions

What social and economic trends do you feel are the most significant? Has downsizing gone too far? How will these trends impact on the labor force as it enters the twenty-first century? How does human resource management make a difference?

What are some of the ways that firms can better utilize the skills and talents of their employees? How can small businesses benefit from better human resource management?

What are the most important changes for the American worker during this century, and what changes do you see as likely in the next 20 years? What are some of the erroneous assumptions often made by management? How have changes in the family resulted in changes in human resource management?

In the past 30 years, the government has taken a more active role in the struggle of minorities and other groups in the workforce. How do you see this effort developing? What changes in policy are likely to occur in the future?

Sexual harassment is a very important area of concern for most organizations. What do you think organizations can and should do about it?

can workers but they are paid only about 70 percent of what men earn. African Americans, other minorities, and people with disabilities have been discriminated against for centuries in American society, to the point where the federal government has been forced to step in and legislate equal opportunity, both on and off the job. Finally, the clash of differing cultures seems ever more pronounced in our society. America has traditionally viewed itself as a melting pot, but it is clear that certain groups have historically "melted" more easily than others, a situation that is reflected in the workplace.

Human resource management plays an important role in industrial America. Business leaders recognize the value of their employees to the future of their organizations.

Has Downsizing Gone Too Far?

Interview | Robert Reich

Streamlining is just plain firing, says the Secretary of Labor, and it has gone too far. But Reich says the president should resort to the bully pulpit before he tries firmer measures to encourage corporations to retain and revalue their employees. Election-year hesitancy?

ROBERT REICH is U.S. Secretary of Labor. A part of this interview appeared on "Frontline," the PBS documentary series.

Q. Mr. Secretary, by conventional measures the economy is doing pretty well. Unemployment is low; inflation is low. There are recent reports that the American middle class isn't doing that badly. Is America as anxious as you've been saying it is?

A. In many respects the economy is doing marvelously well. Unemployment is down to 5.4 percent. In fact, we've had twenty months of unemployment under six percent. We don't have any inflation in sight, and we do have eight and a half million new jobs since February of 1993. That's terrific news. But there is a long-term challenge ahead of us that has to do primarily with a widening gap that has accumulated over twenty years between people at the top and wage earners at the bottom. A lot of people in the middle are anxious, and for two reasons. One, because of the long-term decline in median wages. That's the wage of the person right smack in the middle and everybody below, but also because the rate of permanent job loss is higher in the 1990s than in the 1980s. Most families rely on two wage earners, or they rely on a single wage earner who is the sole parent of that house; therefore, if one wage is lost, that can mean the difference between making ends meet and destitution. So for a whole variety of reasons, there is genuine economic insecurity out there.

Q. Some groups are now saying that wages are not stagnating or falling; they're rising. Some economists are saying that social mobility is terrific. The American dream is as alive and well as it has ever been. Is this true?

A. First of all, you've got to distinguish between average wages and median wages, because so many people at the top are doing so well, the average is pulled up. Shaquille O'Neal, the basketball player and I have an average height of six feet. That's because I'm very short. You've got to look behind averages, and you've got to examine what's happening to the little guy. And in fact we see that, beginning in the late 1970s, median wages began to decline for men. They bottomed out recently. Median wages for nonsupervisory workers, for blue collars, also began taking a dive in the late 1970s and have bottomed out recently. But it means that a lot of workers, particularly those without college educations, are doing worse.

Q. If you read the papers, you see all these studies. Some say wages are down. Some say they're up. Some say social mobility is no good. Some say social mobility is terrific. What are you to believe?

A. I spend a lot of time as labor secretary not only looking at the data, but talking to people around this country, and there's no question that people are better off than they were in 1992. There are more jobs. People feel a little better about their wages and prospects. But over the long term, we still have a major problem in this country, and a major challenge: to restore not just job growth but wage growth. There are a lot of people

> *There is a long-term challenge ahead of us that has to do primarily with a widening gap that has accumulated over twenty years between people at the top and wage earners at the bottom.*

who are justifiably worried about maintaining their standard of living, maintaining their wages. Some people say that social mobility is as great, if not greater, than it was in the 1980s, and that's simply not true. In fact, a lot of evidence indicates that it is harder to move upward if you are near the bottom or in the bottom 20 or 30 percent. And for everybody who is moving upward, there is always an equal number moving downward. So if we see a wider disparity in incomes, that is obviously cause for concern.

Q. Even in the 1990s under the Clinton administration, despite a long economic expansion, despite low unemployment, we aren't seeing the wage increases that we used to see in typical economic expansions of yesteryear. What's going on?

A. Wages for Americans in the top 20 percent of earnings are doing quite well. If you're in the top 5 percent, you are doing extremely well. If you're in the top 1 percent, you are doing better than the top 1 percent has done probably in fifty or sixty or seventy years. But if you're in the bottom 20 or 30 or 40 percent, you're not doing well. If you don't have a college degree, you're probably having an especially hard time making ends meet. We're seeing a wider disparity in this country in wages and earnings. Also in benefits—health benefits, pension benefits. If you're near the bottom, in the bottom third or the bottom half, your benefits are also eroding.

Q. In the meantime, CEOs are certainly in the top 1 percent. Are they making too much money?

A. The salaries they pay themselves are extraordinarily high. I think it's not good for a company in terms of its own bottom line to allow too great a gulf to open up between the compensation of the boss at the top and everybody else. Because what is it that holds a company together? That makes the average worker feel that he or she is part of an enterprise? That they have a common fate? That it is necessary to put in the extra mile to make sure that that company works? It's the sense that everybody is working together, that there is not too great a gulf between people at the top and people at the bottom. The best companies in this country try to encourage a sense of teamwork, of common enterprise, of everybody in the same boat together. You cannot do that if the CEO is earning 140 times what the average worker in that company is earning.

Q. Your own Council of Economic Advisors has been telling us recently that things aren't as bad as the media has been saying. In fact, they say that the American economy is producing good jobs, and they imply that wages are going up. Is that true?

A. Most of the eight and a half million net new jobs added to the American economy since February of 1993 are good jobs. They pay better than average. But the 116 million existing jobs have been increasingly divided between those few that pay better and the larger number that pay less.

Q. But, in truth, we don't know that much about those eight and a half million jobs, do we? We don't really know the wages those eight and a half million net new jobs are paying.

1. HUMAN RESOURCE MANAGEMENT: The Environment

A. We have reason to believe that those are better-than-average-paying jobs because most of them are managerial, professional, and technical. They are the fastest-growing segments of the job market, which is one reason that the wages of college graduates, particularly those with specialty skills, are going up. That's where the demand is.

Q. On the other hand, the median wages of some of these groups have been going down. And that's not measured in the CEA's study. So we don't really know.

A. White-collar workers in the 1990s found that they too were vulnerable, not just blue-collar workers. In the 1980s, blue-collar workers began to feel the pressures of the new dynamic economy in which the old high-volume, standardized, stable mass-production system would give you a job for life. Well, they started losing ground. Nobody paid much attention to them because, perhaps, the media, the professional elites in this country, really didn't hear from blue-collar workers. But in the 1990s, even white-collar managers, middle-level managers, and some senior-level managers started to feel the heat. And once everybody started to feel the heat, then everybody started talking about it.

Q. Some companies are doing a good job. Master Lock, Harley Davidson, Chrysler—they're adding jobs. They're reopening plants or expanding existing plants. They're paying pretty good wages. Why aren't all or even many American corporations doing what Harley, Master Lock, and Chrysler are doing?

A. There are two major reasons why companies are not valuing their employees, treating their employees as assets to be developed instead of as costs to be cut, even though it makes sense for the bottom line. Reason number one is that some companies simply haven't made the change from high-volume, standardized, stable mass production, seeking economies of scale and whose workers are fungible, to more high-value production where the focus is on value for individual customers, where quality matters, and where it's necessary for people on the shop floor to come up with innovations. And when companies make that change in organizational structure, they have to start investing in the skills, dedication, and loyalty of their employees. Otherwise, how do they make it? There are simply no other assets that can give you that kind of value.

There's a second reason, however, why companies find it so difficult to move toward high-value production in which employees are truly the key asset of the company. That has to do with who the top managers are. Now, remember, a lot of the people at the top got there when command and control over large hierarchical organizations was the way things were. They were promoted because they were good at being the font of all wisdom and daring and insight, issuing commands and controls and making sure that everybody followed their directions. They didn't get there because they were good at creating a huge team of people with a common sense of destiny in which workers at the front line were truly valued.

Q. Master Lock is doing pretty well at this. Harley Davidson is doing pretty well. Chrysler is doing well.

> *What is it that holds a company together? It's the sense that everybody is working together, that there is not too great a gulf between people at the top and people at the bottom.*

They seem to be doing it on their own. Why do they need help from government for that?

A. Never underestimate the potential power of the bully pulpit. A president can bring the spotlight of public opinion to bear upon corporate practices that are exemplary, that value employees, that are making money for shareholders, and can just as easily bring the spotlight of public opinion to bear on companies that are being less responsible, treating employees as essentially disposable pieces of machinery.

Q. Are too few companies in America doing what Harley, Master Lock, and Chrysler are doing these days?

A. Too few companies in this country are valuing employees, are understanding that employees are assets to be developed, not costs to be cut. You see, employment costs—wages, salaries, and benefits—comprise almost 70 percent of the total costs of an enterprise. Now the easiest thing in the world for a CEO or a chief financial officer to do is look at that accounting statement and say, "Gee, the way we'd make more money is to squeeze down these payroll costs." It takes a slightly different attitude and mindset and experience to say, "Gee, these are really assets; they're not costs. What we want to do is make these people even more valuable. Give them more skills. Make them feel even more loyal. Because these people are going to be responsible for coming up with the innovations we need. These people are going to be responsible for going the extra mile of helping customers determine what they need. These are the people who are going to make this business go or not go, succeed or fail."

Q. Does valuing the employee work?

A. There is a lot of proof out there that valuing employees, treating them as assets, works to improve the bottom line. Now, is there enough proof out there to convince every chief executive officer? Particularly every one that came up through the old system in which CEOs were the font of all wisdom and daring and insight? And employees were costs to be cut? It's going to take some time. It's going to take an attitudinal shift. It's going to take the spotlight of public opinion on what works.

Q. You think corporate streamlining has just gone too far.

A. I think reengineering or restructuring or downsizing or rightsizing or whatever you want to call it is basically firing, and it has gone way too far. Employees, as I've talked to them across the country, feel that they are not respected, they are not valued, and they are worried about their jobs. They simply feel that the company is no longer loyal to them. Why should they be loyal to the company, they ask me. Why should they go the extra mile? Why should they care?

Q. You think workers have lost trust in their companies? In their managers?

A. Trust is one of the most fragile commodities in any organization, in any culture, in any society. Once trust is abused, once it's lost, it is very hard to regain it, and yet trust is the social glue that keeps organizations together. Employees who trust that management is going to be there for them, who trust that if the company does well, they also are going to do well—those employees are going to go the extra mile. They're going to be innovative; they're going to look for ways to make the company more successful. They're going to feel that one of their primary responsibilities is making that company profitable. But employees who don't feel that the company is going to be loyal to them are not going to go the extra mile. They are fundamentally distrustful.

Q. Are workers more distrustful now than they were twenty years ago, when you were beginning to write about these subjects?

> *More and more employees, workers, average working people I talk to around the country say to me, I'm on my own. I have to look out for number one. Look out for me. The company's not going to look out for me.*

A. I have seen more distrust over the last three and a half years. More and more employees, workers, average working people I talk to around the country say to me, I'm on my own. I have to look out for number one. Look out for me. The company's not going to look out for me. I'm not going to do one extra thing for this company that I don't have to do. Why should I be loyal to this company? Why should I go the extra mile when this company is treating me and other employees like we are disposable pieces of machinery, where there's no loyalty on the other side. Now, those are the companies that are losing ground. They will lose ground over the long term. Sometimes when I walk into factories or offices or retail establishments, I administer what I like to call my pronoun test. I ask the first person I find about the company, and if they use "we" or "our" in describing the company, I know that there is a kind of bond there, an affinity. There's a sense that his or her destiny is bound up with the future of the company. But if they use the pronouns "they" and "their" in describing the company, I know there's a distance. The

1. HUMAN RESOURCE MANAGEMENT: The Environment

employees don't feel that it's their company, and it's going to have a very different result on the bottom line.

Q. Which pronouns are they using these days?

A. I'm struck by how distinct the cultures are. Some companies really have created cultures of community. Some companies are dominated by the pronouns "we" and "our," even big companies. And yet there are other companies that might as well be on a different planet. The pronouns are different. The attitudes are different. People are not feeling that they are valued, and they're not acting as if they are valued.

Q. Not too long ago, you wrote a piece in the *New York Times* suggesting that maybe corporations should be given tax breaks for hiring workers, retaining workers. Is that the role government should play?

A. The first role of government in terms of corporate responsibility is to act as a kind of cheerleader. Use the bully pulpit. Use jawboning. Bringing the spotlight of public opinion to bear on the companies that are doing it right and occasionally the companies that are doing it wrong. Now, beyond that, should there be tax breaks? Well, you know, we have tax breaks for companies to come into disadvantaged areas, enterprise zones, empowerment zones. We have tax breaks for research and development and for investments in equipment and machinery. Should there be tax breaks for more and better investments in employees? I think it's an important question.

Q. Senators Kennedy and Bingaman have recently come out with some proposals about giving tax incentives or encouragement to corporations to adopt more aggressive hiring practices. Is it possible the Clinton administration will endorse any of these?

A. The president is open to any good idea, and again, we have tax breaks for investments in equipment and machinery and research and development, and tax breaks for companies moving into disadvantaged areas. Should there be tax breaks for companies that invest in their workers to a greater degree? Or companies that bring their workers on as part owners? Well, it's an important question. We have not fully evaluated it. But the first step, clearly, is to use the bully pulpit, which the president has been doing. Bring the spotlight of public opinion to bear on those companies that are doing it well: treating the employees genuinely as assets and doing well for their shareholders as a result.

Q. Do we have a new social contract in America between workers and management? Is the old social contract breaking down?

A. There used to be—thirty years ago, forty years ago—an implicit social contract, and although it was never written down, it was understood. It was enforced partly by unions—when 35 percent of the wage force was unionized, that was not an insignificant enforcer—but also by public norms. That social compact said that if the company was doing better and better, workers could be reasonably assured that they would have their jobs and also that they would see better wages and better benefits. That old social compact has come apart. Now we have the spectre of companies

> **The first role of government in terms of corporate responsibility is to act as a kind of cheerleader. Use the bully pulpit. Use jawboning. Bringing the spotlight of public opinion to bear on the companies that are doing it right and occasionally the companies that are doing it wrong.**

doing better and better, and yet some companies—not all, by any means—but some companies are pushing wages down, pushing benefits down, abandoning communities, breaking all of those implicit contractual terms.

Q. Will it correct itself without some kind of government encouragement?

A. The optimistic view is that gradually companies will see the light, that they will understand that the only way they can really make money over the long term is if they treat their employees as assets, if they invest in their training, if they bring them in as partners, if they value them, and also if they value the communities that they live in, because after all, employees and communities are where their customer is ultimately coming from. Good will is very important to the bottom line. Now that's the optimistic view. The pessimistic view is that even over the long term, companies may not fully do what is in the interest of society because investments in employees and investments in communities will never be fully returnable to just the shareholders. There is also a societal stake in all of this. And the true pessimist would say we're never going to get companies to take the long-term view anyway.

Q. And where do you stand on that spectrum between optimist and pessimist?

A. On Mondays and Wednesdays and Fridays, I'm very optimistic. The other days, cautiously pessimistic.

Q. Isn't the economy transforming itself in a healthy way?

A. If you go out and talk to workers across this country, as I have for three and a half, almost four years, and I did it before that, you hear two different stories. Workers who are very well educated, who have the right skills, mostly those in top management positions, or workers who are in good companies that value workers, modern progressive companies—they're upbeat. They think things are eventually going to work out for everybody. But the majority of working people who I talk to are nervous. They're anxious. Yes, the economy is doing much better. Yes, jobs are coming back. Yes, there's no inflation. Yes, wages even are showing a little bit of a rise. But they're nervous about their long-term futures. They look back on the past twenty years, and they just don't know that they're going to be able to keep their job or maintain their standard of living. They're unsure that their children are going to live as well as they. They understand that this is a completely different economy than it was thirty years ago, and it requires completely different skills, completely different attitudes, completely different tools to succeed. They're not sure they have them.

Q. Do you think job training is a big part of the solution?

A. Job skills, education, job training—these are critical to the new economy. If you don't have the skills, if you don't have the right education, you're in trouble.

That's why we are so intent on providing people with vouchers for job training or for low-interest student loans, or we want to make sure that they have a tax break for education and job training. These are not big bureaucratic programs. Vouchers, tax breaks, loans, these empower people to get the tools they need when they need them.

Q. But is job retraining working to your satisfaction?

A. Job retraining is not yet working to my satisfaction. It's working much better than it was in 1992. We pushed the training toward employers, toward real jobs that are out there. We've modeled programs around community colleges, the great unsung heroes in this great transformation of the American work force. But we still need to consolidate all of these job training programs. We need to give people vouchers so they can get the training they need, if they lose a job, when they need it. And we also have to give people tax breaks. A $10,000-a-year tax break for a family for education and training—that's what the president is proposing—as well as low-interest loans. In other words, get it out of the federal bureaucratic system and empower people to get the training they need under the terms and conditions they need it, with good information about what to train for.

Q. Will the jobs be there once they get the retraining?

A. Jobs will be there, but you cannot expect any longer to be able to train for a particular skill and have that skill forever. What you need to train for these days is in the basic competencies underlying a particular area of technology or a particular career. And from that point on, you have to use those competencies to continuously upgrade your own knowledge.

Q. Can workers who are rehired by companies that are doing it right breathe easy? Can they relax?

A. Nobody can breathe completely easy in this new job environment because job security is a thing of the past. This is a dynamic economy. Nobody can be absolutely sure that they will keep a job. But they can at least breathe easier if they have skills and continuously upgrade those skills so that they can get a new job if they lose this one. They need pension portability and health care portability so that if they lose a job, they are not suddenly in trouble and their family is not suddenly endangered. Again, the solution is education

1. HUMAN RESOURCE MANAGEMENT: The Environment

and training, health care and pension portability, and then at the bottom, a minimum wage and an earned income tax credit that at least guarantees that if you fall off the cliff, you will not hit rock bottom.

Q. Why has the administration so vehemently supported the minimum wage this year?

A. The president proposed a minimum wage increase in 1992, and then when health care reform was on the table, when there was a possibility that employers would be providing health care for all employees, we felt that we didn't want to add an additional few pennies to payrolls. But the minute health care was no longer viable, and that very ambitious health care plan, as you recall, did not get enacted, we went back and proposed an increase in the minimum wage in January of 1995. We've been fighting for that for the last year and three quarters. Hopefully, we will get it because Americans at the bottom, twelve million of them, deserve at least a livable wage.

Q. Critics say many of them will lose jobs because companies can't afford to pay them the minimum wage.

A. The minimum wage is heading toward a forty-year low if you adjust for the real purchasing power of a dollar. Now, in 1938 this country decided we'd have a certain minimum standard in terms of child labor (no child labor), that we'd have an absolute floor for wages, and we also established some rudiments of health and safety at the workplace. If you believe in those minimum requirements, you've got to say to yourself, we're heading to a forty-year low. We at least have to make sure that people who work full time don't live in poverty.

Q. Is the administration pushing the minimum wage because it's an election year and it's turning out to be a viable political issue?

A. The president formally proposed a minimum wage increase in January of 1995. Not a month ago, not six months ago, but fifteen months ago, and we have been fighting for it for fifteen months. We almost got a vote in the Senate in November of 1995. We came within just a few votes, but we had to have sixty votes to get cloture. I think that there is a chance now because we're nearing the end of the term, and over twenty House Republicans have turned their tails on their Republican colleagues and joined with us.

Q. Why did the administration call for a conference of CEOs to discuss corporate responsibility?

A. It's very important to continue to put the spotlight of public opinion on those companies that are doing it very well, that are showing the rest of corporate America and the rest of the country that you can do well for employees and for your shareholders, that the two are entirely consistent. In fact, there may be no way to do well for shareholders over the long term unless you are valuing and investing in employees.

Q. Do corporations, then, have a greater responsibility than just making profits?

A. Companies have a primary responsibility to make profits for their shareholders if they are public companies. But the question is, how do you do that and how do you do it over the long term? The only way to do it in this new dynamic economy in which value for customers determines whether you're profitable is by reaching and developing your most precious asset. And that most precious asset, where all of the ideas are going to come from, all of the innovations are going to come from, all of the extra effort that makes the difference between success and failure in the marketplace is going to come from, is your employees, your workers—often your front-line workers. Every other company can get access to the same capital markets, can buy the same equipment and machinery, can go anywhere around the world to get very cheap labor if it wants to. What's the one competitive resource that no other company can easily replicate? What's going to give you as a CEO a long-term competitive advantage? Uniquely? It's your workers. It's their dedication, their loyalty, their skill, their insight, their capacity to work together. That is your competitive advantage. And if you don't know it, you are in trouble.

Does Human Resource Management Make a Difference?

At a time when the numbers of staff in HR departments in several industrialised countries are being reduced – British Telecom, for example, in late 1994 announced plans to cut half of its 4000 personnel staff – the need for academic research into the contribution of the function to the business is more than ever needed. Since several recent studies start with problems of definition, such as, is there a difference between 'personnel' and 'HR'? how would you recognise a human resource strategy if you found one? should a distinction be made between human resource managers and human resource management (which may be a largely 'line' responsibility)?, the academic as well as practitioner debate on those issues is being more fully developed. The question of what is meant by a 'business contribution' also needs definition, if HR responsibility is to be isolated and evaluated. Broad measures of profitability may be less illuminating than more specific indicators to which the HR function might reasonably be expected to contribute.

'Employee relations climate' and 'productivity' were the two measures analysed by the controversial 'big hat no cattle' research by David Metcalf and his LSE team [1]. This utilised data from the 1990 Workplace Industrial Relations Survey (WIRS3) [2] and found that the presence of a personnel manager was significantly associated with a poorer employee relations climate.

The findings were quickly disputed by academics and practitioners on grounds of both interpretation and methodology. David Guest took a lead in this, and was commissioned by the Institute of Personnel and Development to replicate the study and re-examine the findings. The results of this and of several related research studies by himself and others questioned the results in several respects [3]. Some of these related to the handling of the survey data, for although WIRS3 used an authoritative nationally representative sample drawn from over 2000 workplaces, replies to and interpretations of questions were inevitably variable; it focused more on industrial relations than on personnel issues such as selection or appraisal and career management; the definition of personnel manager as 'someone responsible for personnel issues' was too broad to be useful; and the definition of employee relations climate was highly subjective. In Guest and Hoque's re-analysis, taking a narrower definition of personnel, the negative links disappeared and although they were replaced by positive ones, these were generally not statistically significant. Moreover they emphasised that the WIRS survey had only found a 'poor' climate in less than two per cent of workplaces. Controlling for establishment size, industry type and trade union presence, they found that where there was a professional personnel presence, then there was also 'better' personnel practice. The extent to which policies were endorsed at board level and integrated into a coherent strategy was strongly influenced by a personnel director on the main board. There was not enough evidence in WIRS clearly to relate this to business outcomes.

The body of research into links between personnel policy and practice which is gradually being developed tends to focus on company level. One such example was the analysis of case studies of large companies conducted for the WIRS2 study (in the late 1980s). This found that in 30 per cent of cases where there was a personnel director (largely in MNCs), the personnel department was much more involved in policy formulation. Nevertheless, head office HR strategy was very subordinate to corporate business strategy and no clear links were found between the two [4]. A Cranfield study of 30 financially successful companies similarly found many different routes to excellence, but this depended on market conditions not on any clear HR

1. HUMAN RESOURCE MANAGEMENT: The Environment

model. While all the firms took HR issues seriously and had clear policies on management development and on employee involvement, would it have been different without them? [5] Another study, focusing on multi-divisional organisations, concluded that personnel's role in strategy formulation, while often dreamed of, remained marginal. 'Personnel managers are caught in the middle. They know the theory perhaps but have not the power to enact it' (6].

Personnel directors, when asked, tend to see themselves as having more influence than some researchers or line managers perceive. This was found in the Price Waterhouse/Cranfield international study of 1991 and also in a more recent study in Scotland, based on in-depth semi structured interviews with 28 senior personnel directors from the private and public sectors, exploring their understanding of the term HR strategy and issues of its 'fit' with business strategy and the extent of 'integration' within HR policies [7]. The majority saw no difference between HR and traditional personnel, emphasising the continuity (with adaptations) of both objectives and means. The eleven who saw difference, emphasised discontinuity and integration into business strategy but fundamentally the responses of the two groups were similar (and performance pay/appraisal tended to apply only at management levels). Constraints on the adoption of the full HRM model were ascribed to time and traditional attitudes rather than to collective bargaining practices, to which their approach was largely pragmatic. Only a quarter had changed the title of the function and most did so to symbolise change whether or not they perceived difference. For one firm, 'Change to an HR title would be 'Mickey Mouse' and demeaning'.

The main conclusion of the study was that change in the position and influence of the personnel/HR function within the management hierarchy is the key variable explaining the adoption or not of the perceived HRM approach, as at Prestwick Jetstream (a subsidiary of British Aerospace); at Chivas Bros. (a subsidiary of Seagrams) in its move from a production to a customer driven culture; and at Pilkington Optronics with its new 'commercial' focus. The debate over whether there is a difference between HR and personnel seemed largely sterile. Rapid business change with implications for organizational culture was the main driver of change in the personnel role, whether or not the job title changed.

DOES TQM OFFER A NEW ROLE TO HR MANAGERS?

If the traditional personnel management role is declining or being devolved to the line, its future importance may lie in its contribution to Total Quality Management. Wilkinson and Marchington saw a variety of different potential roles, in terms of input levels and influence profiles, that could be played in the implementation of TQM [8]. Literature on the latter tends to concentrate more on technical systems and procedures than on social factors. Vague phrases like motivation, training and commitment tend to remain a black box. The Baldridge and the European Quality Awards allocate 15 per cent-18 per cent of points to HR issues, as well as others to related issues of leadership, communication and strategic planning. Little attention is given to the role of the Personnel function.

Drawing on 15 case studies of TQM in the private and public sectors, during the 1992 recession, all at different 'waves' of its implementation, the authors found two cases of personnel managers being responsible for quality and two in which the quality manager reported to the Director of HR and Quality. Their model, however, distinguished four typical HR/TQM roles: Change Agent (high profile and strategic level) in seven cases; Hidden Persuader (low profile but strategic level) in two cases, chosen by the MD to act as a 'neutral' and a 'sounding board' for the Quality Manager; Internal Contractor (high profile and operational level) which was found in seven cases; and Facilitator (operational level and low profile) which was found to some extent in all cases, and often related to provision of training and communication support for line managers. Each of the roles also had potential pitfalls—either because if TQM went wrong 'high profile' roles were damaged, while if it went right 'low profile' roles were not seen as significant. In some cases different levels of personnel played different roles, or came from different areas over a time period, since TQM is a continuous process.

Conclusions therefore emphasised the dynamics of the role and the 'windows of opportunity' TQM offers to personnel whether at the initiation, decision making, implementing or reviewing stages. While much depends on personnel managers current positions and status (or aspirations) TQM does give scope for a more strategic and initiating role, and possibly a new legitimacy. It should not, however, be seen as a panacea: in most cases TQM approaches are limited rather than transformational in employee involvement terms; TQM can lead to a narrow conformist definition of personnel as the Internal Contractor, existing to serve needs defined by line managers and the procedures of TQM, thus reinforcing a passive, 'reactive' role, rather than a creative one. Personnel needs to maintain its professional integrity and 'cannot simply let TQM define the agenda'.

WHAT ARE THE BEST INDICATORS OF HR EFFECTIVENESS?

A detailed study of effective human resource management in the National Health Service (NHS) explored a range of qualitative and quantitative measures of HRM effectiveness. Since the 'external' (with business strategy) and 'internal' (within the HR policies) integration of HRM is often found to be a guide to effectiveness, four different models of 'integration' were tested: organizational; policy; functional (a professional personnel department); and process (the efficiency/effectiveness of personal service delivery) integration [9].

Definition of measures of HRM effectiveness was particularly difficult: can it be separated from organizational effectiveness? should it be in terms of achieving specified goals? are traditional measures of productivity, turnover and strikes sufficient? is a 'stakeholder' perspective more viable? Eventually reliance was placed on the latter—on the judgment of Board members. In the event, the quantitative measures were least usable because of lack of data or disagreement over the relevance of, say, labour turnover in estimating effectiveness.

A large sample of NHS provider trusts and districts were surveyed by postal questionnaire in 1992—a time of major change aimed at improving management. Analysis of the results involved complex multivariate analysis of the main variables and measures. The contextual variables proved insignificant predictors: there was no evidence that HRM was any more effective in trusts than in directly managed units.

The strongest findings related to the importance of organizational HR integration in predicting qualitative HRM effectiveness—chiefly the existence of written policies, agreed by the Board, on a number of topics. There was a clear link between personnel managers' influence over major policy decisions and effectiveness, but lower level line management decision making had a generally negative effect.

Some links between 'policy integration' and 'effectiveness' were found but were not strong and no association between functional integration and effectiveness existed. Process integration was more important: the efficiency and especially the responsiveness of service delivery by personnel managers had an important link with effectiveness. The existence of a professionally qualified personnel department was unimportant.

The conclusion for personnel managers clearly indicated the need for shared line and personnel policy formulation, and the importance of senior line management ownership. 'Those who formulate policy are more likely to rate it effective'.

A new conceptual model of strategic HRM(SHRM) was developed by LBS/Cambridge researchers to inform their case study data collection. This explicitly set out to relate both external and internal contextual variables to the measurement of significant outcomes, and to distinguish carefully between HR strategy and HR activities. Their model therefore recognised a dichotomy between intended HR strategy and 'realised HR interventions' [10]. Some of the same conceptual issues were also addressed by Lundy, but she also emphasised the need to be aware of trends in management research, in particular that theories about 'strategy' are not all set in the traditional rational decision-making mode; there is a strong school of thought that sees it as incremental and informal and this approach is highly relevant to research into HRM strategy [11].

Attempts to research 'outcomes' of HR effectiveness is also attracting a new wave of American scholars, building on the work of Schuler and of Tsui, in particular. When Peck examined surveys of US executives and HR managers on four dimensions she found that overall HR philosophy (internal to external focus) was not, as expected, related to either organizational strategy, or the employment relationship. 'Staffing policies' were however related to organization strategy; and 'retention policies' to the employment relationship. In general, her findings indicated relationships were more complicated than previous models had indicated [12].

ARE TRADE UNIONS AND HUMAN RESOURCE MANAGEMENT INCOMPATIBLE?

The majority of British private sector establishments (employing over 25 people) are now non-union; and two-thirds of all establishments set up since 1980 are non-union according to the WIRS3 survey, so it is important to know whether HR policies are more innovative or strategic there. Certainly the WIRS survey found that such firms gave fewer rights and benefits to workers and communicated and involved them less. But it seems unlikely that non-union firms are all 'good' or all 'bad'.

Guest and Hoque's analysis of a postal survey of 50 new non-union workplaces (part of a wider study of greenfield sites) therefore considered their adoption of a range of HRM practices and looked at their association with a number of performance outcomes [13]. The study focused on two dimensions: on the degree of integration of HR/business strategies; and on the variation, sophistication and innovation in HR policy and practice. Establishments which were 'high' on both dimensions the authors classified as the 'good' (almost 50 per cent mainly British owned) and those that were low on both as the 'bad' (28/110, often German owned). The 'lucky' were the firms without a clear HR strategy, but a lot of innovative HR practices (27/119); while the 'ugly' or efficiency-driven ones were those with a strategy but a minimal number of policies (8/119).

To measure 'HR' outcomes, eight indicators were chosen relating to commitment, quality, and flexibility; for 'Employee Relations' outcomes the indicators were disputes, turnover and absenteeism; while 'performance' outcomes took various quality and productivity ratings (benchmarks against UK and the world) and the degree of success in weathering the recession. The results show some surprising variations of detail but the overall pattern was as might perhaps be expected, with the 'good' having the most positive HR and Employee Relations and performance outcomes; and the 'ugly' doing better on HR and worst on Employee Relations. In 'performance' terms all the other categories emerged as significantly worse on at least one item, but the 'bad' were overall worst. While these were self reported responses, there was some follow-up by the researchers in certain cases and the conclusion was clear that in new non-union establishments, 'the adoption of an HRM strategy pays off'.

Gall and McKay's study of trade union de-recognition in Britain over the period 1988-1994 followed up earlier studies suggesting a slow but steady increase seemed to be taking place. They found that de-recognition was even greater than previously indicated, but that its nature had changed. Data was obtained from all TUC and non-TUC large unions and the industrial press, but 'counting' was necessarily difficult in multi-plant firms with multi-level and multi-function recognition agreements and the diverse scope of collective bargaining or consultation arrangements [14].

Complete pay bargaining de-recognition was comparatively rare but partial was more common. In general, grade-specific partial recognition dominated especially among professional/managerial grades, although there was also a similar distribution of personal contracts among manual workers. Printing and publishing, shipping, the public sector, certain utilities and offshore oil remained the industrial sectors most affected, but de-recognition was spreading in parts of banking, insurance and the chemical and pharmaceutical sectors, where only Tioxide and Monsanto, medium sized companies, and BP at Barry had introduced complete de-recognition. Most large groups of production workers were unaffected. This means that, (apart from the National Union of Journalists), the large unions have been most heavily affected by de-recognition.

Reasons given by managers are mostly low membership levels and policy decisions to move to a more direct relationship, but managers were often reluctant to be explicit. Tactics ranged from compulsion to financial inducements to sign personal contracts. In about 30 cases union pressures to stop de-recognition were successful but 16 were not, and 43 proposed ballots were not carried through. Legal remedies featured in three reported cases. In general, however, the authors concluded that de-recognition has remained insignificant and marginal outside a few sectors: it should not yet be seen as a major problem facing unions.

New recognition agreements have also been found, despite the difficult environment of the late 1980s. The figures probably underestimate the extent of this, given the number of claims that have been processed by voluntary ACAS conciliation over the last five years, with union success rates varying from 21 per cent to 38 per cent per annum. 105 new agreements were found by the study, covering 23,610 workers.

A complementary study based on more detailed analysis of the WIRS survey evidence, (1984–1990) emphasised the fact that workplaces with falling union membership density outnumbered those with rising density, by about 4 to 1, and were spread over a wide range of industries and workplaces. Major factors associated with this were the demise of the closed shop and marginal de-recognition. Complete de-recognition occurred in 1 in 10 workplaces, especially in the engineering sector in foreign owned firms, but partial in many more, so that the fall in the proportion (86 per cent to 77 per cent) of employees covered by collective bargaining outnumbered those increasing coverage by 26 to 1 [15].

These findings were also reflected in firms in the Scottish study (referred to above) which had all continued to recognise some trade unions, although they had all treated industrial relations as a lower priority issue than in the 1970s. Partial de-recognition however had taken place where membership among certain managerial or professional groups was weak, as at British Rail, British Telecom and Scottish and Newcastle Breweries.

Management policy seemed a less significant influence on Union membership levels than other factors, in new research into the ways in which employee relations were managed in 115 hi-tech firms in the south east of England, 80 per cent of which were non-unionised. This seemed however to be a function of the fact that they were largely newly established, had highly technically qualified staffs, employed relatively small numbers and had not been targeted by unions for recruitment, rather than resulting from new HRM anti-union management philosophies. While such philosophies were found in a few firms, management styles tended to vary considerably with a 'benevolent autocracy' approach being most prevalent. Staff did not join unions largely because they did not see them as useful or relevant. Only weak associations between the presence or absence of unions and the degree of technological and/or organizational change could be found, and these were not uni-directional [16].

Explicit linkage between models of HRM policy outcomes and trade union recognition was tested by some Irish researchers. They tested first a 'simple additive' model; looking for a statistical association between various discrete HR policies on union non recognition. The only significant one found related to the management of reward systems—performance pay and personal contracts. A second model called the 'threshold-fit' model, looked at the incidence of non recognition in firms with a strategic and integrated set of HRM policies. Line management dominance of HRM policy was the only significant factor predicting non recognition but in general the (expected) relationship was not found, perhaps because of the wider framework and traditions of unionised industrial relations in Eire [17].

WHAT IS THE IMPACT OF NATIONAL SYSTEMS ON HRM?

That the pattern of changes in management and industrial relations in Europe was not necessarily leading to convergence was the conclusion of a useful overview study of trends in the twelve EU and seven EFTA countries over the past twenty years. Despite the increasing impact of the European Union (and its various 'harmonization' directives) it found continuing and significant differences between the countries. While there are certainly parallel trends, and the impact of international business, divergence is at least as common as convergence in terms of labour law, works councils, incomes policies and the role of unions. There remains a great deal of scope for EU national governments (and also employers and unions) to exert distinctive strategic choices about HR and IR issues. The signs are that they will continue to do so [18].

Comparisons between the Australian and British industrial relations systems have often shown the similarities between the two heavily urbanised, industrialised parliamentary democracies, with many similar institutions, including strong trade unions. Differences in industrial structure, ownership and size of firms are probably less significant for HR/IR than the different patterns of collective labour law, with Australia having a very strong and centralised system of wages arbitration and trade union rights at industry level resulting in industry wide wage awards and informal workplace bargaining. Comparative statistical analysis of two sets of similar (WIRS) survey data in the two countries on four key dimensions, however, found some unexpected results: that union density was less uniformly distributed in Australia; the position of a specialist personnel manager at the workplace was however more uniformly distributed, but less likely to be found than in Britain. The incidence of industrial action was more widespread in Australia, though more concerned with signalling to the arbitrator than coercing the employer, but labour turnover data was ambiguous: it seemed likely to have been influenced (like strike action) by the absence of 'collective-voice' mechanism in the workplace [19].

A different and more wide-ranging analysis of changing trends in Australian IR/HR over the past decade, concluded that the turbulent economic environment pushed changes in public policy and institutional arrangements (modification of the wage arbitration system and support for enterprise agreements) which interacted with strategies pursued by firms seeking improved levels of productivity and competitiveness. Nevertheless, the resilience of the industrial relations institutions in Australia, particularly the Commission, has meant that their influence was maintained. If there is now a lot of flexibility and decentralisation it is unevenly spread and is still within a largely centralised framework. Changes in the organization of work, in skill formation, the incidence of part-time and casual work, and increases in workplace employee involvement and consultation, are visible but sporadic. Spread of productivity-related wage payment is uneven and performance pay is largely restricted to senior management. Personnel managers have little involvement in strategy formulation. While government has expressed frustration and some employers and unions have wanted to see greater decentralisation more quickly, others are distinctly less enthusiastic about totally abandoning the system of centralised wage awards [20].

National systems and union organization appear to continue to have as significant an influence as human resource managers on patterns of organizational employment policy and practice. Whether and in what ways business efficiency and effectiveness are affected is likely to remain the focus of continuing research in the future.

Sheila Rothwell

REFERENCES

[1] Fernie, S., Metcalf, D. and Woodland, S., 'Does HRM boost employee management relations?', LSE CEP Working paper No. 546, 1994: and 'What has human resource management achieved in the workplace?', *EPI Economic Report*, 8.3, May 1994.
[2] Millward, N., Stevens, M., Smart, D. and Hawes, W., *Workplace industrial relations in transition*, Dartmouth, 1990.
[3] Guest, D. and Hoque, K., 'Yes, Personnel Does make a Difference', *Personnel Management*, November 1994.
[4] Marginson, P., Armstrong, P., Edwards, P., Purcell, J. and Hubbard, N., 'The control of industrial relations in large companies: an initial analysis of the second workplace industrial relations survey', University of Warwick Papers in Industrial Relations, No. 45, 1993.
[5] Tyson, S., Witcher, M. and Doherty, N., 'Different routes to excellence', Cranfield School of Management, 1994.
[6] Purcell, J. and Ahlstrand, B., *'Human Resource Management in the multi-divisional company'*, Dartmouth 1994.
[7] Gennard, J. and Kelly, J., 'Human Resource Management: The Views of Personnel Directors', *Human Resource Management Journal*, 5:1, Autumn 1994.
[8] Wilkinson, A. and Marchington, M., 'TQM: Instant Pudding for the Personnel Function?', *Human Resource Management Journal*, 5:1, Autumn 1994.
[9] Guest, D. and Peccei, R., 'The Nature and Causes of Effective Human Resource Management', *British Journal of Industrial Relations*, 32:2, June 1994.
[10] Truss, C. and Gratton, L., 'Strategic Human Resource Management: a conceptual approach', *The International Journal of Human Resource Management*, 5:3, September 1994.
[11] Lundy, O., 'From Personnel Management to Strategic Human Resource Management', *The International Journal of Human Resource Management*, 5:3, September 1994.

1. HUMAN RESOURCE MANAGEMENT: The Environment

[12] Peck, S., 'Exploring the Link between Organisational Strategy and the Employment Relationship: The Role of Human Resources Policies', *Journal of Management Studies,* 31:5, September 1994.

[13] Guest, D. and Hoque, K., 'The Good, The Bad and the Ugly: Employment Relations in New Non-Union Workplaces', *Human Resource Management Journal,* 5:1, Autumn 1994.

[14] Gall, G. and McKay, S., 'Trade Union De recognition in Britain, 1988–1994', *British Journal of Industrial Relations,* 32:3, September 1994.

[15] Industrial Relations Services, 'Full and Partial Derecognition effects change within the workplace', *Industrial Relations Review and Report 571,* November 1994.

[16] Industrial Relations Services, 'Managing Employee Relations in the Non-Union Firm', *Industrial Relations Review and Report 570,* October 1994.

[17] Roche, W. and Turner, T., 'Testing Alternative Models of Human Resource Policy Effects on Trade Union Recognition in the Republic of Ireland', *The International Journal of Human Resource Management,* 5:3, September 1994.

[18] Clarke, O. and Bamber, G., 'Changing Management and Industrial Relations in Europe: converging towards an enterprise focus?', *The International Journal of Human Resource Management,* 5:3, September 1994.

[19] Whitfield, K., Marginson, P. and Brown, W., 'Workplace Industrial Relations Under Different Regulatory Systems: A Survey-Based Comparison of Australia and Britain', *British Journal of Industrial Relations,* 32:3, September 1994.

[20] Lansbury, R. and Niland, J., 'Trends in Industrial Relations and Human Resource Policies and Practices: Australian experiences', *The International Journal of Human Resource Management,* 5:3, September 1994.

People and Their Organizations: Rethinking the Assumptions

Marie A. McKendall and Stephen T. Margulis

"Come gather round, people, wherever you roam,
And admit that the waters around you have grown.
You'd better start swimming, or you'll sink like a stone,
For the times they are a'changin'."
— Bob Dylan

> It's time to redefine the relationship between worker and corporation.

The ways in which organizations are envisioned and managed seems to have fundamentally changed in the last several years. As more attention is focused on the corporation of the future, it is clear that organizational priorities now revolve around becoming and remaining more flexible. Companies are restructuring in ways that will allow them to respond quickly to turbulent times. To become less encumbered, many have chosen to invest less in human capital. Increasing the use of contingent work forces, reducing the permanent core of employees to a relatively small cadre, and downsizing the organization are a few indications that the manner in which firms view employees has changed. In a similar vein, shorter tenure with any one firm, the increasing popularity of multiple careers, and the revitalization of entrepreneurship signal that employees may be viewing organizations differently as well.

Although we seem quite willing to accept that companies need to assume different forms and pursue new priorities, we remain reluctant to acknowledge openly that such a shift inevitably changes the role a firm can or should play in the lives of those who work for it. Instead, we bemoan the loss of the "good" employee and speculate about how to recreate old bonds.

It is our position that visions of reciprocal "human" relationships between people and organizations, based on notions of mutual commitment and loyalty, are outdated. Continuing to subscribe to them or attempting to recapture them will have serious negative consequences for both parties. Though there is value in understanding history, there are costs in assuming that what worked well before will work well again, if only we can find a way to recreate the past. As the discussion about the organization of the future unfolds, it needs to include an acknowledgment that employees and organizations can no longer be connected to each other as they once were. To this end, we will begin to define a new paradigm that will provide a different basis for viewing employee-organizational relationships.

A BRIEF HISTORY OF THE RELATIONSHIP BETWEEN PEOPLE AND ORGANIZATIONS

The interaction of people and organizations has been a subject of writing and study for about 100 years. In the early twentieth century, the relationship was openly acknowledged to be utilitarian. The company's goal was to secure maximum work efficiency and profits; the worker's goal was to receive maximum financial reimbursement.

During the second half of the century, however, the role of the organization was redefined. Buoyed by an expansionist economy and encouraged by a growing attention to the psychology of employees, firms increasingly took on human characteristics. A great variety of benefits offered by U.S. corporations—including medical, dental, life, and retirement insurance—encouraged employees to view their firm as the Great Provider, and a strong element of paternalism emerged. Employees began to assume that, at least in part, the role of an organization was to take care of those it employed. In return, employees were to be trustworthy and reliable workers, placing corporate interests above personal ones when necessary.

Encouraged by popular writers, and aided by peoples' natural needs and desires, the view of company as family, community, or benefactor continued largely unabated through the 1970s and 1980s. Corporate cultures built on the notion of a reciprocal personal relationship were designed to elicit emotional attachment to the firm. As one personnel manager stated, "My job is to marry them to the company" (Kunda 1992). Companies portrayed themselves as imbued with strong values and desirous of mutual caring, dependency, and respect with those they employed. To cement this bond, they began to employ a "language of loyalty," which included oft-heard metaphors of family, marriage, religion, team, partners, and associates.

It was widely assumed that the commitment and loyalty employees felt toward their firms yielded universally positive outcomes. Managers were admonished to take a lesson from the Japanese and learn how to create "a strong tie that will bind an employee to his company" (Logan 1984). Lewicki (1981) offered a model of how to seduce organizational members into a commitment, declaring that "the more dedicated and loyal members are to an organization, the harder they are willing to work for it and the more stress they are willing to endure on its behalf." An article in *Fortune* heralded a "new age for business" in which the profit motive would no longer be paramount and corporations would be places full of "love and caring" (Rose 1990).

When such notions were first becoming popular, a few lone souls sounded a warning. In 1956, William Whyte coined the term "organization man" to describe the employee who "left home, spiritually as well as physically, to take the vows of organization life." Whyte argued that such fealty was misdirected, stating, "The organization will look to its own interests, but it will look to the individual's *only as The Organization interprets them.*" No one seemed to listen; the term "organization man" almost came to be perceived as a compliment. Similarly, in 1979, Edwards cautioned that companies would inevitably betray bonds of commitment and loyalty because reciprocating them would prove too costly.

> "Employees, regardless of performance or tenure, suddenly found themselves expendable as their corporate 'families' became more willing to sacrifice their members permanently in deference to the bottom line."

As the 1990s dawned, these predictions proved to be correct. Employees, regardless of performance or tenure, suddenly found themselves expendable as their corporate "families" became more willing to sacrifice their members permanently in deference to the bottom line. White-collar downsizing thus became the watershed between organizations and employees, as it conclusively demonstrated to both parties that utilitarian outcomes remained the paramount concern of American corporations.

In the face of widespread anger and disillusionment, a host of articles and books has recently appeared attempting to define a "new loyalty" and a "new trust" between people and their organizations. Why do we continue to use this language and subscribe to these ideals? Is this a model worthy of return? Before we attempt to recapture the past, let's examine the viability of creating a loyal and committed workforce.

THE BENEFITS OF LOYALTY AND COMMITMENT

Organizational commitment and loyalty can produce important behavioral outcomes for firms. Although research results are complex, commitment has been cited as a correlate of a wide range of effective employee behaviors and is a mechanism through which employee behavior can be controlled. First—and most strikingly—studies have shown that organizational commitment is one of the strongest predictors of turnover and absenteeism. Committed people do not leave their organizations, either temporarily or permanently.

Second, identifying with one's company is associated with high levels of organizational citizenship behavior. People who are committed to a firm give generously of themselves and are willing to engage in self-sacrifice on its behalf. Fostering commitment may therefore allow companies to demand extra effort from their employees more easily.

In addition to these important behavioral consequences, organizational loyalty can have beneficial psychological outcomes. The tendency to see an organization as a reciprocal presence can, to some degree, fulfill the human desire to create meaning in human lives. People want to belong to and believe in something greater than themselves; we want to be committed to something worthwhile, and we enjoy sharing a common purpose with others. In addition, research has demonstrated that employees who are highly committed to their organizations have successful careers and report satisfying nonwork lives. Moreover, commitment reinforces a dominant ideology—"Commitment typically is valued by practitioners on normative grounds" (Morrow 1983)—

because it seems like the desirable and moral way to be.

In past decades, organizational loyalty served valuable purposes. As business became concerned about the psychology of employees, it gave managers what appeared to be a caring and moral way to control behavior and elicit effort. And during the years when loyalty and commitment gained popularity, the American business environment was expansionist, markets were open, cycles were predictable, and competition was less fierce. Creating feelings of dependence and loyalty became a way to retain desired employees during a time when corporations could afford to offer long-term security in exchange and there seemed to be no limitation to the demand for American goods and services.

THE PROBLEMS WITH LOYALTY AND COMMITMENT

Though serving corporate purposes, envisioning a business organization as a human entity engaged in a reciprocally committed relationship with employees involves several mistaken notions. Consequently, it has created unintended consequences.

The major problem with the notion of loyalty and commitment between organizations and their employees is that such an ideology ignores the reality of organizational purpose in a capitalistic society. Several decades ago, Etzioni differentiated between normative and utilitarian organizations. The latter, he said, are based on a remunerative arrangement, and the employees' response is generally instrumental or calculative. By contrast, normative organizations control their members by creating a moral orientation to the firm. It is not the employee's work or efforts but the employee's self that is claimed in the name of the corporate interest. Although Etzioni categorized businesses as utilitarian, managing employees through value-laden corporate cultures and norms of reciprocity represents an attempt to elicit a moral and emotional commitment.

Such a focus denies the purpose of a business. Corporations are not self-sacrificing entities whose role is to take care of and protect their "children." They are not human beings with hearts, minds, or souls, and although loyalty may be beneficial in social relationships, one cannot have a social relationship with an organization. The fact remains that corporations are artificial entities with utilitarian ends, no matter what values may be superimposed upon them. Their purpose is to produce a profit, their final responsibility is to their stockholders, and their survival rests on fulfilling those obligations.

Considering the purpose of businesses, then, the anthropomorphism of organizations, the notion of reciprocity, and the resulting loyalty of employees combine to create an inevitable conflict between firms and the people who work for them. Company effectiveness, profits, and survival often necessitate decisions that are not in the best interest of individual employees. We are not saying that organizations are horrible places and managers are unfeeling ogres. Most managers, in fact, care about employees a great deal, but personal feelings must occur in the context of the primary corporate objective. As the last several years have demonstrated, when the interests of the employee and the interests of the company come into conflict, the company will—and should—fulfill its primary role. To claim that such a conflict need never occur is naive and ultimately destructive.

Thus, organizations stand to lose if they continue to depict themselves as something they cannot be. Employees have grown increasingly aware of the inconsistencies between the way businesses portray themselves and the actions they take. They have begun to question the ethics of firms that construct a false image. Organizational rhetoric that promotes mythical reciprocal obligations denotes a lack of respect for employees and creates feelings of hostility, cynicism, and bitterness when the firm fails to live up to the expectations it has created.

Managers, who often feel committed to their subordinates, experience a sense of failure and guilt when they find themselves powerless to change organizational decisions. These feelings of depression, stress, and betrayal are manifested in the entire work force, not just those who are directly affected by a layoff or other adverse decision. If the culture of the organization has been paternalistic, then adverse actions have a much more profound effect on survivors; loyalty plunges most noticeably among workers who were previously the most committed, and performance drops most significantly when a layoff is perceived to be unfair.

> "The notion of loyalty and commitment between organizations and their employees ignores the reality of organizational purpose in a capitalistic society."

Once the perceived contract between employee and organization is violated, survivors often react in unexpected ways. Emotional shock, severe morale problems, feelings of powerlessness, and diminished communication can all operate to decrease productivity. Furthermore, the effects of violated expectations may extend far into the future. A recent study of college-aged children whose parents had lost their jobs revealed that these future employees were more cynical about social institutions and less likely to believe in the value of hard work.

In addition to denying organizational reality and setting up inevitable conflict, allegiance to the desirability of loyalty and commitment has created dangerously dichotomized thinking. Employees have come to be seen as either good and loyal workers or self-centered opportunists. Writers have continued to bemoan the individualistic and impatient nature of American workers. Rowan (1981) decries the "fickle me generation executives" and their loss of "dedication, allegiance, and fidelity." Witten (1989) complains that "the bonds of loyalty and trust have been superseded by self-interest." Demeuse and Tornow (1990) declare that "returning favors and helping out friends is as uncommon today as quilting bees and barnraisings." Such rhetoric leaves the impression that an employee who is not highly committed to a firm will inevitably be a selfish and unproductive detriment. This runs contrary to research indicating that a person can be quite committed to work while feeling no particularly strong commitment toward the business.

Another problem with creating loyalty and commitment through organizational anthropomorphism is that such a strategy emphasizes the wrong outcome. In 1975, S. Kerr wrote the management classic "On the Folly of Rewarding A, While Hoping for B" on the thesis that companies frequently hope employees will exhibit one behavior while they reward and measure something else. The emphasis on organizational commitment is a striking validation of Kerr's theory. What firms really need is people who perform well; but instead of concentrating on performance, it has been decided that performance and loyalty are interchangeable. Research shows, however, that the relationship between commitment and performance is very modest or nonexistent. Other studies have shown that the job insecurity typically associated with low levels of company commitment does not have the reduced performance and strain-related consequences usually hypothesized. One study uncovered no relationship between insecurity and performance; another showed that performance actually peaked at moderate levels of insecurity.

In addition to negative organizational outcomes, there is also some evidence that being a loyal employee can have detrimental psychological consequences. Mandating that employees should be loyal to their organizational "family" inevitably triggers notions of reciprocity. This view of the world fosters an unrealistic perception of what a firm is and produces an unhealthy dependence on an artificial entity. In a case study of a large firm with very strong normative expectations of commitment and family, Kunda (1992) observed that

> . . . if the idea of normative control is founded on the hope of offering members a stable self grounded in a morally sound organizational community, the opposite is produced. Among full members, we find an ambivalent, fluctuating, ironic self, at war with itself. . . . [E]mployees experience a pull that is not easy to combat, an escalating commitment to the corporation and its definitions of reality, coupled with a systematic and persistent attack on the boundaries of their privacy.

When people begin to perceive businesses as personifications, they may identify with them, as they would with another person. Such an illusory relationship produces a false sense of security and predictability, and employees often become willing to engage in self-sacrifice on behalf of the firm. This abdication of personal responsibility and denial of reality exacts an unhealthy price under any circumstances, but given the current priorities of corporations, it sets the stage for massive disillusionment and perceptions of betrayal. When speaking of all he had given up and the family time he had forgone, report Hage, Grant, and Impoco (1993), a laid-off IBM salesman reflected, "I breathed IBM, ate IBM. I went for it hook, line, and sinker." A laid-off employee from another firm echoed the sentiment when he lamented, "I was hurt. After 34 years with the company, I was surprised that it came down to an economic relationship between the two of us. I thought I was in a family kind of thing."

Even under the best of circumstances, a loyal work force does not produce uniformly positive outcomes. Several authors have speculated about the undesirable organizational effects of highly committed employees. A lack of creativity, resistance to change, a tendency to engage in groupthink, insufficient turnover, and the pursuit of improper goals might emerge as unintended byproducts of a very committed work force.

PROPOSALS FOR A NEW RELATIONSHIP

In decades past, it can be argued, the benefits of creating loyal employees outweighed the costs. This, however, is no longer true; in these times of unpredictability, foreign competi-

> "What firms really need is people who perform well; but instead of concentrating on performance, it has been decided that performance and loyalty are interchangeable."

tion, deregulation, crippling debt, downsizings, and hostile takeovers, businesses are acting disingenuously and unethically if they attempt to maintain or recreate feelings of loyalty that they cannot return.

Nevertheless, even the massive downsizings of the last several years have not caused the rhetoric to change. As mentioned before, popular management literature now speaks of the need to generate a "new loyalty" and a "new trust." Again, why do we continue to speak in these terms? What do we hope to gain by continuing to espouse a contract that has incontrovertibly failed? And what, exactly, do these new proposals involve?

Rose (1990) claims that we must rebuild our organizations around basic fundamental values, including trust, respect, dignity, commitment, integrity, and accountability. Love and caring will become motivators, and profit will cease to be the primary goal. In a similar though more sophisticated vein, Aktouf (1992) argues that we must humanize companies through candor, symmetry, equity, and sharing, and that companies must be willing to forgo profits to avoid laying off people. Aktouf concedes that such an ideology cannot flourish in an organization that embraces Western philosophies of economic self-interest; therefore, we must be willing to rethink both workers and organizations.

Recent writings have also advocated covenantal relationships between firms and employees, characterized by mutual commitment, security, and forgiveness—even in the face of disappointing performance. These authors are envisioning true reciprocity. But we maintain it is naive to believe such relationships will become commonplace in the capitalistic framework of American business. To offer this as a prescription on which to fashion a new business relationship is to offer little practical advice.

Another common theme is that to create this "new loyalty," power, knowledge, and autonomy must be shared. This empowerment will be accomplished through work flexibility, group activities, self-managed work teams, expanded training, global thinking, increased communication, strong cultural norms, specific performance criteria, and performance-based compensation systems. We are assured that if these strategies are implemented, loyalty, dedication, and commitment will be restored. Though we certainly agree with the "empowerment" of employees and with many of the proposed means, why should the goal of such strategies be the rebirth of loyalty and commitment rather than the creation of a productive and profitable organization?

Another recommended approach, which also calls for "renewed commitment to the survival of corporate loyalty into the 21st century" (Grossman 1989), involves employees transferring their trust to competent leaders who will communicate and mutually define goals with them. These leaders will then be in a position to reestablish loyalty implementation strategies, truth telling, and long-range planning. What this recommendation fails to note, however, is that individual leaders are constrained by their positions. Ultimately, they must act as agents of the corporation. If they are meant to be autonomous guardians of employees, then how this will be accomplished ought to be described.

When one closely examines these proposals for a new relationship between people and organizations, one does not find much substance in them. We would like to state unequivocally that it should no longer be the goal of a business to depict itself in a manner intended to secure loyalty. Nor should it be the intention of an employee to depend on the corporation or extend loyalty. To travel down that road again invites further disillusionment and betrayal. We do, however, firmly believe it is possible for people and their organizations to engage in a mutually beneficial and productive relationship without subscribing to the reciprocal loyalty myth. In this vein, we would like to offer several recommendations to those who participate in and govern organizational life.

> "It is possible for people and their organizations to engage in a mutually beneficial and productive relationship without subscribing to the reciprocal loyalty myth."

1. Accept that what may have worked before is no longer viable.

We believe it is time to stop blindly assuming that the death of corporate loyalty means we have lost something irreplaceable. Lower levels of commitment may represent a loss, but it is a loss whose time has come. Loyalty can be replaced with other performance-generating methods that free both parties to behave in different—and perhaps better—ways.

2. Portray organizations authentically.

People must hold realistic views and expectations of the companies they work for, or aspire to work for. When people are hired by a firm, they enter into what has been termed a "psychological contract" that consists of the expectations and assumptions each side holds of the other. One of the basic legal and normative beliefs about a contractual situation is that neither party should willfully misrepresent itself. In a capitalistic society, a firm's allegiance to its employees is not likely to supersede its economic interests. So utilitarian organizations should not present themselves in a paternalistic role; they should not expect loyalty and commitment from their members when they do not, and often cannot, make decisions predicated on reciprocating these sentiments.

Businesses must make it clear that while they have responsibilities to fair and equitable compensation, performance appraisal, and employment practices, it is not their obligation to do for their people what those people, as adults, should do for themselves. It is the responsibility of working adults to ensure their long-term financial security, manage their career, and maintain control of their destiny. To abdicate that responsibility is to invite serious personal risk.

3. Monitor attitudes, language, and actions.

If companies expect people to be self-reliant and mature, then managers must be willing to broaden their own views about what constitutes a good employee. It should not automatically be assumed that the best employee is the loyal employee and that the only way people will be productive is to be co-opted or seduced into performing through a strong and paternalistic culture. People are multifaceted; they will perform for many reasons that have nothing to do with being tied into the corporate family. Remember, there is no substantial evidence that organizationally committed people are better performers.

Managers must be committed to dignifying employees by telling the truth. One management technique, the realistic job preview, involves presenting new entrants with accurate descriptions of their jobs and the organizational norms. Extensive research shows that employees who have received a realistic job preview have higher levels of job satisfaction, lower turnover, and lower initial expectations. These realistic expectations, in turn, are a strong predictor of person-job congruence and higher levels of motivation.

Managers, personnel recruiters, and corporate communicators must also guard against making statements that cannot and will not be backed by corporate action. Corporate statements, policies, stories, and language that refer to the company family and assure people that they are the company's most important priority sound pretty, but they also create expectations. Do not talk about the employment relationship as if it were permanent; do not imply that competent performance will ensure an everlasting job. Do not keep unfavorable news from employees because you feel they must be protected or can't be trusted to handle the truth with maturity. Do not allow people to think personal friendships will somehow be able to protect them from adverse corporate decisions.

We wish to be absolutely clear that we are not universally condemning forms of coordination and control based on peer pressure, shared norms or values, and the like. It is, however, incumbent on a firm to make absolutely clear that these forms of control are strategic decisions aimed at achieving goals such as efficiency, competitiveness, information transfer, or flexibility. Because employees have a tendency to construe social forms of control in personal terms, organizations must make their positions abundantly clear. Employees must realize that when organizational self-interest demands legitimate actions that are not in the best interests of all employees, the company will act on those interests. A company that has consistently conveyed that "No" means "No" should not be held accountable for a misguided employee who wants to believe "No" means "Yes." On the other hand, a firm that seduces employees into loyalty but later discovers it has no intention of reciprocating—even for the best of strategic reasons—should be condemned.

4. Recognize and encourage the more valuable forms of loyalty.

People need a sense of meaning in their lives. Though it is unhealthy to search for this fulfillment through organizational commitment, it is possible to find it by becoming committed to the quality and content of one's work or profession. In a corporate world characterized by impermanence and constant change, people must remain employable. This means forming a commitment to becoming skilled in ways that increase the likelihood of future employment. It also means being committed to the principles of service and product quality and producing good work. Indeed, the evidence indicates that these kinds of attitudes are more beneficial to a firm than is blind loyalty.

A review of the literature identifies four types of commitment. First, people can be committed to hard work and can value work for its own sake. Second, people can be committed to a career and feel loyalty to an occupation or a profession. Alternately, people can be committed to a particular job or to the employing firm. Interestingly, work and career foci demonstrate high permanence throughout a person's life, whereas a job focus is of medium permanence and a company focus is characterized by the least stability of all. Finally, people who are committed to their profession tend not to be committed to a firm.

In the light of such evidence, it is time to divest ourselves of the notion that the person who is not loyal to the organization is not going to be a good employee; there are alternate forms of commitment that will ultimately serve both parties better.

5. If you really want high-performing employees, then create the conditions for high performance.

Companies often depict themselves in a manner designed to elicit loyalty because they believe loyalty and performance are correlated. However, as noted earlier, this association has little support. If your concern is performance, then you should become familiar with the conditions that support, encourage, and sustain high performance.

There are many such conditions. For example, job redesign has the potential to increase productivity by about 9 percent; goal setting could increase productivity by about 16 percent; pay-for-performance compensation systems can raise productivity by up to 30 percent. What procedures or combinations of procedures are likely to work best for your firm will depend on your specific circumstances. The point is that there are many management techniques that will foster productivity without creating an unhealthy dependency on an organization.

Contrary to most recent sentiment, we do not think the decrease in corporate loyalty should be bemoaned; we believe it should be welcomed. It is a sign that people are thinking more realistically about businesses, and it releases both parties from impossible expectations.

Given the profit orientation of American corporations, it is foolish to think that a company can or should function as the guardian of individual employees. For that very reason, companies must foster an understanding that keeps them, as organizations, in a proper perspective. This does not mean that people in utilitarian organizations must be vicious, impersonal, or cold. Rather, all employees should be treated with respect, dignity, and fairness; there is nothing about a utilitarian focus that prohibits this. The false promises of paternalism and loyalty are an affront to employees.

We strongly believe that employees and organizations have much to gain from such an approach. By relinquishing the loyalty myth, organizations retain the flexibility to respond to competitive influences without guilt. If they stop creating unrealistic expectations, they will be able to shed the stigma of being seen as the Great Protector that broke all of its promises. Employees, in turn, can stop subscribing to false illusions about their firms and, as a result, can become more responsible for their lives.

All of this, of course, depends on people accepting organizations for what they are—no more and no less. Organizations are creations of society, not ends unto themselves. They provide us with a place to work and a social network. They marshal resources and, through collective action, allow us to produce outcomes that individuals alone could not generate. But they are not a mother, father, sibling, lover, spouse, or friend. To perceive or cast them in such a light distorts their purposes and gives them a power over peoples' lives that they do not deserve and should not desire to have.

References

O. Aktouf, "Management and Theories of Organizations in the 1990s: Toward a Critical Radical Humanism?" *Academy of Management Review,* 17 (1992): 407-431.

S. Ashford, C. Lee, and P. Bobko, "Content, Causes, and Consequences of Job Insecurity: A Theory-Based Measure and Substantive Test," *Academy of Management Journal,* 32 (1989): 803-829.

T. Atchinson, "The Employment Relationship: Un-tied or Re-tied?" *Academy of Management Executive,* 5 (1991): 52-62.

D. Bragninsty, cited in L. Grant, "Finding Hope After Losing a Job," *U.S. News and World Report,* June 28, 1993, p. 48.

J. Brockner, "The Effects of Work Layoff on Survivors: Research, Theory, and Practice," in B. Staw and L. Cummings, eds., *Research in Organizational Behavior* (Greenwich, CT: JAI Press, 1988), pp. 213-256.

J. Brockner, S. Grover, T. Reed, and R. Dewitt, "Layoffs, Job Insecurity, and Survivors' Work Effort: Evidence of an Inverted-U Relationship," *Academy of Management Journal,* 35 (1992): 413-425.

A. Cohen, "Organizational Commitment and Turnover: A Meta-Analysis," *Academy of Management Journal,* 36 (1993): 1,140-1,157.

S. Colarelli, "Methods of Communication and Mediating Processes in Realistic Job Previews," *Journal of Applied Psychology,* 69 (1984): 633-642.

K. DeMeuse and W. Tornow, "The Tie That Binds Has Become Very, Very Frayed," *Human Resource Planning,* 13 (1990): 203-213.

R. Edwards, *Contested Terrain* (New York: Basic Books, 1979).

"The End of Corporate Loyalty," *Business Week,* August 4, 1986, p. 42.

A. Etzioni, *A Comparative Analysis of Complex Organizations* (New York: The Free Press, 1961).

A. Farnham, "The Trust Gap," *Fortune,* December 4, 1989, pp. 56-78.

B. Grossman, "Corporate Loyalty: Does it Have a Future?" *Journal of Business Ethics*, 8 (1989): 565-568.

D. Hage, L. Grant, and J. Impoco, "White Collar Wasteland," *U.S. News and World Report,* June 28, 1993, pp. 42-51.

T. Horton and P. Reid, *Beyond the Trust Gap: Forging a New Partnership Between Managers and Their Employees* (Homewood, IL: Business One Irwin, 1991).

S. Kerr, "On the Folly of Rewarding A, While Hoping for B," *Academy of Management Journal,* 18 (1975): 769-783.

G. Kunda, *Engineering Culture* (Philadelphia: Temple University Press, 1992).

R. Lewicki, "Organizational Seduction: Building Commitment to Organizations," *Organizational Dynamics, 10* (1981): 5-22.

G. Logan, "Loyalty and a Sense of Purpose," *California Management Review,* Fall 1984, pp. 149-156.

W. Morin, *Trust Me* (New York: Harcourt Brace Jovanovich, 1990).

P. Morrow, "Concept Redundancy in Organizational Research: The Case of Work Commitment," *Academy of Management Review,* 8 (1983): 486-500.

B. Moskal, "Managing Survivors," *Industry Week,* August 3, 1992, pp. 15-20.

R. Mowday, L. Porter, and R. Steers, *Employee Organization Linkages: The Psychology of Commitment, Absenteeism, and Turnover* (New York: Academic Press, 1982).

D. Randall, "Commitment and the Organization: The Organization Man Revisited," *Academy of Management Review,* 12 (1987): 460-471.

D. Randall, D. Fedor, and C. Longnecker, "The Behavioral Expression of Organizational Commitment," *Journal of Vocational Behavior, 36* (1990): 210-224.

D. Reichers, "A Review and Reconceptualization of Organizational Commitment," *Academy of Management Review, 10* (1985): 465-476.

B. Romzek, "Personal Consequences of Employee Commitment," *Academy of Management Journal,* 39 (1989): 649-661.

F. Rose, "A New Age for Business?" *Fortune,* October 8, 1990, pp. 157-164.

R. Rowan, "Rekindling Corporate Loyalty," *Fortune,* February 9, 1981, pp. 54-58.

L. Van Dyne, J. Graham, and R. Dienensch, "Organizational Citizenship Behavior: Construct Redefinition, Measurement, and Validation," *Academy of Management Journal,* 37 (1994): 765-802.

J. Wagner and J. Hollenbeck, *Management of Organizational Behavior* (Englewood Cliffs, NJ: Prentice-Hall, 1992).

J. Wanous, "Tell It Like It Is At Realistic Job Previews," *Personnel,* 52 (1975): 50-60.

W. Whyte, *The Organization Man* (New York: Doubleday Anchor Book, 1956).

Y. Wiener, "Commitment in Organizations: A Normative View," *Academy of Management Review,* 7 (1982): 418-428.

Y. Wiener and Y. Vardi, "Relationships Between Job, Organization, and Career Commitments and Work Outcomes—An Integrative Approach," *Organizational Behavior and Human Performance,* 26 (1980): 81-96.

M. Witten, "Whatever Happened to Corporate Loyalty?" *Canadian Business,* 62 (1989): 46-48, 96-102.

Marie A. McKendall is an associate professor of management, and **Stephen T. Margulis** is a professor of management, both at Grand Valley State University in Allendale, Michigan.

Wedding HR to Strategic Alliances

Within the last decade, U.S. companies formed more than 20,000 alliances, but a large percentage have failed. Allowing HR managers to facilitate the relationships can mean the difference between a happy marriage and a messy divorce.

Brenda Paik Sunoo

Brenda Paik Sunoo is senior editor at PERSONNEL JOURNAL.

You've seen them off the highway. You've probably even fidgeted behind one at the nearest pit stop: The long-haul trucker who's tying up the pay phone. He could be calling home. But most likely he's on hold, awaiting his fleet manager's next road assignment. Wouldn't it be great if we could just eliminate the frustration on his end, the manager's and our own? That's just what J.B. Hunt Transport Services, Inc. and IBM did in 1993. A strategic alliance between the two companies produced the on-board computer—a satellite technology that looks like a cellular phone and simplifies the trucking industry's ability to track and assign its drivers while expanding IBM's commercial market.

In addition, Armonk, New York-based IBM also introduced a new software program called Micromap® to simplify the logistics manager's job by sorting through the difficult process of matching loads to truckers. This enabled the computer to consider more than 90 different assignment possibilities. "[The computers] also give us the ability to communicate back and forth with the drivers every minute and at any place in the world," says Steve Palmer, executive vice president of human resources

> **The most important thing is that the purpose be clear. The alliance enables you to throw an anchor into the future and pull yourself towards it.**

and risk management for Lowell, Arkansas-based J.B. Hunt. Already, the technology shared through the alliance has reduced the number of driving miles and has contributed to getting employees home on time. Moreover, the on-board computers have helped to reduce fatigue and the number of highway accidents, he says.

Companies are looking for ways to share resources and opportunities. The strategic alliance between J.B. Hunt and IBM is only one of thousands springing up in the business world every day. One of the most visible partnerships announced recently is the one between Microsoft Corp. and DreamWorks, the entertainment studio founded by producer Steven Spielberg, former Disney executive Jeffrey Katzenberg and music mogul David Geffen. Others include Schering-Plough Corporation and Corvas International; Motorola and various enterprises in China; Amoco and Enron corporations. The list goes on. Today's strategic alliances are cooperative arrangements between two or more companies that want to develop a win-win strategy. Primarily, both sides want to gain access to untapped geographic markets and resources, exercise more control and share risks. They can be created in response to a variety of needs and can take the form of anything from a technology licensing agreement to a full-blown joint venture. Both parties, essentially, want to reduce the time needed to get product to a greater market at the lowest possible costs. According to global management and technology consulting firm

1. HUMAN RESOURCE MANAGEMENT: Human Resources and Corporate Strategy

Booz•Allen & Hamilton, more than 20,000 new alliances were formed between 1987 and 1992. Nearly 6% of the revenue generated from the top 1,000 U.S. firms now comes from alliances. But about 40% of U.S. alliances today are still considered failures because they don't achieve their objectives, says John R. Harbison, vice president for Booz•Allen, based in Los Angeles.

No one knows exactly why they're failing, but industry analysts, business consultants and organizational development specialists are beginning, at least, to understand their nature, to avoid some of the traps and to identify the keys to an alliance's success. Some also advocate a stronger presence of human resources executives. Because most strategic alliances are initially driven by CEOs and marketing and sales executives, HR executives have been underrated and ignored in the process. But, as those involved in alliances are learning, HR professionals—such as the ones from Dresser Industries, J. B. Hunt Transport, Inc. and Lau Technologies—can contribute to an alliance's success at any stage: They can help define the two partners' culture, assess the alliance's business needs and map out a common language. In addition, HR can take responsibility for the usual compensation and benefits issues that would apply to the alliance employees.

"HR needs to get on a really rapid learning curve," says Jessica Lipnack, president of West Newton, Massachusetts-based The Networking Institute, Inc. and co-author of "The Age of the Network: Organizing Principles for the 21st Century." "They need to facilitate interaction and communication and be electronically savvy to connect people and functions at different sites."

Most strategic alliances, says Lipnack, are typically viewed as a *deal.* Executives often don't get down to the level of what it means as far as implementation is concerned. "The most important thing is that the purpose be clear. If the purpose is clear, then everyone involved has a role. The alliance enables you to throw an anchor into the future and pull yourself toward it," she says.

Today, many alliances are formed by larger companies that partner with smaller companies. For example, take a look at Maynard, Massachusetts-based Digital Equipment Corp. Here's a company that recently traveled a very bumpy road. It has posted more than $3 billion in losses in the last several years, has restructured and faced several top-level resignations, and has slipped in ranking behind its competitors, IBM and Hewlett-Packard. To acquire more sophisticated systems expertise, Digital entered into an alliance with Acton, Massachusetts-based Lau Technologies. A company with 200 employees, Lau Technologies was the only minority-owned company of three technology firms designated by the state of Massachusetts as a supplier of personal computers, local area networks and other systems for state-agency purchases. In 1992, it had won a $10 million contract from the Massachusetts Registry of Motor Vehicles (MRMV) to provide equipment for automating the issuance of driver's licenses. Digital provided the stand-alone system, and Lau customized it for the MRMV. By forming an alliance with Lau, Digital was able to take advantage of a state-agency contract targeted for a minority-owned company. It also gained an opportunity to improve its visibility and flash its name on the more sophisticated technology systems provided by Lau. In turn, the smaller company captured a new business opportunity outside of the waning defense industry. (About 90% of the company's revenues still come from producing electronic systems for defense contractors.) "We needed to find new avenues for sharing the burden of defense cutbacks. So we researched what other businesses we could do," says Joanna Lau, president of Lau Technologies.

Human resources, Lau says, plays an important role from a defense conversion standpoint. The skills set of many com-

---

Guidelines for Managing an Alliance

- **Conduct a cost-benefit analysis of favorable and unfavorable conditions. Control them to maximize revenues, minimize costs and lower risks**
- **When possible, start an alliance small and build on trust**
- **Avoid exchanging market access between competitors**
- **Identify and address conflicts over activities critical to success, time horizons or government regulation**
- **Generate widespread internal political support**
- **Place operating managers on the negotiating team**
- **Send divisive topics to higher-level negotiation groups**
- **Structure the alliance with its own board of directors to speed up the approval process**
- **Select a CEO on the basis of appropriate skills, style and ability to develop an understanding of goals and competitive advantages that are to be shared between the alliance partners**
- **Do not require the alliance to prepare two sets of financial control reporting systems, one for each partner**
- **Stay alert to early signs of termination: inflexibility in adapting operating procedures; combative negotiation style; conflict over management appointments; politicking; and a reluctance to reinvest**
- **In the termination process, determine what must be accomplished in order to allow the remaining partner to keep the former joint activity going**
- **When negotiating termination procedures, do not establish a precise termination value formula nor take a detailed, legalistic approach that breeds mistrust.**

Source: The Conference Board

pany employees have drifted from manufacturing to research and development and engineering. "Strategic alliances [spur] innovation, an entrepreneurial environment, more projects and more diverse customers," she says.

Kathleen Camire, Lau Technologies' training manager, says that human resources entered into the two companies' alliance to assist in training.

First, Digital had to train Lau employees to use its hardware equipment. That part was relatively easy. But there were several other Lau employees that had to learn how to train the motor vehicle trainers. "We had to teach 14 [MRMV] trainers how to operate the work station that we were providing for them," says Camire. It was a Windows-based application that allowed an operator to capture a digital image and print a license. The challenge, she says, was to train Lau employees who weren't used to dealing with the commercial side of business. "Before they were trained to do contract-specific tasks like soldering and inspection. Now they had to learn how to set up computers, test software and train others how to use the equipment at the customer's worksite," she says. No longer could these Lau inspectors wear blue jeans and T-shirts to work. "Now, they had to wear a suit and rethink what they were doing. Because we didn't hire people from the outside, we took people already here and trained them to think differently about the way they do business," she says.

Since the alliance, Camire says, HR has spent more time on training, curriculum development, scheduling and choosing the right employees for new tasks. About 30 new types of jobs have been created for internal employees. They encompass customer service, maintenance and installation, software engineering and testing computers. Prior to the alliance with Digital, Lau Technologies didn't even have a customer-service department, she says. "We formed it right before the alliance."

Even rivals can become strategic partners. J.B. Hunt Transport, Inc. also made headlines years ago when it allied with railroad companies to share the freight market. It began with Schaumburg, Illinois-based Santa Fe Pacific Corporation in 1989. Today, J.B. Hunt—a $1.2 billion a year company—has at least nine hauling arrangements and 47 ramp locations with railroads covering the 48 contiguous states, Canada and access to Mexico. Intermodal transportation has become big business at J.B. Hunt and generates more than 30% of total revenues. "We've been given a lot of credit for the [increased] intermodal activity," says Palmer. In the past, the railroad industry had been tarnished by a reputation for high cargo claims, broken freight and unreliable schedules. Then railroad companies like Santa Fe began to change their image by improving their tracks and minimizing the jarring of freight. It also invested in high-speed locomotives to improve its transit time. "In the past, we all competed for the same customers," he says. "But we already had a customer base and a great reputation for service and claims." The bulk of J.B. Hunt's customers were *Fortune* 500 companies with plants all over the country. Santa Fe, Palmer says, had the tracks and the rail expertise. "They used us as the marketing arm to improve their service, and we saved time in delivering freight to our customers. Together, we cut costs for the customer," he says.

From a human resources standpoint, the alliance provided J.B. Hunt's HR managers with better incentives for recruiting, career pathing and retaining employees. Before the alliance, HR was troubled by the high turnover rate among long-haul truck drivers. "We couldn't get them home as often as we'd like," says Palmer. "A lot of drivers would call me fixing to quit. They'd say, 'I need more stability for my family life.' " Long-haul truck drivers of the past would drive 2,500 miles at a time, with home stops about every two weeks. But today's driver is younger, less experienced and more antsy to get home.

With the alliance, HR at J.B. Hunt was then able to create local and regional driver jobs. "It impacted turnover dramatically," Palmer says. At first, the truckers viewed the intermodal services as a threat. Senior truck drivers usually earn up to 33 cents per mile. So when they make a 3,000-mile haul, they earn a hefty sum in addition to various performance bonuses. "They viewed [the alliance] as taking their miles away from them," says Palmer. But after HR had held several orientation and training sessions, the drivers began to see the combined freight service as a career-path opportunity. "Every time we established a rail partner, we gained another rail lane that gave us the opportunity to open up more local and regional jobs." Drivers would still have to pick up the supplier's freight, deliver it to the railhead, unload it at the end of the line and take it to the final destination. In other words, more frequent short shops, rather than one long one. "If we could get them the same compensation *and* home every night, or two to three times a week, that was a big plus."

Parent partners often give birth to new entities. Strategic alliances have often been compared to the dynamics of marriage and the family. Harbison, of Booz•Allen & Hamilton, even describes some of the more common sense traps by using these analogies:

• Picking the wrong spouse: Failing to take the time to select the right partner
• Being vague with the prenuptials: Failing to explicitly agree on objectives and goals
• Being a possessive child: Focusing on one's slice and who controls the baker
• Seeing through the eyes of a juvenile: Not developing much-needed trust
• Causing the generation gap: Relying on inadequate or erratic communications
• Living with the in-laws: Not solving the *protective-parent syndrome.*

Harbison also warns that partners should not be in a hurry to consummate an alliance as in a shotgun wedding. It usually takes about a year to put an alliance together. Armed with an understanding of the motivations for an alliance, it's tempting for companies "to plunge ahead without understanding the perils in the path ahead," he says. "It's dangerous when the selection of a partner drives strategy rather than vice versa," he says.

Ask Paul Bryant, vice president of human resources for Dallas-based Dresser Industries, Inc. He participated in his company's alliance with Woodcliff Lake, New Jersey-based Ingersoll-Rand Company in the mid-1980s. Both were American companies, and both competed worldwide for products. Dresser is known for being a leading international supplier of products and services for the

1. HUMAN RESOURCE MANAGEMENT: Human Resources and Corporate Strategy

oil and gas industry. It offers everything from drill bits to gas pumps to pipe-coating services. Ingersoll-Rand, on the other hand, is a manufacturer of non-electrical industrial machinery and is one of the world's largest makers of air compression systems, anti-friction bearings, construction equipment and air tools.

The seeds of the alliance were planted by the two companies' CEOs. Both had known each other through various industry associations. Because of the downturn in the energy market worldwide, both companies ended up with a surplus of products. "Both sides quickly went from being highly profitable to highly unprofitable. By combining [some facilities], we could put more resources into development and return to profitability as soon as possible," says Bryant, who participated in the planning stages. As alliances evolve, partners often can assume different roles. Some might simply lend a name. Others might invest money, provide expertise or just roll up their sleeves and lend a hand. But regardless of the role, both partners must be committed to the alliance's success. In the case of Dresser and Ingersoll-Rand, the alliance would give birth to a new entity.

The parent companies had to first agree on their strategic goals: To restructure in a way that would reduce the capacity and improve a new product line for their global customers. With the Dresser and Ingersoll-Rand alliance, HR played a pivotal role in the beginning by helping select the remaining sites that would evolve into the new entity known as Dresser-Rand company. The new entity, based in Corning, New York, was slated to manufacture compressors and gas turbines.

"Our philosophy was that the new company had to stand on its own. We decided there would be little interference from the parent companies," he says. Instead, the parent companies would serve as consultants.

Under Bryant's leadership, the then-combined work force of 9,000 [today there are 7,500] would have to be selected. HR had to determine the criteria with which to evaluate them and also establish a smooth transition for their transfer. Because the new headquarters for Dresser-Rand was in a small community, HR made arrangements for temporary housing. Some employees were offered accommodations in local motels within a 15- to 20-mile radius of Corning. The alliance also required that HR design a new set of rules and benefits program. "We had to use grandfathering techniques to look back at each employee's history, pension formula and service credit with the parent company." In other words, the Dresser-Rand alliance was different from an acquisition because a third entity was formed immediately as part of the alliance arrangement.

> **Every time we established a rail partner, we gained an opportunity to open up more jobs.**
> *Steve Palmer*
> *J.B. Hunt Transport, Inc.*

Bryant says that one of the most difficult aspects of any alliance is reconciling two operating cultures. Dresser Industries and Ingersoll-Rand were similar in some ways: Both had a long-service type of culture in which the average employee tenure was about 14 years. Both also came from engineering backgrounds. But the work styles were very different. One was from the East Coast; the other was based in the Southwest. Those regional differences impacted whether employees were more used to a formal or casual way of working, he says. HR facilitated both groups' mingling by arranging special dinners and van pools to the local facilities. "Even though the purpose of the trips was to become familiar with our operations, you get to know each other better after spending two hours in the same [vehicle]," he says.

After serving six years as Dresser-Rand's HR manager, Bryant was promoted in 1993 to his current position as vice president of HR for Dresser Industries. Today, he says, Dresser-Rand is more focused on team building and TQM initiatives that he led before his departure. In addition to the HR department, which includes a staff of 12 professionals, Dresser-Rand also established a quality department run by one vice president and one assistant. "We believe in quality so much that we wanted it to be on equal footing with the other departments," says Bryant, who recommended that Dresser-Rand purchase and implement Corning Incorporated's successful total quality program. "Total quality gave us the framework and initiative to harness our employees. People led teams for the first time and blossomed," he says. Dresser-Rand's alliance has been so successful, that in 1992 the two companies also combined their pump businesses and formed Ingersoll-Dresser Pump after gaining approval from the U.S. Justice Department. Today, IDP is a mammoth global enterprise, with reported sales nearing $900 million, factories around the world and 7,000 employees. By forming that alliance, the two companies were again able to shrink capacity, combine technology and become more cost competitive. In other words, the businesses brought complementary technologies and marketing strengths to the table.

"Strategic alliances are usually set up for one reason. But it often creates so many other possibilities," says Lipnack. Adds Peta Penson, principal of Saratoga, California-based Co-Development International, Inc.: "All of these alliances mean new ways of working together. The most important stakeholders often lie outside one's traditional boundaries. People have reached out to other suppliers and vendors."

Upstart companies team up with global resources. For William Koch, co-owner of Ontario, California-based Rexor Corp., forming a strategic alliance meant partnering with a Korean-American chemist with ties to Korea. Together, they formed Rexor, a small company with five employees that primarily has been a technology research and development firm. Now, the company is proceeding to commercialize by growing single silicon crystals called *boules,* which are sliced into wafers and used to form computer chips. The technology, Koch explains, is one in which Americans have virtually no knowledge. "The people who had been working in this [field] aren't in the United States." Koch's company was exploring a way to grow the crystals in a cheaper and more efficient manner. "Technology is so expensive and so large that it requires more than one single-source provider. In our case, we grow this crystal, which is just one of many steps to get the computer chip to the market place. It requires a high degree of competency," says Koch, whose background is in engineering organizational development.

When Rexor purchased a $500,000 machine to enable the process, the equipment manufacturing representative who came to install the machine had also installed one in India. Koch asked him to recommend someone who might have the required technical expertise. The representative gave him the name of an Indian professional who had been studying the crystal-growing method. Koch flew to India and negotiated to have the Indian join the Rexor staff. That was three years ago. Today, Rexor also is engaged in a strategic alliance with an Indian company that takes the manufactured crystal and converts them into solar cells, then sends them to Korea where they're mounted onto boards and are prepared for worldwide export. "We're getting a price enhancement on our materials by paying a strategic alliance partner a fee in India to do what they want to do—[make solar cells]. Then we pay another enhancement fee in Korea to put them into modules."

The Korea connection was strengthened through the Korean-American co-owners' ties to his native homeland. But even with that cultural advantage and insight, Koch quickly learned that conducting global transactions between two different cultures can still get sticky. "[Americans] have a tendency to do business as a contractual arrangement. Koreans are different. They rely more on verbal agreements. Contracts, dates, checkoffs don't fit well with them. They view it as questioning their integrity. So you never know until the day a project is done, if it's done."

HR can contribute to an alliance's success. As with any marriage, there's no guarantee that strategic alliance partners will "live happily ever after." James Finnegan, director for Cambridge, Massachusetts-based Arthur D. Little, Inc., a management and technology consulting firm, believes the failures boil down to two factors: "After some period of time, either the alliance hasn't achieved its objectives, or it's met the objectives, but one of the two partners has changed its mission." To ensure the best scenario, Finnegan believes HR should participate during the early stages of an alliance. As soon as two or more companies reach a consensus that an alliance is necessary, HR should help define the different cultures and objectives of the *marriage*. Even if an HR professional hasn't participated in one before, some consultants advise that HR aggressively seek the opportunity. HR has often been responsible for its own lack of involvement, says Susan Studd, an organizational development consultant at Intel in Hillsboro, Oregon. What HR needs to do is apply its people skills to the overall business needs of the alliance. "Talk to a senior manager who's participated in one and ask, 'Could you help me understand what worked well and what didn't?' Then, if you hear of a strategic alliance being considered by your company, jump in and ask, 'What can I do to make it more effective?'" advises Studd. "HR's reputation and credibility [in strategic alliances] is still being established. Hopefully, it'll grow over time."

Do Your Human Resources Add Value?

The right game plan can help financial executives make sure they do.

BY MICHAEL DONAHUE

The rapidly changing dynamics of the marketplace are forcing companies to question whether they have the appropriate organization, processes, and technology to deliver human resources (HR) services that add value and are cost effective. Some of the trends driving these considerations are:

- Changing corporate structures resulting from spin-offs, mergers and acquisitions, and joint ventures.
- Demands for cost cutting and administrative efficiency.
- Changing corporate culture and values, which alter the traditional role HR has played.
- Evolving workforce, with nontraditional employment arrangements such as contract labor, part-time employment, telecommuting, and job sharing.
- Growing trend toward employee self-service.
- Maturing market of external service providers.
- Advances in technology, such as sophisticated application software, kiosks, e-mail, groupware, and the Internet.
- Management's demand for measurable added value from the HR function.

Financial executives need to make sure their organization's HR function runs smoothly and cost efficiently. Too often, companies rush toward outsourcing, reengineering processes, staff reorganization, and systems implementation without considering the overall impact on the organization. By performing a structured analysis of HR service delivery, companies often can gain perspective on the proper course to follow to transform the HR function.

MODELING HUMAN RESOURCES SERVICE DELIVERY

An approach that has been used with some of the premier U.S. corporations can help create a game plan for the entire operation rather than one that involves isolated decisions about individual functions. Called a service delivery model, it develops a blueprint for the organization, processes, and technology to be used by HR to deliver services to its customers: employees, line management, and executive management. Under this model, all HR functions are considered, including traditional human resources administration, health and welfare benefits, retirement and retiree benefits, and payroll administration.

Working with a company's internal project team, an external consulting team conducts a detailed review of existing HR functions and makes key operations recommendations:

- Should current functions be maintained or eliminated?
- Should functions be performed in-house or outsourced? Centralized or decentralized?
- How can processes be improved by automating or streamlining them?
- How can technology be applied to improve productivity, quality, and timeliness?

Performing the steps in the following analysis will help companies minimize the administrative burden of human re-

5. Do Your Human Resources Add Value?

sources activities and make processes more efficient and timely for their employees.

- Baseline analysis of company's current processes and procedures; organization and staffing; functional activity analysis; technical systems support; and policies, procedures, and controls. The baseline analysis is the foundation for decision making on the viable options and cost/benefits analysis.
- Benchmark comparison using an HR benchmarking database as well as industry comparative measures, which will help companies assess their position in the marketplace.
- Service delivery options analysis listing the functions the company currently supports and the opportunities it has for supporting them in the future. This analysis is accompanied by a cost/benefit assessment of the options, the recommended approach, and a high-level implementation plan.
- Reengineering opportunities with detailed process flows of current key HR, benefits, and payroll processes and proposed process flows suggesting changes to reduce administrative burden and improve efficiency.
- Business and technology requirements including the application and technical requirements to support the proposed HR service delivery model. Although software is not selected as part of this process, this document may be used to evaluate the capabilities of software vendors and narrow the list of prospective vendors. The consulting team also can provide a company with a list of vendors of application software (HRIS, kiosk) and other technologies (such as voice response, employee self-service) that may be applicable for a particular environment.
- Service delivery model outlining the framework the company will use to deliver HR services in the future and the migration plan to get it there.

These deliverables will provide both financial and human resources executives with measurable value and help them determine a strategy to deliver HR services in the future. This procedure also will assist them in distinguishing the functions and strategic processes, such as recruiting, staffing, and succession planning, within their HR organization that require highly skilled staff and will help add value to those that are largely administrative.

The objective of the service delivery model project is to help transform HR into a strategic business partner by minimizing the effort required to perform the necessary administrative tasks. Eliminating or streamlining the administrative responsibilities of HR allows more effort to be focused on high-value activities such as recruiting, staffing, training, and managing the workforce. Then a decision can be made regarding how to perform the highly routine and transaction-oriented activities most appropriately. Depending on the needs and goals of the organization, these activities may be outsourced, performed centrally in an employee service center, or directed by the employee using employee self-service technology.

To create the service delivery model for an HR function, companies should follow a two-phased approach.

Phase one. Create operations and technology baseline. The initial phase of a service delivery model project investigates and documents current operations. Information on the existing organization is collected through review of existing documents, interviews with staff, and focus groups or surveys. The findings of the investigation will include documentation of the staffing levels, the processes performed, and the existing technology.

Phase two. Develop service delivery model. The second phase of the service delivery model project focuses on determining the optimal method of delivering the services HR chooses to continue performing. This phase may include comparison of benchmark companies' methods of organizing and delivering HR services. Based on the current environment, the objectives and restrictions of the organization, potential models are developed.

Business and technical requirements are defined in this phase. Business requirements are based on the needs of senior management and the HR organization. At this point, reengineering of processes may be performed. Technical requirements consider the existing technical environment and the feasibility of implementing new technologies.

The final step in the service delivery model project is to select the optimal solution based on all the information collected. A cost/benefit analysis is performed on each of the potential options that will result in a recommendation for the HR organization of the future. The recommendation may include a reorganization of staff, implementation of new technologies, or the outsourcing of operations. An HR organization making any of these decisions after such thorough investigation and analysis can feel confident about its actions.

Implementing a new model for human resources delivery could be the answer to reducing HR costs and administrative duties while creating unity among all facets of a company's HR function and within the overall organizational structure.

REAL WORLD EXAMPLE

An international diversified manufacturer suffered from overlapping costs and efforts in a highly decentralized operation (processing payroll and benefits in multiple locations instead of in one place). It could afford to make only incremen-

33

1. HUMAN RESOURCE MANAGEMENT: Human Resources and Corporate Strategy

tal investments in technology. The company was faced with the need to change the decentralized delivery of services dramatically to gain efficiency and cut costs.

The company turned to KPMG Peat Marwick to develop a new model for human resources service delivery. The new model identified $2.5 million in annual savings through the consolidation of field payroll and benefit operations and the outsourcing of several functions. Features of the new HR model include: an alliance of third-party vendors for health and welfare, retirement benefits, and data maintenance working together to streamline HR processes. The company permitted direct contact for employees with benefit providers, reduced efforts at the business unit site, eliminated noncore activities, and reduced the need for future technology spending. As a result, the company saved money on HR costs and reduced the amount of unnecessary labor to reach its goals for phased migration with key benefits within a one-year time frame.

Implementing a new model for human resources delivery could be the answer to reducing HR costs and administrative duties while creating unity among all facets of a company's HR function and within the overall organizational structure. The best way to go about it is to work with a consulting firm that understands the company's needs and that can help it make these critical decisions up front:

- Maintain vs. eliminate functions;
- Insource vs. outsource;
- Centralize vs. decentralize;
- Automate, streamline, or eliminate.

Only after conducting a thorough analysis of the function and its impact on the company can executives make decisions about the best use of their human resources.

Michael Donahue is national partner in charge, World Class Human Resources Practice, KPMG Peat Marwick LLP in Radnor, Pa. He can be reached at (610) 995-4400.

Moment of Truth for the Class of '70

Affirmative action opened the doors and they were the first to plow through—ambitious, determined and prepared. Twenty-five years later, they've achieved the Dream. But can they secure it for their children?

Caroline V. Clarke

They were born in the late 1940s, into a world divided by color—black and white. Given their timing and their race, the white world offered them little and expected even less. But all that quickly changed.

Just as they entered grade school, a victory in *Brown vs. the Board of Education* altered the nation's educational landscape. By the time they were seniors in high school, colleges that had been completely shuttered to their parents were not only considering them, they were recruiting them.

By then, the Civil Rights Act of 1965 had been passed, and the government was putting pressure on white institutions to either admit black applicants or lose federal funding. The incentive opened doors, first at the undergraduate level, then at the graduate level and, ultimately, at the professional level. Blessed with ambition, determination and strong families who instilled in them the value of education, the 11 women and 13 men interviewed for this article became first-line beneficiaries of a new program dubbed affirmative action.

AFROS, PANTHERS AND PROGRESS

Meet the BE Class of '70: Twenty-five members of the generation that led campus sit-ins, takeovers and marches; that joined the Alphas, Deltas, Panthers and SNCC (Student Non-Violent Coordinating Committee); that embraced Black Power and rejected the Vietnam War.

"Affirmative action opened doors that never should have been closed in the first place."

Whether they took center stage, observed from the sidelines, or waged a self-contained battle in the classroom, this group—with very few exceptions—shared a revolutionary state of mind. It apparently served them well.

Today, they are middle-aged (45 to 50); most are married (only four have been divorced); and all but four have children, many of whom are now college age.

In many ways they are classically middle-to-upper class—agonizing over their older children's educational options and goals, chauffeuring their younger ones to Jack & Jill parties and sporting events, serving on local boards and community groups, and juggling demanding careers with full personal interests and agendas.

What is striking about them, though—particularly given that more than half of the group are first-generation college graduates—is the level and consistency of their success. All but four hold graduate degrees (a few hold more than one); their salaries range from roughly $45,000 to about $600,000 a year; 14 of the 25 earn more than $100,000 annually.

Among their ranks are a journalist, three physicians, several corporate managers and executives, a Colorado state Supreme Court Justice, a college president, a handful of successful entrepreneurs—one of whom heads a **BE 100s** company—and one of only six black admirals in the U.S. Navy.

Some of them have appeared in BE before. James Wood's (Morgan '70) family finances were dissected in our October '89 cover story, "Smart Financial Moves For The 1990s." The father of four is an orthopedic surgeon and sports medicine expert who, just last month, moved his San Francisco practice back to his native Baltimore. Ronald Wilson (Stanford '70), a founding partner in the Los Angeles firm of Wilson & Becks, was featured in our exclusive August '93 list of the nation's leading black law firms. And Joyce Roché (Dillard '70), formerly the highest ranking African American executive at Avon, graced both our "21 Women of Power and Influence" (August 1991) and "40 Most Powerful Black Executives" (February 1993) lists.

They are an impressive group, with reason to be proud. But they realize that were it not for affirmative action, they would not be where they are. Unlike younger generations of African Americans, they don't feel that acknowledging the impact of affirmative action on their careers takes anything away from their talent, their intellect or their achievements. They are clear

1. HUMAN RESOURCE MANAGEMENT: Equal Employment Opportunity and Affirmative Action

and unapologetic about what affirmative action did for them. Says Emmett C. Orr (Kent State '70): "It removed barriers that other [white] people didn't have. It opened doors that should never have been closed to us in the first place."

Acknowledging the impact of affirmative action takes nothing away from their achievements

They are equally clear about what it did not do. Contrary to popular belief, it did not enable them to float above basic requirements, advancing on the good will of guilt-ridden white professors and bosses. Quite the opposite. Al Wellington (Oberlin '70) recalls having to cut his summer short by several weeks to take special courses, along with the other incoming black freshmen, designed to "prepare us for what would be this rigorous program that was Oberlin." The fact that Wellington had come within a hair of being valedictorian at McDonald High School (where, as the only black student in his class, he was a star athlete and two-time class president) was never considered.

Joyce Roché still feels anger recalling similar presumptions of inferiority. A particularly stinging experience occurred while she was pursuing her M.B.A. at Columbia University in New York. It involved her grade in quantitative analysis, taught by a professor who Roché says was known "for being pretty good to black and minority students." Roché, who had been a math major at Dillard, had a 'B' going into the final exam, so she was shocked to receive a 'C+' in the course. "I thought, 'How in hell could this happen?' I called the professor and was told he had changed the scale so that all the 'Bs' dropped to 'C+.' In reality, he did pass all of the black students, garnering this great reputation. But he would not give anyone black above a 'C'— we all got 'Cs.'"

"You don't hear this chorus of 'Oh, they're not really qualified,' being applied to women."

Even all these years—a quarter century's worth—later, affirmative action has not succeeded in altering that institutional mind-set, which still views African Americans as inferior at worst and, in the case of real superstars, anomalies at best. "There are attitudes that white people seem unable to get out of their psyche," notes Marian Smith Holmes (Michigan State '70), an assistant editor at *Smithsonian* magazine in Washington, D.C. "You don't hear this chorus of 'Oh, they're not really qualified' being applied to women. The antagonism over qualifications has been aimed almost exclusively at blacks. What else can you attribute that to but racism?"

Reveta Bowers

Personal Stats: 47, married, 2 children
Current Position: Head of School, Center for Early Education, Los Angeles
Education: B.A. Theater Arts, University of Southern California; M.A. Developmental Psychology, College for Developmental Studies
Reflections: When Reveta Bowers entered USC, the most common professional options for women were nursing, social work and teaching. Always one to chart her own path, Bowers majored in theater arts. "USC was a particularly conservative campus," Bowers says, explaining her choice. "The theater arts department was a place of more diversity of thought and action than others on campus."

Although there were "very few" black students at USC then, and the influence of movements such as the Black Panthers "were a part of shaping who and what we all became," Bowers was more troubled by the gap between the haves and have-nots than about the rift between the races. Not surprisingly, though, the haves were mostly white.

"It was very clear to me that political forces were being shaped by economic forces," she recalls. "I was surrounded by students with a great deal of money, whose professional futures were clear. They were not at all plagued by the uncertainties I was. For them, there was a road map and they knew exactly where they were going to be on it. Either places were being held for them at their parents' companies, or made for them at their friends' companies. It was the first time I saw cultural networking. I didn't have a clue."

But Bowers caught on quickly. She logged a short time as a buyer and fashion coordinator for Bullocks (a plum job that resulted from "the convergence of the store needing to integrate its ranks and my having a college degree fresh in my hand"), but quit after a year. She then recalled her mother's sage advice: "You can always fall back on teaching." The rest, as they say, is history.

Bowers ended up at the Center for Education at the behest of a black parent who was concerned that her daughter's private school had no black teachers. At the helm since 1976, Bowers has diverisified not only the staff, but the student body as well. She has made it her mission to be visible (she is a director on many boards, including that of the Walt Disney Co.) and to reach out to parents who are "great believers in public education, but couldn't in good conscience send their children" to the L.A. public schools that served Bowers so well as a child. The pivotal issue for these parents is quality education, not race, Bowers insists, noting, that "those parents who are simply fleeing integration certainly aren't going to send their kids to my school, because I'm there."

Perhaps most important, they say, affirmative action has not yet done what it was most intended to—level the playing field. Now, it seems, it may never get the chance.

Roberta "Bobby" Gutman (Temple '70) is a straight-talking vice president and director of human resources diversity at Motorola Inc., in Chicago. As the only black female officer of Motorola worldwide, Gutman says she is where she is today for two reasons: affirmative action ("which helped open the doors") and results achieved ("once inside, it's all about performance"). Diversity initiatives—Gutman's specialty—are not a replacement for the public policy of affirmative action, she says. "The need for affirmative action is almost as great today as it was 25 years ago," she says. "Has it done what it was intended to? The answer, for anyone who can talk and chew gum at the same time, is no. Because the same basic resistance [to African American parity] is still there." Says Gutman: It needs more time.

And so it was with a sense of anxiety and more than a little ambivalence that the Class of '70 approached their college reunions last spring. As they reflected in lengthy interviews on how far they'd come, as well as the road ahead, some of that old '70s anger began to surface. Anger that a program with such a short history is already being called into question; anger at the racist rhetoric and blatant lies being perpetrated to fuel the debate. The truth, they say, lies in their ongoing individual stories, and those of thousands of African Americans like them. If only we could tell them all.

Unfortunately, space allows us to share just a few (see sidebars).

NEW GENERATION, SAME OLD TUNE

While their anger is palpable, so is their fear. For while this class has come a long way since the vibrant but traumatic '60s and '70s, the rest of the world seems to be circling back. And that does not bode well for their children.

Some seem almost dazed at the speed with which the battles of their childhood have resurfaced—almost as if they were never fought in the first place.

"People are racist and they don't even know it. They judge you based on the color of your skin."

Yvonne Bryant Reece (Spelman '70) came to a painful realization after a recent conversation with her daughter, who went to work at a San Francisco advertising agency after graduating from Stanford in 1992. "She called me and said, 'These people are racist and they don't even know it. They will judge you and promote you based on the color of your skin . . .' and I thought, 'Finally! She understands what I've been saying all along.' " But the relief Reece felt initially was quickly overshadowed by a sense of sadness. "I expected these things to change," says the Atlanta-based branch manager for AT&T's global services network division. "I didn't expect it to take so long."

Carol Oliver

Personal Stats: 46, never married (yet!), no children

Current Position: Manager, Government Programs Administration, Medicare Division at Blue Cross/Blue Shield, Chicago, Ill.

Education: B.A. Sociology, Northwestern '70; M.B.A. Hospital and Health Service Management/Marketing, Northwestern '81

Reflections: Feisty and forthright, Oliver was raised the second of six children in Rankin, Pa., a multi-ethnic working class community outside of Pittsburgh, where even in the '60s, she says, "there was little to march about." In fact, says Oliver, there wasn't much going on, period.

By 17, her life's goal was to pursue speech therapy in a place far from Rankin and her younger siblings. With phenomenal college entrance exam scores of a combined 1475 (out of 1600), she chose to attend Northwestern, entering what she calls "the first real class of black students" the school ever had. The initial experience was a jarring one all around. "We were thrown in with white roommates, most of whom quickly moved out," Oliver recalls.

Trading her pressed-straight hair for a big 'fro (and regarding those who didn't as "not right"), Oliver ditched speech therapy in favor of a combined major in sociology and the newly minted black history. "I was going to be a social worker and go into the black community and save the world," she says. Instead, after a year of teaching special education, she went to Blue Cross/Blue Shield of Illinois as a benefits counselor. "It was going to be my job until my good job came along and, over time, it became my good job."

Except for a bumpy period during the late '80s, when Oliver's position was threatened by a companywide reorganization, she has steadily risen. As one of the first black women managers at the company, she has had younger women—black and white—thank her for nurturing and mentoring them, and for the example she set. But, says Oliver, there were also "always people who noted I was a twofer—black and a woman—and the reference belied my talents and skills. Yet, I know, with all my talent, I would not have been offered the chances I was without affirmative action."

Oliver regards the current threat to affirmative action as "tragic," mainly because parity has not yet been achieved in the workplace. "The glass ceiling for me is lower than it is for others," she says. "That's a fact validated and reiterated virtually every day in some specific way. No matter how much they're 'giving' us, they're giving themselves more. We must never forget that."

1. HUMAN RESOURCE MANAGEMENT: Equal Employment Opportunity and Affirmative Action

Wilhelmina Leigh

Personal Stats: 47, single, no children
Current Position: Senior Research Associate/Economist, Joint Center for Political and Economic Studies, Washington, D.C.
Education: A.B. Economics, Cornell '70; M.A. and Ph.D. Economics, Johns Hopkins '76 and '78
Reflections: Her 16-page resumé is dominated by a list of papers she has authored on the economics of housing, health and urban renewal. A member of Phi Beta Kappa who finished college a semester early, Leigh has also held teaching positions at Johns Hopkins, Georgetown, the University of Virginia, Howard and Harvard.

But what her resumé doesn't detail are the professional slights she's suffered due to her race or gender, and the scars left by her college years.

Says Leigh: "I went to Cornell because my father wanted me to, and because I thought he was the best thing since sliced bread," But the D.C. native was unprepared for what she would find there. "In my imaginings, Cornell was going to be the land of milk and honey, filled with all of these brilliant people. What I found was a mixed blessing. I learned a lot about myself and the world, but a lot of the lessons were very painful.

"In the environment I grew up in, everybody was pretty much the same. In Ithaca, you had to define yourself, and that definition was likely to grow out of what you weren't, not what you were. There were about 40 blacks in [the school of] arts and sciences. For Cornell, it was a real bumper crop, but it felt like very few. My first week there, I just cried."

Cornell was then a hotbed of militant black activism—one of the most striking in the nation. Leigh contributed from the sidelines. Brandishing a weapon, as did some of her peers, "was not my style." Leigh never believed that the sometimes extreme action students took at Cornell, although widely publicized, would have much impact beyond the university. Her doubts were confirmed when she returned to D.C. after graduation. Thus, she says flatly, "I had no ivory tower views of what the world would hold for me. I did not expect to have the same career options as a white male, and I haven't. But I did expect to have more options that my mother, and I have."

Affirmative action dramatically diminished overt racial exclusion, but has done little to alter the racist mind-set, observes Leigh. In her field—in which Leigh is one of few women and even fewer African Americans—Leigh says she has been somewhat "ghettoized" in her research assignments, limited to black- or women-related projects "because it is tougher to be accepted as an expert on other issues." The enemy is still there, she says, but affirmative action has made it harder to pin down.

Ronald Wilson echoes Reece's dismay. Co-founder of one of the nation's most successful black-owned law firms, Wilson grew up in all-black Compton, Calif., and returned to L.A. after graduating Harvard Law School. His first-born, Ramon, spent last spring choosing between offers from Stanford undergrad—his dad's alma mater—and Yale. The elder Wilson could not have been prouder, but he was also wary. "My son has more confidence that I did," Wilson observes. "He's better prepared to deal with the world than I was. I feel good about his chances . . . I feel less good about the world."

Wilson ticks off the daily reminders of unkept promise: "There's no black airline, I look downtown at the skyline—not one black owns any of those buildings. I go to the Lakers game—all the best seats on the floor are occupied by whites. *The New York Times* and the *Daily News* are owned by whites. And I still have to tell my son—as my dad told me—to look out for the LAPD. So, a lot has changed—and not much has changed."

Wilson fears most for those who are situated much like he was back in high school. "The kids coming out of Compton now are not being recruited by Harvard and Stanford and Yale," he says. "Vertical mobility is a powerful thing. It's becoming less and less possible in this country."

Most of Wilson's peers share his concerns, prefacing hopes that their children enjoy a promising, productive future with a prayer of something far more fundamental; that their children are able to successfully navigate the myriad dangers that could cut their futures short.

Rear Admiral Anthony Watson (U.S. Naval Academy '70) grew up in Chicago's now infamous Cabrini Green houses, and returns regularly (his mother still lives there) to encourage its young residents. A few years ago, Watson was escorting a reporter through the development (he abhors the term, 'project'), when they paused to chat with a boy of about seven. "I asked him what he wanted to be when he grew up," Watson recalls. "He said, "Alive." I never forgot that. A seven-year-old should not be preoccupied with staying alive."

Such responses, and a tenable fear about where the world is headed, particularly as it relates to black youth, have fueled the Class of '70's drive to do whatever they can to improve the lot for all African Americans, not just those in their privileged circles. Says Watson: "We not only have to be there to show [young people] an alternative, we have to be there to help them formulate their dreams, so when they respond to questions about their future, they don't do it from the negative or the defensive, but with a real eye toward what they want to do in life."

WHITE FOLKS BENEFITED TOO

In interview after interview, the Class of '70 expressed their disillusionment and then, disbelief that a mere 25 years after kicking in, programs that were clearly aimed at positively impacting the lives of African Americans—such as affirmative

6. Moment of Truth

Carl Robbins

Personal Stats: age 47, married with four children, ages 2 to 12, and a stepchild, 25

Current Position: Senior Manager, Employment, at The Vanguard Group of Investment Companies, Malvern, Pa.

Education: B.A. American History, University of Pennsylvania '70; M.B.A., Labor Relations Management, The Wharton School, '80

Reflections: "I am enraged about all the dialogue that's going on about affirmative action. We are the proof of the pudding. Who succeeds is not merely a question of talent, it's a question of opportunity."

Robbins was born into a close and extended Philadelphia family with West Indian roots and an impressive history rich in intellectual and entrepreneurial pursuits. A national merit scholar in high school, and a self-described "basketball monk" in college, Robbins traced his family's history as a senior-year project.

"At the time, the Nixon administration was touting black capitalism as the wave of the future," recalls Robbins. "Much was being made of self-help and the whole bootstrapper phenomenon." Intrigued, he sought to learn why an old family catering business had not survived. His conclusion: Racism had destroyed the ability of the business to grow and succeed.

Robbins sought his own success in the human resources field, first at the Mobile Corp., then UNISYS and FMC Corp. Today, at Vanguard, he is enthusiastically leading his company's diversity efforts, but admits to being plagued with doubts. "I took an informal survey of the black members of Wharton's class of '73, and almost none of them are working at corporations anymore—they're self-employed. Why? Because it's not a glass ceiling we hit. It's much more profound than that. I'm one of the guys out here waving a big banner at other black folks, saying, 'Come join me!' But sometimes I'm very ambivalent about it.

"In the increasing competition for a limited number of jobs, there's a backlash coming from a small group yelling, 'What about me? We've done enough. I don't want this guilt trip anymore. Why should I give a hoot about someone who's had 25 years of so-called advantage? I've got enough to worry about with my own job and family.' They're totally wrong. And, what troubles me most is that I hear nothing from the business community about why affirmative action needs to be kept in place. It should be graphically, empirically evident that this needs to be kept in place."

---

action—were being torn down. Their list of reasons why it needs to be maintained and, if anything, strengthened, is counted off in personal tales of the chilling effect racism—and exclusionism—continue to have on their lives.

"They could have given my spot to a white person. But they took me. And that was the right choice."

Several mentioned the glass ceiling, although Brenda Armstrong (Duke '70), a physician, likened it to "Plexiglas," noting that "the only thing that gets broken is your back as you keep banging against it." Procter & Gamble recruiting manager Carolyn Thompson (Ohio State '70) observes that while corporate America may be more willing to embrace the cream of the black crop, "We still don't have the opportunity to get the same rewards for being average as the rest of society does."

"We really felt that if we couldn't effect change, we weren't willing to survive."

Alfred Harding (North Carolina A&T '70) maintains that for graduates of historically black colleges, the presumptions about one's ability can be even more damning. Harding, chief of the Program Analysis and Support Division, Office of East African Affairs at the U.S. Agency for International Development (USAID), says that too often during his 25 years at the agency he was given "assignments that seemed geared toward seeing what I could do, or whether I could do them at all." James Wood, who went from all-black Morgan State to being the only

---

"My son has confidence. I feel good about his chances. I feel less good about the world."

African American in his medical school class at the University of California at Irvine, was flat-out told by a pleasantly surprised professor, "We didn't expect you to do so well." Such encounters—such awakenings by white people who had little or no prior contact with black people—only prove that affirmative action has been both necessary and beneficial, says Wood—and not just for African Americans.

"They could have clearly taken my spot in med school and given it to a white person," he says. "But they took me. And

1. HUMAN RESOURCE MANAGEMENT: Equal Employment Opportunity and Affirmative Action

Mamon Powers Jr.

Personal Stats: 47, married, one daughter, 18, and a son, 15

Current Position: President, Powers & Sons Construction Co., Gary, Ind.

Education: B.S. Civil Engineering, Purdue '70

Reflections: Mamon Powers Jr. began working in his father's construction company when he was 11 years old. The lifestyle—being his own boss, running his own ship—was appealing. But his access to it was perhaps too easy for a kid who relished a challenge.

So it was that at 15, Powers spotted his goal after learning that there were no registered black professional engineers in the entire state of Indiana. "I wanted to be the first," Powers says. By the time he graduated from Purdue, then regarded as the nation's engineering mecca, someone else had grabbed that distinction. But Powers felt no less fulfilled. Purdue was no cakewalk for anyone, but for black students—who totaled 130 out of 26,000—the sense of isolation made it tougher.

After a brief stint with Amoco Oil Co. (which offered all engineers deferments from the Vietnam War), Powers rejoined his father in the family business, gradually taking it over and building it to the point where, in 1988, Powers Construction premiered among the **B. E. INDUSTRIAL/SERVICE 100.**

Even though they were well known and respected in the community, financial and entrepreneurial success did not translate into full social acceptance for the Powers family. The most striking evidence of this came in the mid-'80s, when Mamon applied for membership at a country club where several of the local contractor organizations—to which he and his father belonged—held regular meetings.

"I called around to my so-called friends to seek sponsorship," he recounts. "One guy said, 'Well, I'm about to quit,' another said, 'The food's horrible,' another never called back. Then I called our banker. He said, 'No problem, and, by the way, do you know there are no other black members there? If you were white, they would've been after you years ago.' He called back a week later, shaken. He said he didn't know me that well and, therefore, couldn't sponsor me."

Powers countered by calling the newspapers and threatening to sue. He also filed a complaint with the Indiana Civil Rights Commission. Finally, after a lengthy public battle with not one, but two clubs, he was offered and accepted a membership at the Woodmar Country Club. Since 1990, he and his family have been swimming and golfing at the club without incident.

"As I've gotten older, I've realized the world is just not as fair as I'd hoped," Powers sighs. "But the country club incident in particular really left a scar. It let me know that racism is still very much alive and well. On the other hand, in order for us to be effective and productive as a company, we can't let racism become a part of our thought process. If we do, it will hamper us. I tell everyone here, we have to be better than everyone else all the time. And in those fleeting moments when the playing field is level, we come shining through like stars."

---

that was the right choice. And I proved just as valuable to the white community as they were to me. I can't say how often I've talked to white people who have never spoken with an African American, who have never seen a black doctor, no less been treated by one. [Meeting me] has clearly been a plus for them."

SAME WAR, NEW BATTLE

Perhaps most distressing to the Class of '70 is the stark contrast between where we are now and where most of them believed the world would be when they projected 25 years out on graduation day. While the image of their class that lingers in the minds of most Americans is that of a militant generation with a mob mentality, spewing anger and cynicism, sporting wild hair and wilder clothes, their self-image, looking back, is more internally focused. They were really quite hopeful and naive in those days, even idealistic.

Gregory Kellam Scott (Rutgers '70) recalls in detail, with a mixture of deep pride and some lingering awe, his moments as a leader among his school's small but active group of black students. "We believed we could alter the path of history," says Scott. "There was a great deal of change occurring throughout the country and African Americans were in the forefront, with greater influence and power to affect change than others—and more than we have today. We really felt that, if we couldn't affect change, we weren't willing to survive. I really felt that if this country could not tolerate me, I was not willing to pursue a life within society's rules." Scott is now a Justice on the Supreme Court of Colorado.

"I believed that each year would be better than the last. In a sense, they have been."

"Back then, the future seemed wide open," says Henry Gaines (Columbia '70). "You felt anything was possible. We were critical, but also very optimistic. We believed change meant improvement, and felt that we were a part of effecting that change."

Gaines, who went on to Harvard Medical School and is now an internist at Columbia Presbyterian Hospital in New York, as well as a faculty member at Columbia's school of medicine, took an active role in his alma mater's notorious 1968 uprising,

Charles E. Allen

Personal Stats: 47, married, three children ages 12 to 20
Current Position: President and Co-founder of Graimark Inc., Detroit
Education: B.S. Finance/Accounting, Morehouse '70; M.B.A. Finance, University of Chicago '72
Reflections: "When I was graduating high school, it was the heyday of prominent white colleges coming and pulling the best and brightest black students to integrate their schools. I talked to Penn and some others, but I decided I didn't want to be a statistic.

"The last year of Benjamin Mays' presidency was my first year at Morehouse. He was awe inspiring. He would always indicate that Morehouse was a builder of minds, not an athletic machine. We were constantly told we could do anything, be anything. It was a place of ideas and challenges."

Allen says that that rich, nurturing experience prepared him well for business school, where "they went to great pains to explain in detail theories that held that black intellectual capacity was less than white. I will never forget a white professor noting that one had to have the same cultural background as he did to understand the course curriculum. I had a fit. One of my friends had to calm me down. He pulled me aside and said, 'Don't let them provoke you into doing something stupid. Don't let them send you home . . .' "

"I was heavily recruited by banks, including First [National Bank of] Chicago. I arrived there with a blue double knit suit on with a flap over the pocket, a big tie with big birds—partridges—on it, and a big afro. I looked like a country hick, but I thought I was sharp!"

Despite his initial fashion faux pas, Allen moved rapidly through several groundbreaking positions. He served as a vice president and division manager at The Bank of California before becoming president and CEO of First Independence National Bank of Detroit, the ninth-largest black-owned bank in the nation. Now head of his own firm, which manages assets totaling $1.5 billion, Allen believes the future for African Americans lies in the amassing of black capital and the rebuilding of those institutions—churches, schools, businesses—"that we dismantled in our quest for integration." But, he insists, this should not happen to the exclusion of further progress in mainstream sectors.

"There used to be an expression in the pre-affirmative action days that if you struck up a round of 'Dear Old Morehouse' in the post office, you could stop work, because great, bright, promising talent had been locked out of other professional possibilities. That was all changing. What will happen now?"

David R. Jones

Personal Stats: 47, married, two children
Current Position: President and CEO, Community Service Society of New York
Education: B.A. Government Studies, Wesleyan '70; J.D., Yale Law School '74
Reflections: Jones knew in high school that he would become a lawyer and enter a life of public service. It was a family tradition. His father was the first black assemblyman elected in Brooklyn's Bedford Stuyvesant neighborhood—the same camp from which Shirley Chisholm sprung. In the Jones house, the kitchen table was a center of heady political and intellectual debate, from which he and his sister were never barred. They had also met several of the black cultural and political icons of the day, including Josephine Baker and Paul Robeson, both clients of their father.

Jones first found his own stage at Wesleyan, and he rose to the occasion with finesse. He was a leader of the largest black student population in the school's history, helping to found the black student union and its ensuing institutional offshoots. During the summer before his sophomore year, Jones interned with Sen. Robert Kennedy; months later the senator was assassinated. But Kennedy's shocking death—and the other assassinations of that era—did nothing to dampen Jones' enthusiasm for being "a leader for change on both the campus and in American society." In retrospect, he says, "We were naive."

Reality hit hard a few years out of Yale Law School, where Jones had done well and been recruited by New York-based Cravath, Swaine & Moore, one of the most prestigious old-line law firms in the nation. He later published an article detailing what became of his black colleagues at Cravath.

"One committed suicide, one ended up disbarred and homeless, another had a severe mental breakdown," Jones recounts, ticking off the horror stories. Why? "The rules for us were different. You couldn't learn the trade—which means basically making one mistake after another—without it being held against you, used as a reason for not promoting you and not hiring more [African Americans].

"A lot of promises were made—perhaps with real intentions—but then broken. A lot of us got sucked up in this euphoria of opening doors, and then things changed. We had bought into the notion—hook, line and sinker—that this was a meritocracy. Then we got marginalized. It took me years to recover my sense of worth and potential. And I was one of the lucky ones."

At 38, Jones became the youngest and the first African American to lead Community Service Society of New York. Under his leadership, the agency is now the largest of its kind in the nation. A rather vocal opponent of New York's Republican mayor and governor, Jones held a fundraiser last spring to offset CSS' disappearing public monies. It raised more than $380,000 net; a substantial portion came from black New Yorkers.

1. HUMAN RESOURCE MANAGEMENT: Equal Employment Opportunity and Affirmative Action

Brenda Armstrong

Personal Stats: 45, never married, 2 adopted sons

Current Position: Associate Professor of Pediatrics, Division of Pediatric Cardiology; Director of Fellowship Training, Duke University Medical Center, Durham, N.C.

Education: B.S. Zoology, Duke '70; M.D., St. Louis U. '74

Reflections: When Brenda Armstrong was admitted to Duke, her physician father was thrilled. He believed a Duke degree would open doors for his first-born. He had no idea what she would go through to get it.

Armstrong's class of 20 (out of 1,500) doubled the total number of black students at the school, but by year-end only half that number remained. The severe attrition had multiple causes. Chief among them was discrimination. "Advisors would flat out tell you that you didn't have the requisite skills to handle science at Duke," Armstrong recalls. "We also had a number of situations where blacks were brought before the honor board and accused of plagiarism because the teacher felt such work could not have been produced by a black student."

In the fall of 1967, Armstrong helped found the Afro-American Society, which began discussions with Duke's administration seeking specific things: a dorm of their own, a cultural center, more black faculty and administrators, a more inclusive curriculum. On February 13, 1969, frustrated by a lack of responsiveness, 13 black students—aided by others—took over the administration building. Armstrong, then chair of the society, was at the center of the standoff. When the school placed the group on trial internally, all 60 of Duke's black students joined them. They were successfully represented, pro bono, by Julius Chambers, chief council of the NAACP Legal Defense and Education Fund. The experience, says Armstrong, "still drives my career and political involvement."

Graduation proved sobering. "My initial idealism that all of a sudden things would get a whole lot better for us was totally dashed," she recalls. "The only thing I was certain of was that the world would be a whole lot different, and we would have to work hard for whatever we got. I felt a window of opportunity, and a sense that we had to grab all we could before it slammed shut. I've always had a healthy sense of what my father calls paranoia."

The 60 students tried alongside Armstrong in the spring of '69 must have shared that sense. "Between us, we have about 160 degrees," she brags. "People always try to cheapen you with race and gender, but excellence makes it tough for them to stop there."

Still, she admits, even success doesn't dull the sting of racism. "We have never stopped looking back," says Armstrong, who, ironically, has built her career at Duke and is one of a mere handful of black women certified in her specialty. "We still live like we have something to prove."

risking his long hoped for medical career in the process. Twenty-five years later, he says he harbors no regrets.

"I believed that what I did would not just be part of the action, but part of the right action, and that, each year would be better than the last.

"In a sense," he adds, "they have been." The current challenge for the Class of '70—and for us all—is to keep that momentum going.

DOES IMAGE MATTER?

Don't Take People at Face Value

Jennifer J. Laabs

Jennifer J. Laabs is the senior writer at PERSONNEL JOURNAL.

Drew Carey isn't a human resources professional, but he plays one on TV. In ABC's new sitcom, "The Drew Carey Show," Carey is the assistant director of personnel for a Cleveland department store. In the show's first episode, which aired on September 13, Carey was faced with a delicate dilemma: Should he hire Mimi for a cosmetic sales position?

Mimi, a fat woman with big hair and heavy makeup, wants the job. But it's all Carey can do to take the woman seriously because of her dramatic style and presence. Before Carey can get a word in edgewise, Mimi has managed to talk herself into a job—making it clear that she has been discriminated against in the past because of her looks and will not be discriminated against in the same way again.

While this overly dramatic situation was portrayed in a comical light, what makes us laugh is there's a glimmer of truth to the story. At some point in their careers, most human resources professionals have faced a situation in which they were forced to evaluate someone based on his or her looks, not just on qualifications or potential. And they secretly wondered: How fair is it to make snap judgments about people based on their appearance?

If you were behind Carey's hiring desk, would you have hired someone who didn't fit a preconceived idea about what the "right person for the job" was supposed to look like? Have you ever made a snap judgment about someone based on his or her looks and later were proved wrong? Just as there never are black-and-white answers to most human relations questions, it's difficult to determine when a company should evaluate people

> **Appearance is a very personal area of human diversity—with many business implications. If you have image standards, whether hidden or overt, make sure they don't unfairly discriminate against employees.**

based on how they look, or whether to maintain appearance policies in the first place. You might be surprised to learn that there are some solid business reasons for mandating appearance—because those standards can lead to a culture that's uniform and consistent.

But there are other good reasons *not* to judge people based on appearance factors, such as height, weight and grooming. Looks-based judgments tend to inhibit diversity, can be discriminatory and can lead to legal entanglements. Certainly, how a person looks should never be the sole factor in recruitment, hiring, promotion or compensation, but it sometimes is part of the employment decision-making process. Should it be? And if so, when? You be the judge.

Physical appearance affects economic status. Lest you think people *are* judged solely on performance, and not on their looks, consider the following. From infancy, we start making judgments about how people look. Studies consistently show that babies are more attracted to the faces of people who rate higher on the "beautiful" or "handsome" scale than to those who rate lower. They actually will look at a "pretty" face longer, and turn away from a "not-as-pretty" face sooner.

It seems to be an instinct related to the idea of the survival of the fittest. There's something in the human psyche that feels the more attractive you are, the better you'll survive in the world. Therefore, if we align ourselves with the better looking of the species, we also may be better off.

Other studies indicate that when people reach their teens, certain physical traits, such as height and weight, already

1. HUMAN RESOURCE MANAGEMENT: Equal Employment Opportunity and Affirmative Action

inhibit workers' social status and earning potential. For example, a study completed in 1994 by David G. Blanchflower, professor of economics at Dartmouth College, and Dr. James D. Sargent, showed that 16-year-old girls who were in the heaviest 10% of the population earned 7.4% less than their non-obese peers. And, the heaviest teens (the top 1%), earned 12% less. Interestingly, women who still were overweight at age 23 earned 6.4% less than their peers who had never been overweight. It seems that they either never catch up because they're burdened with low self-esteem that continues to affect their performance as time goes on, or employers continually and blatantly discriminate against them.

The study also shows that height was a critical factor in boys' earnings potential. For each 4-inch increase in height, boys' earnings rose 2%. Height, however, didn't statistically affect girls' wages, nor did weight affect boys' earnings.

And statistics don't seem to change as people age. A 1993 study in New England Journal of Medicine shows that the heaviest 3% of women were 20% less likely to be married, had household incomes averaging $6,710 lower than those who weighed less and were 10% more likely to suffer from poverty. To the researchers' surprise, problems such as asthma, diabetes, deformed legs and impaired vision didn't have the kind of impact that weight had.

Height, not surprisingly, seemed to affect men's economic status more than weight. Short men were 10% more likely to be poor and earned about $3,000 less than men a foot taller.

And height and weight aren't the only perceived appearance problems either. Overall attractiveness also affects individuals' economic health. According to a study by economists Daniel Hammermesh and Jeff Biddle—who are aligned with the Cambridge, Massachusetts-based National Bureau of Economic Research—more attractive people earn more and less attractive people earn less. "We were trying to find out how big the relationship was between looks and earnings," says Hammermesh, also a professor of economics at the University of Texas at Austin. "We hoped to see what gender differences there might be." There were, in fact, subtle differences.

The researchers analyzed ratings from three sets of data (two from the United States and one from Canada), in which interviewers had ranked individuals on a five-point scale (strikingly handsome or beautiful, above average, average, below average, plain or homely). Then, taking credentials, occupation and age into consideration, the researchers found that good-looking men and women make close to 5% more than average-looking individuals. Unattractive people, especially men, get less (as much as 9% less). Some of the U.S. data shows that attractive women got about 3% more pay than average-looking women, and homely women got about 5% less than those with average looks.

Whether an individual is classified as good looking is simply a state of being. As they say, beauty is in the eye of the beholder. But money, as they also say, is in the hands of the employer—and should be distributed based on performance and not physical status.

Balancing the legal scale on the issue of weight. Of all the personal appearance topics, weight is perhaps the most delicate. Despite America's preoccupation with slimness, we're collectively getting fatter ("fat," by the way, is the politically correct term). The National Center for Health Statistics tells us that in 1980, the average American man was 5 feet 9 inches and weighed 173 pounds. The average woman was 5 feet 4 inches and weighed 144 pounds. A decade later, the average man weighed 180 pounds, and the woman weighed 153. As of 1993, 68% of all Americans were considered overweight, up from 58% a decade earlier, based on Metropolitan Life Insurance tables. If the majority of people technically are "overweight," who really is the "majority" or "normal?" And what difference does it make in the workplace?

It shouldn't make any difference, unless the overweight condition causes a person to be unable to perform his or her job. The problem is perceptions—and misperceptions. "There are assumptions made that if people are overweight, they can't control their lives, or they're sloppy or lazy," says Anita Rowe, a diversity consultant in Culver City, California. "There's a whole set of assumptions that may be unconscious around this issue."

Says Lee Martindale, a size-rights

Would you have hired Mimi (played by Kathy Kinney) if you were Drew Carey, an assistant personnel director on "The Drew Carey Show?" On the program, Mimi faces appearance discrimination because of her weight and makeup habits. Carey had to decide whether the image his company projects is more important than nondiscrimination standards. Mimi was hired. Do the "Mimis" you encounter at your firm have equal opportunity?

7. Does Image Matter?

activist who lives in Dallas: "I would rather be judged by my work, not my waistline." Martindale, who's also a paraplegic, says she's constantly discriminated against because of her disability and her weight. "I've had employers offer me positions on the condition that I lose 100 pounds. My standard answer is: Fine, I'll do that if you cut off your left arm. It's the same kind of self-mutilation." She explains: "It all boils down to being allowed to contribute based on your talents, not on what you look like."

In a culture in which we're bombarded with social cues saying slim is good, and near-anorexic is better, it's no wonder that much of American society feels woefully inadequate. Yet, we seem to idolize a weight standard that's often unachievable, unsustainable and idealistic. For some, it's an unconscious ideal leading to hurtful bigotry at work.

Take the case of John Rossi, who lives in Chula Vista, California. For 10 years, Rossi worked for Phoenix-based Northern Automotive Corp., owner of Kragen Auto Parts. Four years ago, unexpectedly, Rossi was fired by supervisors in the firm's San Francisco offices—the area where Rossi worked at the time. When Rossi was fired, he weighed 400 pounds. He learned from another manager that his weight played a part in his firing. "He just didn't like the way I looked," Rossi said of the regional supervisor he thinks was behind his termination. "He judged me without even meeting me."

Rossi sued. Supervisors from the firm argued that Rossi was discharged solely for poor performance. Rossi contends he worked his way up from clerk to manager, often doing the jobs of two people. When he could no longer fit into the company uniform, he consistently wore slacks and a tie. Rossi claims he continually was praised for his work during his tenure.

During Rossi's trial, Dr. Richard Kamrath of Walnut Creek, California, testified that obesity can be attributed 80% to genetics and only 20% to environment. After only six hours of deliberation, a jury found that Rossi's weight condition qualified him for coverage under a California law, similar to the federal ADA law, and therefore protected him against discrimination. The California Supreme Court has ruled that under the state law, obesity is a valid disability when it results from a medical condition, rather than a ravenous appetite.

In September, Rossi was awarded $1 million. He will receive $776,739 for emotional distress and $258,913 for lost compensation and benefits. "I hope people are judged on their character and work ethic, not on their appearance," said Rossi after the verdict. The company hasn't decided whether to appeal.

The Equal Employment Opportunity Commission (EEOC) has asserted that obesity—particularly "morbid obesity" (the unforgiving medical term meaning one who weighs twice or more the "average")—should be regarded as a protected disability under federal law. However, neither the Rehabilitation Act of 1973, the ADA, nor the regulations under either statute directly address the question of whether obesity is a disability.

In its first detailed comment on the subject, the EEOC issued a position statement in 1993 in response to the case of a Rhode Island woman who was 5-feet-2-inches tall and weighed 329 pounds. Bonnie Cook had applied for a job with the Rhode Island Department of Mental Health. She was denied employment, and she sued. The court upheld a $100,000 verdict in the case on the basis of the Rehabilitation Act.

The EEOC said that morbid obesity "of sufficient duration and with a significant impact on major life activities can constitute a disability. ... It is not necessary that a condition be involuntary or immutable to be covered under the federal Rehabilitation Act of 1973 or the Americans with Disabilities Act," the commission stated. It compared obesity with alcoholism, diabetes, emphysema and heart disease, all of which have been regarded as covered disabilities, although the conditions "may be caused or exacerbated by voluntary conduct."

Other jurisdictions have issued varying decisions dealing with obesity as a handicap. A leading New York decision declares obesity to be a handicap. A Pennsylvania Commonwealth Court held that morbid obesity may be, but is not per se, a handicap. A Washington court held that it isn't a handicap when the condition is "within the plaintiff's control."

Whether weight is under a person's control or not, what about individuals who are overweight, but don't consider themselves disabled because of it? That was the question ultimately posed by Toni Cassista, a 305-pound woman who went job-hunting. In 1987, Cassista applied for a job opening at Community Foods in Santa Cruz, California. The position involved moving 50-pound bags and produce boxes. She wasn't hired.

Cassista sued, charging that she was denied employment because she was perceived to be physically handicapped by her weight. Store officials testified they were concerned about Cassista's experience and ability to safely perform the job because of her weight. Cassista said her overweight condition wasn't caused by a physiological disorder, and she didn't want to be perceived as disabled.

The state's supreme court emphasized that its task was limited to determining the boundaries of the state's Fair Employment and Housing Act, and that it wasn't free to define "physical handicap" in terms that may be "morally just or socially desirable." Because the state law requires an individual to prove his or her weight is caused by "a physiological disorder that affects one or more bodily systems and limits the ability to participate in major life activities," Cassista's case was dismissed. But the questions remain.

These are questions that the city of Santa Cruz, California, Washington, D.C. and the state of Michigan have decided once and for all. There, you can't discriminate against people because of their

---

"I am a lot like Baby Huey. I'm fat. I'm ugly. But if you push me down, I keep coming back. I just keep coming back." —*President Bill Clinton*

1. HUMAN RESOURCE MANAGEMENT: Equal Employment Opportunity and Affirmative Action

How Appearance Savvy Are You?

Do you consider looks as part of the diversity equation? Take this quiz to find out how you would score in appearance-based situations.

1. When working inside the U.S. business community:
   a. Ability, qualifications and performance are generally more important than perfect grooming.
   b. Fashion usually comes before comfort.
   c. Judgments are made on styles of dress more than achievements.

2. As a middle manager in your Mexican office, you will be expected to:
   a. Dress stylishly. Good clothes and careful grooming are expected of both managers and staff.
   b. Dress for comfort. Mexicans will judge you on your credentials, not how you look.
   c. Dress well yourself and let your staff dress however they please.

3. Employees in your organization are all under 30. You like this young image and feel it sells your product. You:
   a. Are justified in not hiring older people; they may not fit in.
   b. Should hire older people for inside work to create a balance in your staff.
   c. Should disregard these considerations and base your hiring solely on objectives and job-related criteria, without respect to age.

4. People labeled "fat" are less likely to be hired for a job, make less money when they are hired, and are less likely to be promoted. True or false?

5. Men value physical attractiveness and youthfulness in their mates more than women do; women, on the other hand, look for ambition, status and wealth in their prospective mate. True or false?

6. If you want to regularly acknowledge a woman you work with, tell her:
   a. How good she looks or dresses.
   b. Give her feedback on her work.
   c. Treat her like "one of the guys."

7. In a culture obsessed with looks, people with disabilities shed a bad light on the organizations who hire them. True or false?

8. Women of large body size make at least $_____ less per year than women of small body size.
   a. $500
   b. $11,280
   c. $6,700.

Answers are at the end of this article. Questions are from "Diversophy," a game developed by George Simons International in Santa Cruz, California and MULTUS Inc. in San Mateo, California.

---

weight, their height or any other physical condition a person may have been born with. Currently, these are the only jurisdictions having laws forbidding discrimination on the basis of weight and other inherent physical conditions, although others are carefully considering them.

Santa Cruz's city ordinance says: "It is the intent of the city council, in enacting this chapter [9.83.01], to protect and safeguard the right and opportunity of all persons to be free from all forms of arbitrary discrimination, including discrimination based on age, race, color, creed, religion, national origin, ancestry, disability, marital status, gender, sexual orientation, height, weight or physical characteristic ... The council's purpose in enacting this chapter is to promote the public health and welfare of all persons who live and work in Santa Cruz."

The law further indicates that physical characteristic "shall mean a bodily condition or bodily characteristic which is from birth, accident or disease, or from any natural physical development, or any other event outside the control of that person including physical mannerisms."

The law also specifies that employers or labor organizations may not "fail to hire, refuse to hire or discharge any individual" because of these reasons, or "discriminate against any individual, with respect to compensation, terms, conditions or privileges of employment, including promotion."

Although no cases of discrimination have been filed in Santa Cruz on this issue since it was enacted in 1992, plenty have come up in Michigan. James J. Parks, an attorney with the law firm of Gabrian and Parks PC in Bloomfield Hills, Michigan, should know. Parks has represented employees' interests in 15 weight-related cases over the past few years. "It's surprising how people still feel free to treat people differently because of weight," says Parks. "They would never do it with someone's age because they're scared to death [to do that]; they'd never do it because of race, because that's not politically correct, despite bigotry. But nearly everyone feels free to take potshots at fat people. Weight discrimination is the last bastion of discrimination that society permits."

He says he just helped settle a case for a "significant amount of money" against

---

"Michael's appearance makes people think he's gay, but he's not ... you can tell when a person is gay ... You say 'Oh, my God, that guy is gay.'"
—Katherine Jackson (Michael's mother)

Make Sure Your Casual Dress Policy is Non-discriminatory and Jives with Your Corporate Image

Casual dress has been sweeping the country—and dare we say, the world? However, lack of consistency is one of the biggest problems companies have in implementing casual dress policies. Although dress-down standards are spreading like wildfire, they often cause confusion among employees and may send mixed messages.

To help with some of the confusion around what casual dress means, some employers, such as Southfield, Michigan-based Chrysler Financial, a division of Chrysler, have held fashion shows to help employees understand they don't mean T-shirts and ripped jeans when they say "casual." In the process, employers clarify what they really do mean by relaxed dress.

Rockford, Michigan-based Hush Puppies, a division of Wolverine World Wide Inc., is one company that now allows business casual dress Monday through Thursday and "casual-casual" dress on Friday. The firm held a fashion show for employees last year to show what they hoped workers would wear—casual, but not too casual. "We're an international company and we interface with people around the world," says Maggi Mercado, vice president, design director for women's shoes at Hush Puppies. "Therefore, there's a certain level of decorum and polish that's required here." Some clothing items they don't allow: Sandals without stockings, sneakers, leggings, tights, gym wear, cutoffs and ripped jeans.

J. Randall "Randy" MacDonald, senior vice president of HR and administration for Stamford, Connecticut-based GTE, is another enthusiastic supporter of the new casual dress trend. He explained that when GTE was looking for a corporate vice president, they told their recruiter to inform candidates it's company policy to dress casually on Fridays. "I'll tell you that in each case, I came dressed casually the day of the interviews," says MacDonald. So did the interviewees. "Had those people showed up in a dress or with a tie, it wouldn't have affected me one way or the other." He says if people are professional, competent and perform well, that's what counts.

Across America, employees are complaining that with the new casual dress option, they have to go out and buy new clothes just to fit a new corporate image. They say it's especially frustrating after having carefully built a formal business wardrobe over the years. And with the trend toward reduced salaries and bonuses, employees have less disposable income with which to purchase these new clothes. So, don't expect "country-club casual" from a work force who can't afford to shop at Saks Fifth Avenue or aren't comfortable wearing a more elite style. It may end up looking like a case of class discrimination in an organization.

"Nobody's telling [employees here] they have to buy a new wardrobe," says Mercado. "We show them they don't have to go out and buy anything." The firm simply wants to show them a more relaxed way of dressing by pairing their clothing differently. And casual is an option, not a mandate. Employees may still wear their suits if they want to.

It's important that if your company decides on a casual image, executives should also embrace the practice. If the higher-ups are still dressing up, employees will get the idea that to reach the executive suite, they have to dress up, too, regardless of what the company says its standard is.

And if your company promotes a relaxed image, don't have a double standard in rating employees down if they dress casually. You actually may be getting more work out of them, regardless of how they look. Some studies show casual dress actually increases productivity and morale. And many companies are finding that to be true.

Others aren't. "Many of the studies, show wonderful benefits from [casual dress]," says Susan Morem, an image consultant in Minneapolis. "I'm not saying that's not true." But what she's seeing among her clients is that some companies that go from a one-day-a-week casual schedule, to an every day casual schedule, find the overall atmosphere is more relaxed and casual, sometimes leading to lowered standards. She cautions: Just make sure that's the kind of atmosphere you want. —JJL

---

an employer who failed to take appropriate steps to stop harassment (name-calling and malicious statements) of an overweight employee. "It's just like the kind of chiding that happens on the playground," says Parks. "The difference is it can cost employers millions of dollars if they don't stop it." That's money lost in productivity, morale, turnover and lawsuits.

Parks suggests that even if weight discrimination isn't illegal where you work, you should consider adding weight to your company's non-discrimination policy. It will help ensure that employees treat each other with respect. "That doesn't mean nothing bad will happen to you [if you add it to your policy], but it can't hurt," he says. "So why not take that extra step?"

Sizing up the height issue. Just as you should add weight to your policy as something not to discriminate against, it's also wise to recognize height has a diversity issue. Although height isn't a factor in discrimination as often as weight, height discrimination does happen. David Brookfield, for example, who's 4-feet-3-inches, has been told in employment interviews, "You're going to have trouble. People won't hire you because of your height." He says: "That was before the Americans With Disabilities Act [ADA]. Before laws went into effect, people could say those types of things." Now, he says that although it may be illegal to say such things, some employers clearly still think this way and find reasons not to hire people of short stature.

Brookfield, who's a district director for The Little People of America in Anaheim, California, has been employed in the entertainment field for the past several years. He says employers shouldn't discriminate against little people (or "LPs"—the politically correct term) because of

1. HUMAN RESOURCE MANAGEMENT: Equal Employment Opportunity and Affirmative Action

their height. Although height isn't specifically mentioned as a protected category under the ADA, many LPs have non-visible disabilities because of the short stature, such as curvature of the spine or mobility problems, which do give them coverage under the ADA.

Although employers may have to make ADA-type accommodations for some LPs, such as lowering desks and chairs, the accommodations generally are worth the paybacks you get from employing people of short stature, Brookfield says. "I don't want to say we're marketing tools, but [we're] a way for a company to be remembered," he says. "If a little person makes a presentation, people tend not to forget it."

Brookfield says employers need to know that small bodies don't equal small minds. "We're full-grown adults," he says. "We have full-grown minds with the ability to think and sort out problems [just like anyone else]."

Ironically, very tall people don't seem to have the same problem with misperceptions as short people. "As far as I understand, there's no discrimination against tall people in employment," says Ray Wottrich, vice president of publicity for Tall Clubs International, in Stafford, Texas. TCI is a social organization for tall people. "There are studies that indicate the taller a person is, the more likely he or she is to hold a better job and advance more rapidly because there's automatic respect added to somebody when you're looking up to him or her—everything else being equal." But, he says, if people are too tall, they can be perceived as "gawky" instead of "statuesque" and may experience discrimination, too.

A legal look at grooming, appearance and dress codes. Height, obviously, is something a person has no control over. But what about grooming and dressing? Employers should have some rights to regulate these voluntary actions, right? Well, laws governing grooming and appearance are sometimes difficult to interpret, and must be balanced with company standards.

"The general rule is that an employer can regulate how it wishes to have its employees dress and groom, restricted only by general principles of discrimination law," says James Hall, an attorney with the Los Angeles-based law firm of Barlow & Kobata. As you know, Title VII of the Civil Rights Act of 1964 prohibits employers from discriminating against individuals on the basis of race, color, religion, gender or national origin.

In the early days of Title VII, some women challenged employers whose dress codes required them to wear clothing that imposed a greater burden on them than on men. For example, employers who required women to wear uniforms (often revealing or sexually provocative ones), but only required men to wear slacks and shirts, were required to change their policies. And many had to pay lots of money in damages. "So you can't discriminate on the basis of protected classification in drafting or enforcing the grooming rule," adds Hall.

Companies also need to be careful that grooming policies don't discriminate against people's religious persuasions without good reason. In July, a New York federal judge ruled that two guards at Sing Sing prison who were Rastafarians could wear dreadlocks, a common sign of followers of that religion. Prison managers argued that the men's long hair violated the organization's grooming standards—which prohibited spikes, tails and names shaved into hair—and that their hairstyle also signified the guards were "getting down" with black inmates. The judge disagreed saying there was no proof the hairstyle was unprofessional or posed a threat.

Race is another area that appearance standards, unwittingly or not, must be careful not to discriminate against. In one instance, Ann Arbor, Michigan-based Domino's Pizza Inc. had a long-standing, nationwide rule against facial hair. The EEOC challenged the rule on behalf of employees saying it racially discriminated against black males who often suffer from *pseudofoliculitis barbae*, a genetic skin disorder that makes shaving difficult, and even painful.

A 1993 U.S. Court of Appeals for the Eighth Circuit concluded that, in spite of the company's testimony that as much as 20% of its customers have a negative reaction to delivery men with beards, Domino's failed to show a substantial business justification for its no-beard policy.

"The existence of a beard doesn't affect in any manner Domino's ability to make or deliver pizzas to their customers," the judge in the case wrote, adding that the company "makes no showing that customers would order less pizza in the absence of a no-beard rule."

However, the courts don't favor employees in every situation. It clearly depends upon the job and the organization for whom the work is performed. For example, a federal appeals court rejected a race discrimination suit filed by 12 African-American firefighters in 1993. The firefighters had challenged the city of Atlanta's policy that male firefighters must be clean-shaven. They said black men were prone to suffering from pseudofoliculitis barbae and that the policy was discriminatory because of race. The Eleventh Circuit affirmed a district court's grant of summary judgment for the city, dismissing the plaintiffs' argument that the no-beard rule has an adverse discriminatory impact on blacks. The judge in the case wrote that the city proved its shaving rule was prompted by business necessity—a secure seal is needed between the skin and the respirators firefighters wear to protect them from smoke.

Problems over appearance guidelines sometimes can be purely cosmetic. For example, in 1991, an employee of Houston-based Continental Airlines Inc. refused to comply with the company's newly released, 45-page appearance code requiring women in customer-contact jobs to wear makeup. Teresa Fischette, one of the airline's part-time ticket agents in Boston, never wore makeup. When the guidelines were adopted, she didn't change her practice.

According to newspaper reports, the airline fired her. Of the action, Fischette was quoted as saying, "Where does company prerogative step over the bounds into personal choice?" In a letter she wrote to the company's president, Hollis Harris, she said: "My decision in this matter comes from a deep conviction that this policy of requiring, rather than encouraging, women to wear makeup and lipstick is not only unnecessary, but discriminatory toward women. The company certainly has a right to have ... appearance standards, but ... wearing make-up and lipstick should be a personal choice, not grounds for termination." Eventually, the airline reinstated her, but initially stuck with its new guidelines. Whether the company still maintains its strict policy is unknown. Continental has declined to discuss the issue.

Even Burbank, California-based Walt Disney Co., which has strict appearance and grooming guidelines for its U.S. work force, had trouble implementing the same guidelines in France. According to reports, Disney wanted its 10,000 workers in its Euro Disney SCA unit at Disneyland Paris to sign a 10-page addendum to their employment contract called "The Disney Look." The look prohibits men from wearing mustaches, regulates the use of perfume and requires women to wear modest hemlines.

Although the company has been challenged by employees about the same policy in the United States and won, French labor-law inspectors complained the contract was so detailed, it should have been approved by the company's works council before being adopted and implemented. After a former Disneyland Paris executive was fined in the case, the organization implemented a much less stringent dress code in its French operations.

"We think of Americans as being super-independent, but the Europeans absolutely were not going to wear 'le costume,'" says George Simons, a diversity expert and president of George Simons International, based in Santa Cruz, California. "You're going to need a business reason to do any of these things. And a business reason needs to be substantiated."

Even with the potential problems appearance standards may create, Erwin Young, City of Santa Cruz personnel director, argues that employers shouldn't shy away from them. "Those are issues employers should have the right to control," says Young. Although the city of Santa Cruz doesn't have written dress codes for city workers (except those who wear uniforms), Young says employers should be able to maintain appearance codes based on reasonable business necessity. "I mean, if a person is working in a warehouse in the back room, who cares what he or she looks like? But if the person's in a [high-profile job] and serving the public, that's different. If a company wants to portray a certain image, it certainly seems reasonable."

Decide on a consistent corporate image and draft employee appearance standards around it. Having a clear company image is the base from which experts say employers should draft their appearance standards. Whether your firm wants to portray a casual, trendy, conservative or fun image—or any other profile on the image continuum—you need to decide what it's going to be, rather than let it happen by chance. If you don't drive the process, employees certainly will develop an image without you, but it may not be the one you want. While the standard doesn't have to be written, it should be clearly communicated.

This is the position that Jo Anne Dlott, vice president of HR for the Santa Cruz Seaside Company in Santa Cruz, has taken at her organization. Her company has continued to have the same basic appearance guidelines for the 1,000 employees who work in its parks each year during peak season (June through August) as it always has—even after the city's strict non-discrimination code went into effect three years ago. Dlott says they continue to update the guidelines each year as needed.

Dlott says the city's *looks law* hasn't adversely impacted her organization's ability to do business. She testified in city council meetings when the law was up for public hearings. In the law's earliest version, the ordinance would have prohibited employers from discriminating against individuals based on looks for any reason. In the end, the law narrowed it down to not discriminating against individuals because of height, weight or physical characteristics one is born with.

"The city council was really smart," says Dlott. "They listened to everybody, including employers. In the end, they said, 'Look, anything you're born with or happens to you by accident and alters your appearance, we can deal with that. But if you tattoo your forehead or pierce your eyebrows or dye your hair purple and pink, we don't think that's appropriate [to ask employers to overlook].'

"It's been very livable for us from an HR standpoint," adds Dlott, whose organization runs amusement parks in both Santa Cruz and San Diego. "We have a fairly strict personal appearance and dress code. But because we're in Santa Cruz, which is more relaxed, we're far less rigid than, say, Disney." Seaside Company park employees wear uniforms and can't wear bi-level hair, nose rings or a hair color other than one a person would be born with. "Many of our guests come from fairly conservative Fresno, and we basically want to project an image of friendly, well-groomed folk."

And the company's very up-front with its guidelines. "When a person walks in the door and says, 'I want to work here,' we hand him or her a fact sheet so the person knows before even filling out an application, what our [appearance] requirements are," says Dlott.

When violations to the appearance code have occurred, Dlott says it has been up to the offending employees' supervisors to tell the workers it's time for a haircut, to remove their earrings or to change whatever the problem is. A conversation usually takes care of it. When an employee fails to comply, he or she is terminated.

Image experts say companies that take a strong stance on image tend to do better overall because they have a stronger sense of mission and can communicate that better to their customers. "Even if employers don't think image is an issue, it should be an issue," says Susan Morem, an image

> "Averages don't always reveal the most telling realities. You know, Shaquille O'Neal and I have an average height of 6 feet."
> —Robert Reich, Secretary of Labor (4'10" tall)

1. HUMAN RESOURCE MANAGEMENT: Equal Employment Opportunity and Affirmative Action

consultant and president of Premier Presentation Inc. in Minneapolis. "I believe that employees' image should be tied in with the overall image of a company. If companies go to a lot of trouble designing [the physical space of] an office, thinking about advertising logos and such, but forget about their employees' [image], then they're missing the complete cycle that will make it a cohesive image with their customer. It all needs to be congruent." So, be clear about the standards you expect from applicants and employees.

Don't be afraid to include image as part of your diversity literature, either. The Seaside Company, as part of its guest-service training program, emphasizes that its guests are a diverse population and should be treated equally. That translates to workers' diversity as well. "It's really important to treat everyone the same," says Dlott. The idea is that everyone is different and should be treated with respect.

Says Simons: "Try to operate beyond the level of what the law requires to what's going to really work." Have a vision of diversity that includes personal appearance. Then, communicate how it fits into the organization and include it in diversity training. "You want people understanding why they're [being asked to look] the way they do and what advantage it is to them and to the organization," says Simons.

A proactive organization capitalizes on its human resources. "One of the ways we waste resources is by having stereotypical views of other people. We dismiss [people] before we give them a chance to show what they can do and what possibilities they bring to [the company] because they're different." Does it really matter that one of your employees wears a nose ring? If you honestly feel that, yes, it does, then you need to substantiate why that is. If it doesn't matter to the business, but you simply find it distasteful, realize it's your problem, not the employee's. Seek to cultivate personal expression and the diverse flavor it brings to an organization.

"The secret is voluntary synergy, not just voluntary compliance," says Simons. "I'm talking about people building synergy to do what their organization needs to do so they can have a good time, make money and contribute to the world effectively." Simons recommends you become aware of how personal appearances may create unfairness and damage productivity in your organization, and that you see images as diverse.

As someone once said: "If all the tools in your toolbox look like a hammer, then everything will look like a nail." The face of diversity is supposed to look different. That's the beauty of it.

Answers to quiz on page 46: 1.A., 2.A., 3.C., 4.True, 5.True, 6.B., 7. False, 8.C.

The Americans with Disabilities Act and the Workplace: Management's Responsibilities in AIDS-Related Situations

James D. Slack, California State University, Bakersfield

Why should workplace managers bother being concerned about the civil rights of people afflicted with HIV/AIDS? Because it is the law under the Americans with Disabilities Act of 1990 (ADA). In this article, James D. Slack examines the dynamics involved with applying the protections of the ADA to the most vulnerable group of disabled Americans—those who are in the HIV spectrum. In order to implement effectively the ADA in the age of AIDS, managers must be knowledgeable about the nuances of both the law and the disease. Slack concludes that managers must develop a workplace environment that supports and encourages the utilization of ADA-based rights by people with HIV/AIDS and suggests three specific activities which can help establish and maintain that environment.

Because it protects over 43 million people, the Americans with Disabilities Act (ADA) of 1990 has the potential of being the most significant piece of civil rights legislation enacted in the last three decades. ADA is comprehensive in its coverage, but Title I is of particular importance because it guarantees one of the fundamental rights demanded by every group and individual citizen in America: the right to have equal access to jobs and career opportunities. Organizations that are covered by ADA, private entities and public agencies that employ at least 15 full-time workers,[1] are prohibited from discriminating against otherwise qualified disabled Americans in selection, retention, retirement, and termination policies and practices. In addition, otherwise qualified disabled individuals cannot be denied access to various job-related opportunities, such as participation in training programs and workshops or career advancement and professional development activities.

The ADA protects everyone within the Human Immunodeficiency Virus (HIV) spectrum; from individuals just testing positive for the retrovirus to people who have contracted Acquired Immunodeficiency Syndrome (AIDS).[2] Nearly 500,000 Americans have contracted AIDS since the late 1970s; of these, approximately 97 percent are of working age, and 75 percent are in the prime working cohort of 25 to 44 years old (Centers for Disease Control and Prevention, 1995). Although estimates vary,[3] it is quite probable that more than one million Americans are unknowingly infected with HIV. Given the demographic trends of AIDS, it is reasonable to expect the same proportion of people who are HIV asymptomatic to be (or have the potential of being) in the work force and, therefore, contributors to the economy.

This makes the AIDS epidemic a central workplace issue in both the public and private sectors. Although the numbers of HIV-infected people certainly vary according to location, this disease represents a national problem with severe consequences for every community. Considering the social stigma so often attached to having AIDS,[4] as well as the pattern of discrimination against job applicants and employees who are HIV challenged, the promise of protection under this piece of legislation is perhaps more treasured by members of the AIDS community than by any other group of disabled Americans.

1. HUMAN RESOURCE MANAGEMENT: Americans with Disabilities Act

To what degree, and in what manner, will the ADA be applied to workplace situations involving HIV-challenged job applicants and employees? As is the case with so many other pieces of legislation (Van Meter and Van Horn, 1975; Pressman and Wildavsky, 1979; Nakamura and Smallwood, 1980), particularly those that deal with antidiscrimination laws (Saltzstein, 1986; Bullock and Lamb, 1984), ADA will only protect the rights of those in the HIV spectrum if it is understood and implemented effectively at the local level. This article examines management's responsibilities in ensuring the workplace rights of job applicants and employees who have HIV/AIDS.

The Bishop and Jones Study

Peter C. Bishop and Augustus J. Jones (1993) were first to analyze the potential effectiveness of the ADA. Using "prospective implementation analysis," they looked at several factors commonly found to be critical in the implementation process: participation of beneficiaries, clarity of policy goals, specificity of compliance standards, and ability of agencies to monitor and regulate implementation. According to Bishop and Jones, "Congress clearly stated its intent, regulatory agencies developed detailed compliance standards and enforcement mechanisms, and potential beneficiaries are engaged in the process" (1993; 127). Hence, the analysis led them to predict successful implementation.

Because the study was conducted shortly after the passage of ADA, Bishop and Jones admittedly focused only on those variables which tend to affect the early stages of implementation — those at the federal end of the process (1993; 122). Although they did not examine the impact of the local (in this study, workplace-level) implementors, Bishop and Jones suggested that one barrier to effective implementation would be litigation over such issues as reasonable accommodation and undue hardship (1993; 127). The outcome of these issues is affected directly by efforts at the local end of the implementation process.

Furthermore, Bishop and Jones did not focus on the AIDS community as a target group. Major AIDS organizations joined in with other associations of disabled Americans to provide congressional testimony, but it remains unclear whether job applicants and workers in the HIV spectrum will actually use ADA protections. The nature of HIV and the history of AIDS-related discrimination suggest that enthusiastic target group support at the policy-making stage might not translate directly into the full exercise of newly acquired rights at the point of implementation. The fundamental question is, will HIV-challenged job applicants and employees feel sufficiently safe and secure in their respective workplaces to seek the benefits available under the ADA?

In order for the ADA to be implemented effectively in HIV/AIDS-related situations at the workplace, the disposition of the implementors—the knowledge-base and actions of top-level administrators as well as first-line supervisors—will be an extremely critical factor throughout the process. That is, a cen-

> **Effective** *application in the age of AIDS will also be a function of management's ability to understand the nature of the retrovirus.*

tral responsibility of management will be to develop a thorough understanding of the legislation's applicability to HIV-challenged job applicants and employees. As in the case of dealing with all disabled Americans in the work force, managers will need to know the intricacies of the law. But effective application in the age of AIDS will also be a function of management's ability to understand the nature of the retrovirus as well as the many workplace ramifications of its resultant multiple diseases.

ADA and AIDS

Although people with HIV/AIDS are protected by ADA, the disease is unlike many other disabilities. The complex nature of HIV and the multiplicity of AIDS-related illnesses require greater levels of understanding of both the general medical symptoms and the ways in which the legislation should be applied to situations involving specific individuals who are within the HIV spectrum. The need for such understanding becomes readily apparent when three critical components of the law are examined within the context of AIDS: (1) the definition of "disability," (2) the prerequisite of "notification and documentation," and (3) the need to develop specific, "reasonable accommodations."

First, ADA uses the same language as the Vocational Rehabilitation Act to define disability. According to Section 3 of ADA, a disabled person is someone with:

A. a physical or mental impairment that substantially limits one or more of the major life activities;

B. a record of such an impairment; or

C. being regarded as having such an impairment.

To understand how someone in the HIV spectrum can claim to be disabled under ADA, one needs familiarity with the progression of this retrovirus. Typically, HIV occurs in four stages. The first stage, known as acute HIV, occurs six days to six weeks after infection and is characterized by short-term mononucleosis-like symptoms. Generally people are unaware that they have acute HIV. Some people feel like they just have the flu, and others simply do not acquire any of the short-term symptoms.

The second, asymptomatic stage, is characterized by reasonably normal health. People can remain asymptomatic for varying amounts of time, typically anywhere from two to ten years. The length of time spent in the asymptomatic stage is dependent upon a variety of factors, including one's ability to cope with the tremendous levels of stress which normally accompany the knowledge of being infected, the initial strength and stabili-

> The notification and documentation requirement of ADA highlights one of the many ironies of the AIDS epidemic.

ty of one's immune system, the extent to which the immune system continues to be abused, the quality of health and social services available, and the type of medication prescribed and treatment followed.[5]

The third stage is known as persistent generalized lymphadenopathy (PGL). The clinical representation of this stage is the enlargement of various lymph nodes throughout the body.[6] This stage also can last for years, with the person experiencing prolonged swelling of glands. PGL typically marks the beginning of a decline in the number of CD4 T cells, the cells that fight off diseases and viruses. It is the CD4 T cells which explain why glands initially swell (a result of fighting the virus) and the reason why glands remain swollen (a result of the declining number of cells which become insufficient to kill the virus). Hence, the loss of CD4 T cells culminates in the deterioration and ultimate destruction of the body's immune system. As in the previous stage, the rate of decline in CD4 T cells results from many factors.

The fourth stage, full-blown AIDS, is defined by a CD4 T-cell count of 200 or less, whereas most healthy people who are not HIV challenged have a CD4 T cell count of over 1,200. This final stage can also be clinically represented by a host of opportunistic infections, such as pneumocystis carinii pneumonia PCP, and cytomegalovirus (CMV), which cause infections in the lungs, eyes, and other parts of the body. It is also characterized by malignancies, like Kaposi's Sarcoma (KS), purplish plaques that can also occur throughout the body.[7] The final stage typically lasts between two to four years—again, depending on a variety of immunal and environmental conditions. Death is generally delayed until sometime after the development of full-blown AIDS.

Given the various stages of HIV, a job applicant or employee in the HIV spectrum may claim disability under each of the three definitions provided by Section 3 of the ADA.[8] Someone with either PGL or full-blown AIDS qualifies as a disabled worker under the first definition: having an actual physical or mental impairment. However, it is fairly typical for an individual with full-blown AIDS to beat temporarily one or a combination of the opportunistic diseases. The person, for instance, might have KS, but it may be in a state of remission. As such, she or he qualifies under the second definition: having a record of a physical or mental impairment.

An individual who is seropositive but asymptomatic also qualifies as a disabled worker under the third definition: being regarded as having a physical or mental impairment. This situation can include a wide variety of persons who are in the HIV spectrum, ranging from those who are in the asymptomatic stage to people with CD4 T cell counts below 200 (full-blown AIDS) but do not have as yet any symptoms. People in these circumstances are still regarded as disabled under ADA because of the 100 percent fatality rate of HIV infection. Given that perhaps millions of people are unknowingly HIV positive and asymptomatic, this category of disability will become the one most commonly used in the future.

The second issue deals with the ADA requirement of notifying employers, and providing verifying documentation, about specific disabilities (56 Fed.Reg. 35,748, July 26, 1991). While some disabilities are readily apparent and need little further verification, others may not be so evident. This is often the case for people in the HIV spectrum.

Because the majority of HIV-challenged people are asymptomatic, only a nonanonymous blood test can prove the existence of the disability. Even in the case of individuals at more advanced stages, many symptoms and conditions are either psychological or physically unobtrusive.[9] For example, one might not necessarily detect the disfiguring lesions which result from KS except when they emerge on the hands or face. The effects of PCP or pulmonary CMV might also remain unnoticed with the use of prophylaxes. Moreover, the depression which frequently results from constant, swollen lymph nodes, or from learning about another decline in the CD4 T-cell count, may be noted but misinterpreted by management as simply employee moodiness. Hence, PGL or AIDS employees with hidden conditions will also have to provide documentation.

Management is not obligated to protect the rights of disabled individuals when it is unaware of the existence of specific impairments. When verification does not occur, it is possible that some managers will wrongfully discharge the employee; this could be based simply on stereotypes about the disability or fear of imminent health care costs. Hence, the notification and documentation requirement of ADA highlights one of the many ironies of the AIDS epidemic. While the price of protection rests largely on the act of self-disclosure, the social stigma attached to AIDS makes it extremely difficult for many individuals to "stand up" and empower themselves. This situation is exacerbated by the absence of readily apparent and uniquely shared characteristics which, if present, would afford the HIV challenged an opportunity enjoyed by individuals in most other protected groups in society: gaining additional strength and courage from knowing that one is not alone in a particular setting. Regrettably each person in the HIV spectrum must decide in a relative vacuum whether to become a "Rosa Parks" in his or her specific workplace or to simply remain silent and fundamentally unprotected.

The third component, underscoring the complexities and difficulties involved in applying the ADA to HIV/AIDS-related situations in the workplace, deals with the issue of "reasonable accommodation." ADA does not define reasonable accommodation, but offers suggestions and guidelines on how to develop such accommodations. Section 101(7) indicates that reasonable accommodations may include:

1. making existing facilities used by employees readily accessible to and usable by individuals with disabilities; and

1. HUMAN RESOURCE MANAGEMENT: Americans with Disabilities Act

2. job restructuring, part-time or modified work schedules, reassignment to a vacant position, acquisition or modification of equipment or devices, appropriate adjustment or modifications of examinations, training materials or policies, the provision of qualified readers or interpreters, and other similar accommodations for individuals with disabilities.

The law assumes that the responsibility for making the initial attempt at providing reasonable accommodation is in the hands of management. ADA requires employers to take into consideration the nature of the specific job setting as well as the many characteristics and symptoms of the specific disability. However, management is not obligated to provide reasonable accommodation if such modifications do not facilitate satisfactory performance of the essential functions of the job, or if the modifications result in undue hardship for the organization.

Here, too, the nature of HIV complicates the application of reasonable accommodation requirements. Because AIDS is a fatal disease with no cure in the foreseeable future, it is not unusual for the initial diagnosis of HIV to cast the person into a state of shock for a period lasting from several months to well over a year. The only recourse for someone testing positive for HIV is to remain as healthy as possible, minimize the level of stress, find a knowledgeable physician with whom a treatment strategy can be devised,[10] and hope that a cure or at least more effective treatments are developed before he or she dies. It is because of the fundamentally life-taking nature of the retrovirus that HIV-positive job applicants and employees require reasonable accommodations—even in the absence of clinical symptoms. Under ADA, they have a right to receive workplace-related assistance that will help them cope with having a fatal disease and keep them healthier, hence in the asymptomatic stage longer.

The many illnesses related to full-blown AIDS also complicate the rendering of reasonable accommodations. As the immune system deteriorates, opportunistic diseases begin to attack the body sequentially and in combination. Someone with fungal infections, such as candidiasis or histoplasmosis, might require different kinds of reasonable accommodations than someone with viral infections like CMV or shingles. As suggested above, learning that one's CD4 T cell count has dropped dramatically might require additional, temporary accommodations similar to those needed immediately following the initial diagnosis of either HIV or AIDS. Each illness and situation—indeed, each individual—will have to be analyzed carefully in order to determine appropriate and effective reasonable accommodations.

Action Needed by Management

What should managers do to facilitate the effective implementation of the ADA in the case of employees with HIV/AIDS? They need to develop a workplace environment that supports and encourages the empowerment of employees in the HIV spectrum. Three specific activities can help estab-

> The many illnesses related to full-blown AIDS also complicate the rendering of reasonable accommodations.

lish and maintain this environment. First, management should establish a plan of action for dealing with HIV at the workplace. The plan should be tailored to the particulars of each workplace, but generally should include the following four components: (1) a statement supporting the workplace and civil rights of HIV-challenged employees and job applicants, (2) a set of procedures for helping these individuals, (3) general examples of reasonable accommodations which might assist HIV employees and their immediate supervisors in devising specific accommodations, and (4) a plan for providing education to employees and training for supervisors (Slack and Luna, 1992; 306). To further strengthen a supportive workplace environment, the specifics of the plan should be developed and approved by both management and labor. The plan should then be distributed to every employee as part of the personnel handbook.

Second, the education and training component of the plan must go well beyond "AIDS 101." Rather than underscoring only those topics which pertain to modes of transmission and strategies for prevention, focus must be on increasing the level of understanding about those aspects of the retrovirus that have a direct bearing on the productivity, morale, and health of the work force, as well as the processes and practices that are designed to address those aspects of AIDS in a more proactive, supportive, and effective manner. One example of a training workshop that focuses on workplace ramifications of AIDS is in Appendix A.

Finally, workplace managers must devise reasonable accommodations that are job-specific and meet the needs of each individual in each stage of the disease. This is a difficult task, but one which is absolutely essential to prolonging the health of the employee as well as maintaining high levels of morale and productivity. Here are a few suggestions.[11]

Beginning at the asymptomatic stage, reasonable accommodations should focus on minimizing the amount of stress at the workplace and, therefore, helping the employee to maintain a stronger immune system. Having a plan of action in place is the first step in relieving stress and anxiety in that it will help to reassure the HIV-challenged employee of a positive workplace environment. Additional stress reduction measures might include: facilitating the creation of HIV support groups at the workplace, permitting more flexibility in use of sick days for dealing with shock and depression, transferring workers out of jobs that bring them into contact with pollutants or infectious materials, and counseling employees about the negative health consequences of working overtime. Paradoxically, management should try to keep workplace conditions as normal as possible and thereby help to provide a psychologically familiar routine.

Employees with PGL or full-blown AIDS will need an increasing amount of time away from the workplace. Hence, accommodations might entail working at home more often, downgrading to part-time employment while still maintaining benefits, or greater use of flexitime. Because sick-day use will increase, management might consider ways to pool unused sick days from other employees. Depending on symptoms, reasonable accommodations might also entail such simple acts as moving the HIV-challenged employee's work station closer to restrooms, allowing for additional work breaks to recapture his or her strength, or providing brief opportunities for privacy and reflection during the work day. At all stages of the disease, communication between management and the HIV-challenged employee is central to providing not simply reasonable, but effective, accommodations.

Conclusions

It is to be hoped that Bishop and Jones (1993) are correct in projecting success in the implementation of the ADA. After all, the law is supported by a wide variety of interest groups, including those within the AIDS community. Furthermore, both Congress and the Equal Employment Opportunity Commission have provided clear definitions and administrative guidelines. And unlike many other pieces of legislation, the ADA is accompanied with straight-forward oversight and compliance mechanisms.

As with past attempts to implement antidiscrimination legislation, however, local actors will certainly have to play a major role in the process. Especially given the stigma and fears attached to the AIDS epidemic, the responsibilities of the workplace manager in assuring effective implementation of the ADA will be even greater than is the case with other laws. Politics, after all, affects the quality of life for people with HIV/AIDS more than the morbid afflictions that come part-and-parcel with this retrovirus. If managers pursue the spirit of the law, then HIV-challenged individuals will grow increasingly comfortable in exercising their rights under the letter of law. This, it seems, is management's ultimate responsibility.

◆ ◆ ◆

James D. Slack is an associate professor in the Department of Public Policy and Administration at California State University, Bakersfield. Through the department's Institute of Public Administration, he consults with agencies throughout California on the policy and workplace ramifications of HIV/AIDS.

Notes

The author is grateful for suggestions and helpful comments made about earlier drafts of this article by several anonymous *PAR* referees, the editor of *PAR*, and Professor Gregory Butler of New Mexico State University.

1. The ADA does not cover federal employees, Native American tribes, and private membership clubs (except for labor organizations). Federal employees in the HIV spectrum, however, are protected from workplace discrimination and are due reasonable accommodations under the Vocational Rehabilitation Act. (*School Board of Nassau County* v. *Arline*, 1987; *Alexander* v. *Choate*, 1985; and *Chalk* v. *United States District Court, Central District of California*, 1988.)
2. The legislative history makes this very clear ("House Committee on Education and Labor Report" at 52 and "Senate Committee on Labor and Human Resources Report" at 22, 136 *Congressional Record* S9697, July 13, 1990).
3. Estimates range from just a few hundred thousand persons (Fumento, 1990) to perhaps over ten million persons (telephone interview with counselors at the Gay Men's Health Crisis and the San Francisco AIDS Hotline). The CDC estimates that, in the United States, 1 in every 100 men and 1 in every 150 women are probably within the HIV spectrum. All estimates are speculative because the only way to determine the number of HIV-challenged people is by testing everyone at least once every three months.
4. This is due primarily to cultural responses to the disease's initial connection with homosexual behavior and IV-drug use.
5. Several of these factors are supposition. That is, no study indicates conclusively the exact extent to which factors like stress reduction delay the progression of the disease. To one extent or another, however, there is consensus in the medical community that stress has an effect on the health of everyone's immune system. Furthermore, most physicians treating people in the HIV spectrum prescribe activities (support groups, sleep, rest, etc.) designed to minimize the level of stress.
6. PGL is more of a sign than a symptom and, therefore, it is possible for some people to be within the PGL stage (decreasing CD4 T-cell count) and remain asymptomatic. For the vast majority of people with PGL, this stage is characterized by prolonged swelling (equal to or greater than 1 cm) of the lymph nodes with no other signs of AIDS (Stine, 1993; and Cohen *et al.*, 1990).
7. Full-blown AIDS also includes many other symptomatic manifestations, including wasting syndrome, fever, night sweats, and deterioration of the peripheral nervous system.
8. The exception is for individuals in the acute HIV stage. There are simply insufficient levels of antibodies to test positive of HIV at this stage.
9. Psychological issues change with the changes in the disease. The following list is from James Dilley, (1984; 62-76; in Dilley, 1990; 2-5.13.1):
New Diagnosis
   ◆ Affective numbing vs. affective discharge; "denial"
   ◆ Need for emotional, financial, social support; self-esteem
   ◆ Fear of contaminating family, friends
   ◆ Fear of rejection: family, friends
   ◆ Pressure to make complicated treatment decisions
   ◆ Feelings of guilt and self-blame; illness as retribution
   ◆ Is there sex after diagnosis? Life-style changes
Mid-stage
   ◆ Loss of hope; emotional exhaustion
   ◆ More detailed grief work: anticipating and mourning loss of important people and objects
   ◆ Extent of treatment; pain control
   ◆ Unfinished business: life review; putting one's affairs in order
Terminal Care
   ◆ Adequate pain control; personal contact
   ◆ Work with family, friends
   ◆ Death and dying: honoring the patient's wishes.
10. Commonly such treatment strategies entail decisions about antiviral drugs (either azidothymidine, AZT—also referred to as zidovudine, ZDV, or the brand-name Retrovir—dideoxyinosine (ddI), and dideoxycytidine (ddC), PCP prophylaxis (Bactrim or Intron A), and other important secondary prevention strategies such as TB screening.
11. These suggestions are based on conversations with counselors and HIV-challenged people associated with The Living Room (Cleveland), the Gay Men's Health Crisis (New York), the San Francisco AIDS Hotline, the HIV Coordinating Council of New Mexico (Albuquerque), and the Southwest AIDS Committee (Las Cruces, NM, and El Paso, TX).

1. HUMAN RESOURCE MANAGEMENT: Americans with Disabilities Act

References

Alexander v. Choate, 1985. 469 U.S. 287.

Bishop, Peter C. and Augustus J. Jones, Jr., 1993. "Implementing the Americans with Disabilities Act of 1990: Assessing the Variables of Success." *Public Administration Review*, vol. 53 (March/April), 121-128.

Bullock, Charles S. and Charles U. Lamb, 1984. *Implementation of Civil Rights Policy*. Monterey, CA: Brooks/Cole Publishing.

Centers for Disease Control and Prevention, 1995. *HIV/AIDS Surveillance Report*, no. 2.

Chalk v. United States District Court, 1988. Central District of California, 840 F.2d 701, 9th Cir..

Cohen, P.T., et al., 1990. *The AIDS Knowledge Base: A Textbook on HIV Disease from The University of California, San Francisco, and the San Francisco General Hospital*. Waltham, MA: Medical Publishing Group.

DeSario, Jack P., Sue Faerman, and James D. Slack, 1994. *Local Government Information and Training Needs in the 21st Century*. Westport, CT: Quorum Books.

Dilley, James, 1984. "Treatment Issues and Approaches in the Psychological Care of AIDS Patients," In S. Nichols and D. Ostrow, eds., *Psychiatric Aspects of AIDS*. Washington, DC: American Psychiatric Press, pp. 62-76.

———, 1990. "Psychological Impact of AIDS: Overview." In P.T. Cohen, et al., eds., *The AIDS Knowledge Base: A Textbook on HIV Disease from The University of California, San Francisco, and the San Francisco General Hospital*. Waltham, MA: Medical Publishing Group.

Federal Register, 1991. "Equal Employment Opportunity for Individuals with Disabilities; Final Rule." Equal Employment Opportunity Commission, vol. 56, pp. 35725-35756.

Fumento, Michael, 1990. *The Myth of Heterosexual AIDS*. New York: Basic Books, Inc.

Nakamura, Robert T. and Frank Smallwood, 1980. *The Politics of Policy Implementation*. New York: St. Martin's Press.

Pressman, Jeffery L. and Aaron B. Wildavsky, 1973. *Implementation*. Berkeley, CA: University of California Press.

Saltzstein, Grace H., 1986. "Female Mayors and Women in Municipal Jobs." *American Journal of Political Science*, vol. 30 (February), 140-164.

School Board of Nassau County v. Arline, 1987. 480 U.S. 273.

Slack, James D. and Anelia Luna, 1992. "AIDS-Related Documents from 96 American Cities and Counties." *Public Administration Review*, vol. 52 (May/June), 305-308.

Stine, Gerald J., 1993. *Acquired Immune Deficiency Syndrome: Biological, Medical, Social, and Legal Issues*. Englewood Cliffs, NJ: Prentice-Hall.

Van Meter, Donald S. and Carl E. Van Horn, 1975. "The Policy Implementation Process: A Conceptual Framework." *Administration and Society*, vol. 6 (February), 445-488.

Appendix
Managing the Workplace Ramifications of AIDS

Purpose: To prepare management for dealing with workplace situations involving HIV and AIDS.

Goal: By end of training session, participants will have (1) epidemiological, legal, and interpersonal knowledge about HIV and AIDS and (2) understanding of how to apply knowledge of HIV/AIDS to their specific work settings.

Time: This is a one-day (8 hour) workshop.

Module 1. Understanding HIV and AIDS
The general purpose of module 1 is to familiarize workshop participants with (1) some of the fears and myths about AIDS which may impact workplace performance and (2) the realities of what HIV-infected employees experience, which impact workplace performance.

Specific topics include:
1. What is HIV and AIDS?
2. Modes of transmission
3. Progression from HIV to AIDS
4. AIDS-related diseases
5. Keeping workers healthy and productive

Module 2. Managing the Workplace
The general purpose of module 2 is to familiarize workshop participants on how to maintain a productive and healthy workplace. Topics center on the Americans with Disabilities Act (ADA) as it applies to AIDS.

Specific topics include:
1. ADA and the specific work setting
2. Nondiscrimination of HIV-infected employees
3. Reasonable accommodation issues and application to specific workplace and job descriptions.
4. Undue hardship issues and application to specific workplace and job descriptions.

Module 3. Dealing Effectively with both HIV-Challenged and Noninfected Employees
Module 3 shifts focus from the agency level to the supervisor-subordinate level. Using case law in the areas of labor relations, work force management, and AIDS, as well as workplace experiences of HIV-challenged individuals from the community, this module familiarizes workshop participants with one-to-one situations.

Topics include:
1. ADA's requirements of documentation of HIV
2. Sensitivity in dealing with HIV-challenged workers
3. ADA's modification of confidentiality
4. Knowledge about community-based assistance programs
5. Controlling rumors, fears, and behavior of employees who are not HIV challenged.

Module 4A. Developing an AIDS Plan for the Workplace
Workshop participants are divided into two groups. Managers participate in module 4A. Here the basic components of an AIDS plan for the workplace is discussed and applied to each work setting and at the job-specific level. It is emphasized that the purpose of the plan is to maintain a healthy and productive work force while avoiding AIDS-related litigation.

Module 4B. Training the Trainer about AIDS and the Workplace
Training staff participate in module 4B, which focuses on strategies for educating the entire work force on the issue of AIDS. This module includes discussions on how to present AIDS in nonthreatening and nonoffensive ways, yet in ways that are direct and provide detailed information. It also focuses on how the training staff can tap local expertise and resources, as well as how to disseminate information in an effective manner.

Source: Adapted from DeSario, Faerman, and Slack (1994).

Article 9

■ **Managing Them Can Be as Easy as ABC**

Get the Best From Employees with Learning Disabilities

Chances are, you either have, or will have, a few employees who have some kind of learning disability. Educate yourself now on how to manage these employees to peak performance.

Gillian Flynn

Gillian Flynn is the assistant editor at PERSONNEL JOURNAL.

At the Red Lion Hotel in Costa Mesa, California, Robert Suderman is somewhat of a local hero. Friendly, focused and enthusiastic, Suderman is one of those people who just loves his job—so much that he bemoaned all the spare time he had during the end-of-the-year holidays. Suderman's winning streak began in the HR department, where he input personnel file information into the computer. Every day he came in, working steadily and efficiently at a routine task many other employees might have balked at.

Upon finishing that task, he asked for more, this time something extra challenging. Now he assists a payroll professional in the company's accounting department. "Again, the job is a bit routine, but it's something the payroll person was behind on, and it did have some additional steps," says Jan Linville, director of HR. "He's mastered it now and is feeling really good about it. He's performing a necessary function and is helping the staff work more efficiently." But aside from being a tireless employee, Suderman has another quality that distinguishes him: He contributes to the organization despite having a disability that causes him to be a slow learner.

Believe it or not, Suderman's achievement is rare. Even with the passage of the Americans with Disabilities Act, many people who have learning disabilities

1. HUMAN RESOURCE MANAGEMENT: Americans with Disabilities Act

(LDs) remain unaided—mostly because a learning disability isn't as easy to spot as a physical disability. Managers may not be able to identify performance problems as symptoms of an LD, and so may neglect to promote, or even terminate, an employee who's embarrassed to ask for help.

And there are quite a few employees who fall into this category. According to the "Journal of Learning Disabilities," approximately 10% to 15% of employees in any large industry or business have learning disabilities. They need an environment in which they feel comfortable disclosing their disabilities and seeking help. And you need to know how to help them. The much-buzzed-about upcoming labor shortage, a result of baby-boomer retirements, is going to demand you're open to all kinds of workers, including those categorized as slow learners.

Identify and encourage disclosure of learning disabilities. Do you have any employees with learning disabilities? You may or may not know. Most people with learning disabilities look just like everyone else. A learning disability can come in the form of dyslexia, which makes reading difficult and can affect people of even genius-level intelligence (such as Albert Einstein and Thomas Edison). Or it may be more severe, such as disabilities that cause a person to be lower-functioning—though, it's important to note, not to the level of low intelligence or retardation. "It's very difficult to identify people with learning disabilities," says Elaine Reisman, assistant professor at Lesley College in Cambridge, Massachusetts, and director of the *Threshold Program*, a center to aid people with learning disabilities. "People in business can be very aware if someone needs a wheelchair. But if someone is a slow learner because of a learning disability, it's not apparent right away, and you don't know right away what to do about it."

Indeed, with the exception of people whose learning disabilities prohibit them from high functioning, the only way a company would know an employee has an LD is if the employee came forth or if a manager identified certain characteristics as potential links to a learning disability. Of course, the easier of the two would be for the employee to self-identify. This way, any performance issues could be addressed up front before they became problematic. But naturally, many people are reluctant to come forth, afraid they'll be categorized as having inferior intelligence or a lack of education—neither of which is the cause of a learning disability (see definition above).

How to get around the reluctance? Take a cue from Boston-based John Hancock Mutual Life Insurance Co. The company maintains a casual acceptance of learning disabilities that makes disclosure much easier for employees. But even more than that, the company makes it a point to really help workers who have disclosed their disabilities.

An important part in assisting employees to do their jobs is John Hancock's training unit. The company publishes outlines of courses it offers—everything from English as a business language to statistics. Workers simply sign up for what they want. Employees with learning disabilities can also bring their specific challenges to a trainer for one-on-one help. That way, they receive individualized attention for their LD without having to announce to the world they have a learning disability.

What about employees who may have a learning disability, but refuse to disclose it—or even acknowledge it? "That's a tricky one," says Sandra Colley, corporate director of work force diversity at John Hancock. "When the employee won't admit there's an issue and you see him or her heading down a path of not performing well, you want desperately to help. But sometimes you can't get him or her to trust you enough."

In such a case, Colley suggests tackling the problem from a performance-management viewpoint. Point out the areas in which the employee isn't up to par and work with that person on how to improve his or her performance. "You can't just go to someone and say, 'I know you have a learning disability, and I want to help you,'" says Colley. "That's not fair and it won't work. You need to center the talk around being objective, telling the employee what the job requires and what your expectations are. Tell the employee what resources are available. Continually nudge the person to get assistance."

Steve Zivolich, executive director for Irvine, California-based Integrated Resources Institute, a non-profit organization that helps people who have disabilities find employment, agrees it's more important to identify where employees are having problems than to label the specific learning disabilities. "Find out what the issues are so you can assist them," he suggests. "They may not identify their disability by name, they may just say they have trouble sequencing things. That's the key, though, to improving performance."

Still, if you're going to tackle a learning disability from the performance-management angle, it helps to know whether you're actually dealing with an employee who has a learning disability. For instance, there's a big difference between the worker who misses deadlines because he or she lacks the ability to prioritize effectively—and the worker who misses deadlines because he or she is unwilling to do the work on time.

Although it's unwise to place too much faith on managerial detective skills, there are some behaviors that often are signs of a learning disability. To begin with, a person's social skills often can hint to a learning disability. Says Reisman: "People who have learning disabilities tend to have more difficulty in society on a social level. If they have trouble on the job, it's more for social reasons than for inability to do the job."

DEFINING LEARNING DISABILITIES

Learning disability: The most common term used to refer to a permanent condition in which an individual with otherwise good overall ability has difficulty in learning and using certain kinds of information, or in learning in particular ways. While the cause may not be known, it is *not* low intelligence, emotional disorders, poor teaching, lack of educational opportunity, or sensory loss. Some physical, attentional or behavioral characteristics may or may not accompany and complicate the learning disability, such as hyperactivity, distractibility, poor coordination, impulsiveness, and others, but these are not the cause.

—*"You Don't Outgrow It: Living with Learning Disabilities," by Marnell L. Hayes, 1993, Academic Therapy Publications Inc.*

9. Employees with Learning Disabilities

Here are some common symptoms of learning disabilities:

1. The "unfocused or rude" employee who continually repeats things, speaks at inappropriate times or spends unnecessary time at one task may not be doing so by choice. These characteristics can be signs of perseveration or impulsivity, both learning disabilities.

2. The employee who "refuses" to follow instructions may not be insubordinate. Many learning disabilities prohibit people from retaining instructions. They simply can't remember the order in which to do things; they can't "sequence."

3. The employee who has "poor judgment" may just have trouble understanding directions that aren't concrete or specific. For instance, telling these employees they may take a break when they have a reasonable amount of tasks completed won't work—you may have differing definitions of "reasonable."

4. The employee who can't take a hint may not be overly persistent or aggressive. Reisman says many people with learning disabilities have trouble picking up social cues. For instance, saying "How have you been?" may not be interpreted as a greeting, but rather an actual question to be answered. "These are behavioral issues that can be handled easily once they're addressed," says Reisman. "But they do need to be addressed."

Most accommodations are low effort, high payoff. A lot of managers hear the word "disability" and automatically think "accommodation." Cynics wonder how much it's going to cost them; idealists wonder where they can get the biggest and brightest. The fact of the matter is, employees with learning disabilities rarely require much in the way of concrete accommodations—not in the sense we're accustomed to at least. "It's not as if you have to build a wheelchair ramp to accommodate people with learning disabilities," says Reisman. "It doesn't really cost an employer anything—just a little creative thinking."

Case in point: John Hancock. Many of the organization's work units have high volumes in terms of record keeping. For employees with learning disabilities in these units, the paperwork can become overwhelming. Enter an extremely low-tech accommodation: color coding. Files are organized by color to help employees keep straight the order in which they should be handled. In addition, both managers and co-workers keep an eye out for employees who may get frazzled. Managers, for instance, have been trained to dole out the workload in manageable chunks, already prioritized. "Also, if co-workers have a sense an individual is becoming overwhelmed, they'll say, 'Hey,

Strategies for Handling Specific Problem Behaviors

Not all employees who have learning disabilities are going to have the same problems on the job. Yet certain behavioral characteristics do tend to pop up more often among this labor group. In her booklet, "Supervising Employees with Learning Disabilities," Elaine Reisman offers advice on how to best manage specific problem behaviors often associated with learning disabilities. Here's an excerpt:

Insecurity about role on the job and low self-esteem.

Look for opportunities to give positive reinforcement for even small steps in improvement. Be specific about what you're praising. Don't just say, "You're doing a good job." Instead, say, "You handled the data entry well. The typing was neat and correct."

When suggesting changes in behavior, use the "sandwich technique." Start with a positive comment, then explain the criticism, and give a specific suggestion for a way to improve the behavior. For example, "I like the way you greet people who have an appointment with me. But when you come back late from your break, I feel annoyed because I depend on you to be there. Please be sure to stay close enough on break so you can return on time."

Memory problems and inability to follow directions.

- Give step-by-step directions both verbally and in writing. Use illustrations if helpful. Post the instructions where the employee will be using them.
- Ask the person to repeat the instructions to you or demonstrate the task. Encourage questions.
- Be specific in giving directions: "Put these two boxes on the table next to the water cooler."
- Use a checklist to facilitate self-monitoring.

Distractibility and short attention span.

- Assign job tasks that allow for movement. If not possible, suggest the person take a stretch or a short walk after working a set amount of time.
- Try to assign tasks that can be completed in a short period of time.
- Assign the person work locations devoid of excess noise or activities.

Reluctance to ask for information or help.

- Require the person to ask one question a day.
- Praise the person when he or she voluntarily asks for information or help.

Lack of initiative.

- Give the person a list of tasks that can be done without further help from the supervisor.

Perseveration and impulsivity.

- Work out signals, such as a wink or a tap on the shoulder, to alert the person.
- On the job, when these problems occur, immediately identify the behaviors and communicate using the agreed upon signal.
- Suggest that when the person feels the urge to repeat or interrupt, he or she should write out the comment or say it to him or herself.
- Suggest counting to 10 before acting. During that time, the person should assess whether he or she has already made the comment or if this is an appropriate time to interrupt.

Poor judgment in regard to safety issues.

- Point out possible dangerous situations at work. Spell out appropriate responses.
- Role play what steps the person would follow in an emergency.

1. HUMAN RESOURCE MANAGEMENT: Americans with Disabilities Act

let's go grab a cup of coffee,' and get the person to relax," says Colley.

At the Red Lion, one of the company's three LD employees can't read letters or numbers. So managers there gave him a little extra time when he first started the job to memorize the locations of the different banquet rooms in which he works, and they continually give him instructions verbally. Suderman, however, didn't take to verbal instructions as well. When he moved to the payroll department, his job was broken into a series of steps.

For lower-functioning employees, many times, it's behavioral issues that must be addressed. For instance, Reisman mentions a real-life example of an employee labeled as having "poor judgment." The woman was hired as a receptionist because of a good phone voice and clear message-taking. Soon however, a problem arose: She was chatting on the phone an inordinate amount of time. Seems when she was hired, her supervisor had told her it was OK to use the phone "within reason." The woman had no concrete concept of what that meant. The accommodation? The supervisor gave her the translation of "within reason": 10 minutes a day.

It's employees' inability to read social cues that may be one of the biggest problem areas, however. Defined in a general way as perseveration or impulsivity, these characteristics may lead to employees speaking at inappropriate times, repeating things or interrupting. "For instance, you may be having a conversation [with someone else], but if your employee wants to let you know she has a doctor's appointment next week, she'd want to tell you right when she's thinking of it," says Reisman. "She'd interrupt your conversation instead of reading the social cue that you were busy." But again, accommodation is simple: Explain you're busy and should only be interrupted for an emergency. Explain what qualifies as an emergency. Or, if the person tends to perseverate, repeating instructions or questions continually, work out a signal with the employee, such as a wink, that communicates what he or she is doing without embarrassing the employee in front of others (see "Strategies for Handling Specific Problem Behaviors").

Use common strategies to get the most from these workers. Whatever accommodations you make, it's important not to ostracize employees who have learning disabilities. Everyone knows the importance of feeling integrated in the workplace. For employees who have LDs, this is often doubly so. They need to feel welcomed, wanted and reassured. At Red Lion, integration begins right away. Employees with learning disabilities, for instance, go through the same orientation as other employees. They're welcomed in the employee newsletter, and supervisors make sure they see this. They're shown around, introduced to co-workers and given lockers (with key locks rather than combinations for employees who can't read numbers).

"Do anything that would make them feel you thought about them and that would help them feel more secure," suggests Reisman. "That should be done for everybody, but particularly for these people who have so much anxiety about whether you really want them there—even though you hired them."

To help workers with LDs feel integrated, Dallas-based Chili's Grill and Bar chooses not to have too many separate activities for them. Traci Hagan, a regional recruiter, estimates the company currently has approximately 700 employees who have learning disabilities working in the California-Nevada area's 51 restaurants, recruited through the *Team-Works Program*. Although these employees come through the special program, that's about the only thing that separates them from co-workers. "We tell the managers to treat them like anyone else," says Hagan. "Don't say, 'They're the TeamWorks employees.' Some companies do little graduation exercises when their employees who have disabilities complete [training]. We don't. We created the program simply as a vehicle to help our managers find good workers."

At the Red Lion, Linville tries to lead by example. She makes a point of sitting down with employees who have learning disabilities and chatting with them on breaks or in the lunchroom. She encourages Suderman, for example, to bring in the photos he takes as a hobby. "It's important to model that it's OK to talk normally to these employees so others won't be afraid or cautious of approaching them. It's important to let co-workers know these are good people to know."

Speaking of which, do co-workers need training or education about people who have learning disabilities, just as they receive in other areas of diversity? For higher-functioning people with well-managed LDs, most employees would never know or even guess, so the point is moot. Even for lower functioning employees, Zivolich believes specific training could be unintentionally stigmatizing. What he does recommend is explaining to co-workers why certain employees may receive an extra hand.

Rise of the Knowledge Worker—a Threat to Employees Who Have LDs?

The idea of a knowledge-based work force has been rattling around for quite some time now—which may lead many to wonder whether people who have learning disabilities are going to be edged out of jobs soon. Yet most experts don't believe this is of immediate concern.

Sandra Colley, corporate director of work force diversity for Boston-based John Hancock Mutual Life Insurance Co., cites technology not as an enemy wiping out jobs, but as an aid assisting people with learning disabilities. "Although a lot of lower-skill jobs have been lost because of technology, there's really two sides of the coin. Technology can also help people with learning disabilities do their jobs more easily."

Steve Zivolich, executive director for Irvine, California-based Integrated Resources Institute, a non-profit organization that finds employment for people who have disabilities, also agrees that technology can be used to help employees who have LDs. "We have an increased need for service workers. Technology can assist people in these jobs. For instance, a lot of cash registers now have pictures on them. Computers have spell checks. All these things make jobs more accessible for people with learning disabilities."

—GF

9. Employees with Learning Disabilities

> **Most experts will tell you managing employees with learning disabilities is just like managing any other workers—just more intense.**

Reisman agrees the way you handle people who have LDs makes all the difference in how they're accepted in the workplace. "It can work two ways. Co-workers can be resentful, or co-workers can think, 'Wow! This is a place that cares about other people, and if I ever have a need, they'd be considerate of me as well.' It all depends on how the organization approaches it. If it's in a way in which everyone feels their needs are being addressed, the person receiving special attention won't be resented."

Having an accepting workplace sets the groundwork for building on these employees' skills. Once they feel they're truly wanted, they can focus on the task at hand. The best place to begin in encouraging performance is to start the employee with the tasks he or she is best at. Sounds simple, but it's often overlooked in the zeal to push these workers to be their best—and there's nothing more disheartening than over-challenging an employee at the start and later having to demote him or her. "Start off with things they do well and then increase the challenges," says Reisman. "If you're going to hire people who have limitations, then try to fit the job to them or have them do the jobs they can do."

At John Hancock, many employees who have noticeable learning disabilities start out doing administrative tasks and customer-service work. From there, they can move on to do whatever they're capable of doing. "It runs a range," says Colley. "We don't put a cap on achievement."

Looking at Suderman's rise in task work shows how effective give-and-take performance management can be. In his very first days, Suderman was stuffing employee-information packets for the HR department—a task Suderman made short shrift of, proving he could handle more complicated jobs. "He found it frustrating because he was beyond that kind of task mentally," says Linville. After that, Suderman took on increased responsibility.

Most experts will tell you managing employees who have learning disabilities is just like managing any other employee—just a little more intense. For instance, don't make a goal be: "To package error-free letters." Identify each step along the way: Place stamps neatly, seal envelope, double-check address.

In addition, performance reviews should be conducted more frequently—up to once a week when focusing on specific behavioral issues, says Reisman. These performance reviews should be handled as objectively as possible, focusing specifically on the actions to be improved. Hagan says, for instance, that many of the employees who have LDs at Chili's are a little battle-scarred, having been turned down or fired from positions in the past. In fact, 75% of TeamWorks employees had not had a job in the six months prior to coming to Chili's—so they may be more sensitive to criticism.

Linville herself has encountered this problem. She remembers when an employee with a learning disability was reprimanded by his supervisor for something fairly minor. The man came into her office positive he was going to be fired. "So I brought in his supervisor and we all chatted until Paul understood his job wasn't threatened in any way."

Effective management of these employees pays offs. All in all, managing employees who have LDs isn't too tricky a task. But a little extra hand for these employees will take you a long way. At Chili's, where employees who have learning disabilities originally were recruited simply to fight the labor gap, Hagan says plenty of unexpected side benefits have resulted. For one thing, this group's turnover rate is 25% to 30%, a virtual miracle in an industry that usually sports 200% to 300% turnover. "We get valuable employees who are on time, who want to work, who are very loyal and excited to prove themselves," says Hagan.

Hagan adds the arrangement also has unexpectedly benefited managers, maintaining that managers who've worked extensively with employees who have LDs tend to be better at the coaching aspects of managing—important in today's workplace. "Managers need a lot of tools in their toolbox when managing and developing their employees. Working with employees who have LDs helps develop their patience and their motivational and training skills," says Hagan.

Zivolich believes employers will continue to hire people who have LDs to ease the work burden in an effective way. "The more difficult it is for companies to get employees, the more creative they'll become in looking at a wider range of people. But I'd encourage companies to get into this not because they have to but for the positive reasons. With the employers we've worked with, these employees tend to perform as well if not better than their co-workers."

Whether it be to ensure the employees you do have function to the best of their ability or hiring people who have LDs makes good recruiting sense, managing employees who have learning disabilities will take on increased importance. It may take a little extra elbow grease, but it's effort that pays off. Just look at what Suderman has done for his company. "Because of his work, others in the department can focus on their main jobs," says Linville. "He's a high quality employee because—quite simply—he values doing his work well."

Sexual Harassment: Reducing The Risks

Even the smallest company can become the target of a lawsuit.

Sharon Nelton

In San Francisco, a female secretary receives $3.5 million in a sexual-harassment suit against the law firm of Baker & McKenzie.

A male employee at a hot-tub manufacturing company in Los Angeles wins a $1 million lawsuit claiming that his female chief financial officer made regular sexual advances.

In New York, Tiffany & Co., the jewelry retailer, is ordered to pay $360,000 to a former employee who claimed in a 10-year-old suit that she was sexually harassed and then was fired after complaining about it.

These are the kinds of stories that make business owners shudder. And with good reason. The number of sexual-harassment complaints and lawsuits has risen sharply in recent years. The percentage of human-resource professionals who said their departments handled one or more sexual-harassment reports rose from 35 percent in 1991 to 65 percent in 1993, according to a 1994 survey by the Society for Human Resource Management (SHRM).

"There's just a profound trend toward increased filing of [sexual-harassment] lawsuits," says John F. Wymer III, a partner in the Atlanta law firm of Powell, Goldstein, Frazer & Murphy. "People are much more sensitive to this than they've ever been before and much more aware of their rights."

Sexual-harassment law has its roots in Title VII of the Civil Rights Act of 1964, which prohibits discrimination on the basis of sex. Four major events in 1991, however, have led not only to the increase in legal action but also to major shifts in the way we think about sexual harassment.

The topic gained national attention when Justice Clarence Thomas, then a Supreme Court nominee, was accused of having sexually harassed former colleague Anita Hill. Another focus on the issue that year was the U.S. Navy's Tailhook scandal, involving sexual harassment of women attending a convention of naval aviators.

The passage of the Civil Rights Act of 1991 allowed jury trials and "increased the nature and amount of compensatory and punitive damages that employers may be held liable for," according to Joyce Kaser, author of *Honoring Boundaries: Preventing Sexual Harassment in the Workplace* (Human Resource Development Press, 1995).

As more and more cases go to juries and not just judges, Wymer says, the damage awards are increasing significantly. Juries, he says, "tend to be very much inclined to rule in favor of the plaintiff—the employee—and generally not very favorably inclined to rule for the employer."

A 1991 Ninth Circuit Court of Appeals case, *Ellison vs. Brady*, recognized a "reasonable-woman standard" rather than a "reasonable-person standard," promoting the understanding that women may view mild sexual harassment as a prelude to violent sexual assault and feel it creates a hostile work environment.

In a 1993 decision, in *Harris vs. Forklift Systems, Inc.*, the U.S. Supreme Court further changed the legal landscape, rejecting the requirement that a plaintiff had to prove "psychological injury" to establish a claim for sexual harassment.

If you're the owner of a small business, you may be lulled into a false sense of security, thinking that because federal law related to sexual harassment applies only to businesses with 15 or more employees, your company is in no danger of action being filed against it. But Terry Morehead Dworkin, professor of business law at Indiana University, in Bloomington, points out that many state laws are more stringent than federal law and apply to companies with as few as two or three employees.

A business owner may also be misled by the caps that federal law places on damages in harassment cases—$50,000 for smaller companies to $300,000 for the largest. However, Dworkin says, an employee can file a suit under state or tort (wrongful-act) law and receive much larger awards.

The Equal Employment Opportunity Commission defines sexual harassment as "unwelcome sexual advances, requests for sexual favors, and other verbal or physical conduct of a sexual nature" when acquiescence is a condition of getting or keeping a job, a promotion, or a pay increase (*quid pro quo* harassment), or when it substantially interferes with an employee's ability to do his or her work (harassment that creates a hostile work environment).

Acts that result in a hostile work environment create the most confusion because they are less direct and the harasser may be a co-worker, not a supervisor. However, experts generally agree that such behavior as making kissing sounds, verbal abuse, touching, and pressuring an individual for dates can constitute harassment.

You can't protect yourself from being sued, says Dworkin, "but you can help protect yourself from a successful lawsuit if you put certain procedures into place."

Here are some of the steps experts recommend for reducing or eliminating your liability and helping you ensure that your workplace is free of harassment:

Develop a company policy on sexual harassment, and make sure it's communicated to and understood by employees. Your statement should define sexual harassment, make clear you will not tolerate it, describe disciplinary measures that will be taken if the policy is violated, and tell employees how to make a complaint.

Moreover, it should assure employees that their jobs will not be adversely affected if they lodge a complaint. "The biggest impediment to victims coming forward is fear for their jobs, fear they're going to be punished," John Wymer says.

Employees should have someone besides their manager to make a complaint to, says Suzy Hammett, vice president of human resources at Superior Insurance Co. in Atlanta, "because in some cases, it could be the manager harassing them."

Your policy should also inform employees that retaliation by co-workers against an individual who comes forward with a complaint will be treated as seriously as harassment itself, and that false complaints will not be tolerated.

Train managers and employees. All employees must understand what sexual harassment is so they can avoid it or so they can recognize it for what it is if they become targets. Managers, according to Hammett, need training in handling harassment complaints and situations.

Trade associations and other organizations make films and training materials available on the subject. BNA Communications Inc., in Washington, D.C., for example, offers a video training program for employees called "Sexual Harassment Plain and Simple." (Call 1-800-233-6067 for information.)

Take complaints seriously. Investigate them immediately, and take appropriate action. Just talking with a perpetrator is not enough, says Dworkin. "I've never seen a court case that has upheld that as being sufficient." If the infringement is a first-time, mild instance, the harasser can be put on probation. But if it's a severe case—for example, if there is a pattern of harassment—the employee should probably be fired, she says.

It's equally important to take seriously even a suspicion or rumor that sexual harassment is taking place, according to Wymer. "The standard for the law," he says, is that a company "is liable for sexual harassment that it knew of or *should* have known of and failed to [address with] immediate and appropriate corrective action."

As you investigate, respect your employees' confidentiality. And treat the alleged harasser with care, too. "If you move too far too fast and don't protect that person's privacy, they might sue as well," says Wymer.

Also, don't reassign or fire a complainant; keep the person informed of what you are doing to resolve the matter.

Recognize that harassment is not just a crime of men against women. While their numbers are still relatively small, cases involving same-sex harassment or female supervisors harassing male subordinates are on the rise.

If a complaint is lodged, consider mediation. "Mediation is always cheaper than a lawsuit," says Wymer. In a "white paper" on mediation, the Society for Human Resource Management describes it as a voluntary process that allows disputing parties to resolve their conflict with the help of a neutral third party.

But there are some cautions. Mediation is not appropriate when the offender's behavior is so "outrageous" as to require immediate disciplinary action or when either party is unwilling to try the process, SHRM warns. Dworkin also says there's some evidence that women are at a disadvantage in mediation because they have been socialized to be peacemakers or to compromise.

Mediators are listed in the Yellow Pages under Mediation Services. Re-

---

Where To Go For Help

Here are some resources that can help employers create and implement effective sexual-harassment policies:

Books
The following books are available in bookstores unless otherwise indicated:
- *Honoring Boundaries: Preventing Sexual Harassment in the Workplace,* by Joyce Kaser, with Bette George and Arleen LaBella. Clarifies the "gray areas" of what constitutes sexual harassment and includes a sample sexual-harassment policy. Also provides managers and supervisors with guidelines for talking with victims and alleged harassers. Available in paperback for $19.95 plus shipping and handling from Human Resource Development Press, Inc., in Amherst, Mass., at 1-800-822-2801. Ask for ISBN 0-87425-250-4.
- *Sexual Harassment on the Job*, Second Edition, by William Petrocelli and Barbara Kate Repa (Nolo Press paperback, $18.95). Billed as a "step-by-step guide for working women" but valuable to employers and managers for its clear explanations of the law and its listing of state and federal agencies. In bookstores, or call 1-800-992-6656.
- *Step Forward: Sexual Harassment in the Workplace,* by Susan L. Webb ($9.95, MasterMedia). Includes especially useful chapters on handling sexual-harassment complaints and educating employees.

The author also publishes *The Webb Report,* a newsletter on sexual harassment. (See the next item.)

Publications
- *The Webb Report* is a monthly newsletter on sexual harassment. It is aimed at small-business owners, human-resource managers, and government officials. It costs $120 per year and is available from the Pacific Resource Development Group, Inc.; 1-800-767-3062.
- *What Every Employee Ought To Know About Contributing to a Harassment-Free Environment,* a 64-page booklet that tells employees what harassment entails and how to prevent it. Available at $5 per copy (plus shipping and handling) by calling CCH Inc., 1-800-835-5224, Ext. 2091. Quantity discounts available.

Organizations
- The Society for Human Resource Management's publications and conferences frequently feature sexual-harassment topics. For information on membership, contact SHRM at 606 N. Washington St., Alexandria, Va. 22314-1997; (703) 548-3440.
- The Equal Employment Opportunity Commission has more than 50 offices across the country. For the location nearest you, call 1-800-669-4000.
- Trade associations also can be sources of information, programs, and employee-training materials.

1. HUMAN RESOURCE MANAGEMENT: Sexual Harassment

> The real costs of a sexual-harassment case lie in the anger, emotion, hostility, and hurt feelings that accompany it.
>
> —Atlanta lawyer
> John F. Wymer III

gional chapters of the American Arbitration Association can help with referrals, or call the national office at (212) 484-4000.

Take action against third-party harassment. Harassers can come from the ranks of vendors and clients. If a salesman is harassing your employee, says Dworkin, it is appropriate to call the salesman's employer and say, "I don't want to deal with this person any longer."

Consider purchasing employee-practices liability insurance. EPLI, as it is known, protects employers against claims in areas such as wrongful termination, discrimination, and sexual harassment. (See "Protecting Against Employment Perils" in the April 1994 *Nation's Business*.)

Available for only the past several years, the coverage is now becoming more affordable for smaller businesses, according to Dennis J. Donovan, senior vice president at S.H. Smith & Co., Inc., in West Hartford, Conn., an excess and surplus-lines broker in the insurance industry.

Companies with fewer than 50 employees can now buy policies with limits up to $100,000 for premiums as low as $2,500, or $1 million for $6,500 to $7,500. Just two or three years ago, a million-dollar policy would carry a premium of $11,000 to $15,000, Donovan says.

In their efforts to curb sexual-harassment liability, some employers establish policies to discourage romantic relationships between supervisors and subordinates or even institute dress codes.

You may not want to go that far. But you do need to make every attempt you can to keep sexual harassment out of your workplace because the price of not doing so is just too high.

The real costs, says John Wymer, lie in the anger, emotion, hostility, and hurt feelings that accompany a harassment case. As he puts it: "I've seen entire companies torn apart by allegations of sexual harassment, and, frankly, the attorneys' fees are only a small overall cost of [such] litigation."

Sexual Harassment in the Global Arena

When Sexual Harassment Is a Foreign Affair

Sexual harassment can happen between U.S. workers, but in global business situations, it can be even more complex—to identify and to resolve. Here's what you need to know to avoid sexual discrimination liability and increase your company's chances for harassment-free business relationships.

Wendy Hardman and Jacqueline Heidelberg

Wendy Hardman and Jacqueline Heidelberg are senior associates for Ambrose Consulting & Training in Pittsburgh.

Scenario #1: Sandra Whitney is on a three-year, career-enhancing assignment in Mexico for her company and finds herself the target of unwanted sexual attention from her new male manager—a citizen of the host country. Whitney complains to a female co-worker (who's also a citizen), but is told this behavior is "normal." When the behavior persists after Whitney has made it clear she isn't interested, she consults with the human resources manager in her host country. She finds there are now laws protecting women from sexual harassment on the job, although she's assured that her company's policy and the U.S. laws will be maintained.

Scenario #2: Connie Bosworth is working on a team with several men from Europe who have been sent to the United States for six months. Bosworth finds these mens' flirtatious language and gestures charming and endearing, but she feels ambivalent because she realizes that if an American man said the same things to her, it wouldn't be acceptable. Are Europeans bound by the same rules?

Sexual discrimination is a little-discussed problem in cross-cultural relationships. Both of the scenarios above, and other tales of sexual discrimination, are realistic for today's multinational companies and the emerging global workplace. In the past five years alone, the number of female expatriates of U.S. companies has more than doubled according to a recent news item in *The Wall Street Journal* on September 5, 1995. New York City-based Windham International, which

1. HUMAN RESOURCE MANAGEMENT: Sexual Harassment

conducted the survey, predicts the number of expatriate women will reach 20% (of all U.S. expatriates) by the year 2000. In addition, the U.S. workforce is ethnically and culturally more diverse than ever and this trend is expected to continue. As we struggle to understand and negotiate both the subtle and more complicated issues related to sexual harassment in our domestic marketplace, we also must be aware of the added concerns of working overseas with co-workers, customers and vendors of many different nationalities.

To find out what individuals and organizations experience in the international marketplace, we asked several companies to share their stories. As consultants with extensive backgrounds in human resources management and cross-cultural business settings, we also reviewed what has been written on the subject. A key question we posed: "What have you encountered as far as sexual harassment incidents that occurred between people of two different cultures, whether they were employees, customers, vendors or clients?"

While exploring this relatively uncharted territory, several corporate human resources executives from multinational organizations told us we'd have trouble getting any information. Because of the potential liability, and the potential threat to an organization's image, they suggested that candid responses would be scarce. Indeed, the most frequent response we got was that companies had limited experience with the issue, and therefore, they had little to report. The topic of sexual harassment is one that many organizations find difficult to address. And when it's complicated by cross-cultural issues, it becomes even more foreboding.

In fact, several organizations refused to return our calls or stated that they didn't want to participate. Some respondents, including human resources managers at Akron, Ohio-based The Goodyear Tire & Rubber Co. and Chicago-based Amoco Corp., stated they either have had "no incidents" or none that couldn't be handled at the local level.

Is this possible for firms having thousands of employees working both domestically and internationally? Yes, but it's highly unlikely. At Wilmington, Delaware-based E.I. du Pont de Nemours (DuPont), a company noted for its work in sexual harassment training, there were no reported cases of sexual harassment internationally that have reached HR representatives at the corporate level. Bob Hamilton, a diversity consultant with DuPont, conceded that there may have been some situations, but they would have been handled as close to the front lines as possible. He added that third party cases of sexual harassment aren't rare, but DuPont doesn't keep records of these events.

George Krock, manager of EEO and selection at Pittsburgh-based PPG Industries Inc., told us: "In the last couple of years, there have been four incidents involving employees of PPG: two in North America, one in Asia and one in Europe." Similar numbers were quoted by a senior human resources manager in a large pharmaceuticals company: Approximately one to four sexual harassment complaints are filed each year internationally.

Both of these corporations (typical of an increasing number of multinational organizations) employ tens of thousands of employees outside the United States—although many are citizens of the host country. Philadelphia-based SmithKline Beecham, for example, operates in nearly 80 countries and currently has approximately 250 expatriates. When you consider that there are many more expatriate women these days, the actual number of cases of sexual harassment globally seems surprisingly small. Have we triumphed over sexual harassment in cross-cultural settings? Have employers managed to eliminate "unwelcome conduct of a sexual nature," not to mention ridding their workplaces of "hostile or intimidating environments"? Are individuals in cross-cultural work environments more careful, better informed and generally more respectful of each other?

That's certainly one possibility. More believable, however, is the interpretation by one head of international HR for several financial-service organizations over the last several years. He suggests that companies might not have accurate information to report because employees are cautious about disclosing sexual harassment incidents—particularly when they occur cross-culturally. There are many reasons for this. One is the problem that sexual harassment is often under-reported, understated or trivialized—regardless of where it occurs or who's involved. Jim Yates, manager of human resources for international operations with Amoco, says another problem may be the desirability of the overseas assignment. "People may not want to jeopardize their jobs," he says. These positions are highly valued, sometimes taking years to attain.

Training employees about cultural differences before international assignments may help avert problems. Craig Pratt, of Craig Pratt and Associates based in Alameda, California, is an investigator of sexual harassment complaints for San Francisco Bay Area companies. Having been an expert witness in 40 sexual harassment court battles over the past four years, he finds that a disproportionate number of cross-cultural sexual harassment complaints involve perpetrators and victims from differing ethnic, racial or national-origin groups. He often has thought about the complexity presented by sexual harassment situations in cross-cultural contexts. His experiences strongly support the idea that when individuals from two different cultures interact, the potential for problems with sexual harassment is greater, not smaller.

Cultural relativism—the notion that ethics, values and behavior are a function of culture—is one way to understand, and perhaps to dismiss, the issue. In fact, all of the HR and international managers we spoke to raised the notion of a cultural context as central to the discussion. Pratt frequently encounters situations which might be better understood (although not necessarily forgiven) when cultural frameworks are considered. What's acceptable in one culture may be disrespectful and confusing in another. What U.S. citizens may construe as sexually provocative or offensive, for example, isn't shared by most—or even many—cultures.

Bill Ferra, director of U.S. management and development services for Heinz USA in Pittsburgh, reports that Europeans think Americans are "crazy" with all of our laws about sexual harassment. Some behaviors that deeply violate norms of U.S. culture may not be perceived as a problem in another cultural context. In many Mediterranean and Latin countries, physical contact and sensuality are a common part of socializing.

11. When Sexual Harassment Is a Foreign Affair

For example, one Brazilian senior HR executive was surprised when he was admonished for calling the women at work "girls." While this label was appropriate and acceptable in his native culture, he wasn't aware it was insulting to North American women and could contribute to a "hostile or intimidating work environment" by U.S. standards.

Rudiger Daunke, VP of international HR for Bausch & Lomb Inc. based in Rochester, New York, notes that U.S. citizens proceed carefully in their cross-cultural relationships abroad because of cultural differences. The organizations we surveyed unanimously agreed that the incidence of sexual harassment across cultures can be diminished with adequate cultural preparation of employees. Interestingly, many international companies have such programs in place.

Bill Mossett, vice president and director of employee relations and diversity for SmithKline Beecham, says its program *Managing Transculturally*, is currently being rolled out for managers with assignments in the United States and the United Kingdom. This newly instituted program has both a general component as well as culture-specific information. Theoretically, managers might go through it three or four times during their careers—each time they go on assignment to a different country.

Similarly, Amoco offers its expatriates and spouses a two- to three-day, cross-cultural program. The topics covered include such issues as social behaviors, relationships, titles, dining practices and American perceptions. In addition, once a U.S. expatriate is in the host country, he or she receives another cultural orientation.

While this cross-cultural training is a proactive measure that helps diminish the potential for cultural misunderstandings between men and women, it may be inadequate and limited. None of the programs surveyed includes specific information about sexual harassment or sexual discrimination. Moreover, many U.S. companies don't offer stand-alone sexual harassment training (although it's sometimes included as part of diversity awareness training) for their domestic employees. Such training is rarer still for host-country nationals. One exception, DuPont, reports that as many as 90% of its domestic employees have attended sexual-harassment training. In addition, the company says most of its offshore leaders have participated, as well as its international employees on assignment in the United States. But this is rarely the case.

When sexual harassment training is provided, the content is specific to the laws and customs of the United States, *not* to the international destinations of increasing numbers of employees in multinational companies. The sexual-harassment programs in multinational companies—if they're even offered or required—are for domestic, not international employees. And their focus is local, not global.

Another inadequacy to the cross-cultural preparation for most expatriates is that the courses are usually offered for employees on long-term assignment, not for the occasional visitor or business traveler. One international HR executive says that because of the lack of preparation, the occasional visitor becomes the company's greatest liability. He says: "When [U.S. citizens abroad] aren't culturally sensitive, they may use inappropriate gestures or names that can be perceived as harassment, even when it's not intentional."

One example of a cross-cultural preparation course we encountered is the *Passport/Visa Program* used at Amoco for its international business travelers and U.S. employees who host foreign visitors. The passport section is a fairly generic cross-cultural review, while the visa component is country-specific. The organization has visa programs for countries such as China, Russia, Azerbaijan, Egypt, Trinidad and the United States. HR currently is developing programs for Europe and Latin America. Benefits to the learners include being able to "identify, anticipate, avoid, minimize and resolve areas of potential conflict resulting from cultural differences." The only drawback is brevity—the program is only a half-day course.

Finally, cross-cultural training is designed for employees destined for overseas assignments. But it's rarely an option for domestic employees who'll be interacting with foreigners on a regular basis in their jobs.

Should you define sexual harassment by home- or host-country standards? Even when cultural preparation is adequate, it begs the question of cultural relativism. Should an organization operating in a host country with different customs and moral traditions insist that all behavior be measured according to home-country standards? If men and women have interacted in a certain way for hundreds of years in a culture, who shall judge that certain language or behavior is wrong or *bad*? Sexual harassment is one manifestation of sexual discrimination. Values and behaviors about women's rights aren't as deeply entrenched in many societies as in our own.

Mahbub ul Haq, a United Nations development program team leader and the author of a recent U.N. report cited by *USA Today* on August 29, 1995, states: "There isn't a single society in the world that treats its men and women equally, not even by accident." Undoubtedly, expatriate women face unique problems.

Jim Yates of Amoco echoes a common sentiment about the difficulties women encounter cross-culturally: "In some countries, there are barriers that have affected the ability of females to be fully integrated into a project or team." Another senior HR executive notes: "Particularly in 'macho' cultures, it's strange to interact with women in a professional capacity." In these environments, men may take advantage of women because they're accustomed to relating in traditional ways. Even on the egalitarian ground of the United States, the same problems may arise.

Jane Henderson-Loney, of the Timner Consultant Group in the San Francisco suburb of Clayton, California, describes a Middle Eastern-born man working in the United States who was accused of sexually harassing an American-born woman. She remembers him saying: "In my country, women can't behave like this to men!"

Literature on the subject goes beyond mere sexual discrimination. It supports the view that sexual harassment is common in many countries. The *Harvard International Law Journal* reported in 1992: "Sexual harassment is a pervasive problem in the Japanese workplace." In 1991, *IABC Communication World* reported that in Mexico, "sexual harassment has been recognized as a problem, but is accepted in our culture where many men consider themselves superior over women..." The same source reported that a national survey in Austra-

1. HUMAN RESOURCE MANAGEMENT: Sexual Harassment

lia revealed one in four Australian women suffered from sexual harassment at work. Sexual harassment also is happening in Africa. Pratt says when he read the 1992 deposition testimony by a Nigerian woman in preparation for a sexual harassment case, he concluded that it's common in Nigeria—in fact expected—that male supervisors can have sexual access to female subordinates.

> **If sexual discrimination, including sexual harassment, is the norm in some cultures, should it be ignored when it occurs?**

If sexual discrimination, including sexual harassment, is the norm in some cultures, should it be ignored when it occurs? In the book "Essentials of Business Ethics," edited by Peter Madsen and Jay Shafritz, one respected contributor, Norman Bowie, states that he believes universal ethics do exist that should guide business conduct. However, they often aren't obvious, and may be difficult to decipher. Probably every culture would say it believes in, and upholds, the respect and dignity of every human being. It's hard to imagine a society that would openly condone sexual harassment. "The Essentials of Business Ethics" states: "Such moral rules are not relative; they simply are not practiced universally. ... However, multinational corporations are obligated to follow these moral rules."

In fact, the few incidents of sexual misconduct in international situations that we heard about were frequently resolved once the employees were informed that the women in question were offended by the behavior. Senior HR executives from several companies concluded that these incidents often are caused by lack of awareness of cultural differences—they aren't malevolent in nature. Once an explanation is offered and the woman's perspective is explained, the male (the usual perpetrator) is frequently surprised: He's not aware that his behavior could cause such a degree of anxiety or uneasiness. The universal ethic—not to offend—seems to transcend the customary behavior and interaction of a particular culture.

On the other hand, perhaps it isn't so innocent or simplistic. In at least two incidents we heard about, the offender was clearly told that his behavior was unacceptable. The Middle Eastern employee accused of sexual harassment was told—in no uncertain terms—that to continue working for his employer he would have to conform to treating women as total equals, or be terminated. Perhaps the explicit or implied threat of losing a job or a contract results in a change in behavior more often than the desire not to offend. The excuse that it was a cultural misunderstanding and totally unintended, may be just that—an excuse.

Regardless of personal values and beliefs, the employees in question were motivated to change their behavior to conform to the standards that were expected by the company. Most of the organizations we interviewed have explicitly stated values and policies regarding sexual harassment that are maintained worldwide. Several senior HR executives emphasized workplaces should be free of harassment for all their employees. PPG Industries' Krock shares a viewpoint that's typical of his HR peers: "[Sexual harassment] isn't only contrary to our U.S. law, it's contrary to the policies established by PPG Industries. ... We don't believe that employees can operate effectively if they don't feel safe."

Consider the legal and business implications of international sexual harassment. Do the laws worldwide, and in the United States, support companies' internal policies against sexual harassment? The U.S. laws that govern sexual harassment are covered under Section 109 for both Title VII of the Civil Rights Act and the Americans with Disabilities Act (ADA). Section 109 addresses two distinct issues: 1) circumstances in which American and American-controlled employers can be held liable for discrimination that occurs abroad; and 2) circumstances in which foreign employers can be held liable within the United States.

If sexual harassment occurs abroad, American and American-controlled corporations will be covered under Title VII. However, significant interpretation of the law occurs when determining if the company is American-controlled. Section 109 establishes four factors to consider in interpreting whether a company is, or isn't American-controlled. Not all four factors need to be present in all cases:

- Interrelation of operations
- Common management
- Centralized control of labor relations
- Common ownership or financial control of employer and the foreign corporation.

If a workplace is located in the United States, Title VII and ADA apply to a foreign employer when it discriminates within the United States, except when that individual(s) is protected by a *Friendship, Commerce and Navigation* (FCN) treaty. (The FCN treaty grants jurisdiction to one country over another country's corporation, and vice versa.)

In either case, abroad or within the United States, Section 109 doesn't explicitly discuss sexual harassment, although sexual harassment is a part of Title VII. The sexual harassment guidelines that have been issued in this country, increasingly familiar to U.S. employees, have no counterpart in Section 109.

Furthermore, as we mentioned earlier, in most countries there are no laws protecting against sexual harassment in the workplace. A 1992 article published in the *International Labour Review* revealed that in a study of 23 industrialized countries, only nine had statutes that specifically define or mention the term sexual harassment—Australia, Belgium, Canada, France, Germany (Berlin), New Zealand, Spain, Sweden and the United States. The author, Robert Husbands—of the International Labour Organization, based in Geneva, Switzerland—says that the law is in a state of evolution in most of the 23 countries he studied, and that different legal approaches reflect different cultural attitudes and legal systems. In 1994, the European Parliament adopted a resolution to enact legislation obliging employers to "appoint an in-house counselor to deal with cases of sexual harassment." (Belgium is the only European Community country currently with specific legislation on confidential counselors.) This builds on the European

Commission's 1991 Code of Practice to define and combat sexual harassment.

In addition, a November 1992 article in *The New York Times* said: "Legislators in some countries are also reluctant to go too far toward what they see as the desexualization of the United States." When cultures accept and value gender familiarity and unequal roles, it may be difficult to prohibit sexual harassment at work.

The ramifications of sexual harassment when it occurs cross-culturally are more confusing and difficult from both an emotional and legal standpoint. From a business perspective, it's an extremely important area to explore and one that has significant cost implications. With many HR concerns, the human costs of sexual harassment can be high because they directly translate into losses from absenteeism, dissatisfaction and low productivity.

The global nature of the problem adds another cost—expatriate employees are expensive employees. They tend to be high-level and require a great deal of money to support in relocation, schooling their children, tax differences and training, to name just a few. The average expatriate may take approximately $300,000 to replace. When we lose one to a sexual-harassment incident, it's a loss that's costly.

One question mysteriously looms on the horizon of global business: When the practices and laws of two cultures clash, which will apply? This is a question which, apparently, hasn't been widely tested. Perhaps it hasn't even been raised—as some of the organizations we interviewed implied.

It's difficult to believe that a problem that has been so widespread within the United States isn't a problem elsewhere, but the complexities of intercultural socialization blur the lines of what is proper and what is improper. It's HR's job to understand the associated risks when business personnel travel out of— or into—the United States. We also must make training a priority. If our expatriates don't even know which side of the road they'll be driving on when they go abroad on business (or which side of the road their foreign visitors are used to traveling on when they come to the United States), how can we possibly expect them to know what the requirements are regarding intercultural business relationships and the potential for sexually harassing behavior? It's our job to inform our people. Only then can we be sure that the road to international business is a safe one.

Meeting Human Resource Requirements

- Job Requirements (Articles 12 and 13)
- Human Resource Planning, Selection, and Recruitment (Articles 14–16)
- Human Resource Information Systems (Articles 17 and 18)

Organizations, whether profit or nonprofit, are more than collections of buildings, desks, and telephones. Organizations are made up of people—people with their particular traits, habits, and idiosyncrasies that make them unique. Each individual has different needs and wants, and the employer and the worker must seek a reasonable compromise so that at least an adequate match may be found for both.

The importance of human resource planning is greater than ever and will probably be even more important in the future. As Thomas Peters and Robert Waterman have pointed out in their book *In Search of Excellence*:

> Quality and service, then, were invariable hallmarks of excellent firms. To get them, of course, everyone's cooperation is required, not just the mighty labors of the top 200. The excellent companies require and demand extraordinary performance from the average man. (Dana's former chairman, Rene McPherson, says that neither the few destructive laggards nor the handful of brilliant performers are the key. Instead, he urges attention to the care, feeding and unshackling of the average man.) We labeled it "productivity through people." All companies pay it lip service. Few deliver.
> —Thomas Peters and Robert Waterman,
> *In Search of Excellence*,
> New York, Warner Books, 1987

In the future, organizations are going to have to pay more than just lip service to "productivity through people" if they want to survive and prosper. They will have to practice it by demonstrating an understanding of not only their clients' and customers' needs but also their employees' needs. The only way they will be able to deliver the goods and services and achieve success is through those same employees. Companies are faced with the difficult task of finding the right people for the right jobs—a task that must be accomplished if the organization is going to have a future.

Organizations are trying to meet the needs of their employees by developing new and different approaches to workers' jobs. This means taking into account how society, the labor force, the family, and the nature of the jobs themselves have changed. Training and development will be key in meeting future human resource requirements. Employers will have to change the way they design their positions if they are to attract and keep good employees; they must consider how society has changed and how those changes have affected the labor force; they will have to consider how the labor force has changed and will change in the future, with fewer young people and more middle-aged employees as well as dual-career couples struggling to raise children; and they will have to consider how the very nature of jobs has changed in the society, especially from predominantly blue-collar to white-collar jobs.

Human resource planning, selection, and recruitment are going to be even more critical in the future. Companies will have to go to extraordinary lengths to attract and keep new employees. There is no mystery about the reasons for this situation. America is aging, and there are fewer people in their late teens and early twenties to take the entry-level jobs that will be available in the future. Women, who for the past 20 years have been the major source of new employees, now represent almost half the workforce. As a result, new groups must be found, whether they are retirees, high school students, workers moonlighting on a second job, minority group members, people with disabilities, or immigrants. One thing is certain: The workforce is changing and organizations will need to unlock the potential of all their employees.

Another aspect of human resource planning involves both the selection process and the termination process. The days of working for only one company and then retiring with a gold watch and a pension are over. People are going to change jobs, if not companies, more frequently in the future, and many of the tasks they will be doing in the next 10, 15, or 20 years do not even exist today because of technological change. Midlife and midcareer changes are going to be far more common than they have been in the past, requiring people to change and adapt.

Human resources information systems offer important tools in managing human resources. The ability of computers to handle large amounts of data is now being applied to human resource management with very inter-

UNIT 2

esting results. These practices apply to hiring and internal information management and mean greater automation of human resources in the future.

Meeting the human resource needs of any organization in the future is not going to be an easy task. Assuming that the economy continues to grow at an acceptable rate, the need for workers will continue to increase, but many of the traditional sources of supply for new workers will be either exhausted or in decline. For example, human resource professionals know that there will be fewer workers available in the early twenties age group in the next 10 years because there are fewer teenagers today than 10 years ago. Management must plan for this shortage and consider alternative sources of potential employees. In turn, the individual employee must be ready to adapt quickly and efficiently to a changing environment. Job security is a thing of the past, and workers must remain flexible in order to cope with increased uncertainty.

Looking Ahead: Challenge Questions

Job requirements and working conditions have changed over the past several years. What new changes do you foresee in the workplace in the next 10 years?

The first step in the process of working is getting hired; the last step is termination, whether for cause, leaving for a new job, retirement, or a "reduction in force." What trends do you see in the workforce concerning individuals and their careers?

How do you see computerization being applied to human resources, and how will this change human resources?

Manage Work Better to Better Manage Human Resources: A Comparative Study of Two Approaches to Job Analysis

This study looks at the consequences of analyzing the same work with two different methods of job analysis. Position Classification Questionnaire and Task Inventory approaches were used to study the same work functions. The Position Classification questionnaire divided these work functions into sixteen unique classifications for purposes of wage and salary determination. The Task Inventory approach divided these work functions into 28 unique classifications for purposes of developing training programs. The two approaches arrived at considerably different conclusions with regard to how work should be organized into jobs and how jobs should be grouped into classifications. The data collected through job analysis will have significant impact on subsequent human resource decisions. Organizations should take great care in the collection data relating to the work of the organization in order efficiently and effectively manage the organization's human resources.

James P. Clifford

James P. Clifford is a Partner in The Human Resource Systems Institute. He has worked in city government for over twenty years, holding the positions of Human Resources Director, Grants Management Director, and the Director of Employee Development. He has a Master's Degree from Michigan State University in Labor and Industrial Relations.

"Deming (1986) maintains that most variation (over 90%) is due to systemic factors such as procedures, supplies, and equipment not under employee control. Management's job is to reduce the level of variation, and to enlist the help of employees to constantly improve system processes.[1]

The importance of job analysis is well established in the *Uniform Guidelines on Employee Selection Procedures* (1978)[2] and the *Principles for the Validation and Use of Personnel Selection Procedures*.[3] Job analysis is fundamental to documenting valid personnel procedures and actions. Therefore the effectiveness of various approaches to job analysis is extremely important with respect to the management of human resources. In this paper the pros and cons of two approaches are considered: the position classification approach and the task inventory approach. Recently two events occurred which provided an opportunity to conduct a comparative study of the two approaches to job analysis. The first event was when an outside consultant conducted a wage and salary study using the position classification approach, and the second was the establishment of on-the-job training programs for 16 clas-

sifications using a task inventory approach administered by in-house human resource specialists. The two different approaches to job analysis were administered in approximately the same time period, involved the same employees and analyzed the same sixteen job classifications.

A wage and salary study is an effort to determine whether or not an organization's wages are adequate to attract and retain qualified employees. The on-the-job training program is a "job ladder" concept which means that the lower level position is a training position [which] when satisfactorily completed results in a promotion to the higher position. The job analyses were performed for different reasons. The position classification questionnaire approach was used to analyze approximately 300 separate job classifications in the organization to de-

12. Manage Work Better

termine appropriate wage and salary levels; while the task inventory approach, was used to collect data to develop 16 on-the-job training programs.

Alternative approaches to job analysis

The position classification questionnaire approach[4]

"Questionnaires are one of the least costly methods for collecting information. They represent an efficient way to collect a large amount of information in a short period of time."[5] In November of 1990, the consultant conducted meetings with city employees to explain the process of the study and to give instructions on how to complete the position classification questionnaire. The questionnaire included an open ended question regarding work performed. Item 10 on the questionnaire stated:

"Describe below in detail the work you do. Use your own words, and make your description so clear that persons unfamiliar with your work can understand what you do. Attach additional sheets if necessary."

Other information collected by the questionnaire included: name, department, title, work schedule, place of work, full or part-time, allowances, equipment operated, supervisor's name, title of the supervisor, name and title of subordinates, the nature of direction received, contact with people from other organizations, decision making authority, and special physical demands. General supervisors were asked to comment on the accuracy and completeness of the information provided on the form by employees. Department heads were also asked to attest to the accuracy of the information on the form. Employees were required to complete the form and send it to their supervisor for comments. The supervisor in turn sent the form to the department head for comment and it was then sent to the consultant.

In January 1991, the consultant conducted job audits. A job audit is a process to verify the accuracy of the data collected by the questionnaire. Employees interested in discussing the data provided about their job with the consultant submitted their name to the Human Resources Department, who in turn scheduled interviews with the consultant. The consultant interviewed in excess of 33 percent of the work force covered by the study. "Based on the questionnaires and the job audits, the consultant prepared class specifications based on suitable groupings of positions performing similar duties at approximately the same level of responsibility."[6]

The Task Inventory approach[7]

The Union Contract states," . . . the implementation of the consultant Wage Study revealed that the consultant recommended a number of jobs for in-series promotion. The Union recognized the need for training and embraced the proposal to create training programs. A window period of one (1) year from 1/1/92 to 1/1/93 will be used to develop these programs."[8] The training programs were to be developed following a model program which was implemented in the Utilities Department for the Water Service Worker II in 1991.

The procedure for developing a training program required a job analysis of the higher level job. For example, the Water Service Worker II (the high level position) was analyzed in order to establish training objectives for the Water Service Worker I classification. In March of 1992 the task inventory approach to job analysis began for the 16 on-the-job training classifications, approximately six months after the position classification questionnaire study by the consultant had been completed.

Incumbents in the higher level job, or a representative sample of incumbents, were interviewed by in-house human resources specialists. The incumbents were asked to talk about their work while the specialist took notes. The specialist asked questions to clarify comments by the employees. Once the employees were satisfied that most of what their jobs entailed had been discussed, the interview was terminated. The human resources specialist then entered the inventory of tasks into the computer. The employees, who had been interviewed, were given a print-out of the list of tasks and were asked to review them and make appropriate changes. When the list of tasks was satisfactory to the sample group of employees, it was distributed to all incumbent employees for their review and comment. Once the list of tasks was complete, incumbent employees were asked to score the list of tasks for relative frequency and relative difficulty. The employees were asked to score the tasks using a seven point scale from a low of 1 to a high of 7 and place a zero by the tasks which they do not perform. Each of the responses from the employees were entered into the computer. Management employees were then provided with the list of tasks with average relative frequency and relative difficulty scores. Managers were asked to comment on the completeness and accuracy of the list and to identify critical tasks.

Comparative Study Results

The position classification questionnaire approach to job analysis was conducted according to consultant's procedures. The task inventory job analysis was conducted by in-house staff based on a process developed and used two years earlier in the Water Department to design a training program. The consultant was charged with the responsibility to analyze approximately 300 classifications and slightly more than 1000 employees. The 16 classifications analyzed by both the consultant and staff involved approximately 150 employees.

The consultant's study reached the following conclusions regarding the 16 classifications. Eleven of the classifications were unchanged except for title changes for two of the classifications; and five classifications were significantly changed from what they had been prior to the study (Appendix I).

The in-house staff concluded that 8 of the classifications were appropriately classified and should not be changed. This means that the work organized in the 8 classifications, prior to either of the two job analyses, was properly classified; and no adjustments were recommended based on either of the two studies.

Three of the classifications, Utility Maintenance Mechanic II, Laboratory Technician and Water Plant Operator were found by the consultant to be properly classified however, the task inventory approach found considerable variation among the duties depending on the division in which the work was performed. Of the remaining five classifications, the consultant recommended considerable change from what had existed before the wage and salary study.

The eight classifications which were changed either by the consultant and/or in-house staff (see Table I) are discussed below.

Building Maintenance Mechanic II is skilled work responsible for maintaining a variety of buildings and their associated equipment. The consultant, using the position classification questionnaire approach, determined that employees in three departments (Buildings and Grounds, Parks and Recreation, and Parking) performed similar work and should be grouped together in this one classification. The task inventory approach conducted by in-house staff, however, concluded that the work performed in the Parking Department was not comparable to the work performed in the other

73

2. MEETING HUMAN RESOURCE REQUIREMENTS: Job Requirements

two departments. The Parking Department performed only 114 of the total 284 tasks identified by all of the incumbents in the classification. There was only one task performed in Parking which was not performed in the other two departments. There were 222 tasks performed in Parks and Recreation, of which 55 were not performed in Buildings and Grounds; and there were 228 tasks performed in Buildings and Grounds, of which 61 were not performed in Parks and Recreations. There were 167 tasks which were common to both Buildings and Grounds and Parks and Recreation.

Resolution

For purposes of training and the efficient use of human resources, it is not appropriate to train individuals in Parking to become competent in the work in the other two departments. The work in the Parking Department, therefore, was reclassified. The work in the other two departments was determined to be sufficiently different that an employee proficient in one department could not assume the work in the other department without extensive additional training. Therefore, employees will be trained in their "home department." Should an employee desire to transfer from his/her home department into the other department, he/she will be required to serve an apprenticeship to demonstrate competence in the unique tasks of the new department.

Maintenance Assistant II is unskilled/semi-skilled work assisting Maintenance Mechanics. Based on the consultant's study, work performed in five different departments (Streets and Sanitation, Utilities, Buildings and Grounds, Parks and Recreation, and Traffic Safety) was similar enough to group employees into a single classification. Based on the task inventory approach, human resource specialists found that the work among departments was highly diverse. A total of 276 tasks were performed by the Maintenance Assistant II's in all five departments. In Traffic Safety, only 67 tasks were performed, and only one person in that department held that position. In the Utilities Department, there were eight employees; and they did an average of 189 tasks, with one employee performing as few as 88 tasks and another employee performing 248 tasks. Streets and Sanitation also had eight employees with the title of Maintenance Assistant II, with a low of 33 tasks and a high of 139 tasks. Sixteen of the 22 employees with this title worked in either Streets and Sanitation or the Utilities Department. They performed a total of 239 tasks among them with 113 tasks common to both departments. Buildings and Grounds had four employees and performed 116 tasks, of which 93 were in common with Streets and Sanitation and Utilities.

Resolution

The work in each of these departments was sufficiently different that it could not be assumed that an employee who was trained and determined proficient in one department could be deemed proficient in another department without additional training. Employees will be required to demonstrate proficiency in the unique tasks of the new department during a probationary period.

Utility Maintenance Mechanic II is a skilled technical position responsible for maintaining the buildings and equipment for the collection and distribution of water and wastewater. All of the employees in this classification are in a single department, Utilities, but in three separate divisions. This position was studied by the consultant, but no changes were recommended with the exception of a title change. The consultant found the work to be sufficiently similar in the three divisions to consider it a single classification. Based on the analysis by in-house staff, which was part of developing a training program, the work performed by employees in this classification is significantly different among the three divisions. It is clear that an employee trained to perform the activities in one division could not be considered competent to perform the activities in either of the other two divisions. Unique tasks for each of the three divisions were identified along with universal tasks which were common to all three divisions. There were 146 universal tasks and 56, 67 and 25 unique tasks for the various divisions.

Resolution

It was determined that once an employee was determined competent in one division and wished to transfer to another division, the employee would be required to demonstrate competency in the unique tasks of the new division during a probationary period.

Equipment Operator II is a skilled job requiring the operation of a wide variety of motorized equipment. Equipment Operator II's are in three departments (Streets and Sanitation, Parks and Recreation, and Sewer Maintenance) and were grouped together under the position classification questionnaire approach into a single classification. Based on the information collected via the task inventory approach by the human resources specialist, significant differences were identified. Equipment Operators in the Parks and Recreation department were performing duties more similar to those of Groundskeeper II than to Equipment Operator II's in the other two departments.

Resolution

When training was considered, it became apparent that it was not efficient for the employees in Parks and Recreation Department to learn to operate the variety of equipment other Equipment Operators were expected to operate in Streets and Sanitation or Sewer Mainte-

Position Title	Position Classification Questionnaire Approach	Task Inventory Approach
Building Maintenance Mechanic II	Work performed in: Buildings and Grounds, Parks and Recreation, Parking was similar	Buildings and Ground - 228 tasks. Parks and Recreation - 223 tasks; Parking - 114 tasks (113 tasks common to all groups)
Maintenance Assistant II	Work performed in: Buildings and Grounds, Parks and Recreation, Traffic Safety, Utilities, Streets and Sanitation was similar.	Buildings and Grounds - 116 tasks. Parks and Recreation - 129 tasks. Traffic Safety - 67 tasks. Utilities - 248 tasks. Streets and Sanitation - 139 tasks. (No tasks common to all groups)

Table 1 (continued)

Table 1. (continued)

Utility Maintenance Mechanic II	Work performed in: Water Pumping, Water Distribution, Wastewater was similar.	Water Pumping - 202 tasks. Water Distribution - 171 tasks. Wastewater - 213 tasks. (146 tasks common to all groups).
Equipment Operator II	Work performed in: Streets and Sanitation, Parks and Recreation, Sewer Maintenance was similar.	Streets and Sanitation - 103 tasks. Parks and Recreation - 100 tasks. Sewer Maintenance - 98 tasks. (51 tasks common to all groups)
Sewer Maintenace Worker I	Work performed in: Streets and Sanitation was different from that of Equipment Operator II in Streets and Sanitation	Streets and Sanitation - 52 tasks.
Groundskeeper II	Work performed by: Parks Caretaker II and Cemetery Caretaker II was similar.	(Through reorganization these were combined in the same classification). Groundskeeper - 84 tasks.
Laboratory Technician II	Work peformed in: Water distribution and Wastewater was similar.	Water Distribution - 122 tasks. Wastewater - 101 tasks. (36 tasks common to both divisions)
Water Plant Operator II	Work performed in: Water Distribution and Water Pumping was similar	Water Pumping - 269 tasks. Water Distribution - 91 tasks. (69 tasks common to both divisions).

nance. The Equipment Operator II's in Parks and Recreation have been reclassified to Groundskeeper II's.

Sewer Maintenance Worker I is responsible for the maintenance and upkeep of the sewer system. This classification is only in the Sewer Maintenance Department. During the interview with in-house staff, Sewer Maintenance Worker I's made the comment: "They do everything an Equipment Operator II does plus work in the sewer." By comparing the task inventory data of the Sewer Maintenance Worker I with that of the Equipment Operator II for the Streets and Sanitation Department and the Sewer Maintenance Department, the statement was verified to be accurate. The task inventory of the Sewer Maintenance Worker I included the majority of the tasks of the Equipment Operator II plus the additional tasks of sewer maintenance. While it is not unreasonable for one position to encompass the duties of another position, it does raise the question of compensation. Upon review, it was discovered that the Sewer Maintenance Worker I was compensated at the same level as the Equipment Operator II. Usually, the job with the greater responsibility receives a larger compensation in recognition of the additional responsibility.

Resolution

The positions, Equipment Operator II and Equipment Operator III classifications will be combined, increasing the responsibilities of the Equipment Operator II position.

Groundskeeper II is unskilled/semi-skilled work performed in the maintenance of grounds and buildings. The consultant combined the Park Caretaker II classifcation with the Cemetery Caretaker II classification into the newly titled classification, Groundskeeper II. The task inventory approach conducted by in-house human resources specialists agreed that the work was similar and that it was appropriate to combine the two classifications.

Resolution

No changes required.

Laboratory Technician II. This is semi-skilled work in laboratories in the Water Distribution division and the Wastewater Treatment division of the Utilities Department. Based on the results of the Position Classification Questionnaire, the work of this classification in these two divisions was similar. Based on the results of the task inventory approach, there was considerable difference between the work in the two divisions. There were 122 tasks performed by the Water Distribution division and 101 tasks in the Wastewater division. There were, however, only 36 tasks common to both divisions suggesting that the work of the two divisions is more different than similar.

Resolution

The work in the two divisions was sufficiently different that it could not be assumed that an employee proficient in one division would also be proficient in the other division. If an employee transfers from one division to the other division the employee will be required to demonstrate proficiency in the unique tasks of the new division.

Water Plant Operator II is a skilled job operating a very complex water pumping and distribution plant. Water Plant Operators are in two different plants of one division of one department. Based on the results of the Position Classification Questionnaire, the work of this classification is similar. The results of the task inventory approach concluded that there is considerable difference among the two different plants. Water Plant Operators in the pumping plant perform 269 tasks while employees with the same classification in Distribution plant perform 91 tasks. There were 69 tasks common to both plants indicating that the work is more different than similar.

Resolution

An employee proficient in one plant will not be considered proficient in the work of the other plant. If an employee transfers from one plant to the other plant, the employee will be required to demonstrate proficiency in the unique tasks of the new plant.

2. MEETING HUMAN RESOURCE REQUIREMENTS: Job Requirements

Summary

The same jobs were analyzed with the position classification questionnaire and the task inventory approaches. The reasons for the analysis were different. One analysis, the position classification questionnaire, was conducted as part of a wage and salary study; the task inventory approach, was used in the development of training programs. The two approaches resulted in very different conclusions. Many of the jobs, which were grouped into the same classification as a result of the wage and salary study, were inappropriate for training. The dissimilarities were so significant that the organization adjusted its personnel practices regarding the policy of employees transferring from one position to another in the same classification. Employees, who wish to transfer from one department, division or even work station to another even though they hold the same job title, are now required to serve a probationary period in the new job. One classification, Building Maintenance Mechanic II, was divided into two classifications. The classifications Equipment Operator II and Equipment Operator III were combined into a single classification. Of the sixteen classifications studied by both approaches five classifications were revised significantly from what they had been prior to the position classification analysis and eleven classifications were unchanged. Based on the task analysis approach four of the five classifications changed by position classification questionnaire were significantly changed for a deviation rate of 80 percent. Of the eleven which were unchanged by the position classification questionnaire approach two classifications, Laboratory Technician I and Water Plant Operator II, were found to have significant differences within the same classification so as to treat them as separate classifications as far as training is concerned. Of the total universe of work that was studied by both approaches to job analysis the Position Classification Questionnaire approach organized that work into sixteen unique classifications. The Task Inventory approach organized that work into 28 unique classifications. This is a significant rate of deviation.

Conclusion

The Uniform Guidelines on Employee Selection as well as the *Principles of Validation and Use of Personal Selection Procedures* stipulate that job analysis is an essential element to validation of any and all major personnel activities. The quality of data collected during a job analysis is, therefore, critical to the quality of subsequent personnel decisions and actions. Comparing two different methods of job analysis demonstrates that there are considerable differences in the results depending on the method used. The results of the two different approaches used in this study indicate that personnel activities may be greatly affected depending on the method of analysis used. In this instance, the method of analysis had a great affect on the development and implementation of training. It is reasonable to assume that the method of job analysis will also affect other personnel decisions such as recruitment, compensation, promotion, and performance evaluation. Edwards Deming states, "I have seen elaborate plans based on shoddy data. Could be subject to 25 percent error in either direction, and nobody knew. Nobody even thought about the infirmities of the data."[9] This study documents that not all job analyses are the same in terms of the accuracy and reliability of the resulting data.

In the interest of improving an organization's ability to manage its human resources, it is important to recognize that the quality of managing the work of the organization may have a great deal to do with the quality with which an organization manages its human resources. Failure to manage work well may limit an organization's ability to effectively manage its human resources. To the extent an organization incorrectly defines or records work, or improperly organizes it into less than efficient jobs, then the subsequent human resource decisions will be suspect. Decisions, which are based on inaccurate data about the work of the organization, may not only be unreasonable and ineffective but may be counterproductive to the interests of the organization.

The quality of job analysis is also very important to the employee. The job is where the employee and the organization come together. The job is the domain of the employee and is an expression of the employee. It is that segment of the organization which the employee controls and manages. The employee will know when work is not well understood and managed. The employee will conclude, and rightly so, that the organization does not value his/her work when it does not accurately analyze and manage that work. If employees believe the organization does not value their work, there is little reason for the employer to assume that employees will value the work of the organization.

When employees are trained to perform duties for which *they are not responsible*, time and money will be wasted. When employees are not properly trained for duties for which *they are responsible,* there could be serious consequences. When employees are left to their own devices to "learn the ropes," they are bound to make unnecessary errors and may become improperly trained. Organizations which fail to train employees effectively project an attitude of indifference toward the work force. When management makes decisions based on inaccurate data, such as decisions regarding training, there is not only the potential loss of time and money; but there is also the potential for loss of confidence in management. "The job of Management," according to Deming, "is to replace work standards by knowledgeable and intelligent leadership. Leaders must have some understanding of the job."[10] Otherwise, management will be perceived as not knowing what they are doing and failing to carry out the essence of management due to inaccurate data.

Organizations need to recognize that jobs are dynamic and change over time. Therefore, in order for organizations to hire and train employees to perform those jobs in the most efficient manner, data regarding the work of the organization needs to be current and accurate. Spending time, energy, and money up front for an accurate job analysis and a procedure which permits the analysis to be updated easily, may pay large dividends in the long run. Organizations are subject to ever increasing change in the economy, methods of production, communication, the work force, as well as in laws and regulations and in the expectations and needs of employees. Organizations should be prepared to react to and accommodate these changes. In order to react efficiently to change and respond positively, organizations need to make decisions that are based on current accurate data.

An organization which defines its work accurately should be in a position to make reasonable, efficient human resources decisions. The organization should be in a position to hire, train, evaluate, and compensate its human resources in an effective, efficient manner. An organization, which makes decisions based on accurate data, should reflect a respectful concern for the efficient use of its human resources and establish confidence in its employees. Philip Crosby defines quality, "Quality is conformance to requirement; it is precisely measurable; error is not required to fulfill the laws of nature; and people work just as hard now as they ever did."[11] Accurate and precise job analysis should contribute to the quality of data used to make human resource decisions. Improve the quality of human resource decisions and an organization should improve the quality of human resource management. As Deming states, "We can no longer tolerate commonly accepted levels of mistakes, defects, material not suited for the job, people on the job that do not know what the job is and are afraid to ask, handling damage, antiquated methods of training on the job, inadequate and ineffective supervision, management not rooted in the company..."[12] We must constantly question the processes which we use in managing work and how we manage our human resources.

Appendix I

Position Classification Questionnaire

Implemented Changes

Revised Classification	Revisions
1. Equipment Operator II	Combine: Equipment Operator II, Public Works Maintenance Worker II, Water System Mechanic, Sewer Maintenance Worker I, and Storm Drain Maintenance Worker.
2. Maintenance Assistant I	Combine: Public Works Maintenance Worker II and Building Custodian II.
3. Building Maintenance Mechanic II	Combine: Maintenance Painter, Carpenter, Maintenance Mechanic II, Park Maintenance Worker II, and Building Maintenance Supervisor I.
4. Utility Maintenance Mechanic I	Maintenance Mechanic (no change)
5. Wastewater Plant Operator II	No Change
6. Water Plant Operator II	No Change
7. Water Service Worker II	Utility Service Worker II (Title Change)
8. Lineworker II	No Change
9. Meter Reader II	No Change
10. Groundskeeper II	Combine: Park Caretaker II and Cemetery Caretaker II.
11. Laboratory Technician II	No Change
12. Real Property Appraiser	No Change
13. Chemist II	No Change
14. Planner II	No Change
15. Draftsperson II	No Change
16. Sewer Maintenance Worker I	Combined with Maintenance Assistants

Notes

1. Bowman, James S., At Last, an Alternative to Performance Appraisal: Total Quality Management, *Public Administration Review*, Volume 54 Number 2, p. 130.
2. Uniform Guidelines on Employee Selection Procedures (1978), *Federal Register*, Vol. 43, No. 166-Friday, August 25, 1978 pp 38290–38315.
3. Society for Industrial and Organizational Psychology, Inc. (1987). *Principles for the Validation and Use of Personnel Selection Procedures*. (Third Edition) College Park, MD: Author.
4. Yoder, Dale Ph.D. *ASPA Handbook of Personnel and Industrial Relations*, Volume I, Washington, D.C., 1974, p. 4–54.
5. Grant, Philip C., *Multiple Use Job Descriptions: A Guide to Analysis, Preparation, and Applications For Human Resources Managers*, Quorum Books 1989, p. 76.
6. Consultant Report, unpublished, September 1991, p. 3.
7. Ibid, p. 4–64.
8. *Agreement Between The City of Grand Rapids and The Grand Rapids Employees Independent Union, 1/1/92–12/31/94*, p. 90.
9. Walton, Mary, *The Deming Management Method* 1986, New York, p. 48.
10. Deming, W. Edwards, *Out of the Crisis*, Cambridge, MA, MIT Press, 1986 p. 75.
11. Crosby, Philip B. *Quality Is Free: The Art of Making Quality Certain*, New York, 1979, p. 8.
12. Deming, W. Edwards, *Out of the Crisis*, Cambridge, MA, MIT Press, 1986 p. 26.

Family or Work?
A Matter of Priorities

Eugene H. Fram and
Francena L. Miller

The authors are, respectively, J. Warren McClure Research Professor or Marketing and professor emeritus of sociology, Rochester (N.Y.) Institute of Technology.

SMALL BUSINESS owners and managers urgently need to make contingency plans to accommodate growing employee demands for family-related leave time and schedule flexibility. Those who do not are shortchanging their companies and possibly compromising their firms' futures. The biggest issue, often overlooked, in a small business is how to get work done productively when a key employee needs to be absent to solve a family problem. Another top concern is how to accommodate schedule changes for employees who find normal business hours unworkable for their family situations.

The *Wall Street Journal* noted in 1994 that small businesses appear ready to cope with the requirements of the Federal Family and Medical Leave Act (FMLA). Yet, few seem to realize that dealing with the legislation's provisions on an "as needed" basis, without contingency plans, is not enough.

Societal pressures are building that will force smaller organizations to realize that employees' family problems increasingly will conflict with maintaining productivity in the workplace. Greater numbers are seeking a better balance between family and work obligations, as evidenced by the wide support for the FLMA.

In the past, the interests of labor and management frequently collided over these issues, with key workers in small companies often bowing to the needs of their employers. In the future, though, this likely will be reversed.

The workforce is continuing to undergo restructuring. More women—the traditional caregivers in American society—are employed either full or part time. The number of two-income families is growing, and the amount of men taking more responsibility for daily child care is escalating.

Because of the complexity of modern life and changing interfamilial expectations, employees are finding an increasing variety of family-based reasons for being absent from work or requesting alternate schedules. According to one human resources manager, workers' family problems usually follow a similar pattern: The younger group tends to have more marital and child-raising problems. The 30-39s are running into school and behavioral difficulties with their kids hitting their early teens or late adolescence. The 40-49s are having to cope with both their children and aging parents, while the 50-plus group has to deal with their parents and their own health.

The over-all issue of dependent care is a family and a business concern of increasing dimension. Any working parent who has lost a babysitter or other child care provider with little notice can testify about the emotional havoc created. For adults, job responsibilities suddenly collide with the mandatory care needs of young children. Since the U.S. has a growing population of older persons, elder care also is becoming an increasing consideration.

Although small businesses appear willing to cope with the requirements of the FMLA, few appear to have thought about many of the implications. Are they ready to face the increase in complicated requests for work schedule flexibility? Are they prepared to accept an attendant reduction in productivity during the temporary loss of a key employee? Are they in a position to attempt to mitigate potential production losses through advanced planning?

Without sufficient tactical planning, most substitutions of a key person or changes in work schedule are likely to lead to production slippage. From a productivity viewpoint, a temporary replacement almost never is equal to an experienced employee. Even if the temporary person is another employee who was cross-trained to do the work in emergencies, production slippage probably will occur somewhere in the system.

To determine how organizations are responding to employees' critical family needs, in-depth interviews were conducted with human resources managers at 14 small firms or autonomous divisions of larger companies. All have reputations for being "family friendly," and eight are family owned. The basic approaches they utilized included telecommuting, hiring temporary personnel, cross-training, job sharing, and offering special services. In all examples, the solutions were determined only after a problem arose, but in some cases, managers developed creative solutions others can copy.

Telecommuting. In one company, a manager caring for a baby was able to work with her staff from home, via telecommuting, and limited coming to the office to two or three days per week. In another situation, a firm retained the services of a writer, through telecommuting, when the staff member moved to another city because of a spouse's job change.

Obviously, telecommuting won't work if a manager has to supervise a factory production line. Nevertheless, it does present a positive, inexpensive alternative (currently about $2,000 for good basic equipment) for companies wanting to retain the active participation of certain key personnel. The cost/benefit of investing in electronic equipment should be considered in company contingency planning programs.

Smaller firms need to be alert to issues inherent in the use of flexible working arrangements, however. Suzanne Fields, a columnist for the *Washington Times*, warned that, when flexible working arrangements are not offered to others working under similar conditions, hostility can develop: "The latest strains in workplace strategies pit men against men and women against women.... Conflicts arise if there's a disparity in productivity and effort. No one complains about a guy coaching his son's Little League team or his daughter's basketball team—as long as it doesn't mean a colleague has to write the brief he should have, entertain his customers, or take his weekend calls.... Nearly two-thirds of workers in the United States are without children under the age of 18. Priorities change. So do attitudes. One size does not fit all."

Temporary personnel. Hiring a temporary person is another obvious alternative, but small firms must be aware that training time for a temporary employee can be considerable, and it also decreases productivity for the trainer. In many smaller organizations, where it is common for an individual to do a number of tasks, the training should be recognized as a complex job, with cost and productivity implications.

To avoid problems inherent in hiring temporary personnel, one of the firms in the survey made a conscious decision to build extra capacity into staffing. An executive of the firm noted: "We used to staff right where we had to be. So if anybody got sick, if anyone went on vacation, right away, it was kind of a crisis. The day-to-day work just didn't get done. So in the last four to five years we've increased our staffing to the point where some minor illness doesn't turn into a real problem."

Another manufacturing firm employs "floaters" who can handle several job tasks. These persons have up-to-date skills and quickly fill the gap when someone becomes ill or must leave immediately because of a family emergency. The same company also trains college students during summer months to replace vacationing employees. If an emergency arises when the school year resumes, students are contacted about working on a fill-in basis. The plant has some flexibility in using student-workers because it has a three-shift schedule.

Some businesses have been able to find unique sources for developing pools of temporary workers. One uses the local school district's list of substitute teachers to find persons who want short-term work. Another option is to utilize retirees, especially those who need relatively little training.

A third possibility is to consider allowing an employee to work when the company is not open for business. One firm permitted a permanent worker to work unsupervised from three to seven in the morning. The unusual arrangement allowed the employee to attend to child care duties during the day and also earn a part-time income. The human resources manager described the employee as a "diligent worker," but indicated that such an arrangement would not be suitable for everyone desiring it.

Cross-training. To mitigate emergency conditions, employees can be cross-trained. This is especially desirable where the job requires a great deal of teamwork. On the negative side, cross-training can involve extra costs which a smaller firm may be unable to support. One respondent also warned that some jobs may not be suitable for cross-training because of the technical expertise required.

An excellent way for a small business to begin thinking about personnel flexibility is to examine the job and assess the time it effectively takes the individual holding the position to do the work. It is possible that some employees who want time to devote to family concerns may have grown more efficient in their jobs over time, so that their work can be completed in a shorter time period. One human resources manager described such a situation: "Jane works in the office and has been here about eight years. At this point, what used to take her eight hours a day, she can get done in five, and it just works out great for her and for us. And now that her kids are getting older and can stay more by themselves, she can give us more hours. She's becoming more flexible for the company."

Job sharing is feasible for some positions, but not for others. One company encountered problems with two people sharing a single job in engineering, but found it succeeded for office workers. Another reported that two employees, needing time for children, share one job, each putting in 21 hours a week. Both are paid for an extra hour a week to have a luncheon meeting, outside the office, to coordinate their efforts.

Another firm allows a production control job to be filled by two persons, one working part time for a total of 24 hours a week. The other 16 hours per week are covered by a full-time employee who has other duties during the rest of his workweek. When the full-timer has to be absent, the part-timer puts in a full 40-hour week.

Offering special services. A few innovative small businesses have taken an approach to responding to family needs that others could find beneficial. One of the 14 firms interviewed has 80% of its employees in the 30-39 age bracket. The company has found this particular group has a high divorce rate. Management noticed that, for about a five-month period, newly divorced employees were "here physically, but not mentally." To assist workers through this period, and improve productivity, the firm tries to facilitate employee-counselor contact to help new divorcees deal with their emotional and financial woes. The organization indicates that it has had some real successes as a result of the program.

Other innovative options exist for small businesses. A few might pool resources and offer some type of dependent services, especially those related to child care. Small firms located in a specific geographic area, for instance, might work together to offer a cooperative day care center or organize elder care support groups. These actions not only would help their own workers, but can make the immediate area more attractive to potential employees.

In today's time-stressed society, employees appreciate services that save them time. A group of small businesses could encourage, for example, a dry cleaner to open nearby. Company cafeterias could consider selling packaged dinners for evening family meals.

Xerox Corp., at its research facility in Palo Alto, Calif., not only stocks library books on parenting, but also offers lunch-hour parenting courses. According to the company, communication between parents attending these courses improves and pays dividends in the form of reduced stress.

Contingency planning

"Finding solutions that get the work done and help in family situations is one of the biggest management challenges of the day," *Business Week* (June 28, 1993) concluded. Larger firms seem to be rising to the challenge. Aiming to become a "family friendly" firm by employing "work-family coordinators" has become an organizational posture used by some corporations. DuPont, a leader in this area, has a Director of Work Force Partnering who negotiates with management on family-related issues. These come to management's attention through questionnaire data or through reports from 50 work-life committees at DuPont plants.

Small businesses don't seem to be responding to social pressures in the same way. Media reports indicate only some concern about having to offer job-protected leaves to persons who aren't sick—*e.g.*, new fathers. Obviously, some small firms don't perceive how stressed working parents with new babies can be.

2. MEETING HUMAN RESOURCE REQUIREMENTS: Job Requirements

None of the 14 organizations interviewed had developed any contingency plans for the temporary loss of key employees or more flexible scheduling for workers with special family needs. In fact, none even thought contingency plans to be very important. Several said that contingency planning would mean they were putting company practice "in stone." The same firms reasoned that some employees would manipulate the system, placing employers in the uncomfortable position of having to develop alternative solutions.

Nearly all managers interviewed said they felt most family-related employee problems could be handled if their company employee policies were "flexible." Yet, one particularly aware manager noted that flexibility, in itself, is not a panacea: "It's going to be a [shop floor] nightmare in some cases. It's going to take more work. . . . If someone on shift one comes in a half hour early and leaves a half hour early, the same thing must happen on the second and third shifts. . . . You have to move three [persons]."

One executive explained his technical firm's lack of planning by saying, "We won't have any suggestions until we're confronted with those [family-employee] situations. We just haven't had any. If we knew what area it was going to happen in, we'd plan for it. But we just don't see a need." Yet, the same executive noted elsewhere in the interview that the company had to cope with scheduling problems arising from family situations.

Two organizations reported taking tiny steps in the right direction by doing some formal training in family awareness. A third had conducted employee focus groups on family problems. One human resources person stated: "Until recently, the expectation was that key people would learn how to deal with family issues by osmosis; the culture would determine their policies. However, last year, the company brought in a consulting firm to conduct a regular seminar on management sensitivity."

Slowly, a few small businesses are recognizing the need to change their approach to meeting employees' family needs. In the not-too-distant future, it may be hoped that others will begin to see the value of adopting contingency plans that can be implemented when employees face family crises.

From the interviews with the 14 firms, it appears that when family issues do arise, they often are handled on a decentralized basis. A decision by an employee's supervisor is key to any option, and, in some cases, obtaining leave time or a more flexible schedule involves a departmental negotiation process.

If a company wants to develop a contingency plan, its first step should be to identify the major types of family-related concerns, where they are occurring, and other potential problems. For instance, if a large portion of the middle management group consists of younger women, pregnancy leaves will have to be a consideration. The current practice of decentralized decision-making may not give a clear picture of the extent of family pressures. Consequently, a formal company-wide review of the firm's experiences must take place.

Once all major problems have been identified, those requiring quick management action should be addressed first. Others should be discussed with employees, and they should be asked to offer their reactions and propose solutions. If, for example, numerous workers are abusing alcohol, a discussion with an employee group wouldn't necessarily be helpful in deciding whether the firm needs an employee assistance program. The need is evident.

On the other hand, if job scheduling has become an issue because some workers have serious child or elder care concerns, discussions with employees probably would provide some insightful solutions. These discussions should be handled carefully to avoid having a few individuals push their own agendas.

After listening to its employees, a small company may determine that the supporting resources needed are not available. This can lead to some discontent, even if the resource problem is talked about openly. If handled well, though, these discussions can boost employee morale because they show the employer cares that workers face serious problems. It is equally important for employees to understand that a financially healthy company should care about its workers, but that financial health is based on the firm's ability to achieve quality productivity in every facet of its operation.

Once possible financial risks have been assessed and adjustments for employee time schedules completed, a small business needs to make contingency plans for each of the key managerial and line personnel who might have to be absent for an extended period. The plan should show:

- Who replaces each key employee.
- The projected impact on productivity if a temporary person fills a vacant position, or if more than one temporary person is needed to fill the slot.
- A job description for the person serving as a replacement and assignment of other duties to specific individuals.
- A priority listing of duties that might have to be postponed.
- The names of individuals who could serve as back-up replacements in the event the primary candidate is unavailable.
- Productivity benchmarks that need to be reviewed continually in the absence of the key employee.
- The name of the person responsible for evaluating and supporting any temporary employees.

In many small businesses, senior managers may have to be the working substitute. Consequently, they must be prepared to work on the factory floor, handle daily customer phone calls, or to do other jobs using somewhat rusty skills. Serving as a replacement may be physically and psychologically difficult because they still will need to fulfill their management responsibilities. On the other hand, it can be beneficial to staff morale to know that management is willing to share the load.

While no organization can plan for every situation, a small business should anticipate such possibilities as long-term leaves for key employees and work schedule flexibility for those with difficult family problems. Management can not afford to ignore the social pressures that increasingly will affect its ability to maintain productivity.

Article 14

How To Recruit Online

Surfing the *Net* with online services is the newest recruitment technique. It can yield many good resumes—and candidates—but only if you know the right strategy.

Shannon Peters Talbott

Everyone's talking about online recruitment. It's simple, right? Just post your openings on the Internet, and wait for resumes to flood in via e-mail. It sounds so easy. But wait—how do you decide where to post your ads? Which site on the World Wide Web is best for you?

The options are endless: *Monster Board, E-Span, Career Magazine, Job-Center, Career Mosaic,* plus dozens of others. All of the Web sites offer different services at different prices—but they all promise to provide the best candidates.

In reality, there's no one right place to do online recruitment. Instead, each organization must design an online recruitment strategy to meet its own needs, then find a service to match. By following the steps below, you'll have a clearer understanding of the selection process, and you'll likely find an option that will provide the best online results for your organization.

Step 1: Familiarize yourself with the Internet. Systems West Computer Resources in Salt Lake City first tried to recruit online in mid-1994, when few companies had moved into this new recruiting arena. Its first attempts weren't particularly successful. In early 1995, however, CEO Nancy Halberson redesigned the company's strategy, and recruitment went back online. Now, Systems West receives approximately 40% of its incoming resumes through e-mail, and the company is finding online recruitment a great source of applicants. The key, explains Systems West consultant Dave Madsen, is understanding and experimenting with the Internet. For human resources professionals to use the Internet's recruitment services successfully, they first need to learn the basics.

"A lot of HR professionals don't understand the Internet, so they try to delegate it," Madsen says. "[Many] people haven't touched it, yet they try to use it for recruitment and then are frustrated with the results."

It's important not to delegate Internet recruitment. "Go to a class and get comfortable with the technology—even if it means sitting down with a college student for [several] hours and just learning what the Internet has to offer." The key is: Don't be afraid to learn the basics. Once you pick up a rudimentary understanding, you'll be able to better use the tools—and the language—of the Internet. It's important in forming your online recruitment strategy.

Step 2: Research the market. Once you've mastered the basics of the Internet, discover what the Web can offer you in terms of recruitment. Most active electronic recruiters suggest you use an online index or directory to find out which recruitment services are available. A popular directory is *Yahoo!*—developed by Stanford University, in Stanford, California—which can be accessed by visiting the Web address: http://www.yahoo.com. Other similar resources are *Lycos* (http://lycos.cs.cmu.edu) and *WebCrawler* (http://webcrawler.com). By searching relevant keywords—such as "jobs," "employment" or "careers"—HR professionals can find out just what options exist.

Hilary M. Bencini, vice president of Miami-based Uniforce Staffing Services, conducted this type of search before she selected an online service. "We did a generic search to get an up-to-date listing of all the Web sites dealing with employment," she said. "From there, we visited each site to get more information." Bencini, who does approximately 45% of her recruiting online, recommends this approach to anyone interested in the electronic approach to staffing: "It's essential that recruiters research the various services to obtain specific information on the size and makeup of the candidate pool," she explains. "Also, by doing a generic search and visiting each site—then calling representatives to get more information about each individual service—firms can determine whether the services fit their budget and provide the expected results."

Step 3: Define your target audience. To determine whether a specific service will meet your expectations, you must first define your needs. As Bencini notes, an important consideration involves your target audience. Each company has its own unique recruitment needs, and these require exposure to different types—and numbers—of applicants.

For some users, the greater the exposure, the better the site. Take, for example, Scott Stevenson, technical recruiter for Federated Systems Group in Atlanta. Because Stevenson isn't looking for employees from a specific geographical region, he selected a service that would give him the most exposure possible. *E-Span*, one of the online Web sites, maintains a presence on the Web and on four of the major online services (CompuServe, America Online, e-World and GEnie), so when Stevenson posts jobs on the service they're distributed to a larger audience. "We're primarily looking for folks who have a technical background, but we wanted a site that would reach a lot of potential applicants," he says. "There are many bulletin boards and online services that our ads get dumped onto after we post them. Because our service provides this option, it gives us the exposure we want and helps us find the right people."

Madsen agrees that access to these Internet users is important: "We wanted to see which services were pulling resumes from the large service providers, because more people are using these resume-posting services. This was a consideration when we chose where to post our openings."

Although many recruiters share these concerns, totals may not always be key. In addition to looking at the number of visitors to a site, companies also should try to ascertain who those visitors are. As John Sumser, president of Internet Business Network in Mill Valley, California, notes: "Some services measure their effectiveness in size and volume, and they have databases that are as large as five years' worth of Sunday classifieds. Traffic does matter, and high volume is sometimes a good sign. But, what HR people need to worry about is finding the right traffic every time."

For the most part, this message isn't new. Like newspapers or magazines, most Web sites attract a certain segment of the population. Some are oriented toward a specific industry; others are geared toward college graduates. Some services only reach a certain geographical area. The important thing is that

> **You can run all the ads in the world for nuns in *Playboy*, but you won't get any applicants.**

recruiters identify each service's target market before advertising. Although many services claim they're national, the majority of registered job hunters often come from a limited geographical area. Bencini says to ask for this information when you call the service representative: "If you're trying to recruit someone from Michigan, you shouldn't be spending advertising dollars on a service that targets the New York metropolitan area. It can't hurt to get a geographical breakdown of the candidate pool to determine if applicants come from the area you desire."

Finally, Sumser notes that recruiters are facing an imbedded racial and gender bias when recruiting online—regardless of which service they select. "The Internet is most commonly used by young, white males," he warns. "In two years, this may not be true, but right now, it's something to think about."

Overall, the message is this: If your advertisement isn't reaching your target audience, you're unlikely to fill your job openings, regardless of the volume of Web users. As Sumser illustrates, "You can run all the ads in the world for nuns in the back of *Playboy*, but you won't get any applicants, even though the magazine's circulation is huge." For best results, define your audience then find a Web site that most closely matches your description. Target industry-specific sites, such as *Tech Web* for technical experts or the *Franklin Search Group* for biotech, pharmaceutical and medical professionals. For college recruitment, look into sites such as *JobTrak* and *Job Web*. The key to success is narrowing your search. "You have to be sophisticated about the market," Sumser says. "This begins with understanding exactly what candidates you're seeking."

Step 4: Determine your search needs. You can narrow your search further by studying the features offered by each service and selecting one that appeals most to you. Each service works in its own way: Some store resumes in a database, and registered employers perform searches for qualified applicants. Other sites allow employers to create profiles of their companies and post their jobs—allowing applicants to send resumes directly to the company when positions are of interest to them. Finally, some services also perform what is called job-matching, storing resumes and job postings online and actively contacting both parties when an applicant looks right for a job. For many recruiters, this latter approach is a major benefit. "Active systems really help with tracking," says Madsen with Systems West. "You can see the activity, because the services send you matches. It's nice to go to your e-mail and know there are seven or eight resumes waiting for you every morning."

Bencini agrees, calling active matching an "invaluable tool." However, she warns: Most often, matching services operate according to keywords, which recruiters use to describe their openings. "Success depends on your ability to identify keywords appropriately," she says. Bencini advises HR professionals to avoid general job titles such as "administrative assistant" or "technical support specialist." Titles mean different things

> If you haven't yet joined the Internet revolution, consider testing the water—at least with a little toe.

to different people, and you may end up with many resumes you don't need. "You do want to encompass as many qualified people as possible, but you have to be careful," she warns. "If you list something general like 'computer programmer,' you will get all the resumes with that description, regardless of their experience or the other qualifications you need. Not all of the keywords must be present on a resume for it to be considered a match."

What words are appropriate? Madsen says to use only nouns. "HR people have been trained to write job descriptions in flowery paragraphs," he says. "Forget that, and think in terms of nouns to describe the skills and qualifications needed for the position. This will get you a better bunch of applicants."

Step 5: Compare costs. With all of these options and different types of services, it's no surprise that the costs vary immensely. In fact, some services are free, while others charge thousands of dollars. When selecting a service, it's important that you ask about the pricing philosophy for each site and stay within your budget. For Bencini, the charges for matching services are worth the investment: "Some services provide free access to posted resumes, but I haven't found them especially useful," she says. "What you will find is that some resumes are posted on spec—and a candidate may or may not be a serious job hunter." Instead of spending time wading through these free resumes, Bencini prefers to pay a service to perform matches for her. "Passive searching can be a real time waster," she adds.

At present, the greatest problem with the cost of online recruiting is predicting what you may get for your money. "As of now, there aren't any decent effectiveness statistics," says Sumser. "Be prepared to get silence on the other end of the phone if you ask these services questions about their effectiveness. They'll give you lots of numbers and percentages, but 'Does this work effectively?' isn't easily answered."

Step 6: Continue experimenting. No matter which online service you choose, remember the Internet is constantly changing. According to the Internet Business Network, the Internet is growing at a monthly rate of 12%. And lots of people are logging on. A survey by CommerceNet/Nielsen Internet Demographics tells us that 17% of people aged 16 or older in the United States and Canada (approximately 37 million people) have access to the Internet—and 11% of the same group have used the Internet in the past three months. Tomorrow, these numbers will be even higher. Because of this rapid growth, human resources professionals should frequently reevaluate their online recruiting choices.

Bencini, at Uniforce Staffing, says she's continually considering new options for her company: "The Internet is growing by leaps and bounds, and a Web site that wasn't successful for you two months ago could be your best option today," Bencini says. "Be sure to return to the search engines often to reassess your approach."

Perhaps the most important fact to remember as you navigate the Net is: There aren't any simple, straightforward answers. Only by thinking through your expectations—then experimenting with a variety of services—will you discover the sites that meet your recruitment needs. If you haven't yet joined the Internet revolution, consider testing the water—"at least with a little toe," says Sumser. Try a few services and track your results, especially before committing to a long-term contract. Over time, you'll find a strategy that works for you.

Unlock the Potential of Older Workers

■ You're Going To Need Them

For too long now, we've kept mature employees in frustrating confinement. But business can no longer discount this group—HR will need to refocus its recruiting, training and retention.

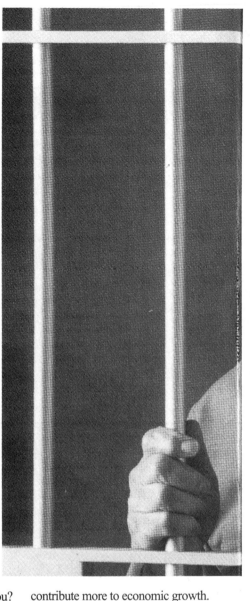

Charlene Marmer Solomon

Companies don't seem to know what to do with them. Ineffectively recruited, ineffectively retained, they have been confined to the fringes of the organization by employers—or have been unintentionally barred completely. They are older workers, and companies had better sit up and take notice. Their ranks are swelling, and this rapid growth will continue as the oldest of the 76 million baby boomers born between 1946 and 1964 begin hitting their fifth decade. According to the Washington, D.C.-based American Association of Retired Persons (AARP), one in eight Americans is older than 65, and by 2030 that figure will rise to 20%. Already, people older than 55 account for 20% of the U.S. population.

What does all this have to do with you? A lot. This labor force will become absolutely critical to your business in the next few years—for several reasons. First, older people are staying in the work force longer than ever before. Thanks to laws such as the Age Discrimination in Employment Act, people in most professions are no longer forced to retire, and they're enjoying extensive protection of pension benefits.

Technology is also playing its part. The information revolution is creating jobs that are less physically demanding, so individuals will work longer, and older workers will contribute more to economic growth.

But there's a second piece of the puzzle that soon will make mature workers indispensable. Because of the baby bust, major labor shortages loom on the horizon. With 76 million boomers and only 56 million baby busters (born between 1965 and 1976) to take their places, companies trying to fill entry-level positions will be searching mightily for viable candidates to fill those slots.

Unfortunately, there are still many barriers to employing mature workers. Today's workplace isn't particularly friendly or accessible to older people.

> **Major labor shortages loom ahead. With 76 million baby boomers and only 56 million baby busters, businesses will need to recruit and retain older workers.**

15. Unlock the Potential of Older Workers

There's no reason to bar older workers from your company—but many reasons to swing the door wide. AARP surveys of management find that most employers value their older workers for such characteristics as experience, skills, productivity, low turnover and an excellent work ethic.

They suffer from great earning disparities with younger workers. They're forced into uncomfortable decisions by rigid scheduling structures. The option—either retirement or full-time work—causes many to shy away from employment. Finally, many myths and prejudices about older workers keep them from the workplace. For instance, a 1989 report by the Bureau of Labor Statistics, "Labor Market Problems of Older Workers," indicates that many older workers who want to find jobs give up because of age discrimination.

So just because companies will need older workers and this group is eager for employment doesn't, unfortunately, mean the problem is solved. Organizations that want to successfully employ this segment of the labor force must recognize the particular needs of older workers and create policies to ensure their success.

Recruiting, training, managing and retaining all must be approached with a bit of a twist. Companies that do it right—such as McDonald's, Home Shopping Network, AT&T, Texas Refinery Corp. and Good Samaritan Hospital—will tell you a little extra effort pays off.

Before you do anything else, dispel the misconceptions. Older people are constantly being questioned about their ability to stand up in the work force. The older the person, the greater the skepticism. Even a July *Time* magazine cover story on presidential candidate Bob Dole chose to focus on age: "Is Dole Too Old for the Job?"

"The biggest barriers to the employment of older workers are myths about productivity, safety and costs of employing these workers," says Catherine D. Fyock, president of Prospect, Kentucky-based Innovative Management Concepts and author of the book, "America's Work Force is Coming of Age."

Yet none of these rumors have proven to be substantial. For instance, AARP states that workers between the ages of 50 and 60 stay on the job an average of 15 years, and their attendance is as good or better than other groups. Safety also should be of limited concern, according to the AARP. In most occupations, mature workers have a *lower* accident rate, with workers 55 and older accounting for 13.6% of the work force but for only 9.7% of on-the-job injuries.

Finally, there's little proof that older workers cost more to employ. For instance, the belief that older workers cause increased health-care costs—one of the most tenacious myths—has proven to be unfounded by several studies. In particular, one by Yankelovich, Skelly and White Inc. showed that health-care costs between 30-year-old males, women with dependents and 65-year-old retirees are about the same. It also proved that 55-year-olds are the least costly of all groups. And, in a number of surveys, according to Fyock, respondents revealed that even if health-care costs were higher, the advantages of employing mature workers offset any additional cost because of lower absenteeism and turnover.

These concerns aside, there still remains a lingering theory that older Americans either don't need or don't want to work. This too is untrue. According to AARP, 3.5 million people aged 55 and older were below the poverty line in 1985—with the rate being higher for those older than 65. That translates into nearly one-fifth of the older population. Indeed, for many older workers, there's great financial need to gain employment.

Plus, many want to work. They like the idea of dipping a foot back into the labor pool, or even remaining there for the long haul. In a 1981 Louis Harris poll, 79% of those aged 55 to 64 and 73% of those older than 65 said they'd prefer to work part time. In a 1983 AARP survey, 74% said they'd prefer working to retiring. The stance was still strong in a 1988 AARP study, in which 40% to 50% said they'd work past retirement age if they could have flexible schedules, part-time and temporary employment.

So the first step is an important one: Acknowledge and dispel the myths about older workers. Educate yourself and your company. "One main issue is awareness," says Fyock. "Sometimes it's just talking about these kinds of things in a discussion group or in a classroom setting. People will suddenly realize that they've been operating with these kinds of assumptions or biases or stereotypes. HR people really do need to get educated on the issues of aging and an aging work force."

Recruiting older workers: Unleash your creativity. Just as you'd alter your recruiting approach for college students or working mothers, companies must adjust their efforts to attract older employees. Consider what they want (flexible working hours, for instance) and where to find them (older communities, for example).

One company that takes these ideas seriously—to its success—is Clearwater, Florida-based Home Shopping Network (HSN), a cable television company. Calling itself an "electronic retailer" that broadcasts 24 hours a day to more than 70 million American households, the company has tremendous staffing needs for people to answer phones and take orders for merchandise.

"We needed a flexible part-time work force to answer the telephones during the peak periods," says Mount Burns, a company HR representative. "We're located in an area where there are many retired folks who need and want a little extra income. We knew they were there, but we didn't know how they'd get hold of us."

Fourteen Steps in Managing an Aging Work Force

1. Understand the changing work force.
2. Implement the Age Discrimination in Employment Act and understand its implications for management policy and practice.
3. Know the facts about the normal aging process.
4. Prevent work-induced stress detrimental to older workers and encourage effective stress management.
5. Know the health-related cost/benefit issues of older workers and use cost-management strategies.
6. Use objective performance appraisals.
7. Offer well-designed retraining programs and encourage older workers to participate.
8. Implement alternative work schedules.
9. Use knowledge of life stages for job assignments and team building.
10. Conduct management training on the subject of aging to prevent age discrimination and to encourage effective use of older workers.
11. Use community resources for future employment and career-development opportunities for older employees.
12. Examine labor's history, policies, needs and services regarding older union workers.
13. Capitalize on older workers' desires and abilities to extend their working career.
14. Offer comprehensive retirement-planning programs.

Source: Helen Dennis' book, "Fourteen Steps in Managing an Aging Work Force," (Lexington Books, 1988).

In 1990, the company established Prime Timer, a program that invites people older than 55 to become part of their work force. It encourages them with policies such as flexible and part-time jobs and by recruiting practices that systematically seek out seniors.

Burns, himself 67 and formerly retired, took on the task of recruiting. First, the local television station ran spots publicizing the company's needs. Then Burns visited the various community agencies that served older adults, such as the senior-citizen centers at each of the county's seven or eight cities. Burns contacted each center's director and developed slide presentations to show people exactly what the job entailed. He worked with the Chamber of Commerce, and he also attended Senior Job Fairs and placed ads in local newspapers. Basically, HSN combed the area for potential applicants.

The company has been successful—both in quantity and in quality. Its first training class, which began on March 21, 1990, had 12 people; today more than 500 individuals have come through the Prime Timer training program. Burns himself moved from a two-day-a-week slot to a full-time human resources position and a role as the Prime Timer coordinator. In addition, according to Burns, the Prime Timers who were hired in 1992 had a 30% lower turnover rate than other hires—and these are individuals who range up to 84 years old.

HSN's recruiting success is largely a result of its commitment to and understanding of the older population of workers. The company creates policies that address their needs for varied schedules and responsibility, and it recognizes that mature individuals are a very diverse group and require different recruiting techniques.

It's important to remember that although some recruiting generalizations can be made about older workers, individuals in this group are as varied as any other large segment of the population. They include people who are in mid-life career changes, early retirees, older retirees, displaced workers and people who've never worked outside the home before. Each group has its own motivations to work and benefits needs. In addition, each group has its own concerns about Social Security benefits and how those will be affected by employment (see "Part-time Work Protects Social Security Benefits.")

Fyock, who had years of experience developing programs for older workers at Louisville, Kentucky-based Kentucky Fried Chicken, suggests that recruiting messages are extremely important. Mature adults work for several reasons—financial needs, security requirements, social needs and self-esteem. Recruitment messages should not only segment the market, but also speak to those needs. These messages can be presented at a variety of venues such as job fairs, through direct mail or via a hotline.

For instance, Fyock helped develop strategies that located older adults in the course of their daily activities. KFC made presentations at senior centers, at coffee-klatch meetings, at mall-walker groups. The company targeted certain neighborhoods in the community that had pockets of older people.

"Generally, HR people have never targeted older adults," she says. "In fact, the whole notion of targeting [seniors] may be new and unique. So you want to focus your thinking on how you can reach older adults, what they're doing, what their daily activities are like and how you can reach out to those individuals. You even can create messages that are appealing to them."

Oak Brook, Illinois-based McDonald's Corp. has long been admired for its success in targeting mature individuals. And so it should be. Company founder Ray A. Kroc was 52 when he established the company in 1955. McDonald's ReHIREment program was formed in the '80s when the company recognized the employee shortage it was facing. Now ReHIREment entices older individuals to rejoin the work force, or to join it for the first time, as in the case of many homemakers. "We looked at other markets and found that we already had many successful older workers in our restaurants, and we could probably find ways to recruit more," says Barry Mehrman, employment development consultant for McDonald's Corp.

But McDonald's had to overcome some interesting recruiting challenges. For instance, one of the corporation's unique aspects is that approximately 40% to 50% of its employees are young—in high school and college. Mehrman says that when young managers in their 20s sit down to interview someone old enough to be their parent or grandparent, it may be awkward. To alleviate that problem, the company works with the managers to rehearse scenarios. It also adjusts some of its selection questions. For instance, it isn't much use to ask a 65-year-old who's com-

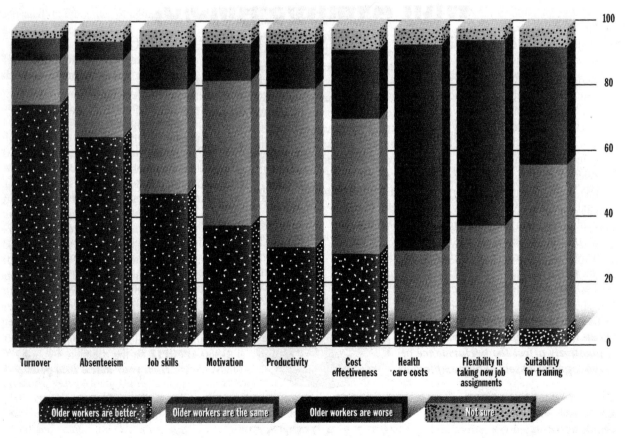

Older Workers Often Outscore Average-aged Workers

The perceived benefits of employing older workers outweigh the perceived liabilities, according to a survey of more than 400 HR executives. In such important areas as turnover, absenteeism and job skills, older workers received higher ratings than average-aged workers. Although some executives hold views that older workers are undesirable in certain areas—such as health care and job flexibility—these have largely been proven false (see main story).

Source: The Conference Board: "Availability of a Quality Work Force"

2. MEETING HUMAN RESOURCE REQUIREMENTS: Planning, Selection, and Recruitment

ing out of retirement to work part time what his career goals are or what he wants to do in the future. "We found you really don't need to approach it like that when you're interviewing," says Mehrman. Instead, McDonald's developed specific recruiting materials to help older candidates talk about how they can share their skills and experience with others; they sell McDonald's as a career opportunity based on scheduling flexibility and the fact that they help individuals so they don't jeopardize their Social Security earnings.

To minimize older workers' fears of moving into the work force, McDonald's also sets up a buddy system so that each older worker has someone to help acclimate him or her to the way things are done at McDonald's. Workers can choose one restaurant position that they're particularly interested in, or they can choose to learn a variety of positions. The company's approach to recruitment works: Today, more than 40,000 senior employees serve McDonald's customers worldwide.

Training: Establish adult learning goals. Regardless of age, training and retraining employees ensures that they remain up to date on new skills and refreshed on old ones. Training older workers isn't too far a reach from training younger ones. Many companies use this three-pronged strategy:
- Continually training mature workers who've remained in the work force
- Training new hires
- Training supervisors on how to manage older workers.

Continued training is key for workers as they mature on the job. According to AARP, the three common mid-career problems that lower productivity are career burnout, career plateauing and career obsolescence. These can be alleviated substantially by career management and effective training.

The first situation, career burnout, requires early diagnosis and intervention. It can be helped by job redesign or rotation, since burnout is usually associated with high-pressure jobs. Temporary assignments, reassignments as mentors or trainers, stress management training and sabbaticals also can be of use.

Career plateauing can be addressed by assigning employees to projects that use their special skills. For instance, if an individual is skilled at sales but has been doing it for many years, the person could be assigned to a new advertising campaign for the company. This way the employee continues to sharpen his or her skills—but in a new way with a new approach. In addition, alternative career paths, as well as opportunities for training and development, can also thwart career plateauing.

Career obsolescence requires retraining to sharpen existing skills or supply new skills. Other solutions are to encourage employees to take classes to keep up with new developments, join professional organizations and consider career contingency plans. Employers may also consider offering career-planning workshops or starting an information center.

When it comes to training new hires who are older, the process isn't actually too much different from training new hires who are young. Find out what areas they need to work on, and then jump in. For instance, AARP studies show that many managers view older workers as lacking technological skills. But that didn't stop HSN from hiring them. The company designed a very specific training program to teach people who'd never used a computer before exactly how to handle the data entry the business required. In addition, the company reminded managers that training older workers shouldn't be approached too differently than any other training. "We put a lot of supervisory personnel through a [sensitivity] course so they would know how to react to these individuals and how they should be treated—not as school children but as adults," says Burns.

In general, when training and retraining older workers, remember this: While adult learners have different needs, most older adults thrive in a friendly, supportive learning arena. They need to know why they're learning something, what they're learning and how to apply it. Adult learners need to build on past experiences. The challenge is to incorporate all of these aspects into a creative, supportive learning climate.

You can best create this climate by following these five suggestions:

1. Identify employees who need training and help with career development
2. Motivate employees to take advantage of training programs
3. Improve flexibility and capacity of employees to learn new skills
4. Modify training to accommodate employees with special needs
5. Determine cost-effectiveness of training and employee development.

McDonald's McMasters programs, active in California and Washington, D.C., provide training exclusively for older workers. Candidates are screened through

---

Part-time Work Protects Social Security Benefits

How would you feel about taking a job if it meant losing a dollar for every three you made? A bit hesitant probably. But that's basically what happens when older people return to full-time work after retirement—due to regulations on Social Security.

Social Security benefits are kept in check by an *earnings limitation*—a cap on how much a person can earn in a year without it affecting Social Security. In 1995, the earnings limitation for a beneficiary aged 65 through 69 is $11,280. For workers younger than 65, the limitation is $8,160.

When older employees begin earning more than these amounts, they're in effect "penalized." For employees younger than 65, their Social Security benefits are reduced by $1 for every $2 they earn over the limitation. For workers aged 65 through 69, benefits are reduced by $1 for every $3. When an employee hits 70, Social Security benefits are no longer subject to limitations.

Although many older employees decide to work full-time in spite of the earnings limitations, most still appreciate companies' giving them a choice. Allowing older people to work part-time or on an independent-contractor basis demonstrates that the company acknowledges older employees' positions—and attracts and retains a whole group of people that less flexible companies will miss out on.
—GF

15. Unlock the Potential of Older Workers

state and local agencies (including the Department of Aging and AARP), and referred to the company for interviews. The program includes coaching by McDonald's managers, who provide one-on-one training for these candidates for a four-week period. They also receive classroom instruction, operational demonstrations and training in a variety of positions. They learn how to use the restaurant's computerized cash register system, and how to make salad and cook fries. Orientation for all workers lasts about two hours, and the training focuses on hospitality skills and customer service—two areas that older workers tend to excel at anyway. "From a generational standpoint, people who are in their 60s and 70s are absolutely outstanding when it comes to being friendly and offering quality service," says Mehrman. At the end of the program, McMasters employees have a graduation ceremony. They're then integrated into the work force at the restaurant at which they were trained.

But managers must also undergo training if older people are to successfully acclimate to the workplace. McDonald's recognized this fact: Like HSN, the company provides sensitivity training to restaurant employees and managers to dispel myths and answer questions about older workers. McMasters managers are encouraged to schedule team-building sessions involving older workers, other restaurant employees and the management team. "We try to create a family feeling in the restaurants, and one of the important aspects of that is respect," says Mehrman.

McDonald's managers also are trained to recognize the different management issues regarding mature workers. For example, mature workers tend to have a lot of social needs. For management, this means that supervisors must be trained to look for different goals that older people may have. Mehrman provides an example: "We promote internally. So a lot of young people learn skills and want to move up. That's different for someone who's coming back after retirement to work part-time. So, you're not going to say, 'Gee, you're doing a great job, do you want to be a swing manager?'" They may not want that additional responsibility or time frame.

However, managers must also be trained to keep an eye on older workers who want the opportunity. In the Chicago area, for instance, McDonald's hired a retired international banker who'd worked all over the world. He was originally hired as a regular crew person but then decided that he wanted to become a recruiter. He's now working full time doing recruiting and building relationships with schools and other organizations.

Managing and retaining seniors: Know what's important. Managing and retaining mature people is another facet that requires HR know-how. Fort

> **Many retired folks need and want extra income. We just didn't know how they'd get hold of us.**
> *Mount Burns*
> *Home Shopping Network*

Worth-based Texas Refinery Corp. is respected for its policies regarding seniors. Indeed, the company's No. 4 salesperson is 74 years old—and this employee isn't alone. With a sales force of more than 3,000, the company has held on to 500 members who are 60, 70 and 80.

Company President Jerry Hopkins will tell you the reason the company works so hard to hold on to its older workers is pure business. TR believes that older people are more inclined to be self-starters and interested in establishing long-term relationships with clients. "Their age is immaterial to us," says Hopkins. "We put a great deal of value on life experience, and we think that in relationships, often an older, more experienced person probably has a distinct advantage."

Most of these older individuals are hired as independent contractors who receive commissions and benefits based on their sales. Many work demanding full-time schedules—such as Bill Shapiro, a 75-year-old sales representative who has been with the company 31 years. The definition of self-starter, he averages 55 hours a week, drives 100 miles a day and can drive as many as 300 to 400 miles to do business. Shapiro still climbs ladders to do roof inspections of industrial buildings.

Others take advantage of the independent contractor status to work flexible, part-time hours to protect their Social Security. This option is a key provision to Texas Refinery's retention. According to AARP, one of the most significant factors that stands in the way of employment is that older workers are forced to choose between full-time work and retirement. They express a preference for phased retirement and reduced work schedules.

As Texas Refinery illustrates, flexible work arrangements that can be adjusted by each individual are an important component of retention. Companies can use a variety of flexible options, from job sharing and on-call work, to part-time and phased-in retirement.

But flexible work arrangements are only part of retaining older workers; another is an atmosphere that respects and values seniors. A corporate culture that accepts and encourages aging workers describes Los Angeles-based Good Samaritan Hospital. Take Inez Hamilton, for instance. She may be 76 years old, but you'd never know it by the work she does. As an instrument technician for Good Samaritan Hospital, Hamilton is responsible for the exacting and critical task of cleaning and preparing surgical instrument trays. Day after day, from 2 p.m. to 10 p.m.—and sometimes more—Hamilton cleans and sorts scalpels and scissors, forceps and needles. The great-great-grandmother of four continues to be so skilled that the cardiac surgeon she worked with previously called her out of retirement to work for him again when he changed hospitals.

The hospital's embracing attitude is one that keeps older workers around. Says Margaret Hambleton, director of compensation and benefits: "Many of the people who work directly with patients tend to stay in the positions much longer. We have many employees who've been with us for 35 years, and we appreciate having employees who continue to remind us of our history. We encourage our older workers to stay on with us."

How does the hospital encourage them? Although the administration is care-

2. MEETING HUMAN RESOURCE REQUIREMENTS: Planning, Selection, and Recruitment

ful not to compromise patient care, it helps to create an environment that accommodates some physical limitations of the older worker. For example, a nurse's aide will help move a patient or change bedsheets for a mature individual who has trouble with those strenuous activities.

The hospital also keeps a close eye on pay equity for its work force—15% of employees are older than 55; 6% are older than 65. Although the company works with a merit-based pay system, Hambleton says that it's careful to be sure the pay levels for senior workers keep up with those of the younger staff. At one time, younger workers tended to be "leap-frogged" in and often were put at higher rates. This was especially true with nurses who were in serious demand.

That kind of pay environment no longer exists at the hospital; Hambleton says it now makes a special effort to maintain pay equity. The hospital does an annual performance review and, at the same time, determines that salaries of long-time employees don't lag behind younger—or newer—workers. While pay is merit-based, Hambleton and the director of human resources go through the entire employee population by hire date, seniority and number of years of experience to ensure that salaries are fair—that individuals don't fall behind simply because they're with the organization longer.

Perhaps most importantly, the corporate culture simply values seniors. For example, during the hospital's cultural-diversity week, it highlights older workers as part of the cultural richness. "We talked about some of the needs of the older worker, and about making use of older workers. [We talked about] their history at the hospital and using them as mentors. It was really an education," Hambleton says.

The hospital also sponsors a mentoring program that works informally to acknowledge the experience of seniors. "All patient care people require a mentor as they go through their orientation. They go through a period of up to six weeks during which they have a buddy who's one of the best performers and someone with a lot of knowledge. Often our older workers [act as buddies]."

Just as many younger people have concerns about interviewing people twice their age, so can younger-to-older management raise some concerns. Joan L. Kelly, manager of the Business Partnerships Program at AARP, explains that this is, in fact, a major management hurdle. "Sometimes you find younger managers saying,

How Companies Perceive Older Workers

In 1989, the American Association of Retired Persons (AARP) commissioned the Daniel Yankelovich Group Inc. to update an earlier study called "Workers Over 50: Old Myths, New Realities." The firm sampled 400 companies from a wide range of industry sectors and of various sizes, and interviewed the HR decision-makers about their perspectives on older workers. Here are the results.

The HR people felt older workers have:

Good attendance and punctuality	91%
Commitment to quality	89%
Solid performance records	87%
Loyalty and dedication	86%
Great deal of practical, as well as theoretical knowledge	85%
Ability to get along with co-workers	79%
Solid experience in job and/or industry	78%
Emotional stability	76%

On the other hand, HR people tended to give older workers lower marks for the following:

Good educational background	36%
Physical agility	29%
Desire to get ahead	27%
Feeling comfortable with new technologies	22%

However, all of these marks were up from the previous survey: education up 19%, agility up 7%, desire to get ahead up 9% and comfort with new technologies up 12%.

Source: The Daniel Yankelovich Group

'I feel like I'm supervising my mom or dad,' and they feel a little remiss to do that. But, we need to remember there's respect due on both sides. Age has nothing to do with it. It gets back to respecting all employees and being even-handed with your treatment of everyone."

Says Fyock: "One of the biggest issues is that different aged workers tend to share certain value systems based on the beliefs at the time in which they grew up. Younger workers tend to share a [core of similar] values; older workers do as well."

One of the big problems with managers is that they sometimes don't understand differences that are generationally based—yet to effectively manage, they must acknowledge them. Fyock recalls a time at KFC when many managers were so accustomed to the value systems of young people that when older adults entered the work force with different values and different ways of looking at work, they needed to completely rethink how to manage those individuals.

For example, young people almost always responded positively to a participative management style, whereas older adults sometimes found it a little confusing. "First of all, participative management may not have been used throughout their years in the workplace," says Fyock, "and also they have a very strong ethic of respecting authority. They may even feel that participatory management is almost an abdication of authority."

Furthermore, she says, older adults generally place a high importance on work. They see it as a duty, a responsibility, an important part of their life. Younger adults may tend to see work as a means to an end. It should be fun, it should be exciting, it should be more than just the work itself. Their views about authority may also be vastly different. "We talk about how young people see authority as a sort of necessary evil, something that must be tolerated, something that also should be questioned and challenged. Older adults tend to see authority as something to be respected and valued."

When you have differences like these, it's important that everyone recognize them. Moreover, young managers need to understand the influences and backgrounds of their different employees

15. Unlock the Potential of Older Workers

and understand those biases when attempting to manage them.

Yes—even in retention and management, much of the key to success resides in dispelling prejudices about mature employees. The AARP recommends that age stereotypes can be overcome through education, communication about the problem, participation in task forces to investigate the problem, rewards for managers who fully train and utilize the talents of older individuals and strict enforcement of age discrimination regulations. In situations in which younger people supervise older workers, AARP suggests a frank discussion and open communication between the two. It also suggests that one way in which younger people may overcome problems is to utilize the older employee's expertise. For instance, if the older person has a background in teaching, the younger person could ask for some input on a company training program.

What's the bottom line on all this? Brush up on marketing your company to older workers, rethink your current policies and re-examine your beliefs about mature employees—because HR professionals are going to need the skills to work with older people. "In the next 15 to 20 years, one out of every four employees is going to be over the age of 55. It means a whole new workplace for us, with a whole new set of needs. It's going to be a very big issue," says Fyock.

So open your doors to these workers. Invite them to the table. You can't afford to keep them on the fringes any longer.

Charlene Marmer Solomon is a contributing editor at PERSONNEL JOURNAL.

How To Assist Senior Workers

- **Understand older workers—who they are and what they want**
- **Review retirement policies and flexible work options. Consider restructuring jobs to allow for part-time, flextime, phased retirement**
- **Look at attitudes of supervisors and younger workers toward older employees**
- **Check if your recruitment techniques are reaching seniors**
- **Examine benefits packages. Do they fairly reward and motivate?**
- **Examine training techniques. Presentation styles and tools needed may be different**
- **See if your retirement and pre-retirement policies mesh with corporate goals and employees' needs.**

Based on ideas from Catherine D. Fyock's book, "America's Work Force is Coming of Age" and Helen Dennis' book, "Fourteen Steps in Managing an Aging Work Force."

Article 16

Attracting the Right Employees— and Keeping Them

Employers are experimenting with everything from pre-employment tests to random acts of kindness to discover the tie that binds.

Gillian Flynn

Gillian Flynn is an assistant editor at PERSONNEL JOURNAL.

Every organization has its star employees. They may be the folks sitting in the senior ranks at headquarters. Or they could be the high-potential new kids on the block. But they all have something in common: The ability to continually outperform their peers, the determination to constantly strive for improvement and the creativity to reinvent their job tasks.

Unfortunately, they may lack a quality just as important to your business: company loyalty. In these days of downsizing, belt tightening, and limited advancement openings, your best and brightest could be turning a roving eye to other opportunities. Think it won't happen to you? Think again. Because when businesses began to hack away at the employer-employee contract, they may have cut some of their losses, but they also severed a work-force mindset: Today's employees put their own welfare before their company's, and if that means packing up and heading somewhere else, then so be it.

With limited resources and a finite supply of talent, companies must pay extra attention to getting the right employees—and keeping them.

Smart companies recruit employees they can retain. Dallas-based Texas Instruments was hiring more than 3,000 college graduates each year back in 1984. One decade and several downsizings later, the company extends only about 200 job offers to college grads each year. With this limited recruitment effort, retention depends on getting the right people in the right job in the first place. "The requirement has changed," says Dan McMurtrey, manager of placement services with TI's corporate HR department. "It's not: hire 200 good students. It's hire 200 superb students."

Unfortunately, not too long ago, Texas Instruments' recruitment strategy wasn't reaching the superb students. The company was visiting a limited number of campuses and administering an assessment test battery that took more than three hours for students to complete. "We were taking an awful lot of flack in working with campuses. Students didn't like it, deans didn't like it. This battery was worse than any final exam these students would take," says David Current, manager for TI corporate university relations.

That way of testing created a twofold problem. First, it restricted the number of students that TI could reach; second, it didn't give candidates much of a feel for what TI was like as a company, and it certainly didn't promote the company's best attributes. Current decided that for successful recruitment, TI would need a tool that would assess the student's fit with the company while serving as an introduction to Texas Instruments. But, in order to engage a large number of students in the first place, it also had to benefit the candidates. Says McMurtrey: "We said 'How do we package some sort of approach so that the student will want an assessment test?' It seemed ludicrous at the time, but we think we've done that."

The result was "Engineer Your Career," a tool that assesses candidates both professionally and personally for their fit with TI while introducing the student to the company's culture—and providing career planning information. The kit, designed by Personnel Decisions Inc., contains a disk which opens up a brochure that tells the student a little bit about TI— its products, its history, its values.

Following the introduction is a self-selection tool. "This gives the student an opportunity to basically open the doors of Texas Instruments, look inside and see what our environment is," explains Current. In the self-assessment, candidates respond to 32 questions about work preferences, such as work environment, working conditions and relationships. In answering, they also may respond to what degree they agree or disagree. For instance, one question asks how the candidate feels about smoking in the office, and the student can reply with a response from strong agreement to strong disagreement. At the end of this section, the computer displays a bar-like code to show the candidate's relative compatibility with the company. If there's a potential problem, it informs the student of this. So in the case of smoking in the office, if the student responded that he or she felt strongly in favor, the computer would signal that TI has a non-smoking environment, which may be an issue for the student. It also highlights strong matches. By being honest and open about TI's work environment and expectations, the company effectively allows a job candi-

> **By having students apply for jobs on disk, we can reach a wide range of universities. We can find the applicants who are the best, who fit the best.**

date "inside" the company, so the applicant can make an informed choice rather than finding out too late that the situation won't work.

Following this section is a built-in resume writer for the student to complete, followed by job opportunities that are currently available at TI. Because the job listings are on disks, TI can update them each time it issues a new disk. A "career mapper" section gives TI further information about a candidate's skills and interests to better match the student with openings.

All students who complete the "Engineer Your Career" program and mail it to TI receive direct feedback on their fit—as well as a manual that informs students on getting started in the work force. "We think we've packaged assessment and product advertising in such a way that it's desirable even if the individual doesn't want to come to TI," says McMurtrey. "It's a useful, initial graduating-senior self-help kit."

TI is currently introducing the disks to campuses where it does not usually recruit, and is awaiting the results. McMurtrey predicts that the Engineer Your Career program will benefit recruiters on three levels. First, TI may use the disks to prescreen candidates in deciding which students they want to interview when visiting campuses. Second, TI can use the personality assessment to screen out individuals who just wouldn't fit, no matter how well-qualified they are. For instance, the company is evolving toward self-directed work teams, so a person's inability to be a team player would definitely weigh against him or her. "Our decision to select an individual certainly won't be based just on skills; it will be biased heavily toward such things as interpersonal relationships," explains McMurtrey.

Finally, by providing an honest view of TI values and culture, students go into the process with open eyes. Says McMurtrey: "Many may decide to self-select out, and that's good. It's going to increase the quality of the face-to-face interviews that we do have on campus."

Current sees nothing but benefits from the new process: "This disk is an important tool. We can't continue to use the same apparatus to mount a campaign at a wide range of universities. It's cost prohibitive. With this approach, you can effectively reach every campus in the nation. This will allow us to find the ones who are the best, who fit the best, and allow us to engage those individuals."

Another company using testing in its recruitment process is ServiceMaster. The Downers Grove, Illinois-based company, which employs people for pest control, lawn treatment, and cleaning services, knows that to run a successful business, each of its 36,000 employees must have certain work ethics.

For one thing, these employees, who often work at people's houses and businesses unattended, must be trustworthy and responsible. "Our first objective is to keep risky employees out of the organization," says Bill Selkirk, senior administrator of loss control, claims and safety management. "We believe that every applicant is a potential success or a potential loss. We want to make sure that we're on the potential win side of the picture."

Pre-employment testing plays a major part of ensuring retention. Screening out those who will not succeed with the company saves it time and money. ServiceMaster's test screens for seven risk factors not wanted in the organization. These are:

- Theft
- Drug Use
- Violence
- Poor customer relations

16. Attracting the Right Employees

- Poor work values
- Unsatisfactory cognitive skills
- Unsafe work habits.

The test, developed by London House, doesn't just cover whether a worker has engaged in certain activities in the past, but whether the candidate has a propensity toward certain behavior or even tolerance of it. For instance, to keep drug users out of the company, ServiceMaster goes beyond physical testing to find candidates' psychological viewpoints. "Alcohol or drugs are only tested for during a short window of time in a person's application process," says Selkirk. "We look at a person's attitude toward alcohol or drugs. If they are tolerant of it in the workplace, we don't want them. This doesn't mean that they take drugs or alcohol, it just means that they have that propensity."

Attitude toward safety was another important issue in employee retention. Because 90% of workplace injuries are due to people's behaviors and attitudes, rather than any sort of malfunction, screening out candidates who ignore safety considerations is a must. And it worked: After the test was in place, ServiceMaster enjoyed a 44% reduction of injuries in those employees hired by testing.

Just as important, the test enabled ServiceMaster to extend employment invitations to only those employees who indicated that they would stay with the company for a substantial amount of time. This is significant, because ServiceMaster is in an industry that traditionally has trouble with retention. "Being a housekeeper is not exactly most people's ultimate goal in life," says Selkirk. "So for many, many people it's a stepping stone. We really want to control that. We want people who want to be in a service-minded career, who are not ashamed of being a housekeeper or a maintenance mechanic or a bug sprayer. We want people who have a high level of service-mindedness and low turnover propensity, who will give their best no matter what job they have in life." The testing has helped screen out these job hoppers: The company went from turnover rates of about 180% a year down to about 14% after testing.

First impressions can make or break a relationship. Every good salesperson knows the customer makes a decision to buy sooner rather than later. Likewise, employee loyalty needs to be cemented in a new hire's early days. With a good initiation, the company can continue to build employee loyalty from the beginning. With a shaky introduction, the company must backpedal to right its wrongs before it can proceed. Corning Inc. has made a strong commitment to getting employees off on the right foot. After implementing an orientation program in 1983, the Corning, New York-based company watched retention rates rise 25% among employees who underwent orientation.

So important is a smooth introduction to Corning that orientation is the first thing an employee does. "They don't even report to their place of work the first day," says Susan Richter, senior education consultant. Instead, orientation classes are available each Monday, with only two new hires necessary to form a class.

On the first day of orientation, new hires are steeped in the Corning culture. They learn about its history, heritage, values and the various positions within the company. On the second half of the day, they take care of some business like signing up for benefits and receiving their security badges.

The new hire also receives a new-employee workbook, which covers each of the seven learning modules that new employees will go through, along with questions and summaries of each section. Richter says that the workbook gives orientation a sense of validity—it seems like a carefully thought-out program rather than a series of time-consuming lectures. "It's designed to let employees know what is going to happen throughout the orientation process—and the fact that it is indeed a process. It's not something you just go through, sit there and be done with it."

Corning then waits six weeks before finishing the remaining five modules of orientation. This time period allows the new employees to become more familiar with the company as well as to spend some time learning about their new division. At the end of the six weeks, all those hired within a six to eight-week time period attend a two-day orientation session. They begin the day learning about Corning's performance development and review process—what to expect and how to prepare for it.

Because diversity is high among Corning's values, new employees also attend a module called Valuing the Individual. Here, employees break into three groups and discuss the advantages and disadvantages of being a white male, a woman and a minority at Corning. Richter says this module is particularly important in opening the diversity discussion among new hires and sending a signal that Corning values diversity. "It's a real eye-opener for some people who think that there are no disadvantages to being a white male. Well there are. Or those who think there are only disadvantages to being a woman. Well that's not true, there are advantages to being a

> **New employees decide within the first six or eight weeks whether they're going to stay at a company. Orientation gives people the sense of belonging.**

woman at Corning as well," says Richter.

The second day begins with teaching new employees how to read parts of the annual report so that they understand what it means to them as an individual and how their actions effect the company. Speakers introduce such simple ideas as encouraging doublesided copying to save paper and discouraging first-class flying on business trips. This is important, because spending habits at an employee's former company could be very different from what's accepted at Corning. This makes it clear from the start what is OK and what is not.

Because new employees may feel hesitant about using the company's resources at the beginning, a person from the Employee Assistance Program tries to encourage the program's use. Says Richter: "It really makes everyone as an employee feel that if they're just having a really rotten day, and they want someone to talk to, these people are here to listen. You don't have to have a drug problem or be in bankruptcy or have marital problems. They really eliminate some of the myths that are there."

Finally, members of Corning's research and development, and engineering groups present some of their projects. "It really is a big show and tell," says Richter.

"They set up a table full of products. For some people this may be the only time they see some of the end products that Corning sells. A lot of people are familiar with the cup or plate that Corning sells, but they're not familiar with headlamps or TV tubes or cellular ceramics." Again, it's a matter of making the employee feel familiar with the company.

Richter says that although orientation is currently only for salaried employees, Corning is looking into shaping up its non-salaried employee orientation as well. She says that Corning's orientation plays a major role in employee retention. It provides new employees with a lot of contacts within the company, and it ensures that they have a smooth move into the culture. "Employees decide when they join a new company within the first six or eight weeks whether they're going to stay at that company. That first impression is such a lasting impression, which is why we try to get the orientation done in that time frame. It gives people the sense of belonging and being valued and important. We try to capitalize on that."

A little attention goes a long way. Turnover doesn't always happen right away. Most employees want to make their situation work, and leave only when they feel they have no other choice. The Big Six accounting firm Deloitte & Touche discovered a major problem of this sort two years ago: It was losing its women employees.

It wasn't that the Wilton, Connecticut-based company was hiring unevenly; in fact, for the past 10 years, approximately 50% of its new hires have been women and because it takes about 10 years to become a partner, the firm was expecting to see an increase in the number of women coming up the pipeline for candidacy to partnership. Instead it was seeing a decline. "That concerned us from one primary standpoint," says Jim Wall, national director of HR. "We were having a talent drain of capable women. We had to do something about it."

Deloitte & Touche took action. It launched a Task Force on the Retention and Advancement of Women to find the problem and fix it. It retained the services of such groups as Catalyst, the Charles Rogers Group and Work/Family Directions. It also interviewed women at all

16. Attracting the Right Employees

levels of the company, as well as women who had left the firm.

What they discovered were three main areas of complaint. Although work-life balance did play a part, it was really the work environment and what they felt was limited advancement opportunity that had women up in arms. They felt they were being left out of both informal networking and mentoring systems. Fixing this would be a challenge, because the exclusion was subconscious rather than deliberate. "In a male-dominated business society, men network, and often do so—I don't believe intentionally—but often at the exclusion of women," admits Wall. "Informal mentoring systems within the firm worked better for men. Men tended to sponsor other men. Mentoring occurred as a more natural process for men than it did for women."

To solve this problem, Deloitte & Touche knew it could do nothing less than retool the work environment itself. Beginning in early 1993, it made some changes. One such change was a renewed commitment to flexible work arrangements, such as reduced workload and flextime. The firm also developed plans for company-sponsored networking and formal career planning for women. Also, the firm's 5,000 partners, senior managers and managers attended two-day workshops concerning "Men and Women As Colleagues," at a price to Deloitte & Touche of about $3 million.

The result? Retention of women at all levels has risen, and for the first time in the history of the firm, turnover rates for senior managers—the last position before partnership—have been lower for women than men. Deloitte & Touche is finding that retaining talented women also attracts talented women: It now has the greatest number of female employees in the Big Six. Says Wall: "The external recognition in the marketplace is helping us retain people. It's helping us develop our own business. It's helping us tremendously in recruiting. The business reasons for doing this are coming home very quickly."

But it's not just women who need a commitment from their employer. All employees want recognition. All employees want to feel their employer takes an interest in their career. And today that desire for attention is elevating from a plea to a demand. "There's been a change in the employer-employee contract," says Lincoln Norton, CEO and chairman of HRSoft, Inc., which produces HR planning software systems. "Retention today is more about what's in it for the employee. Vertical growth in a downsizing environment doesn't happen. So when you're down to that, the employee has to say, these are the reasons I work for this company; I'm learning, I'm growing, I'm evolving."

Kansas City, Missouri-based Hallmark works hard to identify its high-potential employees early on to ensure they are challenged and kept interested. It's a major part of the company's culture for senior managers to identify these employees, and take them under their wings, nurturing them into the company. "It ranges from inviting them onto special project teams or planning sessions or finding reasons for them to make presentations at higher-level staff meetings to senior execs," says Dave Pylipow, director of employee relations.

Pylipow estimates that the senior-level execs at Hallmark could name right off the top of their heads the 15 most important players in their divisions for the long-term. "Once they identify a high-potential, they begin to figure out 'How do I keep that person plugged in?'" says Pylipow. "Most of those folks just crave the opportunity to show you what they can do, and respond well when they know they're being recognized." Hallmark has indeed tapped an important part of employee retention. In a Robert Half survey of 150 executives, 34% said that it was lack of praise or recognition that most often caused employees to leave a company.

On top of providing this sought-after attention, Hallmark has a number of other initiatives to direct its employees toward a future with the company. For instance, Hallmark's profit-sharing system provides larger chunks of money to employees the more years they rack up.

We were having a talent drain of capable women. The informal mentoring and networking systems within the firm worked better for men than women.

Also, to demonstrate the value it places on long-term employees, the more seniority a worker has, the more steps must be taken for any termination proceedings. Wall himself must sign off on any termination for employees at Hallmark two to four years. If an employee has been with the company five years, it takes two vice presidents to approve termination. "Employees here know they're going to be treated fairly," says Wall. "It doesn't mean we don't fire people, because we do, but anybody who does lose their job has had a very thorough review of their case." This process not only emphasizes the importance of tenure, it also provides employees with a sense of security and the freedom to share thoughts or to disagree with superiors without worrying about it coming back to haunt them.

Finally, Hallmark celebrates seniority by recognizing employee anniversaries. In particular, the 25th anniversary brings a big celebration, with an appearance by the chairman of Hallmark if possible. Little gestures like recognition and praise have reaped big rewards for Hallmark—it has a turnover of only 5-1/2%—and 3,000 employees, some now retired, have made it to the 25-year mark with the company. "Folks tend to stick around for quite a while, so we think we're doing something right," says Pylipow.

With employees quickly becoming business's greatest asset, employee retention must become a company's highest priority. It's not enough to hope employees will stay. HR must give them the reasons to stay.

CATCH THE WAVE AS HR GOES ONLINE

Cyberspace offers new frontiers in recruiting, networking and information gathering. In fact, going online is changing the HR function at companies such as Cisco Systems, Hydro Quebec and Lotus Development.

Samuel Greengard

It's just another day on the Internet. Inside the offices of Hydro Quebec, a large Canadian utility, Michel Mantha is surfing his way around the world, and he's now looking for the next great wave. Sitting in front of his computer, the HR research adviser is browsing the Internet's World Wide Web and using its sophisticated hypertext links and graphics to boldly go where HR has never gone before. With the click of a mouse button, he's inside the U.S. government's server in Washington, D.C., examining a schedule of upcoming HR conferences. Then, instantly, he's off to Cornell University in New York, looking at the latest reports issued by the Glass Ceiling Commission. A few minutes later, he's made a lightning-fast pilgrimage to The Quality Wave, an index of sites containing information on TQM, educational programs and business theories.

Every time Mantha sees something that piques his interest, he simply clicks on a highlighted word or graphic image—including high-resolution photographs—to obtain more information. The text pours onto his computer's screen, at which point it can be printed or saved for future reference. And if it so happens that he's jumping to another Web site, the system transports him there at warp speed—efficiently and invisibly, regardless of whether the computer is located in Boston or Bombay. Of course, the World Wide Web is just one portion of the Internet. He also uses the Internet for *E-mail* and to subscribe to *newsgroups* that keep him informed on the latest industry buzz (see "What's All This Talk about Gophers? The Lowdown on Online Lingo," for definitions of italicized terms). "It's a remarkable way to do research," he states. "It's a revolutionary step forward."

Cyberspace. It's certainly not the final frontier, but it's fast becoming an important part of the corporate arsenal—and psyche. This international network of computers is opening new doors and new opportunities for human resources professionals who have the equipment and the mindset to venture into the online arena. Today, a growing wave of HR managers are going online to recruit personnel, conduct research using electronic data bases, send E-mail, and engage in valuable networking and discussions. Using the Internet—which connects upwards of 28 million people and 3.2 million host computers in 70 countries—as well as commercial services such as CompuServe, Prodigy and America Online, these pioneers are venturing into a revolutionary new world where data and information flow at the speed of light.

"It's changing the way people work and think," says Stephen Gibson, publisher of *Online Sources For Human Resources*, an interactive online guide and associated monthly newsletter that offer HR cybernauts tips and information on how to better use the Internet. Adds Michael Rowe, marketing director for E-Span, an online job-placement service that represents dozens of major corporations: "The online world represents a tremendous opportunity for HR. It's one of the most powerful tools one can have at his or her disposal. Every day, more and more people realize just how powerful this medium is. They're getting beyond the novelty and hype and discovering that it offers solutions to real problems."

But all the gain doesn't come without a good deal of pain. Taking the plunge into the online world can be difficult, confusing and time consuming. Not only must one decide what type of service or provider to use, it's also necessary to learn how online systems work and how one can use them to achieve results. That often translates into learning how to use new software and understanding the finer points of online etiquette. It also means reengineering the way processes work within HR, or even adopting an entirely different way of thinking. And, as with any new medium, things don't always work as billed. Many online products and services aren't as useful as their promoters might like you to think.

Yet, those who have embraced the online world to recruit, research and trade information insist it's a giant step forward. As Tim Johnston, manager of university relations for Advanced Micro Devices (AMD) explains: "The entire world is at your fingertips."

The Internet and online services offer HR a wealth of opportunities. Venturing online isn't a particularly complex task in itself. At the most basic level, a computer, a *modem* and the right kind of software can open the door to the vast world of cyberspace. Those on a network at a major company often can wade into the Internet via a direct connection. Using a program designed for today's graphical interfaces, such as Windows or the Macintosh, it's possible to position a cursor on text, icon or graphical image, click the mouse, and travel from one topic, forum or site to another. Interactive and flexible, it allows an end user to gather data—or provide it—quickly and effortlessly. And, depending on the nature of the service, it's possible to connect with others who share similar interests. You might call it the realization of Marshall McLuhan's Global Village.

And that's fundamentally changing the workplace of the 1990s. Although many of those who subscribe to online services use them for reading news, tracking stocks, exchanging gossip, playing games and pursuing interests and hobbies, the online world increasingly is oriented toward business. Just browse the Internet's World Wide Web, an environment that offers dazzling graphics to complement an almost endless stream of text, and it's clear that a growing number of companies are viewing the medium as a way to promote themselves and their products. The list includes organizations as diverse as AT&T, Honeywell, IBM, Eastman Kodak, Microsoft, Ford Motor, Pizza Hut and Ernst & Young.

But the Web isn't strictly a marketing tool for Big Business. In the HR arena, sites such as Career Mosaic, Job Web and the Monster Board offer employer profiles, job openings, career information and human resources forums. In addition, there are long lists of consultants and services peddling their wares and offering their expertise on everything from training to career development. There also are govern-

Traveling the Infobahn: What You Need To Go Online

Despite the complexity of today's computers and the seemingly arcane language that defines the Internet, venturing online isn't particularly difficult—especially for those using a Macintosh or a PC with the popular Windows operating system. Here's what it takes:

You need a way to access the online world: A freeway on-ramp of sorts. If you already have a computer at your desk, that's a good start. To go online, you will either need a direct connection via an existing network or a modem to dial into the Internet. A direct connection is extremely fast, but it's usually limited to large companies that can afford the expensive hardware. If your company can provide this capability, it's best to discuss it with someone in information systems. If you will be accessing the Internet via a modem, try to use at least a 14.4k *bps* device, preferably a 28.8k bps. Transferring huge amounts of data and graphics takes time—particularly when the Internet encounters heavy use during peak hours. A faster modem also can reduce costly online time when accessing commercial services such as CompuServe (800/848-8990), America Online (800/827-6364), Prodigy (800/776-3552), GEnie (800/638-9636) and e-World (800/775-4556). It allows you to download files in less time.

Entering cyberspace is like learning to drive—you have to know how your vehicle operates. If you're interested in using a commercial online service, you simply need to load the appropriate software into your computer, enter a password and a local telephone access number, and log in. If it's a Windows- or Macintosh-based version, such as WinCim or MacCim on CompuServe, the program will likely self-install and take you through the necessary steps to get online. From there, it's a simple point-and-click process. Costs vary, but a minimum of $8 to $10 per month is the norm for basic access. If you wish to have direct Internet access, which is free of charge, you still need to have a service provider, such as Netcom (800/501-8649) or Delphi (800/544-4005). At present, the only major commercial online service with full access to the World Wide Web is Prodigy, although AOL and CompuServe will soon follow suit (they now offer access to FTP and *Gopher* capabilities). Commercial services generally charge $10 to $25 per month for a basic level of service, which often includes several free hours.

You need a vehicle to enter the info superhighway. It's possible to access many online services using a basic telecommunications program or the Terminal program that's built into Windows. But unless you're a propeller head who thrives on typing arcane commands into a computer and dealing with the complexities of cyberspace, it's best to use software designed specifically for the task. For the Internet, you will need a special program that manages *TCP/IP* connections. In Windows, it's called *Winsock*, and more than a dozen firms offer a version of it. Internet providers often make it available as part of a package of software that includes several other programs, including Eudora (E-mail), Ewan (Telnet), Archie and Veronica (Gopherspace) and Mosaic or Netscape (World Wide Web). Of course, commercial services are happy to provide you with copies of their E-mail programs—which makes the service more appealing for you, and more profitable for them.

Maneuvering the highway may require a map. Once you're online, you need the right tools. Otherwise, it's a little like trying to see the sites of Paris on foot and without a map—you will occasionally bump into something interesting, but you will also spend a great deal of time staring at sidewalks and fire hydrants. Indeed, it's best to learn how to use online directories, reference guides, and online search features. For example, on the Internet, a service called Yahoo (developed by Stanford University) offers a sophisticated indexing system that can lead you to tens of thousands of sites. WebCrawler and InfoSeek are a couple of others. And don't neglect a good book, such as *Zen and the Art of the Internet* by Brendan P. Kehoe, *Navigating the Internet* by Mark Gibbs and Richard Smith or *The Internet Yellow Pages* by Harlan Hahn and Rick Stout. You may still get lost every now and then, but in the end you'll find the routes that get you where you want to go.

—*SG*

2. MEETING HUMAN RESOURCE REQUIREMENTS: Information Systems

ment sites, including OSHA, where an HR practitioner can stay informed on current regulations, directives and even scan OSHA notices in the Federal Register. It's possible to jump from one subject or service to another in a matter of seconds—by simply clicking a mouse button. Meanwhile, other portions of the Internet—such as *FTP*, *Usenet* and *Telnet*—offer a mind-boggling array of additional resources. You can access *mailing lists* for your specific interests, along with newsletters, academic studies and an array of background materials.

The breadth of the material truly is astounding, especially if you consider that the Internet is only one piece of the online puzzle. Commercial services such as CompuServe, Prodigy and America Online also feature career centers, companies promoting goods and services, and forums for discussing a wide range of HR-related topics. They're easy to access and relatively inexpensive. And those who wade online agree that these services are becoming more powerful all the time. Today's generation of Windows and Macintosh software provides an easy way to navigate online quickly and seamlessly. DOS and UNIX users also can take advantage of proprietary software designed to enhance and simplify the process.

Cyberspace is a new recruitment source. Not surprisingly, many within the HR field are beginning to take notice of the vast online universe. And recruiting is perhaps the hottest area of all. Step inside the Menlo Park, California, headquarters of Cisco Systems, a fast-growing, internetworking firm, and you're likely to see the HR department of the future. Almost all open positions are posted on the Internet—on the firm's own World Wide Web *homepage* and on various career services. Net browsers can view as many as 400 ads at any given time.

And, apparently, a lot of people like the idea of looking for work online. The company receives as many as 700 resumes electronically every month—approximately 30% of the total it receives overall. Some months the figure has reached 50%. All resumes automatically are routed into a Resumix system, where they can be recalled at a moment's notice—whether at the Bay Area headquarters or across the country at the firm's Boston or Raleigh sites.

"Company recruiters no longer have to spend their time scouring resumes to find the appropriate candidate; they simply can fill the position," says Barbara Beck, vice president of human resources. "Going online has provided us with a tremendous boost in productivity. It's facilitating communication, and it's making it easier for everyone to use HR services. It allows us to add maximum value. We're working very hard to stay ahead of the technology curve and have an extremely sophisticated human resources organization."

Indeed, Cisco's Web site, besides displaying the job listings, contains information about the company's products, its financial data, its culture and history. "And that saves a lot of time for HR, which no longer has to field as many inquiries," Beck says.

Another HR person who finds online recruiting particularly appealing is Elaine Hart, manager of recruitment for Staples, the nation's third largest discount office-products superstore chain. In March, the Framington, Massachusetts-based company joined the Monster Board, a career center and job-placement service on the Internet's World Wide Web. Hart typically posts listings within Staples' homepage; when job seekers browse through, they're able to click on an icon to go to the company, and then search job openings by region, category and other parameters. They're also able to get information on the company itself.

"It's a way to demonstrate that the company is on the leading edge of technology, and it's a way to make the entire recruiting process more efficient," says Hart. Indeed, when an applicant responds to a posting, the E-mail message is routed directly to Hart's computer. A process that can take weeks using traditional methods—newspapers, trade ads and paper-based resumes—now can take only hours. That allows Staples to find qualified applicants far more quickly. In addition, electronic postings create greater flexibility. Hart can modify or remove an ad if it isn't working or if a position is filled.

Recruiting online saves time, reduces the amount of paper Hart must handle and lowers administrative costs. But, more importantly, venturing online allows the company to reach an expanded audience. Already, she's receiving as many as a half dozen electronic resumes and applications a day. And virtually all of those who respond to the online ads tend to be highly educated, well trained and perfectly comfortable with computers and online services—a set of skills that's becoming crucial in the 1990s. Of course, many technical specialists—particularly in computer hardware, software and networking—gravitate to online forums, making the medium a particularly fertile area for mining prospects.

This is true for college recruiting as well. Just ask Johnston. Recruiting from college campuses always has been grueling for him. Every time the manager of university relations sets up a job-fair booth, it takes hours to organize the display and get all the brochures and paperwork in order. Then there's the arduous task of conducting one interview after another—a dozen or more in a single day isn't unusual. There's travel time, hotel stays and a steady crush of paperwork to follow up on. By the time he gets back to his office in Sunnyvale, California, he's typically buried in work. "It isn't especially cost effective or time effective to hit the road," says Johnston, "but it has been a necessity."

Johnston is hoping to change all that. Just more than a year ago, AMD began designing an alternative to the traditional recruiting model. Although the firm continues to seek young talent by participating in more than 30 job fairs each year, it also has ventured into the far reaches of cyberspace. The $1.6 billion corporation, which produces computer microprocessors and other high-tech devices, has begun recruiting online.

Using the Internet's World Wide Web, AMD lists information about the company, the culture, its officers, its compensation and benefits, and other areas of interest to job seekers. If an individual is interested in one of the positions listed, he or she can apply directly from his or her computer. And when AMD needs a specific position filled, it broadcasts the news to college job-placement offices and key professors all across the country via electronic mail.

"We have a network in place that allows us to automate recruiting and reach the right people," Johnston says. "It's redefining the entire process. Electronic media never will replace human interaction, but it's clearly going to play a key role in the way AMD and other companies handle HR-related tasks. It's effective, it's efficient, and it saves time and money. Online capabilities allow a greater level of sophistication, and that is increasingly important as everyone battles for a competitive edge."

That's a concept that's well understood at Lotus Development, the Cambridge, Massachusetts-based software giant. It posts ads for approximately 20 positions a year online, but the number is increasing rapidly. "We advertise through all avenues," says Christine Leonardo, director of strategy and programs in the human resources department. "We use Internet job postings and traditional newspaper and magazine ads, as well as recruiting at conferences. It's important to have a balanced approach. But the dramatic increase in the number of people online, especially on the Internet, is making electronic recruiting more attractive all the time. The Internet is an outstanding tool."

One of the big advantages to advertising positions online, Leonardo points out, is that it eliminates many of the space constraints of advertising in a newspaper. Most companies that sell online space don't severely limit the length of the text. And if a company sets up its own site on the World Wide Web, or rents space on the Monster Board or a similar service, it can provide as much information as necessary about the company, culture, benefits and any open positions. "You put an ad in a major newspaper and wind up spending a fortune without saying much of anything," she says.

Recruiting online requires instituting new procedures. When Lotus decided it would go online, it turned to an employment service called E-Span—a four-year-old Indianapolis company that has become a leader in the emerging world of online employment services. Leonardo must simply write the ad and send it to E-Span along with instructions on how to categorize it, and the firm posts it in its job libraries for as long as four weeks. E-Span also provides expertise on how to use the online world more effectively. Because it has a presence on CompuServe, America Online, GEnie and the World Wide Web, more than 10,000 job seekers access E-Span's Interactive Employment Network every day. Leonardo sees it as a winning proposition. "Many of these are highly qualified people you wouldn't otherwise connect with," she says.

It's an approach that appeals to growing numbers of recruiting specialists. Rowe says that the number of ads the agency posts now runs between 500 and 600 a week, and has increased tenfold during the last 18 months. "It's a tremendous opportunity to capitalize on technology and use it to HR's advantage," Rowe says. "Paper-based systems aren't going to go away any time soon. There's still going to be a demand for newspaper and trade ads. But this certainly fits into the changing corporate paradigm."

A paradigm that Lotus' Leonardo knows well. Approximately 30 electronic resumes land in her computer every week—and the number continues to grow. After reviewing a resume at her PC, she passes it on to an assistant, who imports it—along with those received by fax and through the mail (the latter are scanned in)—into a resume-tracking program. Then, her department can use key word searches to find qualified applicants in a matter of seconds. It's efficient enough that Leonardo hopes to increase the number of resumes that enter the system electronically in the months and years ahead. That could eliminate extra administrative personnel, including temporary help during peak periods.

"Online recruiting has many advantages," states James C. Gonyea, author of the *Online Job Search Companion* and president of Gonyea and Associates, an online career service headquartered in New Port Richey, Florida. "You literally can create a job listing and post it within minutes. You have access to millions of people, and it's generally less expensive than conventional methods, which require a greater support structure. Online systems require less clerical staff and less paperwork." He believes, too, that image enters into the equation. "If you're looking for people with a high level of skill—particularly in technical fields—recruiting online shows that you're on the leading edge."

Indeed, those who conduct online recruiting say that although the typical ad doesn't elicit the same level of response as an advertisement in a newspaper because far fewer people surf online channels than read newspapers, in most cases, the response is more focused—and the level of candidates often is higher. "You often find people who are very adept and knowledgeable," says AMD's Johnston. (Before you dive headfirst into the Internet, however, you may want to give it some more thought.)

But recruiting online is a somewhat different ball game than posting ads in a newspaper or a trade publication. Gonyea points out that it's necessary when writing an ad to go online to make sure that the wording and terminology elicit the desired response. Because resumes must be entered into a searchable data base, key words are crucial. "If you're interested in hiring an administrative assistant, but the position might also be referred to as a secretary, you want to make sure that both words are contained in the ad," he says. "Otherwise, a highly qualified person searching for the word *secretary* online might miss the ad when they conduct a search." And the same goes for anyone searching the data base within the company. "Without strong indexing, you aren't going to pull a list of all the qualified candidates," he warns.

Gonyea also suggests that firms posting ads online should have the capability to receive resumes and inquiries via E-mail. "The last thing people want to do if they're at their computers and they see a listing they're interested in, is print their resume and mail it or fax it. When E-Mail capability is missing, it's an indication that the employer isn't really confident or fully conversant in the technology. It can be perceived as a problem. If a company opts to recruit online, it should put all the pieces in place to do it right."

Recruiting online is easy—but it can cost you. The cost of establishing an online presence for recruiting purposes can vary greatly. The least expensive option is simply listing an open job in a professional online forum and an Internet newsgroup. That costs nothing, and thousands of such listings are visible on any day of the week. Turning to an outside agency such as Gonyea and Associates and E-Span, which can ensure that millions of users are exposed to the ads, can

2. MEETING HUMAN RESOURCE REQUIREMENTS: Information Systems

cost from $75 an ad to $3,000 or $4,000 a year for unlimited advertising. A few firms charge as much as $10,000 a year. A company that chooses to establish a homepage on the Web's Career Mosaic or Monster Board will likely fork over anywhere from $1,000 to $10,000. And organizations intent on setting up their own Web site can spend considerably more. Although a Sun Microsystems or Hewlett-Packard workstation sitting on a desktop can become a server on the Web—thus supplying text and graphics to others on the Internet—it's far more challenging to develop an eye-catching interface and link data effectively. As a result, the expertise of an outside consultant or agency often is required.

Still, accessing online services is simple. Venture into E-Span's CompuServe site, and you're greeted with a main menu that lists various tools: an introduction to the service; What's Happening at E-Span; Resume Rules; Successful Interviewing; Networking; Tips for Searching E-Span; and direct access to E-Span's Job Search data base. By clicking with your mouse on the topic of interest, you're led through various menus—accessing information along the way. Once you've entered the actual job data base, it's possible to browse ads by subject—marketing, computer programming, education and media are just a few of the categories included—as well as by region. A typical ad offers a page of information about the open position, as well as the company or organization. In most cases, an E-mail address complements telephone and fax numbers, and addresses.

Navigating the World Wide Web isn't any more difficult. With software such as Netscape or Mosaic and powerful online indexes such as Yahoo, it's possible to find HR-related sites and then click through menus and hypertext links to find desired listings. In addition, many companies—including AMD, Amdahl, Intuit, McCaw Cellular, General Electric and Schlumberger—offer their own listings within larger sites that provide information on products, services, investor relations and an array of corporate matters. In most cases, it's possible to contact the HR department directly from the Web site.

What's allowing HR professionals at these firms to move so seamlessly into online publishing? Gibson credits the emergence of *HTML (Hypertext Markup Language)*, a typesetting language that has become the standard for documents on the Internet. Just by executing a simple command, it's possible to convert a Microsoft Word or Novell WordPerfect document into an ASCII format that harnesses the Web's hypertext and graphics capabilities. No sophisticated programming needed, no lengthy conversions with expensive software.

"The landscape is changing," says Gonyea. "The old world order of storing resumes in filing cabinets is disappearing. Electronic methods of collecting, storing and recalling resumes and employment data are playing an increasingly significant role. Many companies are beginning to realize that they must complement conventional approaches with an online presence. Otherwise, they're likely to miss an important segment of the job market. And, as time passes, it's going to become a standard way for all companies to do business."

HR professionals are going online to network and gather information. Hunting job candidates in cyberspace is only one part of the overall picture. As HR professionals become more knowledgeable—and comfortable—with the technology, they're venturing into other online areas. Some of the most popular uses for the Internet and commercial online services are professional forums, *bulletin board systems (BBSs)* and discussion groups. In most cases, HR professionals freely share information on topics as diverse as training and development, HRMS, payroll and benefits, and legal requirements. By posting a question in the appropriate location, it's possible to have responses in a matter of hours rather than days or weeks. Often, illuminating discussions develop.

"It's a powerful medium for networking and trading information," says Gibson. "In many respects, it's like having a workshop or conference available any time of the day or night. Instead of making 10 or 15 telephone calls to colleagues to discuss an issue, or searching through reference materials to get the latest information on a hot topic, it's possible to have it at your fingertips with almost no effort at all. It's like opening a window to a world you never knew existed."

Mantha knows just how powerful the medium can be. The HR research adviser spends an hour or more logged onto the Internet daily. Responsible for researching a variety of HR subjects, including TQM and business process reengineering, he checks more than half a dozen different bulletin boards, where he exchanges news and information with colleagues from all over the world. In addition, he subscribes to more than half a dozen electronic mailing lists, including Cornell University's highly respected HRNet, and reads other newsgroups by accessing a part of the Internet known as Telnet. The newsgroups include discussions and information on topics as diverse as best practices and performance management.

"It's enabling me to do things I wouldn't otherwise be capable of doing," remarks Mantha. "It's providing a tool that allows me to do my job more effectively and more quickly than others who aren't online." A few months ago, for example, when Hydro Quebec needed to develop an employee satisfaction survey, Mantha found himself wading deep into the Internet. Seeking other corporations with at least 20,000 employees that had conducted comprehensive census surveys, he posted a query on an Internet newsgroup. Within 24 hours, 30 HR professionals responded, including top managers at Federal Express and United Parcel Service. Says he: "I didn't need to research the issue any further. All the information I needed was there. Without the Internet, I would have been forced to make dozens of phone calls and check back issues of magazines and newsletters."

And that wasn't a one-time event. During the last year, Mantha has connected with senior human resources executives at Motorola, IBM and other major corporations. "I have developed my own online network," he says. Yet discussions with colleagues are just part of the Internet's allure. When Hydro Quebec wanted information on diversity and women's issues, Mantha logged onto a Cornell University Web site that offers academic papers, government reports and research on the issues. He downloaded two dozen reports—many between 50 and 100 pages—printed them out and handed them to his boss.

They were used by several colleagues and served as background material for a presentation at a conference. "There's no question that I could have gotten the same material by writing and requesting it. But it would have probably taken weeks instead of minutes," he says.

At Cisco Systems, Beck and human resources managers routinely check other companies' Web sites, organizations, associations and government pages so they can do benchmarking and other research. "It's a powerful tool you can use without ever leaving your office," Beck explains. Her staff also uses E-mail with attached files to send and receive documents and information with dozens of other high-tech companies. "If a compensation analyst needs to get information from another firm, they often do it using E-mail and the Internet. It's quick and it's easy."

Though Beck and Mantha are particularly adept at using online services, they're certainly not alone. Approximately 10% of Hydro Quebec's HR department currently has Internet access—and the number is growing rapidly. At Cisco, virtually everyone has access from their desktop. Outside these companies, online use is also on the rise. Subscriptions to Cornell's HRNet have increased from approximately 600 to 1,400 in 18 months. And on Prodigy, where the Society for Human Resource Management (SHRM) launched a professional HR forum last December, more than 6,000 individuals have accessed the service.

Although increasing, these numbers are still low. "There's an opinion that the HR profession has been a bit slow to

What's All This Talk about Gophers? The Lowdown on Online Lingo

Along with new skills, HR professionals who want to surf the net must learn a new language. Here's a glossary of terms you might need to navigate the Internet and commercial online services:

BBS (bulletin board system) An electronic system that allows users to exchange messages and information.

bps (bits per second) A measurement that indicates the speed at which data is transferred by a modem.

Broadband Network A network that can handle multiple signals at the same time—using separate channels to transfer data, voice and video.

Chat The ability to "talk" in real time to other users by typing messages at the terminal.

Cyberspace The whole range of information resources available through computer networks.

Domain The official Internet name of a computer as used in E-mail messages. The domain immediately follows the @ symbol.

E-mail (Electronic Mail) A system of sending messages from one computer to another via online services or over the Internet.

FAQ (Frequently Asked Questions) Documents that list and answer the most common questions on a particular subject or about a particular site. A regular feature on Internet Usenet articles.

FTP (File-transfer Protocol) Allows Internet users to transfer files from one computer to another using a telephone line or a network connection. FTP is able to check if information has been received correctly.

Gateway A computer that connects one network to another, despite the fact that both use different protocols.

Gopher A menu-based system for searching the Internet. Gopher is a client-server style program, which requires that the user have a Gopher Client program.

Homepage An organization's site or presence on the World Wide Web.

HTML (Hypertext Markup Language) The coding language used to create pages for the World Wide Web. It uses codes that allow the display of fonts, layout, graphics and hypertext links.

HTTP (Hypertext Transfer Protocol) The system that allows World Wide Web pages to be transmitted over the Internet.

Hypertext A method for writing and displaying text and graphics that allows users to click on an element and jump to related documents or images. On the World Wide Web, that allows users to move from one server to another, across countries and topics.

Listserv Programs that automatically manage mailing lists. Functions include adding and deleting subscribers, and distributing messages to list subscribers via E-mail.

Mailing List An E-mail address that remails all incoming mail to subscribers interested in the given topic.

Modem (MOdulator, DEModulator) The device that allows a computer user to connect to other computers via phone lines.

Newsgroup A bulletin board system that allows users access to discussion on a given topic.

PPP (Point-to-Point Protocol) A method of connecting computers together over phone lines. Used to connect individual PCs to the Internet.

SLIP (Serial Line Internet Protocol) Allows a computer to connect to the Internet via a serial line. Similar to PPP.

Snail Mail Traditional mail services.

TCP/IP (Transmission Control Protocol/Internet Protocol) The basic protocol that allows computers to communicate over the Internet.

Telnet A first-generation program that allows a user to log on to other computers on the Internet.

Usenet A system of distributed bulletin boards, usually referred to as newsgroups. Using a program called a newsreader, it's possible to view messages.

WinSock (Windows Sockets) A standard for controlling the way Windows interacts with TCP/IP. A WinSock program manages Internet sessions when connecting via Windows.

WWW (World Wide Web) A sophisticated hypertext system that allows users to browse the Internet, viewing text, graphics and video, and receiving sound. Programs such as Mosaic and Netscape allow users to have access to the full capabilities of the WWW.

—SG, with contribution from Matisse Enzer/Internet Literacy Consultants.

2. MEETING HUMAN RESOURCE REQUIREMENTS: Information Systems

catch up to the computer revolution," says Mike Frost, manager of the SHRM Forum. "Unfortunately, most in the profession simply aren't using the computer to the extent of its capabilities. An online forum, among other things, encourages people to think about their computer as more than just a word processor or a data base. It's a way to tap into lots of useful information and resources right from your desktop. It's a way to exchange information, at a time when the flow of information is crucial. With the Internet, you don't need a plane ticket or a hotel reservation to participate in a conference."

The same goes for many independent BBS sites, where HR professionals can log on to electronic bulletin boards with a modem and access reams of data. "The HR profession relies on networking, information chasing and people knowing other people," says Robert Keach, president of HRCOMM, a Pleasant Hill, California, service with more than 350 active members. "The online medium is a natural marriage between the technology and the HR profession. It's a way to shrink the world and greatly expand connections—rather than finding yourself limited only to the cards you can fit in your Rolodex."

HRCOMM offers an array of features for HR professionals—all at no cost. It's possible to search the *National Directory of Compensation & Benefit Surveys*; advertise a job opening; search for a new job; conduct, participate and view custom-designed online surveys; track down consultants, contractors and other experts; download files and software; and engage in discussions on virtually any HR-related topic. Companies promoting their services online fund the BBS. "People only now are beginning to get a sense for what the technology can do for them," explains Keach.

Access reams of information via cyberspace. As the Internet, commercial services and independent BBS sites expand, the level and quality of information also is improving. As Mantha illustrates, it's now possible to conduct serious research using the World Wide Web and other parts of the Internet, such as FTP (File Transfer Protocol), which allows public access to remote computers. Venture into the U.S. Department of Labor's Occupational Safety and Health Administration's Web site and you'll get a good idea of what's available. OSHA posts the text of the Occupational Safety and Health Act of 1970 (including Amendment 1990), OSHA notices contained in the Federal Register, the Field Inspection Reference Manual, corporatewide settlement agreements, and an assortment of directives, documents, regulations and interpretations. The Web site is updated twice a week.

For an online user, navigating OSHA online is as simple as clicking the appropriate menu and reading text. It's also possible to use built-in hypertext links that allow you to jump to a variety of other OSHA-related services and sites, including the Office of Information and Consumer Affairs, the agency's Draft Ergonomics Proposal, and an extensive list of publications and booklets on a wide range of safety- and health-related topics. Other links can lead a user into scores of government data bases, including FedWorld, which serves as a repository for a seemingly endless supply of federal-government statistics, data and information.

Government sites aren't the only place to find useful information, either. Many independent companies—including consulting firms—post reports and surveys. And articles from business publications offer information on a wide range of HR topics. The Internet's electronic newsstand includes *American Demographics, Executive Female, Sloan Management Review, Inc.* magazine, and dozens of other publications. CompuServe features *Forbes* and *Industry Week.* And America Online offers *Business Week, Time, San Jose Mercury News, ABC News* and many others. Frequently, it's possible to search back issues by keyword for specific topics.

Archival data bases, such as CompuServe's Magazine Database Plus and Business Database Plus, also can provide articles—particularly on mainstream topics such as benchmarking, pay for performance, TQM, business-process reengineering and an array of other topics. Using key words to search a topic, it's possible to download stories and print them on an "as needed" basis—almost always for a fee. More sophisticated services such as Nexis Lexis and Dialog offer even more advanced—and expensive—capabilities. Says Gibson: "The problem isn't finding information, it's sorting through everything to find the right information."

In fact, experts say that a few minefields await lackadaisical cybersurfers. One of the biggest problems, argues SHRM's Frost, is that the Information Superhighway can easily become the Misinformation Superhighway. "Just because you find something online doesn't mean that it's current or accurate. There's a lot of garbage masquerading behind fancy graphics and interesting hypertext links. Unfortunately, information has a certain legitimacy when you see it online. But that doesn't mean that it has been researched or that it's being presented by a legitimate authority."

That's the hype factor. Although the breadth of online resources is remarkable, depth is sometimes lacking. Differentiating between a five-star site and a one-star site requires patience and critical analysis. Yet it isn't the only concern. It's also important to pay attention to copyright laws and take care when reposting information online. The ease with which data can be copied makes it ripe for copyright abuse. And, finally, there are plenty of challenges in simply learning to navigate the Net. The sheer size of the online world is daunting, and there is etiquette—more often referred to as "netiquette"—you must adhere to. Users who fail to follow accepted procedures invite the wrath of others—known on the Internet as "flaming." "It's a little bit like learning to ski," says AMD's Johnston. "It is frustrating at first, but if you stick with it you will learn how to do it and it will become fulfilling. There is a ton of information out there, and the tools for obtaining the information are getting better all the time."

Online ability is changing the HR profession. HR professionals who venture online say that they can't imagine doing things any other way. With AMD's recruiting moving heavily online, Johnston can focus on ways to do his job more effectively. By broadcasting information to university job-placement offices and key professors, he's able to reduce the time it takes to fill a position and zero in on top candidates more effectively. "I'm spending far more time using E-mail than the telephone. Although there are occasions when the phone is useful, E-mail is faster and more efficient," he states.

And that's just the beginning. With the company's Web site, he doesn't have to worry about constantly updating brochures—an expensive and time-consuming task. "You create a four-color brochure, and it's out of date as soon as it's printed," Johnston says. "Online, we can change data or a graphic overnight at minimal cost." Similarly, he isn't burdened with trying to ship endless boxes of materials to job fairs. He simply directs potential recruits to go online and check out AMD's Web site—which includes video clips, sound bytes, full-color graphics and text. In fact, it's possible to learn about AMD's Austin, Texas, facility, and then use a hypertext link to jump into the city's site, which discusses housing, education and recreational opportunities.

Lotus' Leonardo is convinced that the online world represents the future of HR. Soon, applicants will be able to directly access the company's homepage on the Web and find job openings and career opportunities. By clicking appropriate buttons, individuals will be able to receive further information and fill out online forms. They will be able to apply directly, without using E-mail, *snail mail* or faxes. And, today, when Leonardo needs detailed information on the industry and current trends, she uses the Internet and other online services to access newsletters, magazines and even newspapers such as *The Wall Street Journal*. Says Leonardo: "Going online doesn't eliminate human interaction, it simply makes it more efficient."

Which is precisely the idea. "This is completely revolutionizing the workplace," says Steve Scott, manager of technical recruiting at Staples. "It's creating possibilities that couldn't have been imagined just a few years ago." Concludes Gibson: "The human resources field has lagged a bit as far as getting online, but it now has an opportunity to catch up and take advantage of the tremendous capabilities. It's an extremely powerful tool that fits perfectly into the philosophy of eliminating inefficiencies and becoming a strategic partner. Like it or not, it's here to stay."

So grab your mouse and hit the surf—cyberspace awaits you.

Samuel Greengard is a contributing editor to PERSONNEL JOURNAL.

Interactive Benefits Systems Save Time And Dollars For Employers, Employees

MIRIAM BASCH SCOTT

New technology is enabling employees and benefit plan administrators to obtain immediate answers and results, thus saving time and money. Easily accessible and complete information is important in this age of increasingly complex benefits choices, reduced staff, and diverse work forces with varied needs and expectations.

Interactive systems, computer systems with which employees can directly "interact," are increasingly popular tools to meet the needs of plan administrators and employees. According to a 1993 Conference Board survey of 70 large employers, the percentage of companies using computer software for benefits communications was expected to reach 43% in 1993 and 1994, a major jump from 23% in 1991 and 1992. The percentage of large employers using voice response systems was expected to increase from 53% to 71% during the same period. In a voice response system, recorded voice messages prompt and respond to the caller's instructions as they are punched in on the telephone.

With the appropriate software, employees can obtain benefits data through personal computers (PCs) at their own workstations or at accessible kiosks. Or, at a lower cost to employers and perhaps greater psychological accessibility to employees, a voice response system allows employees to transact their benefits business through a familiar instrument: the telephone. The data obtained through the phone system is collected in a dedicated PC that can process the information according to the plan administrator's needs.

WHAT THEY DO

Interactive systems allow employees to obtain information immediately and privately and to review various potential scenarios before making a decision. In addition, such systems can be adapted to communicate in foreign languages as necessary.

An employee can access an interactive system by using a Social Security number, a personal identification number, or a password.

Because interactive systems handle routine tasks efficiently and accurately, they free up staff to answer employees' more detailed questions and to work on benefits planning. They also reduce dramatically the amount of paperwork necessary in benefits administration.

Interactive systems aid in obtaining employee feedback, thus easing plan evaluation. For example, the systems incorporate reporting functions that help identify problem areas as revealed through employees' frequent inquiries on a specific benefit or issue. A system also can be used to conduct employee surveys quickly and inexpensively.

Interactive systems also may be used to convey important information faster than other traditional printed communications.

The Segal Company's version of a telephone-based voice response system, *SegalVoice*, can be used 24 hours a day with any touchtone phone. *SegalVoice* can provide employees with personalized or general benefits information. It can handle enrollments, including automatic issuance of confirmation statements, for even the most complex benefit choices.

Segal recommends that prior to implementing a high-tech system, employers first evaluate their existing communications program and their employees' likely reaction to such a system. Some work forces may prefer dealing with a person rather than with a "machine."

Another issue in implementing an interactive system is cost. A customized program can cost $5,000 for a simple application, but can exceed $50,000 for complex packages, Segal says. In evaluating the options, employers must look at the potential savings, such as reduced administrative time and, perhaps, reduced staffing needs. Voice response systems generally divert 70% to 80% of the transactions that ordinarily would be made through benefits staff, consulting firm William M. Mercer, Inc., asserts.

While the cost of a customized program may be prohibitive for small employers (those with fewer than 500 employees), such employers instead could resort to existing products, such as general planning computer programs, offered by major investment and accounting firms for a nominal fee.

DEFINED CONTRIBUTION

Defined contribution and Sec. 401(k) retirement plan administrators have found interactive systems particularly useful. Defined contribution plan administration requires fairly complicated and very time-consuming steps, including processing information on new enrollments, payroll deductions and changes, and participant request for transfers, loans, or yield information. Furthermore, large amounts of information must be transferred to recordkeepers and plan trustees.

High-tech systems can make defined contribution plan administration much more efficient and timely. With such a system, employees may process transactions whenever they are ready, not just during business hours, and complete those transactions within days, rather than weeks or months. And employees can keep track of account valuations on a more current basis (often daily, but more commonly monthly) and make adjustments as necessary.

In reducing manual processing, high-tech systems lead to improved quality and reliability, experts and users agree. Furthermore,

---

Do-It-Yourself Federal Budget Balancing

Would you like to know the effect on the federal budget of raising the Social Security retirement age to 70? Or the impact of eliminating congressional pensions? No need to call your elected representative—just dial up the Internet.

Budget Shadows, a computer game that calculates the long-term budget impact of program cuts and tax breaks a player decides to implement, was introduced by Sen. Bob Kerrey (Neb.) of the Bipartisan Commission on Entitlements and Tax Reform and former Sen. John C. Danforth (Mo.), who had been a commission member until his retirement. In December, the commission sent a letter to President Bill Clinton advising him of the group's failure to agree on a recommendation for curbing entitlement spending (see *EBPR*, January 1995, p. 14).

According to Mr. Kerrey, "Anyone with access to a computer can sit down with this model, tune out the demagogues, and devise a plan to prevent changing demographics in the 21st century from bankrupting entitlement programs." Players win by accumulating 100 points, although that only ensures that by 2030 the deficit will not grow; balancing the budget requires 115 points. The game allows players to make cuts from among four categories: Social Security, health care, tax expenditures such as tax credits and mortgage deductions, and other federal entitlements like Medicare.

One demonstration of the game indicated that cutting congressional pensions had a negligible effect on the deficit and gained a player no points. However, raising the Social Security retirement age to 70 increased a player's score by five points.

Budget Shadows can be downloaded from the World Wide Web Homepage on the Internet and is scheduled to become available on disk and CD-ROM. For information, call the Bipartisan Commission on Entitlements and Tax Reform, (202) 224-2300.

2. MEETING HUMAN RESOURCE REQUIREMENTS: Information Systems

because employees easily can make changes in elections or investments with a high-tech system, employees feel empowered and responsible for their own financial future.

Saint Joseph's Hospital, a 600-bed facility in Denver, used an interactive voice response system to process 1994 flexible benefits enrollment for its 2,100 employees. Previously, Saint Joseph's would hire temporary workers for a two-week period each year to answer employee questions and assist with forms processing.

TECHNOLOGY IN ACTION

Using the Human Resources 2000 (HR 2000) package, a product of Software 2000, a Hyannis, Mass.-based firm, and Telephone Inquiry Payroll Personnel System (TIPPS), a product of Computer Communications Specialists, Inc., a Norcross, Ga.-based firm, Saint Joseph's employees input flexible benefits enrollment information directly into a central computer (an IBM AS/400). The hospital also plans to use the interactive voice response system to verify employment, to respond to employee inquiries, and to complete employee surveys.

"Our goal was to maximize productivity by reducing the time spent processing flexible benefits paperwork," said Julie Goodwin, the hospital's HR information center manager. "Interactive voice response technology not only helped us achieve that goal, but also increased overall employee response and data accuracy. We've also received positive feedback from our employees; many called us to comment on how well the system worked for them."

Software 2000/TIPPS features include the ability for rotary phone callers to move through the system menu with voice commands instead of touchtone, a tool for modifying the TIPPS script to the specific needs of a plan sponsor, and multiple language capability including French, German, and Spanish. TIPPS connects the central processor to telecommunications systems via turnkey PC software and hardware.

For more information about *SegalVoice*, contact Carole Henson, voice-technology services manager, (212) 251-5482; for more information on Software 2000/TIPPS, contact Gail M. Fulcinity, Software 2000, (508) 778-2000.

Implementations Show Technology Is Information

Increasingly, the sole function of new technology in employee benefits is to improve information delivery. This is true, whether an employer wants to know where its highest claims costs are occurring, or an employee wants to know how best to invest in a Sec. 401(k) plan, or a third party administrator needs to produce a Form 5500 for a client.

For example, J.C. Penney's most recent technology acquisitions have included a variety of imaging systems to track various forms that need employee signatures. Some of these are enrollment forms for health and retirement plans, personal identification number (PIN) authorization forms, beneficiary designation forms, consent forms for benefit distributions, and change of address forms.

Instead of verifying and checking these forms manually, Penney now can retrieve scanned forms through its computers, track the process of enrollment, verify signatures, and alert benefits personnel when necessary signatures have not been obtained.

R.R. Donnelly & Sons also has used technology as an information tool in several benefits areas. First, in 1993, the publishing and printing firm opened a retiree information center for its 5,000 employees. The center is staffed ten hours per day and uses an 800-telephone number to allow retirees quick and free access to Donnelly retirement information.

For its active employees, Donnelly has established a benefit information line for its defined benefit and defined contribution plans. The information line now includes interactive voice response, which provides employees with account balance information and allows financial modeling. The line also includes the ability to complete transactions, make loans, and perform pension modeling.

WHAT'S AVAILABLE

The following list of available human resources software technology, prepared by Lawson Software, provides further evidence of the primacy of information processing in benefits technology:

• *Artificial intelligence.* Permits companies to analyze data for trends or anomalies; serves as an early warning system to identify potential problems.

• *Executive information systems.* Allow CEOs and other top management to use benefits data for planning and budgeting.

• *Modeling/forecasting systems.* Use historical information to plan for the future.

• *Electronic mail.* Permits the routing of memos, reports, and other information quickly and efficiently; reduces paper and work flow bottlenecks.

• *Centralized data bases.* Eliminate duplicative systems that cause mistakes; increase accuracy of and access to information.

• *Integrated payroll, human resources, and benefits systems.* Reduce the need for data entry; permit easy, flexible analysis of all information about employees.

EXECUTIVES WANT INFORMATION

In a 1994 survey of *Fortune* 1000 human resources executives, 67% of the respondents said that the demand on human resources departments for useful, strategic information is greater than ever.

However, only 29% of the responding companies reported that they have the technology to provide executives with the needed information. The survey was conducted by Lawson Software and the Deloitte & Touche Center of Expertise in Human Resources.

The survey also provided the following information:

• About one-quarter of the respondents said that their company routinely uses human resources information in business and strategic planning.

• Among companies that have state-of-the-art technology, 79% said that they could produce human resources information for strategic planning, but only 49% routinely do so.

• Technology enhancements that the respondents said they expected to be installed within the next three years include kiosks, imaging systems, forecasting and modeling software, and executive information systems.

• More than one-third of respondents could not provide a return-on-investment figure for human resources technology. Of those who could estimate returns, 33.9% said the return for each dollar spent was 25¢ or less, 25.5% estimated 26¢-50¢, 17.6% said 51¢-$1, and 23% said their return from technology was more than $1 for each $1 invested.

More information on the survey may be obtained by contacting Lawson Software in Minneapolis, (612) 379-2633.

Creating a Productive Work Environment

- **Motivating Employees (Articles 19 and 20)**
- **Facilitating Communication (Articles 21 and 22)**
- **Leading and Directing (Articles 23 and 24)**

Whenever anything is being accomplished, it is being done, I have learned, by a monomaniac with a mission."
—Peter Drucker

For years, management theorists have indicated that the basic functions of management are to plan, direct, organize, control, and staff organizations. Unfortunately, those five words only tell what the manager is to do. They do not tell the manager how to do it. Being a truly effective manager involves more than just those five tasks. It involves knowing what goals to set for the organization, pursuing those goals with more desire and determination than anyone else in the organization, communicating the goals once they have been established, and having other members of the organization adopt those goals as their own.

Motivation is one of the easiest concepts to understand, yet one of the most difficult to implement. Often the difference between successful and mediocre organizations is that people in successful organizations are motivated. They are enthusiastic about the company, about what they do for the company, and about the company's products or services. Effective organizations build upon past successes, recognizing the truth of the old saying, "Nothing succeeds like success." If people feel good about themselves and good about their organization, then they are probably going to do a good job. Whether it is called morale, motivation, or enthusiasm, it still amounts to the same fragile concept—simple to understand, difficult to create and build, and very easy to destroy.

In order to maintain a motivated workforce for any task, it is necessary to establish an effective reward system. A truly motivated worker will respond much more effectively to a carrot than to a stick. "Turned-on" workers are having their needs met and are responding to the goals and objectives of the organization. They do an outstanding job because they want to, which results in an outstanding company.

Perhaps the single most important skill for any manager, or, for that matter, any human being, is the ability to communicate. People work on this skill throughout their education in courses such as English and speech. They attempt to improve communication through an array of methods and media, which range from the printed word, e-mail, and television, to rumors and simple conversation. Yet managers often do not do a very good job of communicating with their employees or their customers. This is very unfortunate, because ineffective communication can often negate all of the other successes that a firm has enjoyed. Managers and the firms they represent must honestly communicate their goals, as well as their instructions, to their employees. If the manager does not do so, the employees will be confused and even distrustful, because they will not understand the rationale behind their instructions. If the manager is successful in honestly communicating the company's goals and ideals to the employees, and is able to build the motivation and enthusiasm that are necessary to successfully accomplish those goals, then he or she has become not just a manager but a leader, and that is indeed rare.

Leadership is probably the least common of all human characteristics. Leadership has been studied for centuries in Western civilization, going back at least to Plato's *Republic* and the concept of the "philosopher king." But this quality is only poorly understood at best. Leaders do have certain obvious abilities, such as the ability to communicate and the ability to motivate. However, they also have something else. True leaders have a vision, a purpose, a direction, something that Martin Luther King called a "dream."

Creating a positive work environment is not easy. Communicating, motivating, and leading people, whether employees, volunteers, citizens, or Boy Scouts, is difficult to

UNIT 3

do. However, managers are faced with the task of doing exactly that.

Looking Ahead: Challenge Questions

Getting people to accept ideas and adopt them as their own is one of the most difficult tasks facing management. What are some things you might do to motivate employees, especially in a downsizing environment?

What strategies could you employ to communicate more effectively with your peers or your instructor? What things can destroy effective communication? What roles do trust and rumor play in organizational communication?

Leadership may be the rarest of all human abilities. How would you seek to establish yourself as a leader? Give examples of outstanding leadership in today's world.

Article 19

The Top 20 Ways to Motivate Employees

T-shirts, turkeys, and other gimmicks won't work for today's burnt-out employees, say motivation experts surveyed by IW. It's time to get back to the basics.

Shari Caudron

#1
GIVE EMPLOYEES THE INFORMATION THEY NEED TO DO A GOOD JOB.

THE TITLE ON JIM DAVIS' BUSINESS CARD used to read "vice president of sales," a position in which he managed more than 30 people from a prestigious corner office. The then-29-year-old was an ambitious corporate climber, motivated by promotions and all the status that accompanied them. That was two years ago, before his company was acquired by Houston-based Enron, one of the largest natural-gas companies in the world. Today, he works in a modular cubicle no larger than any other cubicle in his department. His title has been downgraded to director. And the number of his direct reports has been slashed to just five employees. Talk about demotivating. Although Mr. Davis understands these changes had nothing to do with his performance and everything to do with corporate restructuring, "It's still pretty shocking when it happens to you," he says. "Your ego suffers . . . and your image of yourself is blown apart."

Mr. Davis is not alone. Employees at every level in corporate America have seen promotional opportunities vanish as companies struggle to become leaner, more agile, and more competitive. In manufacturing companies in particular, employees have weathered countless layoffs, they've suffered through reengineering and job redesign, and all their expectations about their careers and career advancement have been tossed out the window. Whereas job security and promotions used to be almost guaranteed, today there's no such thing, and employees are wondering why on earth they should work so hard when the rewards seem so few and far between.

The result is a workforce with a motivation problem the likes of which U.S. management has never seen. Unfortunately, too many companies are facing this challenge the wrong way by attempting to fire up today's workers using yesterday's motivational techniques. Company T-shirts, Christmas turkeys, and employee-of-the-month programs may have made people feel good when times were good, but today's jaded workforce requires a more back-to-basics approach. As Philip Berry, a director of human resources for Colgate-Palmolive Co., New York, explains: "We need ways of motivating people to understand and work within the new organizational structures we've created, and in my mind that kind of motivation is very simple. It boils down to respect for the individual."

But what, exactly, does respect for the individual entail? To learn what the fundamentals of motivation really are, INDUSTRYWEEK surveyed some of our country's top motivational gurus, including authors, academics, consultants, and trainers (see "IW's Motivation Experts"). Our question was simple and straightforward: "How do you motivate today's burned-out employees?"

We took their comments, advice, research, techniques, and case studies and blended them together to come up with our own top-20 list of the best motivators. As we discovered, there is no one-size-fits-all approach to motivation. Instead, it is a process in which successful managers employ a combination of several approaches. On its own, any one of our motivators is a good start. Put them together and look out!

Whether we admit it or not, all of us are internally driven by the question: "What's in it for me?" For this reason, the

#2 PROVIDE REGULAR FEEDBACK.

first step toward creating a motivated workforce should be to hire self-motivated people, says Gerald Graham, dean of the W. Frank Barton School of Business at Wichita State University. He says these people can be identified "by taking a look at their history and experience."

Unfortunately, with the exception of a greenfield manufacturing site, a company probably isn't going to have much opportunity to start fresh with a new, entirely self-motivated group of people. For most managers, the employees they have are the employees they are stuck with, and the trick is to find ways of accelerating their internal drive to succeed. And before attempting this, managers must know the kinds of behaviors they want to motivate. Is it cost reduction? Quicker turnaround on projects? Increased customer satisfaction?

Once the objectives are known, managers can **(#1) give employees the information they need to do a good job.** This includes information on the overall goals and mission of the business, the work that needs to be done by particular departments, the specific activities individual employees should concentrate on, and why any of this information is important in the first place. Bob Nelson, author of *1,001 Ways to Reward Employees*, says that open communication helps employees feel they are in on key decisions about the business and helps them to understand the whys and wherefores of business initiatives.

The information should come not only at the front end of a project or task, he adds. It should come midway through the effort and again at the end. In other words, managers should **(#2) provide regular feedback.** As Ken Blanchard, author of *The One Minute Manager*, stresses: "Feedback is the breakfast of champions." It gives employees a way to measure their own performances. Nothing is more demotivating than finding out what a bad job we did after a project is complete and there is no longer an opportunity to fix any problems.

Because employees who do the work are the experts on the work being done, managers should **(#3) ask employees for their input. Involve them in decisions that affect their jobs.** "People have to feel like a part of their environment," Mr. Nelson says, and nothing is more flattering or generates greater buy-in than being asked for opinions.

"Creating an environment where people can share their ideas is the most motivational thing we do around here," adds Lois Kilsey, vice president of operations for Neptco Inc., an electronics-component manufacturer in Pawtucket, R.I. "And there's nothing very sexy about it. It's really a very basic motivational technique."

This spirit of open communication and two-way information sharing is even more motivational when it becomes an integral part of doing business. Therefore, a company should **(#4) establish easy-to-use channels of communication** that employees can use to express their questions and concerns and get answers. Employee hotlines, suggestion boxes, surveys, small-group forums, and question-and-answer sessions with the president are some of the formal ways a company can encourage employees to speak up. But managers should also encourage employees to voice their opinions on an informal basis by maintaining some type of "open-door" policy.

One of the most important objectives of open communication is for managers to **(#5) learn from the employees themselves what it is that motivates them**. Because each person's internal motivators are different, the rewards offered for a job well done must be customized. A secretary who makes $24,000 a year may be extremely motivated by the promise of a $2,000 bonus, whereas a $100,000-a-year professional probably wouldn't be.

Mr. Nelson asked one of his employees what would motivate her to do a good job on a certain project. "She told me greater visibility in the company would be rewarding," he says. After she finished the project, Mr. Nelson went to the president of the company armed with specific information about the employee and the project she'd just completed. He then asked the president to stop by her office as soon as possible to personally congratulate her for doing such a good job. The result? "She was flying high for weeks afterward."

"Resist preconceptions," adds Saul Gellerman, author of *Motivating Superior Performance*, "and demonstrate your respect for individuals by responding to signals they put out about how they want to be treated and the kinds of work they want to do." In other words, managers should **(#6) learn what on-the-job activities employees choose to do when they have free time**, and then create opportunities for them to do those activities on a more regular basis. A salesperson who chooses to call on larger potential clients, for example, may be excited by the challenges presented by bigger accounts.

Three years ago, Wichita State's Dean Graham surveyed 1,500 employees in a variety of work settings to find out what they considered to be the most powerful workplace motivators. Their response? Recognition, recognition, and more recognition. According to his study, the top motivator is a form of recognition that costs no money and that is for managers to **(#7) personally congratulate employees for a job well done.** These congratulations should be offered immediately and should be specific as to why the work was so exceptional.

One way to ensure recognition is provided in a timely fashion is to maintain frequent contact with subordinates. Managers should **(#8) recognize the power of their physical presence.** Employees like frequent contact with their managers, however brief, because it subtly indicates that the manager recognizes the importance of their work. "When I chat with you I'm investing the most important thing I have, and that is time," says Mr. Gellerman. "It underscores the importance of our relationship, and it demonstrates my concern for your work." Frequent contact also allows employees to bring important matters to managers' attention and to get help with problems when they occur.

If in-person recognition of employees is impossible for some reason, managers should **(#9) write personal notes to them about their performance**. This demonstrates that the manager not only recognized they did a good job, but that their work was so good that he or she felt it necessary to take the time to tell them so in writing. Additionally, because

3. CREATING A PRODUCTIVE WORK ENVIRONMENT: Motivating Employees

#13
HAVE THE TOOLS AVAILABLE TO DO THEIR BEST WORK.

written congratulations are tangible, the "feel-good" benefits last much longer.

Considering how powerful one-on-one recognition is, it comes as no surprise that *public* recognition can accelerate an employee's drive to succeed even further. When managers **(#10) publicly recognize employees for good work**, they are telling employees that their achievements are worth everyone's attention.

Because teams are a fact of life in many companies today, recognition efforts must also include them. People like the camaraderie of celebrating success with others, so recognition efforts should **(#11) include morale-building meetings that celebrate group success**. These celebrations don't have to be elaborate to be successful. It's simply enough to let teams know on a timely basis that they are doing a good job.

Because nothing saps employee motivation quicker than boring, routine, unchallenging work, if companies want employees to do a good job, they should **(#12) give them a good job to do**. It makes sense that people who enjoy their work and who believe in the importance of their contribution are going to be more highly motivated than people who don't care. Managers shouldn't let employees stagnate but should show them how they can grow with their jobs and give them opportunities to learn new skills.

The next step is to make sure employees **(#13) have the tools available to do their best work**. Nothing is more demotivating than having to work with outdated computer programs, old technology, and shabby tools. Companies that invest in state-of-the-art technology tend to be exciting places to work. Having top-of-the-line tools also makes employees proud, and great motivational power accompanies an employee's ability to boast about his or her job.

Up to this point, we've been talking about initiatives managers on their own can undertake to motivate employees. But it would be an oversight to neglect the influence of corporate culture. Together, company policies and management practices have an amazing ability to either support or undermine individual motivational efforts.

"You have to create an environment where people want to do good work and not one where people do good work because they have to," explains Russell Justice, technical associate with Eastman Chemical Co. in Kingsport, Tenn., an INDUSTRYWEEK "America's Best Plants" selection in 1991 and a 1993 winner of the Malcolm Baldrige Quality Award. "When we began to change our environment here, we started seeing dramatic improvements in the quality of work within about six months."

A company that lacks an inspirational ambiance can improve by using any combination of the next seven techniques, starting with **(#14) recognizing employees' personal needs**. "We're dealing today with employees who have special needs, including single mothers, dual-career couples, and disabled individuals," Mr. Gellerman says. "We need to accommodate people whenever we can because it demonstrates our concern for them as human beings." Employees will be more motivated to work for a company that acknowledges and cares for their personal needs by making arrangements for such things as on-site day care, flexible working schedules, and special equipment.

Although there's a lot more talk today about performance-based management, the idea of **(#15) using performance as the basis for promotion** is still pretty revolutionary. Too many old-line manufacturers, particularly those that are heavily unionized, still promote people on the basis of seniority. Instead of motivating people to excel, this approach merely encourages a sit-and-wait attitude.

And speaking of performance, a company should **(#16) establish a comprehensive, promote-from-within policy**. As Gary Dessler, author of *Winning Commitment*, says: "Many employees will ultimately measure their firm's commitment to them by the degree to which they had the opportunity to achieve careerwise all they were capable of achieving." People stop trying in a hurry when they see jobs they are qualified for go to individuals from outside the company.

Such policies should also address job security—something everybody is concerned about—by **(#17) emphasizing the company's commitment to long-term employment**. Include statements such as, "Stable employment and the continual well-being of our employees are essential and can be obtained through steady growth of the company."

Mr. Dessler, who calls this a "lifetime-employment-without-guarantees" policy, says such statements indicate to employees that they are ultimately responsible for their own job security but that the company will do all it can to facilitate long-term employment.

Job security closely corresponds to our most basic human need—survival—as well as another important need—affiliation. For many people, work is both a way to make a living *and* a way to connect with others. A company that **(#18) fosters a sense of community** has gone a long way toward creating the kind of organization that people want to work for. Backstabbing, office politics, and low morale will rob motivation from even the most achievement-oriented people. Reorganizing into teams is one way to create camaraderie, but a company also should educate employees about the importance of recognizing *each other's* work.

It would be an oversight to overlook money as a motivator, although most of the current literature on motivation downplays its significance. "Most companies can match the amount paid to employees by their competitors," Colgate-Palmolive's Mr. Berry says, "but you can't always replicate the environment that motivates people to better results and greater job satisfaction.

Furthermore, adds Mr. Gellerman, "It takes large sums of money to produce small performance changes that are usually pretty brief. It isn't cost effective." Why? Mostly, it's because of the way financial-incentive programs are structured. Giving everyone the same bonus at the end of the year, for example, can be extremely demotivating—when high performers see low performers getting the same amount, they have no motivation to continue their good work.

When done right, however, money can be extremely motivating, says Tom Wilson, president of The Wilson Group in Concord, Mass., and author of *Innovative Reward Systems for the Changing Workplace*. "On a scale of one to 10, I'd rank money as No. 2 or 3," he says. The way to start getting the biggest bang for a buck is to **(#19) pay people competitively, based on what they are worth**. If employees feel appropriately compensated, they won't be so preoccupied with their paychecks, and a company will be able to get the most from nonfinancial rewards.

But even with a competitive salary structure a company can motivate people to greater gains by **(#20) giving them a financial reason to excel by offering them a share of the profits**. However, the activities that have an impact on the bottom line must be clearly identified, because employees must know what they are working toward. Furthermore, for money to be truly motivational the amount must be significant.

More than one-shot solutions, these ideas must be used continually to be successful. As Aubrey Daniels, an outspoken advocate of positive reinforcement and author of *Bringing Out the Best in People*, says, "At the end of every working day, people leave either more motivated to come back and do their jobs again tomorrow or less motivated as a result of what happens to them that day. Performance is about *what happens every day.*"

Furthermore, there's nothing revolutionary about these techniques. Motivation is really about treating people with dignity—something today's burned-out, shell-shocked employees desperately need more of.

"I think the cloud of downsizing and restructuring has a silver lining," says Reid Zeigler, senior manager of visual communications for Merck Research Laboratories in Rahway, N.J. "It has forced us back to the basics. It's amazing what happens when we listen to employees, ask their input on decisions, and give them regular thank-yous. When you think about it, motivation is really very simple."

IW's Motivation Experts

In compiling our list of top-20 motivators, we surveyed a variety of authors, consultants, trainers, and academics. Our panel of experts includes:
- Gerald Kushel, author of *Reaching the Peak Performance Zone*.
- Saul Gellerman, consultant and author of *Motivating Superior Performance*.
- Gary Dessler, author of *Winning Commitment*.
- Video Arts Ltd., producers of "The Best of Motives" video training program.
- Bob Nelson, vice president of Blanchard Training & Development Inc. and author of *1,001 Ways to Reward Employees*.
- Tom Wilson, president of The Wilson Group, a consulting firm that specializes in the development of innovative reward systems.
- Chet Holmes, president and CEO of Kaleidoscope Media Group Inc., an international consulting company that has developed a 12-step motivational program for sales personnel.
- Gerald Graham, dean of the W. Frank Barton School of Business at Wichita State University, who has extensively researched employee motivation.
- Aubrey Daniels, author of *Bringing Out the Best in People*.
- Bill Byham, president and CEO of Development Dimensions International and coauthor of *Zapp!: The Lightning of Empowerment* and *Heroz: Empower Yourself, Your Coworkers, Your Company*.

THE TOP FIVE DEMOTIVATORS

1. Offering "jelly-bean" rewards.
That is, giving everyone—regardless of individual performance—the same rewards at the end of the year.

2. Not being specific or timely about praise;
for example, telling people they did a good job on a project that was completed two months earlier and neglecting to tell them why the job was good.

3. Using threats or coercion to get work done.

4. Breaking a promise.

5. Treating employees in a bureaucratic way instead of as individuals.

Empowerment

MYTH OR REALITY

Address by MICHÈLE DARLING, *Executive Vice President, Human Resources, CIBC*
Delivered to the Human Resources Professionals Association of Ontario, Toronto, Canada, February 14, 1996

Empowerment is a concept that we hear a great deal of today as organizations seek answers to the challenges of the 90's. Is empowerment truly the key to creating energy, excitement and commitment in organizations large and small? Or is it just a slogan, a new buzzword of the times? For many, the jury is still out.

So, what's the trouble with empowerment?

Why is it that a recent study in the United States revealed that employees felt it was more myth than a reality in their "empowered" organizations?

We probably don't have to look much further than our own organizations to trace some of the clues to the real story on empowerment. In my own company, and in work outside CIBC I've logged many insights on our continuing journey towards empowerment. I'd like to share a few quotes:

"Empowerment is just another Human Resources idea. We need strong leaders, we need strong controls, and we need to make decisions quickly."

"Empowerment is simply good common sense. Employees should be able to do what is needed for their customers without asking head office for permission."

"I believe in empowerment. But my manager takes away from my empowerment by cutting costs, bringing down hard budgets, and making decisions that I don't agree with. How can I feel empowered in this kind of environment?"

"The problem isn't with the concept of empowerment, but with the concept of organization. We still try to pour this thing called empowerment into the old organizational forms, with the same systems and processes that supported command and control. No wonder it doesn't often work."

Sound familiar? The themes emerge time and again.

The need for controls.

The role of leadership.

Personal ownership of work and of the customer relationship.

Acquiring the tools, budget and resources to get the job done.

Breaking down the old organization paradigm and building a new one to unleash the potential of our people.

I'd like to talk about each of these themes today in the context of our experiences, including hard-learned lessons, and successes at CIBC.

My proposal to you is that there isn't one, single golden lever that switches on an empowered organization. Empowerment is the result of aligning all of an organization's systems, processes and people practices against a new organizational paradigm. The fabric of empowerment is interwoven with all of the themes I've just mentioned.

But first, there's a fundamental question we haven't yet addressed. Why empowerment? Why should we invest our energy in and endure the pain of shifting our fundamental organizing concept?

The answer is that change, on a massive scale, is making it an imperative. There is not an individual, family, business or government that does not feel that the scale and pace of change around us seems greater today than at any previous time.

We are living through one of those epoch periods of history when our mental mind maps change. We have grown up in a system of order and hierarchy which no longer seems to work or fit our environment any more.

I suspect that, wherever you come from, CIBC's view of the environment is very similar to your own. We have experienced an exponential increase in competition as a result of deregulation and new entrants to our business.

All of us, as consumers, have become more demanding as choice opens up and pressure on our time causes us to want it "our way". Nine to 3 p.m. banking doesn't wash with our customers anymore. We are all increasingly caught between a clock and a hard place.

All of us, as employees, expect to be treated as individuals who have our own needs and our own lives. Receiving a letter from Human Resources telling you that you're moving next month to Sudbury doesn't do that.

Banking is no longer a monolithic, one-size-fits-all business of lending and deposits. At CIBC, we are a consolidation of nearly 30 different businesses, including insurance and securities. Each business has its own products, culture and labour market.

Our customers and our employees, are not exclusively white Anglo-Saxon males any more. CIBC is both part of the multicultural reality of Canada today and of the shift in values around women in the workplace and women as financial decision makers.

Early on, we realized that grappling with these issues would have to go far beyond tweaking business strategies and the structure of our organization. We had to make some fundamental changes.

We knew we had to shift away from a bureaucratic focus on internal matters to making the external world the centre of attention. But where would our competitive advantage lie in a world of accelerating change?

We decided that we could not become a financial leader in the long term by taking a product-driven approach. After a great deal of soul-searching, we decided that CIBC's strategy was going to be based on delivering that most difficult thing of all. The thing that would require us to re-tool every aspect of our culture, processes and organization. The thing that was so difficult to pull off, that if we did do it, it would be very difficult for a competitor to pose a challenge.

We decided to compete on the basis of delivering customer satisfaction.

We sensed that to do this, we had to unleash the potential and creativity of all our employees. Everything about CIBC would have to be re-aligned to support excellent customer experiences, rather than traditional bureaucratic processes.

We believed we could achieve this if we created an organizational environment that would encourage broad-based creativity, innovation, problem-solving and problem resolution within an appropriate control framework.

But how would we get there?

Our customers had the answer. They told us that they wanted to deal with bank representatives who were knowledgeable and committed to service. But more than that, they had to be capable of making decisions, on the spot, that the organization would stand behind. Waiting two weeks for head office to approve a car loan was, quite simply, not on.

The implications for CIBC were staggering. Rather than abandoning decisions to the gauntlet of approvals, our people were asked to assume ownership of the customer relationship. They would become decision makers. They would become the bank for our customers.

I believe this is the essence of empowerment — the transfer of decision making and ownership from managers to those individuals who have the knowledge and ability to most appropriately make decisions. It implies trust in other people's abilities, and indeed, in one's own abilities. It goes beyond the act of delegating tasks to within the hierarchy, to a new philosophy of partnership within work groups and between managers and employees.

This became our definition of empowerment at CIBC.

And so we began our journey. A journey that includes about 40,000 travellers. Along the way we hit the inevitable pothole, or have to pause to re-examine the map, and we check to see how everyone is adapting to life on the road.

Our ongoing dialogue on how we're doing surfaces many of the same questions over and again. Let's return now to some of the themes that have been top of mind with CIBC employees.

The first is controls. How far should we go in removing the rules in an empowered organization? In an industry like ours, there are some very firm boundaries. The key lies in defining these boundaries, outside of which one may not tread, while at the same time allowing for tremendous flexibility within that framework.

The president of our insurance company uses a term called the "Empowerment Coral" to define the concept. The framework sets out three non-negotiable boundaries.

At the top is the business strategy and plan, which defines our customer focus and business priorities and guides individual and team activity.

On the right hand side are CIBC's values. Every action taken must reflect our commitment to stewardship, respect for every individual, the encouragement of initiative and creativity and excellence in everything we do.

At the bottom of the coral we are bound by the regulatory and legal framework of the industries and markets in which we do business.

The fourth boundary is a flexible one. It can expand or contract to make the empowerment coral larger or smaller. It is directly dependent on the capability of an individual, relative to the skill and knowledge requirements of the job they do. If, for example, I am a new customer service representative and am entering the job with the minimum required capability, this boundary will contract. As a seasoned pro, the boundary will be set much further to the left.

This model also helps to clarify one of the challenges associated with empowerment. When individuals have more latitude to make decisions, the organization must also allow people to make mistakes. One can look at this model as a helpful way of understanding where CIBC is willing to allow people to make mistakes, and where mistakes will have serious consequences.

The W. L. Gore Company in the United States uses another analogy to reinforce the concept of boundaries and risk with their "Waterline Principle".

Imagine an organization as a ship sailing on the ocean. All of the personnel on board, in carrying out their responsibilities, are obviously cognizant that putting a hole in the side of the ship is not a desirable thing to do!

When working above the waterline, however, making a mistake and creating a hole in the side of the ship will have no serious consequences. We'll have the time to repair the hole, learn and sail on.

Below the waterline, an action that creates a hole could quite literally, sink us.

I know we can all think of examples in our companies and in our careers that help illustrate the point. One of the most powerful examples I can think of is the Tylenol scare that seized the entire continent in the early 90s. The entire management team at Johnson and Johnson was clearly working at the waterline.

And knowing the risks, they first consulted their company values to establish the boundary, or waterline, below which they would not work. Second, empowered teams across the organization were formed to break down the issue and contribute equally to the decision that would ultimately result in removing Tylenol from every shelf in North America.

Ownership of the problem was broad-based, the decision was a courageous affirmation, the company's commitment to its customers and values.

What could have been a fatal blow to the brand actually served to generate high trust in the ethics of the corporation and a gain in market share.

Communicating boundaries and ensuring controls are in place is part of the pivotal role that leadership plays in the empowered organization. But leadership is also the key to so much more.

We recently conducted a survey of our branches to learn, from a practical standpoint what drivers were necessary for delivering a very high level of customer satisfaction.

Our research team quickly reached a point where they could literally walk into the front door of a branch and sense immediately if it was a high performing or "best practice" branch.

This sense of purpose and energy prompted one of our researchers to ask an employee in one of these branches what the secret was. The teller pointed to the manager's office. "It's her," she said.

One of our greatest learnings has been that supportive and empowering leaders are the key to creating effective and empowered organizations.

3. CREATING A PRODUCTIVE WORK ENVIRONMENT: Motivating Employees

We found that in our best practice branches, leadership provided the appropriate balance between direction and discipline, and individual freedom.

This initial research prompted us to undertake a more comprehensive study at CIBC to understand and measure the impact of supportive and empowering manager behaviors and key organizational outcomes related to productivity. Dr. Linda Duxbury of Carleton University and Dr. Christopher Higgins of the University of Western Ontario directed the research which involved approximately one quarter of CIBC's 40,000 employees.

The results are being compiled now, but early indications confirm a very strong link between supportive, empowering leadership behaviors and high organizational commitment, productivity, role clarity, reduced stress and lower work/family conflict.

Dr. Duxbury's research has found that supportive manager behaviors in one corporate culture may not be the same as in another. She has however, documented a consistent core of behaviors that will lead to higher employee productivity, and a second group that will undermine employee productivity. These findings are based on the responses of more than 25,000 employees at over 40 Canadian corporations.

What makes a supportive manager? A supportive manager is one who:

Provides positive feedback;
Recognizes that an employee has a life outside work;
Engages in two-way communication with employees;
Mentors employees;
Shows respect for employees, and
Empowers employees.

A non-supportive manager is one who:
Displays poor interpersonal skills, which means focusing on the negative rather than the positive being inconsistent giving poor direction;
Focuses on hours of work and not on output;
Shows lack of respect for employees;
Does not empower employees.

If it is leadership that builds the bridge toward effective, empowered organizations, then you have to pay more attention than ever before to creating and sustaining leadership — the right kind of leadership.

CIBC's Leadership Centre is a clear signal of our commitment in this area.

But our real commitment is in the allocation of time and energy.

This is the third year of operation. Over 4,000 managers have attended Foundations of Leadership, our flagship program, designed to break down traditional mindsets about the organization and teach empowering leadership behaviors.

Teams also use the centre for planning and advanced programs address the additional challenges of leadership during times of change. By the end of this year, we expect that over 7,000 people will have participated in programs.

The success of our approach at the Leadership Centre has been documented in another piece of research. At CIBC, four out of ten participants in our leadership programs declare significant behavioral changes when they've returned to the work place.

Moreover, six out of ten employees who report to those managers have observed behavioral change that is in line with CIBC values and a more empowered workplace. To set these results in context, the Centre for Creative Leadership in North Carolina have found that three out of ten participants indicate they had significantly changed their behavior.

We've established the importance of aligning controls and leadership with empowerment. What about the role of the individual contributor in the organization?

In our ongoing dialogue with managers who have participated in programs at the Leadership Centre, we have sometimes heard the lament that leaders go back to their units prepared to empower the team, only to encounter resistance from their employees.

There seem to be three issues. The first is that employees can interpret empowerment as an abdication by their managers of a role that is rightfully the leader's. The second obstacle is a fear of retribution if mistakes are made. And, finally, hierarchical systems can breed a high comfort factor among employees.

One of the tools we provide managers to help align the team and move forward is our Focus Will Capability Model. The leader helps individuals find focus and direction within the overall goals and objectives of the organization. The commitment or will to strive toward that goal is supported by our environment and leadership style. The capability of individuals and the team to take on more is a planned and an ongoing journey.

Leadership development, enhancing capabilities, and shifting employee mindsets about the organization and their careers has been supported by a myriad of supporting programs and policies which we've developed over the past five years. The success of empowerment depends as much on this infrastructure as any other theme we've discussed today.

Although we've created it one step at a time, we have done so within a comprehensive framework that promotes a positive, empowered and productive employee environment at CIBC.

The overall model that we've created has seven key components:

First and foremost is our commitment to effective leadership. I've talked about the Leadership Centre, and this area also includes support such as our succession planning process and tools, as well as manager selection.

The second area supports strong two-way communication. Human Resources, business leaders and our corporate communications teams all share responsibility in supporting this area.

The third encompasses a group of policies and practices that support a key corporate objective — to become the employer of choice. I'd like to talk more about this area in a moment.

The fourth relates to our performance management, rewards and recognition programs where we are shifting our compensation philosophy and programs from a culture of entitlement to one of personal responsibility and performance-based rewards.

Confidential employee support is available through our employee helpline for personal and family issues and a second service provides confidential support and counsel in resolving workplace issues.

We also provide professional support services to our leadership team in the area of employee relations.

Finally, we have built a monitoring and measurement framework that not only tracks our progress toward our strategic goals in people management, it also provides the critical information required to keep the overall system aligned and relevant to the needs of the organization and our people.

While we don't have time to talk about each of these areas in detail today, I would like to spend a few moments on our approach to learning, and on our policies related to career development and resourcing which support our journey toward becoming an empowered organization.

It is no longer possible, nor desirable, to direct from head office the learning and careers of 40,000 employees who are involved in over 30 businesses. To reinforce the shift we must make from that old paradigm to a modern one, I often tell my colleagues that learning is not the filling of a pail, but the igniting of a fire.

We are moving quickly away from classroom-based training. In 1993, we finished a program to define the required competencies for most jobs at CIBC. A supporting individual development planning guide now provides employees with a clear target of what they need for their own development.

To support employee learning we also built 14 Employee Development Centres across Canada. These centres are a cross between employment agency and a library staffed by consultants. They provide employees with guidance and assistance in using learning tools.

On the career development side, we've made some tremendous breakthroughs. In 1993 we switched on the most advanced staffing network in the world. After two years of development, CIBC has an IVR computer-based staffing network. This enables managers to advertise vacancies across Canada using a terminal. And it allows employees to phone enquiries into the system and to receive, automatically, faxed job specifications.

To support these related systems, CIBC has an open staffing policy. We feel that we need to attract the very best candidates for every position. To do this, we have a policy which treats each employee with the same respect that one would give an outside candidate. All jobs up to and including senior vice-president are posted.

So, what does real empowerment look like in practice?

Our customers will deal with employees who will own all aspects of providing the solutions to the customer's needs.

Our employees will have control over much more of their lives and will know the boundaries of what they can do and what they are responsible for.

They will be supported by managers who will be able to provide clear direction, remove obstacles and make management decisions within a well understood framework that is clearly communicated throughout the entire organization.

As we move toward this vision, we are measuring our progress. "How are we doing?" is a question that is on my mind daily.

Our progress in building individual commitment to our business goals, comfort with taking on risks, full ownership of a job and of the customer relationship was recently measured in our employee opinion survey — Open Forum.

The results are quite extraordinary.

Over 93% of employees said they were clearly prepared to be held accountable for the decisions they made. 80% said they have the authority they need to carry out job responsibilities compared to an external benchmark of 72%. And over 85% said they know the impact of different customer categories on our financial performance.

While the level of personal empowerment is clearly aligned with our direction, the survey also revealed some less positive categories related to the availability of tools and resources required to get the job done. It is perhaps an indication of where we are on the empowerment journey. Individuals feel personally empowered, but are still coming up against obstacles in the organization.

We're currently piloting an empowerment survey and one of the early findings appears to confirm that one's sense of personal empowerment is also linked to how easy or frustrating it is to get work done outside the unit. This speaks to another sub-theme, the requirement for alignment across units and through interdependent teams.

What I have been discussing is the application of theory in an organization of 40,000 people. This is difficult work, which takes longer than anyone would hope.

Momentum has to build in a large organization.

For a time, there is little visible sign.

But then it begins to emerge.

When it does, there is so much energy behind it that it becomes very powerful.

Just as I opened with a few employee quotes, I'd like to close with a statement which, I think, serves as evidence that we are close to, or even at, that breakout point.

It is a statement made by one of our managers at the end of a session at the Leadership Centre.

"As your manager, I am committed to my role to inspire a shared vision and to work with you in a strong team environment. I will work with you to provide clear objectives and remove obstacles to achieve and sustain financial growth and personal development. My role will be to support all staff by empowering all employees using positive reinforcements, honest feedback, and recognition. I will role model CIBC's values by focusing on the customer and taking ownership of our actions to continuously improve the way in which we deliver our services."

Is empowerment a myth or a reality? As we continue our journey and invest the energy and talents of the people of CIBC, I believe we move empowerment closer to a reality every day.

This individual's commitment to herself, to her staff and to you as customers is one of thousands of achievements, large and small, that are testament to our success. Thank you.

Social IQ And MBAs

RECOGNIZING THE IMPORTANCE OF COMMUNICATION

Address by ROBERT L. DILENSCHNEIDER, *Chairman of the Dilenschneider Group*
Delivered at the Fordham University's Graduate School of Business, New York, New York, February 27, 1996

Thank you for that kind introduction. And I'm honored to be invited. There used to be a story going around. Some versions of it were about Babe Ruth. Some about Mickey Mantle. I'll tell you the Mantle version.

Mickey was hitting the cover off the ball. Reporters kept on bugging him, "Mickey, Mickey, how do you do it?" Mickey ignored them. But not for long — he himself got to wondering: "How do I do it?"

When Mickey had it all figured out he called the reporters. Right after that Mickey went into a slump. And the reporters hated his explanation.

The lesson we're suppose to learn from this story is: Don't analyze.

Well, I think that lesson is dead wrong.

Analysis is one of the most important tools business has. I believe — and by your participation you believe — that analysis can improve performance. And during your time at Fordham you'll learn how to use a broad range of analytic tools.

Today, I want to talk about another tool I believe in.

Since there's so much team work going on you've probably heard already about this tool. It's hot.

When I was in graduate school, they called this tool: "Communications" or "human relations principles."

Then they started calling it: "Interpersonal skills."

Now they're calling it: "Social intelligence" or "emotional intelligence." They're finding that your social or emotional IQ is more important to your success than your grey matter.

About a year ago Daniel Goleman published a book called Emotional Intelligence. That book has been discussed everywhere from the cover of Time magazine to business periodicals like Fortune.

What Emotional Intelligence does is explain in scientific terms what many of us have known intuitively. And that is: How we perceive ourselves and how we act with other people determine our success. Your cognitive IQ could be 145 and you could get a doctorate in business. But, you'll never be able to break away from the pack unless your interpersonal skills are top-drawer. The business world is full of wounded warriors who focused solely on their work — not people — and they never got a shot at the gold.

A few weeks ago, in the "Managing Your Career" column in The Wall Street Journal, a survey was cited by the National Association of Colleges and Employers. The survey found that managers rated oral communications as the most important skill for career success. Notice the managers didn't rate "outstanding work" as number one.

There are many of those studies being published today. With things moving so quickly, with so many virtual teams, someone with a low social IQ can no longer play the game.

Today I'm going to focus on four aspects of communications or social IQ.

• First of all, we'll look at why social intelligence or communications is a prerequisite for professional success.

• Next, we'll examine why your generation has tremendous advantages in communications. In fact, you have it over all 12 of the generations in America who came before you. Incidentally, I hate the term "Generation X." But I'll use it here just because it's become standard.

• Three, we'll see how you can leverage your strengths in communications to build relationships with the powers-that-be — that is, the baby boomers. Right now baby boomers are the gatekeepers at doors you want to enter.

• And, four, let's look at how you can boost your social intelligence score. For most of you it's already high, but it can get even higher. Who knows? You may turn out to be one of the geniuses in social intelligence like Dale Carnegie or Ronald Reagan.

Okay, communications. Why does social intelligence matter so much?

Look at those who've made it in business: Jack Welch, Bob Lutz, Geoff Bible and Oprah Winfrey. They all are outstanding communicators.

Now, how about those who never really reached their potential in business: John Akers, Chris Steffen, Bill Agee and Jim Robinson. All good people but they all have communications deficits.

In essence, communications is two things.

• One, communications is the ability to read or decode signals others give out. The baby cries. The mother figures out that the signal means: "Feed me."

• And two, communications is the ability to project signals so that we get our messages across. The mother sends a signal to the toddler: "It's time you learned to feed yourself."

Today, watch for nonverbal cues — facial expression, glint in the eyes, energy level, tone of voice, body tension, posture and hand movement. What do these signal regarding feelings about the audience? Do I respect you? Is this something I have to do? Could you be valuable to me in my network?

Okay, what happens if you miss or misinterpret signals coming in from the outside?

Well, what happens if you're at a railroad track crossing and you miss the signal that a train is coming?

Right: Splat. A disaster happens. When there's a missed signal, the consequences can be severe. For instance:

• You don't pick up that your subordinate wants sympathy about his health problem. He spreads it around that you don't care about your people. It becomes difficult for you to recruit people to come into your department.

21. Social IQ and MBAs

- You don't pick up that the boss wants you to be upbeat about the product the company is developing. So, you let him know you're convinced that new jeep will never get off the drawing board. Since then the boss is standoffish. From other sources you hear that the boss considers you an obstructionist.

- In running your small business you miss the fact that your potential clients need a lot of hand-holding. You'd rather spend your time perfecting the software you develop. The business goes belly up. In short, a low social IQ has big-time consequences.

Now let's look at what can happen if you're not giving off the right signals about yourself.

- Maybe your nonverbal cues such as facial expressions or body language are telling your subordinates you're unhappy in the job. The word gets around. You become a lame duck.

- You want people to feel welcome dropping by your office in your home. Being an entrepreneur is lonely. But when they come, you don't offer them coffee and you emphasize how much work you have to do. They stop dropping by.

- Your boss is so tense. If only he would open up and let you know what the problem is. Then it occurs to you that you've never been open at work either.

Offices, including my own, are full of people giving off misleading signals. I have one employee who's proud of her high intelligence. Unfortunately, she never displays it. It's masked by her anxiety.

Why do we get so many bad connections in our signal systems?

Answer: There are deficits in our communications skills. Some part or parts of the system aren't working.

In Emotional Intelligence, Goleman explains that communications skills are rooted in four capabilities.

The first capability is knowing your emotions and controlling them. That's a tall order. And you'll spend the rest of your life working on that. Self-knowledge plus self-control. I wish I could give every one of you that gift.

Capabilities three and four are the ability to recognize emotions in others and be able to respond appropriately. This is usually called "empathy." And it's the foundation for the quality of our relationships. If I could tell a new account rep in my office one thing I would say: Put yourself in the clients' shoes and consider how things look from their point of view.

Why don't more people have these four Abilities down cold?

Well the number-one reason people make a mess of social interactions is that they are preoccupied with themselves.

Knock, knock.

Someone's home but they're too busy with themselves to notice that a person's at the door.

When people are trapped in themselves, all their energy is going into monitoring themselves. Instead their focus should be on what's going on outside them.

Also, they might have missed all the nonverbal cues because they take words too seriously. Words that are spoken are a very small component of what's really going on. In fact, in many cases words should be totally ignored and the nonverbal cues analyzed. We are in the political season. Do you remember what any of the Republican candidates are saying? Or do you remember "how" they appealed? Remember Ed Muskie standing in the snow? What did he say? Few remember. But we all remember what happened. If they're firing you, ignore what the manager is saying. Watch the body language. That tells you how far you can push them in giving you a better package.

To raise their social IQs people have to start thinking of their environment as a movie. The scene is always changing. But you can't afford to miss any element in any scene. All that material represents clues about how to interpret what's happening.

In athletics, we say: "Keep your eye on the ball." Here in communications we say, "Keep your eye on the picture."

Another reason people miss the boat on signals is their training or conditioning. Somewhere along the line, they were encouraged not to notice what was really going on. So, they became socially retarded.

To redevelop the capacity to read an environment, people should play the game I call: "Watch the Picture." It requires a few patient friends to join in with you. Rent a movie. Then try to determine what's the manifest content or what's going on, on the surface. Then look at what is the hidden content or what's going on below the surface. What's the real story? Everyone in the game makes their interpretations of the same scenes. And then everyone compares notes. In this way you can train yourself to understand how others might feel.

Another reason people are poor at signal-getting and signal-giving is that they're not living in the moment. Top communicators like CNN's Larry King stay in the here and now. King is not three minutes ahead of reality — or ahead of his guest. By projecting into the future, poor communicators miss what's in the present.

To stop fleeing the here and now, people have to get comfortable in their own skin — so they stay grounded in the present. Several of my clients had this problem. One tried exercise. Another tried praying. Another became engrossed in volunteer work on behalf of animals. All those strategies worked for them.

Now, let's move to you. Why does Generation X have such a high social IQ? Think about how you grew up versus how the baby boomers grew up.

You had it tough.

Maybe your parents got a divorce and the family income went from middle class to poverty.

There was probably no one home when you came from school. You made supper.

You took care of your little brother.

And, you didn't have time to analyze what was screwed up about your mother or father or society.

And when you entered the work world there wasn't much out there except McJobs.

Also, when you were born TV had already been established. You spent years studying that media, including the commercials. That made you savvy consumers.

High tech was also part of your life from an early age. You're the one who programs the VCR right?

Baby boomers, on the other hand, were born into an affluent economy. The Great American Jobs Machine was working overtime. Blue-collar workers at General Motors could catapult their family into the middle class. In fact, good jobs were so plentiful that baby boomers had the luxury of angst about finding "meaningful" work.

The media covered the baby boomer's every move. When they exchanged their hippie beads for pinstripes, that made the covers of magazines.

And baby boomers had heavy-duty issues like Watergate and Vietnam to contemplate. They began to question every-

3. CREATING A PRODUCTIVE WORK ENVIRONMENT: Facilitating Communication

thing, including their parents, their lifestyle and the goals that society told them to embrace.

This generation also saw life symbolically. To them, the suburbs represented what was wrong in the post-modern age. For you, the suburbs is a place to live.

In contrast, baby boomers aren't as visual as you. They're still a print generation. And they aren't as at-home as you with high tech.

Now let's look at the advantages your background has given you when it comes to communications.

- First of all, you're not as self-absorbed as the baby boomers. That means you have a greater capacity for empathy. And that also means you make more accurate readings of what's out there.

- Secondly, you have more self-control. Baby boomers struggled with the existential necessity of "being yourself." Some actually decided it was a moral imperative to "let it all hang out."

- Third, you're pragmatic. Usually you accept life as it is and have no special problems with authority. That allows you to get a clear view of the terrain. You're not superimposing what "ought" to be on what is.

Baby boomers tend to view things through the filters of their idealism and rebellion. They don't see the boss as the boss. They see him as Richard Nixon or as their uncle Raymond.

Your generation's take on bosses is that they are simply a component of your job. And they, like every other part of your job, must be managed. If you're an entrepreneur, that would apply to clients.

- Fourth, you have no ambivalence about money. You're convinced it's a good thing, especially since you didn't have much of it growing up.

Also, you see money not so much as a symbol but as a means. Money lets you buy all those electronic gadgets that you love. Your straightforward take on money helps you see the work world as purely business, not personal. That helps you put boundaries on the kind of signals you give off at work. And that gives you more control over your professional image.

- Fifth, you're highly visual. Being visual lets you take in the whole picture when you're interacting. You always see the big picture and the frame around it.

Therefore, you tend to "frame" issues in your communications. That framing makes it easier for you to explain things to others. As a result you come across as brighter than people who can't explain.

Also you can see beyond the words. If a memo comes to you, you can bypass the bureaucratic messages and surf to the big picture. You're the one they go to in the office when they want to decode a remark their boss has made or a memo that's gone out about expense accounts.

- Six, you're at-ease with technology. When you get voice mail, you're not irked. You never had trouble navigating the Internet. This high-tech prowess allows you to be effective communicating in any medium. I bet you were the first one on your block with a pager.

As each new communications technology comes out, you're going to be on the first wave. It will take earlier generations longer to adjust to it.

These communications strengths can help you deal with the baby boomers.

When I was starting my business career and right up until my early 40s, there were people who helped me. Helped me a lot. They had the time and the interest to teach me the ropes and to open doors for me.

Today, there aren't many people, in corporate or in entrepreneurial enterprises, who have the time or the interest to help you.

They see themselves in a survival mode. And they're convinced the bulk of their energy has to go into keeping their lifeboat in good shape.

And they aren't putting out any welcome mats for you to step into their lifeboats. Theoretically, the baby boomers should be your mentors. They might have been that — had there not been a global economy. The global economy with its increased competition changed the game.

Jobs and entrepreneurial enterprises have become volatile. And we all have to work harder — and smarter.

But you can tap into this resource — the baby boomers. You can build bridges to the baby boomers.

To do that, you have to put yourself in their shoes and see how the world looks from their perspective.

When you apply the big "E" — or empathy — to baby boomers you'll realize:

- For baby boomers, life didn't play out as they expected. They're confused, resentful and frightened. They probably would enjoy having someone like you from another generation to help them sort out what they feel.

This means you have to learn to become a good listener. Leaders get to be leaders by listening to people and finding out what they want.

Baby boomers will welcome the opportunity to download on you. Most of their lives they've been center stage and they feel almost entitled to plenty of attention. If you're willing to give them that attention, you may be able to develop alliances.

- Secondly, the baby boomers aren't getting any younger. Some have actually hit the 5-0 mark. And aging has thrown these former members of the youth culture into a tizzy.

You can build bridges between their mindsets and your generation's mindsets.

You can point out what's similar between the generations. You can casually introduce them to your generation's performers, heroes, gods and goddesses.

If all this occurs gradually, you may get baby boomers interested in you. They're very alert. They'll "get it" that you are available to be their guide to this brave new world of rapid change and technology.

- Third, the baby boomers see your youth as the force that's pushing many of them into early retirement.

Well, you can demonstrate that careers aren't a zero-sum game. You can indirectly point out how your success doesn't diminish theirs. Figure out how in your profession, the pie is getting bigger, not shrinking. And believe it. Actually, it's true many new types of jobs are being created to replace those that vanished.

- Fourth, baby boomers still often feel like aliens around technology. If you can slow down, then you can calmly show them the inside scoop on high tech.

Suppose, for instance, you notice a baby boomer is still relying on DOS rather than using Windows. You can approach the issue by claiming that DOS has gotten a bad rep since Windows came on the scene. Talk up the virtues of DOS. Then slide in some pluses Windows has to offer. Sit down with the baby boomer and give a very elementary lesson in Windows. Offer to come back in a few days. Eventually, you could form a bond.

It's irrelevant how mean-and-lean the workplace has gotten or how competitive it's become for us who are self-employed.

It's also irrelevant how nasty people are at work or what lowlifes clients are.

What does matter is how you "frame the picture." You can focus in on one or two baby boomers and put a frame around them. You can focus in on your goal to get two years in General Motors or five years running a plastics business. That's all that matters: How you frame your experience.

Those are just a few suggestions about how to persuade baby boomers to help you. There are plenty of good books out there on persuasion. One is Roger Dawson's Secrets Of Power Persuasion. Another is Allan Cohen's and David Bradford's Influence Without Authority. Browse around the business section of a super book store and you'll find other useful guides.

Now, before I wrap up, let's look at how you can raise your social IQ.

- First of all, you have to relax. Do you know that relaxed people come across as brighter than anxious people? If you are calm, you'll have easier access to what you're feeling. And you'll have more self-control. Also, if you're not racing inside, you'll be able to stop and take the time to understand what's going on in others.

In all my years of business I have rarely seen a tense person get to the big time — and stay there. They flame out. That's because a high level of tension interferes with getting and receiving signals. If you see that you're misinterpreting signals, stop. Find a way to calm down. Then start again.

- Next, practice the 2 Rs: Giving people recognition and rewards. That's the best way to touch others and make them part of your professional network.

If your colleagues have said something brilliant in the meeting, let them know that you noticed. Tell others about what was said. This will put you on the high ground. You'll be perceived as a "decent human being" and "fair." People will be attracted to you.

And there are ways you can reward others without coming across as manipulative. If someone has done a bang-up job on a report, treat her to lunch. Or ask him to present highlights from the report at the staff meeting.

I have a freelance writer whom I wanted to reward. I kept my eye open for the right opportunity. It came when I had dinner with a CEO. I told him about her. Then I told her what I had told him about her. I was able to give her what she really wanted: More business. This transaction enhanced our relationship. She now goes through more trouble to get me what I want.

The 2Rs can work — upwards, downwards and sideways. When dealing with a subordinate, though, you have to be careful that you don't come across as condescending. And in dealing with superiors you have to make a judgment call as to when it's appropriate for you to comment on their performance.

- Third, join groups. It could be your condo board, a church organization or a study group. Analyze the dynamics. Who's getting what from whom and how are they pulling it off? Look at the influence you have. How can you increase that influence? The more you analyze, the more you'll notice. Look for:
  - The leaders in the group
  - Who's after power
  - Who's losing power
  - Who has credibility
  - Who is using "porcupine power" — or the power of being an obstructionist to get their way. Incidentally, journalist Hedrick Smith wrote The Power Game back in 1988. It talks about porcupine power and tons of other influence strategies. The book is dated in terms of the people he uses to illustrate points. But it's a good read.
  - Also look at who's the peace maker in the group and what they get from that role
  - What's the "cost" of being in the group? If you can tolerate another textbook, there's some good material out there on group dynamics. One is Donelson Forsyth's Group Dynamics.
  - Another interesting aspect of groups is shifting roles. Are you becoming less of a malcontent and more of a leader?
  - Is the group beginning to end? What would it take to get it going again? And what would be the cost of that?
  - The fifth way to raise your social IQ is what I call: Fake it 'til you make it. It buys you time and lets you exercise self-control until you have more information to go on. Or until you make a decision about what to do.

When I was starting out in a public-relations agency there was a senior vice president there who was successful and well respected. He was also very positive. Right out of Norman Vincent Peale.

Since I was young and somewhat cynical I wondered why he wasn't more cynical. There wasn't one lemon which he couldn't use to make lemonade.

After a couple of years he and I developed a friendship. I got up the nerve to ask him about his positive take on life.

I'll never forget what he told me. He said that when he started out, at another agency, he considered himself the voice of reason and truth. He would let them know when they were violating his standards for excellence or when their code of ethics seemed tarnished.

After he was kicked out of there, he got smart. He got it: In business they don't like negatives. So, he began to make a conscious habit of always being positive. At first it was fake it 'til you make it. Then it became easier. Soon, it even made sense to him: If he spoke in a positive manner, he would really think in a more positive way.

Think of this: Giant corporations pay Booz-Allen and other consultants millions of dollars to be critical of them. And, guess what? They're not paying their workforce a dime for this service. Why work for free? Be positive, not negative.

Being positive helps us be less hard on people. I have a subordinate who drove me crazy. Then I tried looking at her strengths and either her faults disappeared or I just didn't notice them anymore. She's terrific now.

To wrap this up, let me say that, if your social IQ is high to begin with, you'll soar.

But if your social IQ is lower than you'd like it, well, go about boosting your IQ slowly. Observe how others handle situations and imitate them. There are many courses and workshops about this. Keep your eyes open for them. Dale Carnegie Seminars are repositioning themselves so they can now offer an up-to-date version of what you need.

Not too long from now, a few of you from this group will emerge as social geniuses. Your colleagues probably already know who you are. What's important is that you yourself recognize this talent in yourself and nurture it. It's a precious gift.

Thank you for your attention.

Handling Communication Problems

W.H. Weiss
W. H. Weiss is a consultant in industrial management. He has written many articles and books on human relations, supervision and management. His latest book titled "Plant Supervisor's Complete Desk Book" was published by Prentice Hall.

Getting through to people is the most difficult part of the job for many supervisors. The matter cannot be taken lightly because no single aspect of the supervisor's job can contribute to career success as much as being an effective communicator. Since communication on the job is so important, it should be promoted and encouraged at every opportunity. To do so, supervisors should be aware of the barriers and how to overcome them. They must continually look for and practice ways to keep communication channels open. Being informal and available to discuss almost any problem has proven to be of value.

You and other supervisors need to know the answers to the many problems of communicating on the job. Here are some suggestions on how to handle the most important ones.

Promoting Upward Communication

Your job of supervising is much easier if your people keep you informed. You will have the facts that will help you make decisions, and you will be able to foresee problems that could arise. For these and other reasons, it is to your advantage to promote upward communication from your people at every opportunity. The best way is to always be available and receptive to people who want to talk. Listen to all your people's ideas regardless of how illogical or impractical they may sound. Listen also to their complaints, and answer them promptly.

When people learn that you respect their opinion and are interested in their welfare, they will not hesitate to give you information, particularly if you show you appreciate it and tell them so. If they learn also that you are fair and honest, they will not hold back on telling you about mistakes rather than trying to cover them up.

To most workers, the supervisor will always be the boss, and it behooves them to say what the boss likes to hear and do what the boss wants them to do. It may be to some workers' interests to withhold certain information lest it be used against them or against others in the same work group. This psychological barrier to upward communication is simply fear. Successful supervisors do something about it by continually working toward ways to eliminate or reduce that fear.

You can promote upward communication also by being decisive on the job and confident that what you say and do is right. People usually have few fears when their leaders are positive in giving orders and directing work. When workers know that they are doing their work correctly and to their supervisor's liking, rapport improves and teamwork is given a boost. People just naturally communicate more

22. Handling Communication Problems

when they feel secure. If you want employees to freely communicate, keep up the morale and place a high value on their three strong desires:

- To be recognized and given appreciation for work done.

- To be kept informed so they are "in" on things.

- To receive friendly, sympathetic advice on personal problems.

Carrying On A Conversation Easily

Being a good conversationalist helps your image and makes you welcome at both business and social functions. It also makes it easier to communicate your thoughts and ideas because your listeners will pay more attention to what you have to say. You can develop the technique of easily carrying on a conversation if you work at it. Here are a few dos and don'ts:

- Be aware that an interesting conversationalist conveys a sense of leaving many things unsaid. Telling everything can be tiring for many listeners.
- Never interrupt someone who is speaking. Waiting your turn makes what you say more interesting when the right moment comes.
- Add some body language occasionally to your words. You'll put some sparkle into your message and it will help you when you want to be emphatic.
- Refrain from raising your voice to get attention. It's a sure way to run most people off.
- Ask a close friend if your voice is shrill, harsh, too loud or too soft. Knowing about these faults makes them correctable.
- Avoid making remarks that make listeners uncomfortable. Think twice when you feel impelled to state unpleasant facts.
- Hold up when you sense you are monopolizing a conversation. Your listeners' minds may begin to wander. Worse, you will become boring.
- Minimize your use of slang and cliches. Although such words may make it easier to express yourself, they are dull to your listeners. They also convey the idea that your vocabulary is limited.

Improving Your Verbal Communication Skill

If you are concerned that you may not be fully accepted as a leader because your verbal communications are not as good as you'd like them to be, you must work at improving your perception of what it takes to put your ideas across and to be understood. One of the best ways to do this is to pick the words you will use in advance. Giving clear instructions will result in maximum comprehension by your listeners. You want to prevent their attention from wandering, and you want your message to be understood.

In trying to put across an idea or to persuade somebody to your thinking, recognize that people may be biased, prejudiced and have preconceived ideas. These barriers to understanding complicate your efforts to communicate clearly because people may not listen carefully, if at all, to an idea, theory or viewpoint they don't agree with.

It's better to avoid speaking rapidly when you give instructions because there are some people who need extra time to think about what they have heard and to fix the information firmly in their minds. There are those who find it difficult to understand instructions unless the instructions are given slowly, even repeated. Some people also have poor retention abilities, so if you give them two assignments or more at a time, you run the risk of having them forget some parts of the jobs.

If you want to avoid any misunderstanding, try not to get too technical. Unless you are talking to a skilled technician, you are likely to lose your listener with your words and phrases. Using slang is one thing; using jargon that is unfamiliar to the receiver is a waste of time.

Many employees want to be involved in any new job or assignment. They also want to know what goals they are expected to reach. These people will respond quickly if you give them more information relative to their assignments. They will listen intently, and they will absorb your instructions with less difficulty.

To get people into the proper frame of mind to accept and understand assignments, communicate frequently with them. Also, show a consistent willingness to answer their questions when they ask them. This paves the way for them to start listening as soon as you begin talking — thus the communication time can be shortened.

Try to pick the best time of day when you want to verbally communicate with individuals or groups. Mornings are usually best because by afternoon, your thinking and reasoning faculties can be dulled from several hours of hard work. In the morning, you will be fresh and your listeners will be more receptive.

3. CREATING A PRODUCTIVE WORK ENVIRONMENT: Facilitating Communication

Deciding How Much To Tell People On The Job

Today's employees want to know how what they do contributes to the whole of their company. They also want to know what people in other departments are doing. They like to be "in" on things whether or not they are involved. Most people in management positions recognize that knowledge is a good motivator and morale builder. Still, the question remains of how much people on the job should be told.

Although more and more emphasis is being placed today on keeping employees fully and completely informed, you can't tell everybody everything. It's not necessary to give people a lot of unwanted details. Information can be put into three categories when deciding what to pass on to your people.

1. That which they should have to properly do their work, such as how machines function, where supplies are, what forms should be used, when jobs must be completed and similar information which relates to their specific job.

2. That which they should know because they might be affected, such as an expansion in the department or company, a rearrangement of work areas or an increase in a production quota.

3. That which they would find helpful in relating to their position and contribution to the organization, such as information about the company' goals and achievements, sales, new products and profits.

Generally, you should see that employees are given information in the first two categories. The amount of information of the third category which you should tell depends on the interests of the individuals. Those who are creative and innovative, such as research and development people, would welcome news about new products or services the company offers. Almost everyone should want to know how the company is doing profitwise and what the future looks like. Most employees are more interested in their company than you suspect.

Avoiding Overcommunicating

Some supervisors, in their eagerness to be clear and completely understood, may overdo it and thus cause themselves other problems. It's

> *"These barriers to understanding complicate your efforts to communicate clearly because people may not listen carefully, if at all, to an idea, theory or viewpoint they don't agree with."*

easy to keep talking past the point of accomplishing your objective, especially when you are explaining something or giving instructions. Talking too much can become a habit that is hard to break.

Overcommunicating is undesirable for two reasons. First, it diminishes the interest of your listener in what you are saying. Second, it tears down all of the communication gains you have achieved up to that particular point. Thus by talking too much, you become ineffective in a skill that all supervisors need.

People overcommunicate when they excessively repeat themselves and when they expand their messages beyond what is necessary. The problem with saying too much is that it confuses your listener. This happens when much of your explanation is unnecessary. Because you continue to explain, your listener attempts to attach some additional significance to your words. Although it's dangerous to assume people know what must be done, at the same time you don't want to endlessly repeat something which they already know.

Instruction time can be reduced by checking beforehand to ascertain whether or not something is already well-known.

There are several things you can do to avoid overcommunicating. If you sense that you are doing too much explaining, repeating or expanding your messages, adopt the following procedures:

1. Expand your vocabulary. Better word usage will cut down the time and words you need to make your point.

2. Spread out the information you want to pass on over a period of time. Your listener will more easily understand it and remember more.

3. Put across a message more effectively and faster with a model, drawing or some other type of visual aid. In addition to reducing the amount of talking you must do, these things often are much easier to understand.

Leadership

SEVEN BEHAVIORS FOR MUDDLING THROUGH

By JAMES R. HOUGHTON, *Chairman and CEO, Corning Incorporated*
Delivered to the Senior Leadership/Corporate Transformation Conference, Harriman, New York, April 11, 1996

Good morning ladies and gentlemen. I'm delighted to be here. This meeting is organized around a particularly vital and exciting topic — senior leadership and corporate transformation. I'm going to transpose those topics, however. First, I'll discuss my views on the transformation of corporations. Then, I'll talk about my vision of what it takes to be a senior leader in today's corporate environment.

As we stand at the door to a new century, it's useful to look back and check the century we're leaving. One hundred years ago, the United States was primarily rural and agrarian. People lived on farms. They worked the fields or toiled in small workshops. Markets were local and the workforce was largely homogenous. Formal education was pretty informal. It usually ended at an early age.

By the start of the 1900s, the Industrial Revolution had changed all that. The body and the soul of America were transformed. Millions of workers and their families migrated to our shores — attracted by opportunity, by jobs. These workers brought a tremendous capacity for work. They helped this country grow great. However, many of them did not know the language; few had any education. These factors — combined with the prevailing psychology of the day — resulted in the creation of large, hierarchical organizations. Workers were considered little more than cogs. Leaders were expected to be commanding and authoritative, armed with all the answers.

But of course, all of that has changed with the advent of the Information Age. In fact, it's my belief that the world's new emphasis on information has caused two major paradigm shifts in the business arena.

The first is globalization. Access to information has made national borders meaningless. Meanwhile, this shrinking of the world has increased, by orders of magnitude, the competitive stakes for which we play. No market is protected anymore. Competitive threats appear daily in the form of new technologies and new global contenders. Today, firms in every region of the globe can access any market. They can bring to bear the power of new technologies; of low-paid, highly skilled workers; and large amounts of capital.

How can we respond? With a continuing thrust toward world-class quality. Now a lot of people have written about quality and frankly I wish I could use a different word. People's eyes glaze over when they hear the word quality.

You know the story about the Frenchman and the Japanese and the American who were all captured by hijackers. They were asked what they would like as a last wish before they were killed. The Frenchman says, "I want to hear the Marseillaise one more time." The Japanese says, "I would like to make a speech on quality." The American says, "Please shoot me before I have to hear one more speech on quality." So, although we are all veterans of quality, and we're dealing with error rates in the parts per million, I think it is important to keep looking to get more from quality.

Beyond production of perfect products and services, what else can quality give us? Well, I believe quality will allow us to meet customers' needs even before they know they have them. I believe quality will lead to higher levels of employee involvement and training. I believe quality will allow us to fully develop the potential skills and talents of all our employees. There will be no more "check your brains at the door" as you come to work. I love the phrase I heard once, "When you hire a pair of hands, you get a head for free. Use it."

At Corning Incorporated, quality has led to goal sharing and profit sharing. Everybody from senior leaders to the shop floor participates. We've achieved flatter organizations with fewer bosses, more teammates. Our plant in Blacksburg, VA, for example, that has two levels of employment. It has the plant manager and it has teams. It's a very different way of operating.

That leads me to the second paradigm shift occurring in business today. Simply put, in addition to globalization, businesses are facing an unprecedented emphasis on the importance of highly skilled labor. Lester Thurow of MIT has published a book called Head to Head. In it, he writes:

The skills of the workforce are going to be the key competitive weapon in the twenty-first century. Brain power will create new technologies, but skilled labor will be the arms and

3. CREATING A PRODUCTIVE WORK ENVIRONMENT: Leading and Directing

legs that allow one to employ the new product and process technologies that are being generated. Skilled people become the only sustainable competitive advantage.

Products can be made and shipped from almost anywhere. This can be advantageous for business. However, just as capital and technology flow around the world at lightning speed, conceptual workers — those people who primarily use their heads to get a job done — are mobile and enjoy ever increasing choices as to where they live and work. These conceptual workers are ones who have doctorates in highly specialized fields, or they're talented or trained in marketing, finance, information services, or production management.

At Corning, conceptual workers form a growing percentage of our workforce. For example, in 1972 one-third of our workforce was made up of conceptual workers while two-thirds were people who basically used their hands. Today, that is completely reversed. Two-thirds are conceptual workers and one-third uses mainly physical skills.

Conceptual workers have many opportunities and can sell their skills to the highest bidder, either in money or in the intangibles of the workplace, or both. If we're honest with ourselves, individual businesses need this group of mobile workers more than they need us, so we had better pay attention and prove our worth.

Moreover, if you look at the demographics of the year 2000, it is no surprise that an increasing number of people entering the workforce are going to be women and people of color. To avail ourselves, therefore, of the entire pool of talent out there, we cannot rely only on white males. To attract the best talent we must demonstrate that we really believe in and practice diversity in the workplace.

Now, if you buy the fact that knowledge or skills may be, ultimately, the only competitive advantage, then you must intensify your efforts to truly value "the individual."

Talented individuals will choose a friendly environment where everyone has a chance to succeed to her or his highest potential. Conceptual workers will be drawn to a company that makes them feel appreciated and gives them the independence and flexibility to make decisions at the level where the work is being done. They will not be attracted by hierarchy, but by horizontal structure. They will not be attracted by security, but by the opportunity for personal growth. They will not be attracted by homogeneity, but by cultural diversity. Also, they will not be attracted by work alone, but by a perceived balance between work and leisure.

How will traditional businesses need to change in order to keep pace with these challenges? I believe we'll need to adopt a new concept of loyalty and obligation. Companies can no longer guarantee job security — if, in fact, they ever could. What they can and should guarantee is the provision of opportunities for personal and professional growth. In addition, companies must provide the tools by which each individual can attain life-long training, so that his or her skills are constantly upgraded to meet the requirements of the job at hand.

Ultimately, companies should strive to make employees eager to stay, but ready to go. This is a big shift. It moves responsibility from the company to the individual to take advantage of opportunities.

In the Harvard Business Review, Chris Bartlett describes it as a shift from "guarantee of employment to commitment to employability." This will not be easy because it flies in the face of the old paternalistic, controlling, "cradle-to-grave" thinking.

We must increasingly think of all employees as professionals. With high performance work teams in both manufacturing and administrative settings, we need to entrust employees with strategic ownership of the business. Without question, this makes for a more inventive company, one that is able to respond to the requirements of a diverse global clientele. Even investors are beginning to appreciate that a company's real investment today is no longer in machines, but in the knowledge of the worker.

Workers today — whether they are equipped with "conceptual" or "physical" skills — must be capable of thinking for themselves. They must be able to make critical decisions about their customers and their immediate work environment. They must possess "transferable" skills and be able to apply knowledge gained in one situation to very different situations. All of this behooves us to make life-long training of each and every employee a priority — and not just for basic skills. The new way of working will require new skills such as empathy and listening. These skills can and must be learned with the same level of priority we put on technical skills.

Perhaps most important, as we turn the corner on the next millennium, companies need to own up to their social obligations and responsibilities to workers. If we ignore this responsibility, it may be taken away.

There is a great euphoria about "market economies" and "globalization." Corporate strategists proclaim the wisdom of comparative advantage, of leanness and meanness. If one can get software development done as well and cheaper in Bangladesh than in Silicon Valley, so be it. If one has to announce a massive layoff as earnings are rising, well, that's good for shareholders — almost always the stock price goes up with such an announcement. However, that kind of game cannot go on forever. Society will not stand for it.

I am all for bolstering the economy of India or China, or wherever — but we cannot forever neglect or ignore our own infrastructure, or our own people. If we take a totally free market view, over time our political institutions will inject themselves into the process, more than they already have — and that would be the worst outcome imaginable.

Already there are questions being raised in this country about why the real income of average Americans is shrinking when corporate earnings, the stock market, and CEO salaries are all growing. If we in business do not show a sensitivity to this issue, and to the fate of our current workforce — whether it be in France, the US, or Japan — then someone is going to make some rules we don't like. Jobs will be protected, borders will be closed, and we'll be back in the Economic Dark Ages. Thus, companies face the difficult, but necessary, task of balancing the need to be global players and the need to ensure a healthy workforce where we operate.

Regarding a healthy workforce, the sorts of changes I'm talking about invariably are accompanied by stress at every level of the organization. Even though employees will have to take a much more proactive role in their own careers through constant renewal and life-long education, this does not lessen the organization's role. Companies will have to apply resources to deal with stress. Leaders will need to be sensitive and sympathetic, and help their people through it. Companies will also have to show responsiveness to employees' needs outside the workplace. This means ongoing support for work-family balance, for flexibility in dealing with individual needs and concerns, and even for continued financial support of the infrastructure in communities where we operate.

Does this sound soft? Too humanistic and liberal? Believe me, it is not. Valuing the individual and a continuing focus on people is a hard-nosed strategy that leads to a competitive advantage and long-term shareholder value.

So far, I hope most of what I've said has elicited a nod of recognition and the thought, "That's right. That's how it is." Now let's take a look at ourselves, as leaders, and see how well equipped we are to manage these new organizations we're creating.

We have traditionally viewed leaders as "heroes" who come forward in a time of crisis to resolve a problem. If we are lucky, we get a Cincinnatus or a Washington, who uses power wisely and lays it down when the job is done. If we are unlucky, we get a Hitler, a Stalin or a Mao. In between are those who can lead only through hierarchical rigidity.

By focusing on the leader as hero, we stress the short term, and we assume the powerlessness of those being led. We also ignore the many other positive examples of leadership history has to offer.

What if we look at leaders like Pericles and Lincoln, Pope John XXIII and Gandhi, Corozon Aquino and Mother Theresa, Hesburgh and Conant, Watson and Sloan? What do these people have in common? What can we learn from their leadership model? I think I can boil it down to seven leadership behaviors. Of course my original list was a lot longer, but we humans can't seem to remember lists of more than seven things, so I've made it easier on myself and on you by categorizing. Let me go through each behavior.

The first one is an adaptation of justice Learned Hand's wonderful description of liberty. He said, "The spirit of liberty is that spirit which is not too sure it is right." I would say that the spirit of true leadership is the spirit that is not too sure it is right — all the time. I like the ring of that because I believe leaders who are not sure they are right are leaders who listen.

History tells us that those in positions of leadership who do not listen, fail. Being a good listener is no guarantee of success, but I believe lack of this characteristic is a fatal flaw. Not being too sure you are right all the time also frees you to take risks, and to take the heat gracefully when things go wrong — as they inevitably will sometimes when you're dealing with ambiguous situations.

In fact, it's important to understand that compromise and "muddling through" are acceptable as long as your basic values and goals are not compromised. As a leader, you need to model this behavior, and become a catalyst for change, a champion of new ideas, a supporter of unconventional thinking. When you don't have to be right all the time, you can also teach your people to ask for help when needed and shamelessly accept it. You can also encourage them to ask, "What needs to be accomplished here?" rather than "Who's in charge?"

That brings us to the second critical leadership behavior: Be a team player — and pay attention to the bench. Of course there is an inherent paradox in being a leader in a non-hierarchical organization. While your relationships with others must be as egalitarian as possible, you'll also be held to higher standards than anyone else.

As you establish the values, create the vision and set the standards for performance. You'll be judged not by your talk, but by your walk. So you better put the best interests of the company and its people above yourself. Sure, I grew up in an age where protection of turf was the bottom line. I know that's a hard habit to break. But turf wars only divert your resources from the real war zone: the marketplace. So, as a leader, you have to demonstrate that personal success comes only from group success.

You also have to keep an eye on the future and develop strong subordinates for succession. Any winning team has a bunch of strong players waiting on the bench. So watch for people smarter than you — these may be your future leaders — coach them, mentor them. Take chances, especially with young people. You can often get uncommon results from common people, but only if you believe that developing people is one of the most important jobs you have.

If you really want to be successful in this ambiguous world we live in, you'll develop this third critical leadership behavior in yourself. Namely — balance deliberation with action.

Yes, you have to be a strategic thinker. Yes, you have to use your intelligence and experience to make good judgments. Yes, you have to think always of the vision and communicate it in a way that people will understand. But in addition to conceptualizing, deliberating, and communicating, you must be swift to action.

Hold yourself and others accountable for great performance over time. Concentrate on high impact opportunities and be oriented at all times towards achievement. Demonstrate your beliefs through your actions. In a word, commit.

Okay. So far I've told you that as a good leader, you must not be too sure you are right all the time. You must be a team player and pay attention to your bench. You must balance deliberation with action. What else makes a good leader?

Filtering everything through a broad-minded widely experienced world view.

This fourth leadership behavior accounts for the fact that you don't see too many 20-somethings running large corporations. It takes time to rack up experience in both line and staff positions, to gain exposure to various disciplines, to develop an appreciation of different cultures, and to be comfortable traveling and working in the "global village."

These are all prerequisites for leading a multifaceted, global enterprise. How else will you gain international experience to apply to business dealings? How else will you practice true diversity as a real competitive advantage? How else will you develop the skills it takes to manage alliances, joint ventures, trading partnerships and all the other forms that business relationships take these days?

In fact, these days there is one dimension of society and business that Cincinnatus and Washington and Lincoln never had to deal with. That is, of course, technology. To be a leader today, you better make technology your friend. That's the fifth leadership behavior we need to cultivate, because whoever "obsoletes the existing," wins.

How do you "obsolete the existing"? You understand and know how to deploy technology. You believe in innovation as a way of life, and you think big. But you also don't innovate for innovation's sake. You make the critical linkage between technology and the marketplace, and you use technology to become the low cost producer.

Because ultimately, you have to adopt the sixth leadership behavior, and that is: Don't forget the bottom line. Be financially adept.

Develop good analytical skills, get comfortable using basic

3. CREATING A PRODUCTIVE WORK ENVIRONMENT: Leading and Directing

financial tools; understand financial markets; and use economic data and trends to your advantage. But in addition to seeing the big picture from 10,000 feet up, you also need to be able to zero in on the details. Counting your pennies is a good place to start. You'll have to be comfortable with P&L and balance sheet management.

Now, what did I leave for last? What's the final advice I have for anyone interested in being a great leader? It's this: Leave your office once in a while.

Sure, hard work never killed anyone, but why take a chance? Create a balanced, healthy lifestyle. Take care of your physical condition. Pick up a hobby or two. Of course, if it makes you feel better, you can always tell yourself that these other interests give you new perspectives to apply at work.

Also, don't forget the community. Be a good corporate citizen. Contribute your time and your money to some worthy cause. Share your management expertise with a educational or cultural institution. If nothing else, they usually appreciate you more than your business associates. You might even consider running for elective office.

Finally, learn to laugh at life's quirks, and especially at yourself. Be always an optimist, especially in the darkest hour. And show your appreciation, especially for any luck that comes your way.

So what can we conclude about all this? For one thing, as good leaders we should not be too sure it's right. Or maybe we should not be too sure that, even if it is right, that it will stay that way.

Leaders, especially in transformed organizations of the future, will undoubtedly require other behaviors we haven't even considered yet. It's at times like these that I realize how important corporate values are. The leadership behaviors I've suggested or any future behaviors, should always be tested against your corporate values.

I'm fond of saying that our values are the buoys in an ever-changing sea of commerce. If you value quality, if you value the individual, and if you value performance, I believe you'll be able to achieve the great feats of leadership that I've been able to achieve. In other words you'll muddle through somehow.

NOT ENOUGH GENERALS WERE KILLED!

Peter Drucker

OVER THE YEARS, I HAVE DISCUSSED with scores—perhaps even hundreds—of leaders their roles, their goals and their performance. I have worked with some exceedingly bright executives and a few dummies, with people who talk a good deal about leadership and others who apparently never even think of themselves as leaders and who rarely, if ever, talk about leadership.

The lessons are unambiguous. The first is that there may be "born leaders," but there surely are far too few to depend on them. Leadership must be learned and can be learned.

The second major lesson is that "leadership personality," "leadership style," and "leadership traits" do not exist. Among the most effective leaders I have encountered and worked with in a half century, some locked themselves into their office and others were ultragregarious. Some (though not many) were "nice guys" and others were stern disciplinarians. Some were quick and impulsive; others studied and studied again and then took forever to come to a decision. Some were warm and instantly "simpatico"; others remained aloof. Some spoke of their family; others never mentioned anything apart from the task in hand.

Some leaders were excruciatingly vain—and it did not affect their performance (as his spectacular vanity did not affect General Douglas MacArthur's performance until the very end of his career). Some were self-effacing to a fault—and again it did not affect their performance as leaders (as it did not affect the performance of General George Marshall or Harry Truman). Some were as austere in their private lives as a hermit in the desert; others were ostentatious and pleasure-loving and whooped it up at every opportunity. Some were good listeners, but among the most effective leaders I have worked with were also a few loners who listened only to their own inner voice. The one and only personality trait the effective ones I have encountered did have in common was something they did not have: they had little or no "charisma" and little use either for the term or for what it signifies.

All the effective leaders I have encountered knew four simple things:

1. The only definition of a leader is someone who has followers. Some people are thinkers. Some are prophets. Both roles are important and badly needed. But without followers, there can be no leaders.

2. An effective leader is not someone who is loved or admired. He or she is someone whose followers do the right things. Popularity is not leadership. Results are.

3. Leaders are highly visible. Therefore they set examples.

4. Leadership is not rank, privileges, titles or money. It is responsibility.

REGARDLESS OF THEIR almost limitless diversity with respect to personality, style, abilities and interests, the effective leaders I have met, worked with and observed also behaved much the same way:
■ They did not start out with the question, "What do I want?" They started out asking, "What needs to be done?"
■ Then they asked, "What can and should I do to make a difference?" This has to be something that both needs to be done and fits the leader's strengths and the way she or he is most effective.
■ They constantly asked, "What are the organization's mission and goals? What constitutes performance and brings results in this organization?"
■ They were extremely tolerant of diversity in people and did not look for carbon copies of themselves. It rarely even occurred to them to ask, "Do I like or dislike this person?" But they were totally—fiendishly—intolerant when it came to a person's performance, standards and values.
■ They were not afraid of strength in their associates. They gloried in it. Their motto was what Andrew Carnegie wanted to have put on his tombstone: "Here lies a man who attracted better people into his service than he was himself."
■ They submitted themselves to the "mirror test"—that is, they made sure that the person they saw in the mirror in the morning was the kind of person they wanted to be, respect and believe in. This way they fortified themselves against the leader's greatest temptations—to do things that are popular rather than right and to do petty, mean, sleazy things.

FINALLY, THESE EFFECTIVE leaders were not preachers; they were doers. In the mid-1920s, when I was in my high school years, a whole spate of books on World War I and its campaigns suddenly appeared in English, French, and German. For our term project, our excellent history teacher—himself a badly wounded war veteran—told each of us to pick several of these books, read them carefully, and write a major essay on our selections. When we then discussed these essays in class, one of my fellow students said, "Every one of these books says that the Great War was a war of total military incompetence. Why was it?" Our teacher did not hesitate a second but shot right back, "Because not enough generals were killed; they stayed way behind the lines and let others do the fighting and dying."

Effective leaders delegate a good many things; they have to or they drown in trivia. But they do not delegate the one thing that only they can do with excellence, the one thing that will make a difference, the one thing that will set standards, the one thing they want to be remembered for. They do it.

Developing Effective Human Resources

- Training Employees (Articles 25 and 26)
- Career and Staff Development (Articles 27 and 28)
- Appraising and Improving Performance (Articles 29 and 30)

Every organization needs to develop its employees. This is accomplished through a number of avenues, including formal corporate training, career development, and performance appraisal. Just as the society and the economy will continue to change, so will the human resource needs of the organizations. Individuals and their employers must work together to achieve the effective use of human resources. They must plan together to make the maximum use of their abilities so as to meet the challenge of the changing environment in which they live.

American industry spends approximately the same amount of money each year on training and developing employees as is spent by all colleges and universities combined. It also trains roughly the same number of people as there are students in traditional postsecondary education. Corporate programs are often very elaborate and can involve months or even years of training. In fact, corporate training and development programs have been recognized by academia for their quality and excellence. The American Council for Education has a program designed to evaluate and make recommendations concerning corporate and government training programs for college credit. And corporations themselves have entered into the business of granting degrees that are recognized by regional accrediting agencies. For example, McDonald's grants an associate's degree from "Hamburger U." General Motors Institute offers the oldest formalized corporate degree-granting program in the United States, awarding a bachelor's in industrial management; Ernst and Young offers a master's in accountancy; and a Ph.D. program in policy analysis is available from the Rand Corporation. American industry is in the business of educating and training employees, not only as a simple introduction and orientation to the corporation, but as a continual and constant enterprise of lifelong learning so that both firms and employees can meet the challenges of an increasingly competitive world. Meeting these challenges depends on knowledge, not on sweat, and relies on the ability to adapt to and adopt technological, social, and economic changes faster than competitors.

There is an important difference between jobs and careers. Everyone who works, whether self-employed or employed by someone else, does a job. Although a career is made up of a series of jobs and positions over an individual's working life, it is more than that. It is a sense of direction, a purpose, and a knowledge of where one is going in one's professional life. Careers are shaped by individuals through the decisions they make concerning their own lives, not by organizations. It is the individual who must ultimately take the responsibility for what happens in his or her career. Organizations offer opportunities for advancement and they fund training and development based on their own self-interest, not solely on workers' interests. Accordingly, the employee must understand that the responsibility for career development ultimately rests with him- or herself.

One of the ways that organizations can assist in the career development of their employees is to engage in appropriate and effective performance appraisals. This process benefits both the employee and the employer. From the employer's perspective, it allows the organization to fine-tune the performance of the individual and

UNIT 4

to take appropriate action when the performance does not meet an acceptable standard. From the employee's perspective, appraisal allows the individual to evaluate his or her situation in the organization. Appraisal will indicate, in formal ways, how the individual is viewed by the organization. It is, for the employee, an opportunity to gauge the future.

To ignore the development of the potential of the employees of any organization is to court disaster—not only for the organization, but for the employee. People who have stopped developing themselves are cheating themselves and their employers. Both will be vulnerable to changes brought on by increased competition, but the workers will be the ones who join the statistics of the unemployed.

Looking Ahead: Challenge Questions

Organizations spend a great deal of money on training and development. Why do many organizations feel it is necessary to provide courses in-house? Why do other organizations spend money on outside programs? Why might the training programs of some firms be inadequate, even though a great deal of money is spent on them? What are some of the questions organizations should be asking of their training and development operations?

What are your career plans, and how do you plan to implement them?

Performance appraisals can be difficult, especially if they are not positive. How would you handle an essentially negative performance appraisal, both as the appraiser and the appraisee? How can organizations improve performance appraisals? How might a poor performance appraisal lead to a charge of discrimination?

Send Managers Back to School At the Local University

Institutions of higher learning can be a valuable source for training managers. Here are some guidelines to understanding how to create a partnership between your organization and a university.

Fred Maidment

Fred Maidment is Associate Professor and Chairman of the Department of Business Administration at Park College in Parkville, Missouri. He received his B.S. from New York University, his M.B.A. from Baruch and his doctorate from the University of South Carolina. He has written extensively on training and is the editor of Annual Editions: Management; Annual Editions: International Business; *and* Annual Editions: Human Resources.

When human resource professionals are seeking training and education for managers in their organizations they will often look at many sources including in-house, outside consultants and professional associations. One resource that should not be overlooked, however, is university education programs for practicing managers.

More schools are offering programs designed for managers in business and industry for the following reasons: they help to establish and maintain contact with the corporate world; they assist the college in faculty development; and they operate at a profit, bringing additional fund to the college in the form of fees.

• They enhance the reputation of the university among a potentially large and important source of financial and other support.

Human resource professionals are charged with helping managers stay current with what is going on in their particular field, whether technical or managerial in nature, and these programs at colleges and universities provide certain advantages by:

• Eliminating the distractions of the job while in the seminar.

• Presenting the material in a highly efficient and organized way.

• Allowing the manager to learn in an environment that is less threatening.

• Permitting the manager to discuss his or her situation in a "neutral" setting.

• Helping managers actually learn something that will help them on the job.

Human resource professionals need to be aware that management training programs vary greatly in terms of cost and time that the manager and/or his or her company must invest.

Some of these programs can take several months, such as the one at Harvard University, where the manager actually becomes a student, living in a dormitory for several months, to a single day or half day. Expenses for the program can range from less than $100 to thousands of dollars.

Colleges usually present the programs on campus, but it is not unusual for the institution to go off campus and do the program at a hotel, convention center or some other facility.

Course Requirements

University-based management education programs have the advantage of carrying the institution's name as a kind of endorsement of the program, but the human resource manager needs to be aware that these programs are often not examined with the same rigor as the regular course work.

The fact is, that university education programs for practicing managers are in the same market and subject to the same pressures as the programs from vendors other than universities, such as professional associations, or consulting firms and have the same problems:

- As with all management education, the level of instruction is very uneven. Just because some professor has been teaching a course to 20-year-old undergraduates or 24-year-old graduate students does not mean that he or she will do a good job instructing managers.
- The programs are market-driven. They present programs based on topics that the college thinks it can sell.

In addition, human resource professionals need to acknowledge that university-based management education programs have certain problems that are unique to them:

- They are not the main business of the university. These programs are viewed as ancillary enterprises and often do not have the full support of the university.
- Many university administrators do not understand industry, and, indeed, some harbor anti-business attitudes. Remember, the radicals of the sixties are now in their 40's and 50's. Many of them are still in colleges as administrators and faculty.
- Because these programs are not the major emphasis of the institution, they can be subject to the political whims of the administration. A change at the top can kill the program.
- These programs do not necessarily have a committed constituency inside the university and that includes the business school faculty. A phenomenon in education for business is that many of the faculty have never been in business. They may suffer from the 27 year-old Ph.D. syndrome.

Today, it is possible, and indeed not unlikely to find marketing professors who have never sold; professors teaching banking who have never worked in a bank; and lawyers teaching business law with little or no experience in contracts.

- Just because a program is sponsored by a college does not mean that the school is presenting the program. Some schools simply sub-contract this activity to seminar-producing organizations. Conversely, it is not unknown for private organizations to approach universities for their endorsement, and the use of their name in exchange for a fee or royalty.

While people in human resources may sometimes find it difficult to judge the quality of university management education programs, especially if the topic is outside of their expertise, there are some things that a human resource manager can do to help determine the quality of the program:

- Find out the name of the person who is actually teaching the course. Any seminar is only as good as the instructor. See if you can get a copy of the instructor's resume, publication list, etc.
- Ask the vendor for a list of students and firms who have been through this particular seminar with this instructor. If this is the first time this particular seminar is being offered, ask for a list from other seminars. They may, legitimately, refuse to give these lists to you, but it does not hurt to ask.
- Contact the instructor directly and determine what he or she plans to do in the seminar. The outline in the brochure and reality may be very different.
- Determine whether students will be evaluated. This is rare, but if you are paying to send employees to school, you will want to know how well they have done. Programs are often very reluctant to do this because a bad grade usually means that people from that firm will not return, because the risk is too high from both a career and personal perspective.
- Remember, price and reputation do not ensure quality in management education. Some of the very best instruction may be obtained at institutions of less than national standing, while some of the worst is very expensive and at well known and highly regarded schools. The reverse is, obviously, also true.

HR professionals, and the organizations they represent must learn to be effective and efficient consumers of education and training, as with any other item that is purchased by industry.

Chevron Trains for Redeployment

New Skills Equal New Opportunities

By Gillian Flynn

It's a slippery, scary workplace world out there. Job categories, entire occupations, can slide into extinction in the time it takes to make your morning coffee. The best self-defense against a moribund career: skills, and lots of them.

Enter San Francisco-based Chevron Corp., a company succeeding in the unstable slicks of the oil industry. We all know the embattled state of the trade as a whole—in the past five years, repeated restructurings and downsizings have kept most oil companies from regaining firm footing. Chevron itself hasn't been impervious to the turbulence. But it has handled it laudably, always with an eye for avoiding layoffs. It has done so by building on that basic idea: The more skills employees have, the safer they are.

Through a special program instituted in 1992, Chevron has rematched employees with jobs internally, encouraging job-hopping from company to company. The matches don't have to be perfect—skills training smooths the rough edges. Employees who can't find another Chevron job are still offered opportunities to develop more marketable skills for job-hunting on the outside. The effort has protected hundreds upon hundreds of workers from the unemployment lines—and saved Chevron millions of dollars in severance payments.

To be so unlucky: Chevron just has too many high performers. Since the late '80s, the oil industry has been beleaguered indeed. Many divisions at Chevron found themselves serving up severance packages and outplacement programs. It wasn't that the employees weren't great; the company just had to slim down to stay alive.

In 1992, the corporation began to ask itself if this was the only way. The company as a whole wasn't undergoing a downsizing; different divisions within the company were. Often, while one operating company was cutting its headcount, another was aggressively recruiting to keep up with demand.

Houston-based Chevron Production Co. was one of the first to come up with the idea: mixing and matching employees from one unit with another. "The process was based on the premise that these are highly skilled, bright people, and should we not think of using those skills in other operating companies," says Sam Fortune, manager of human resources for the Gulf of Mexico business unit, Chevron Production Co.

For instance, in production operations, a large number of employees are petroleum engineers with college degrees. Chevron's refineries have traditionally recruited *chemical* engineers. But with some training and assistance, couldn't a petroleum engineer fill the void? If it could work, it would be a win-

UPGRADE SKILLS

Chevron USA had bright, qualified employees—in all the wrong places. Some Chevron units had too many; others too few. Instead of laying off here and hiring there, the company trained employees to take jobs outside their specialties or in other Chevron companies.

ning situation all the way around: An over-staffed company would cut headcount without layoffs, an under-staffed company would hire an employee already familiar with Chevron operations and the employee would hold onto his or her job.

Companies within Chevron were categorized as either supply (needing to cut headcount) or demand (needing to staff up). Within every operating company, *redeployment coordinators* were identified. Both demand and supply organizations had coordinators—high-level individuals who would negotiate matches.

The demand companies remained skeptical at first, on two counts. One: They were concerned about how far employees should try to stretch—would they try to jump entire job categories unqualified? Two: They were a little suspicious that "surplus" employees might be low performers who supply companies simply wanted to get rid of.

Chevron responded from the top level. The company made it clear that it was going to at least try this plan. To ensure its use, HR set up a job bank—demand organizations were required to first post their jobs in the database before they hired outside the company. To further alleviate any doubts, the company ruled that if relocation was involved, the supply company would pay for it—for both exempt and nonexempt workers. Chevron was ready to start its grand experiment, and an experiment it was. Says Fortune: "I have to admit, initially it was all theory. We just put the theory into practice and crossed our fingers."

Employees identify skills they have, train for those they lack. While most demand companies originally searched for technical matches, many found they were swayed equally by an employee's "softer" skills: the ability to work in teams, to solve problems, to lead people. Field operators from production headed to refineries to train as board operators. Former techies were jumping into marketing positions whereas before only those with business degrees were hired. "Companies found that what was more important than the degree in many cases was the type of individual and the dimensions of their behavior," says Fortune. "They could actually be trained without a lot of effort to fit into a marketing environment."

Part of the redeployment coordinator's job was to help identify as many skill areas as possible. Coordinators received reports from employees' former supervisors and interviewed the employees to find out what kind of job they wanted and were suited for.

Jim Brady, manager of Elk Hills oil field in Bakersfield, California, found himself as the redeployment coordinator

At Chevron, overstaffed operating companies can transfer employees to other units, which train them for the skills they need in their new jobs. For instance, a chemical engineer may head to a new position in another operating company ramping-up for a new project in another part of the world.

for the entire western business unit when more than 150 people were "surplused." He spent nearly 70% of his time for six months functioning as a coordinator. He says an important part of the program was this self-assessment process—identifying everything an employee had going for him or her. "The first thing we tried to tell employees was that they weren't being cut off because they weren't good," says Brady. "We told them, 'You've got skills that someone's going to want. All you have to do is identify those skills and find out what the other organizations need.'"

Of those that entered the redeployment and training program, Brady estimates that 80% found another job within the company. Those who weren't redeployed often were partly culpable—they were too rigid in their job interests or relocation destinations. "But people who truly, actively worked with the system, almost all of them were placed," says Brady.

Whenever possible, surplused employees were immediately released from their job duties so they could spend the full six-month grace period looking for an intracompany job. This allowed them to be free both for meetings with coordinators and interviews with interested demand organizations. For the period of highest intensity, May 1992 to May 1993, 1,050 individuals were redeployed, spanning job categories as broad as geologists, engineers, technicians, pilots, secretaries, information-systems specialists, offshore oil-platform workers and even more.

Some supply companies assisted employees in enhancing their marketability by offering their own training. For instance, one unit realized its employees were short on computer competencies, skills many demand companies were recruiting for. It hired Manpower Inc., the staffing firm, to teach onsite classes in computer-software programs such as *WordPerfect* and *Lotus*. During a six-week period, more than 200 training sessions were offered. Of the trainees

4. DEVELOPING EFFECTIVE HUMAN RESOURCES: Training Employees

taking all four courses, more than 85% found jobs.

Most often, however, training was handled by the demand organization. Take the case of Dave Reeves, a *redeployee* whose background was in health and environmental resources. He hired on at the El Segundo, California, refinery for a position as a reliability analyst. Not a perfect fit, but he met the refinery's basic criteria: a suitable technical background, good communication and problem-solving skills. However, he still required some training. "His background wasn't a refinery background," says his supervisor, Brian Garber, lead fixed-equipment analyst. "There were many processes here he wouldn't understand."

So Reeves underwent several weeks of education: process training (on how the refinery operates), reliability-candidate training (covering basic job skills and expectations) and incident training (instruction on identifying causes of system malfunctions) as well as safety, all conducted in the refinery by trainers or by Garber.

Garber says the time and cost of training was a worthwhile trade-off. Reeves was up and running quickly—both because he was familiar with Chevron and because he had a high-achieving personality. "Dave was making big, big changes around here in the first year," says Garber. "We had training in place that helped him get a good foot on the ground, but his progress was accelerated by his work ethics."

Despite success stories like Dave Reeves, redeployment wasn't a complete success—not all employees were good fits. But most demand organizations will tell you that the good ones more than made up for the poor ones. Sue Nutter, section supervisor for the environmental operations unit at El Segundo refinery, also supervises a redeployee. Roger Hahn came to the refinery from a production area, but glided through the training and readily applied it. He became such an asset to the division, Nutter actually created a new job for him, upped his pay and gave him supervisory responsibilities. "He was such a pleasant surprise," she says. "I have absolutely no complaints. We made out like bandits." Would she do it again? "If I could identify a good-fit candidate like Roger, I would definitely do it again."

Chevron's strategy of mixing and matching employees with jobs works in a large part because it has so many businesses running on different cycles, such as this unit in the republic of Kazakhstan, formerly in the Soviet Union. Here, employees return to their homes in Kul'sary, Karaton and Sarkamys.

Chevron even provided training opportunities for employees who weren't vying for a job within the company. An educational assistance program reimbursed 75% of tuition, books and fees—even for up to two years after termination—to employees taking courses that would enhance their opportunities for finding a job outside the company. Employees with bachelors' degrees who wanted to become teachers were reimbursed the cost of obtaining their teaching certificates.

Chevron's generous training and education efforts helped employees acquire marketable skills—which landed them jobs inside and outside of the company. Just as human resources had hypothesized early on, it was a winning situation all around. Demand companies have been extremely satisfied overall, says Fortune. "They've seen the benefits of getting an employee who knows the company, who has a track record and can bring quicker success than bringing in a new hire and starting fresh," he says.

Employees also have been satisfied. Some of Brady's redeployees have contacted him several years after their transfer to tell him how thankful they were for the process. In general, the workforce rests easier knowing that the redeployment option exists if ever they're surplused. Many check the job base regularly anyway, just to see what skills are in demand or to identify opportunities for job enrichment.

Chevron, as a company, has benefited in a variety of ways. For one thing, its workforce is more highly skilled as a result of the redeployment process. The effort also saved the company approximately $25 million in severance costs alone, and earned it kudos in the U.S. Department of Labor's *Guide to Responsible Restructuring*.

For organizations interested in a similar approach, having a variety of businesses running on different cycles as Chevron does is a definite plus. But Fortune believes the effort can work for most companies: "The biggest step rather than the size of the company is committing to at least making an effort to try it. You need top management support—saying, 'Before we let these people go, do we have needs elsewhere they can fill?'"

Today's job market is all about skills—how many do you have and what can you do with them? Chevron's answer to that question in 1996: Lots.

Gillian Flynn is the assistant editor at PERSONNEL JOURNAL.

Women in American boardrooms
Through a glass, darkly

WALK up to the directors' suites of a big American corporation, and the women toiling there will mostly be secretaries, caterers and cleaners. Go down a floor or two, and the situation changes: women account for 48% of managerial and executive positions and 52% of professional ones. The "glass ceiling" that once appeared to block women's advancement is cracking as women hammer on it from below. Indeed, a glass ladder might now be a better metaphor: women can climb to the top, but the upper rungs are slippery.

So far, few women have climbed all the way up. A government-financed Glass Ceiling Commission last year estimated that they held only 5% or so of senior executive positions. That is not entirely surprising. In 1992 the average age of senior corporate women was 44; in the same year, the average age of chief executives in the 1,000 biggest public companies was 56. The advent of large numbers of senior female executives is simply too recent to show results.

The experience of the early pioneers is promising. In a survey of 217 Fortune-500 companies, Roy Adler of Pepperdine University found that women who got their MBA degrees between 1955 and 1970 had outperformed men. Although women accounted for fewer than one in 25 students of the class of 1970, for example, one in ten of those who had made it into the top 20 in their company was a woman. "For nearly every year," Mr. Adler concludes, "a woman is two or three times as likely to reach top management as her similarly prepared male counterpart."

There are other signs that women are gaining ground. According to a salary survey published last year in *Working Woman* magazine, pay for female executives has increased by 18.3% since 1993, compared with 1.7% for men. From 1982 to 1992, the number of female executive vice-presidents doubled. And once a few women infiltrate managerial ranks, others will follow. Heather Haveman of Cornell University found that the more women there are at a particular level, the more likely other women are to be hired or promoted to that level; and the more women managers, the more likely women are to sit on the company board.

Until now, women managers have generally been concentrated in a few areas, especially the public sector, where women from minority groups are particularly likely to make their careers. Women are also more likely to be managers in fields in which there are lots of women to manage: health, say, rather than steel making. That may change as women acquire qualifications in subjects that were once exclusively male. In 1971 women took only 1.1% of advanced degrees in engineering, for example; by 1992, that figure was up to 14.8%. Women also take almost half the law degrees in America, and more than a third of advanced degrees in business and medicine.

But in spite of this progress, the lives of male and female managers remain stubbornly different. Men continue to rise further and faster than women in corporate America. A study of male and female 1982 MBA graduates from Stanford University found that, though 10% of the women had become vice-presidents by 1992, 23% of the men had; for chief executives, the figures were 2% and 16% respectively. Male managers are also better paid: another study of 676 MBA recipients who had worked continuously since taking their degrees between 1975 and 1980 found that women earned 19% less than men. A quarter of those women believed that sex discrimination had blocked their promotion.

Could they be right? Certainly, companies place a premium on having a core of long-term, highly committed executives in strategic positions. Women may be excluded from these key jobs—but sexism is unlikely to be the only reason. Another explanation is that women are more likely to choose (or perhaps be nudged into) public relations, personnel and similar fields, which are not usually the careers from which chief executives are drawn.

Even if sexism disappeared from corporate boardrooms tomorrow, the Fortune

4. DEVELOPING EFFECTIVE HUMAN RESOURCES: Career and Staff Development

500 might never see 250 chief executives in skirts. Two-thirds of all graduates in business and similar subjects are still men. Men rarely have to balance the demands of work and family, as women often do.

Men also seem more committed to their careers. They work more hours than women and spend more years in the workforce. They are hungrier for success: a 1992 management survey found that women were one-third as likely (14% to 44%) as men to aspire to be top dog. Blame babies for the difference: women are more likely to take time off, to work part-time, or switch to a less demanding job during child-rearing years. Indeed, for some well-heeled men, a stay-at-home wife has become a yuppie status symbol.

Moreover, those women who have climbed the ladder do not always feel comfortable with their success. Among lawyers, for example, an analysis of American Bar Association surveys from 1984 and 1990 found that, after controlling for other factors, the hourly pay and promotion prospects for men and women were basically the same. Nevertheless, women were much more likely to leave their firms and to be dissatisfied with work.

Corporate America is still a man's game, so it is hardly surprising that men are better at playing it. Jean Lipman-Blumen of the Claremont Graduate School has found that women use formal processes to seek promotions, while men tend to use informal ones—and the old boys' network remains highly effective. The biggest rewards still tend to go to the aggressive, damn-the-torpedoes management style that men so often adopt.

Uncomfortable in a male world, female executives are more likely to move on than their male colleagues. Judith Rosener of the Irvine school of management at the University of California finds that female executives leave because they feel that they are undervalued, or that they do not fit in. They often move to smaller firms in which the hierarchy seems more permeable, or start their own businesses.

In fact, American women are setting up shop on their own at an awesome pace. Since 1987, the number of women-owned firms has increased 78%, to 8m, and employment has more than doubled, to 18.5m people. That sex discrimination has played a part in promoting this entrepreneurial surge is strongly suggested by a survey of women entrepreneurs which found that their biggest problem, by a wide margin, is being taken seriously. If today's small businesses grow into tomorrow's corporate giants, American men could find that their occasional sexism has brought down the wrath of the goddess Nemesis on their heads.

EXECUTIVE WOMEN CONFRONT MIDLIFE CRISIS

It is a time of reckoning for the first big generation of women to hit the age of 40 in a business suit. But for many career women, even talking about it carries a whiff of betrayal.

Betsy Morris

Shoya Zichy's pale-yellow living room on the Upper East Side has become an unlikely refuge for some of the best and brightest career women in New York City. In the past year they have made the pilgrimage here, sometimes in groups, sometimes alone, to visit with Ms. Zichy—to sip her wine, take in her oil paintings, seek her counsel, or counsel each other. Here they can share their darkest secrets; they can be outrageously un-PC; they don't have to make any apologies.

They are serious career women. They are trailblazers. They think lateral moves are for losers. But increasingly they have become unhappy with their lives, and some of them have made big changes.

Adrienne Glasgow, who'd been manager of international finance at Borden and treasurer of Reeves International by age 35, has recently quit her job as chief financial and administrative officer of her family firm. "I wasn't fulfilled," she says. Now she is consulting.

In May, Claire Irving started her own white-collar-crime detective agency. She bailed out of the mergers and acquisitions business eight years ago ("It wasn't burnout, it was boredom") and took a step toward self-determination by joining an investigations firm. Running her own show, she finds, is even better: "I am now doing it for me."

Françoise Jeanpierre, an MBA and a Fulbright scholar, left a promising career in international banking to start a consulting business two years ago. "I was often moving through home," she says. "I needed to *be* home."

And Ruth-Ellen Simmonds, who'd established herself as a turnaround specialist, walked away from an offer to become vice president for marketing at GTE Information Services. "I only have a finite amount of time. I really don't want to do the corporate b.s. over and over and over again. It's a waste of time. It makes me crazy. I need more to life than that."

REPORTER ASSOCIATE *Ruth M. Coxeter*

Such sentiments had puzzled Ms. Zichy, even though she herself had taken about as dramatic as possible a midlife U-turn seven years ago. She had been an international banker and a vice president of American Express Bank when she quit and moved to Rockport, Massachusetts, to devote her time to painting. She thought her own experience rather unusual until she returned to the business world as a consultant last winter. "Here were all these extremely talented women," she says—women with MBAs; women with a dozen or more years in; women with executive positions; a surprising number of them without children and all the attendant work-family problems. They should have been on top of the world; instead, many of them were miserable.

"I started asking myself, 'Why are so many of these brilliant women burning out?'" she says. And she started building a new business—a combination of personality testing and counseling—to try to help them. It has been a land-office business so far: She's counseled 200-plus clients since the beginning of the year, many of them members of the Financial Women's Association of New York.

IT IS CLEARLY a time of reckoning for baby-boomer businesswomen—the first big generation of "skirts," as they are still called in some corporate circles, to hit the age of 40 in a business suit. In many cases, the soul-searching has little, directly, to do with frustration about the glass ceiling. In very few cases does it seem to stem, directly anyway, from so-called work-family struggles. It can be tangled up with those issues, and it is frequently misdiagnosed, but this widespread angst is really something else: Large numbers of women find themselves going through the kind of midlife crisis their fathers and grandfathers went through. "Suddenly women know what men have known all along: that work is hard; work takes a lot of time; work isn't always a day at the beach," says Sharon McGavin, once a senior vice president at Ogilvy & Mather and now chief development officer for the American Red Cross in Greater New York. As former Labor Secretary Lynn Martin puts it, "Women are more aware of what's on the gravestone, which is not 'I worked for IBM.'"

These midlife crises are ultimately not about retreat but about redefinition. In great numbers, women executives emerge from this period making decisive midcourse corrections. Many have simply wearied of the male-dominated game and seek to do business more on their own terms. They change not only their jobs but their ideas of success as well. Some abandon the corporate ladder for the entrepreneurial shoestring. Some take the skills they have learned in business and apply them to more altruistic callings. A much smaller number than people generally think retreat to hearth and home.

Deloitte & Touche got a big surprise, for instance, when it decided to explore the reasons for unusually high turnover among its own up-and-coming female employees. As is true in many companies, executives there assumed women were bailing out mostly for family reasons. What the firm found, however, was that more than 90% of the Deloitte refugees it surveyed were working elsewhere; only a handful were home with small children, and most of those planned to go back to work. The generation of women that blazed new trails into the corporate suites is, evidently, blazing its own trails out.

To get a better snapshot of the phenomenon, FORTUNE enlisted Yankelovich Partners to survey 300 career women, ages 35 to 49, about their thoughts and feelings as they enter midlife. About 94% of the women surveyed were managers or executives. Nearly half had salaries of more than $60,000. The extent of their angst was astonishing. All but 13% said they had made or were seriously considering making a major change in their lives. Almost a third said they frequently felt depressed. More than 40% said they felt trapped.

4. DEVELOPING EFFECTIVE HUMAN RESOURCES: Career and Staff Development

MORE THAN half the women surveyed had friends or colleagues who were getting a divorce or seeking therapy. A third said they had friends who were having an affair. While personal issues were certainly a factor—a majority said they felt they were getting old and less attractive—much of their dissatisfaction stemmed from work. About 45% said they had started their own business or changed jobs, or were seriously considering doing so. Nearly 40% said they had gone back to school or taken a sabbatical, or were seriously thinking about it. A majority said they didn't have enough of a personal life. A third said they were bored. Their restlessness seems to be particularly acute right around age 40, and starts to diminish around age 45.

In most cases, motherhood had little correlation with the frustrations; women with and without children felt similarly. Nor did the glass ceiling seem to be much of an issue. While half felt their workplaces too dominated by men, more than 70% expected to make major career advances in the next five years.

In sum, the usual suspects can't be blamed; something new is afoot here. "There is some kind of profound something going on—a reassessment, a rethinking, a big gulp, whatever," says Ann Clurman, a partner at Yankelovich. "It is not biological. It has to do with self-image and the workplace. And I find this astonishing."

Confronting the problem can be especially hard for career women because any exploration of it leads almost immediately into dangerous territory: sexism, feminism, family, class (can anyone but whining yuppies afford to worry about such matters, much less take time off or jump career tracks?). Many women shudder at the very term "midlife crisis," associated as it often is with the worst kind of self-absorbed male behavior.

Furthermore, discussions of midlife crisis carry an unavoidable undertone of betrayal for this generation of women, which poured hopefully into the work force in the 1970s. It was a group imbued with 1960s idealism and haunted by the specter of Ira Levin's *The Stepford Wives*—desperate to get out of the house. And business was like a big fraternity rush: Women, whether as novelty items or not, were actually being invited to join such traditionally male clubs as the FORTUNE 500 and Wall Street.

"There was so much hype, so much hoopla along the way," says Jeri Sedlar, who was editor-at-large of *Working Woman* magazine until her own midlife reassessment four years ago led her to form an executive search firm with her husband. "I think it was pushing us on." The ambient enthusiasm may have unrealistically raised expectations of the role work and career could play in the lives of women, especially as the climb got steeper, the pyramid grew narrower, and the thrill of the chase faded away.

It was psychoanalyst Elliott Jaques who popularized the term midlife crisis in 1965—and defined it as the point at which people stop growing up and start growing old. It generally happens in the mid-30s, he said, can last for some time, and is different for different people. Depression, often in milder forms, is actually a much more common symptom than a new Porsche. Dr. Laurence Steinberg, psychology professor at Temple University and co-author of a recent book about midlife crisis called *Crossing Paths*, estimates that about 50% of all women and 40% of all men will go through some "significant reassessment" of their lives at this point. About 15% of both groups will have a full-blown crisis.

AND YES, for some men that will be quite spectacular, involving sports cars and mistresses. But one of the more startling things about men these days is that most apparently are suffering silently. Midlife crisis "isn't as in vogue for men this decade. They are in a struggle for career existence," says Jean Hollands, who runs a corporate-counseling and executive-coaching firm in Silicon Valley (see "Men at Midlife: Crisis? What Crisis?"). Many men in this age group were raised to see themselves, as their fathers did, as the family's major breadwinner. And many, drawing on the experience of their fathers, expected to achieve far more than they have—if not in title and pay, then at least in terms of job security and stability. But many have been shaken by the corporate reengineering of the past decade with all the attendant layoffs and insecurity. Executive women in this age group are in a different situation. Starting out with much lower expectations, many got further in their careers than they'd imagined. They took risks; often the risks paid off. Despite widespread frustrations about discrimination in the workplace, many still seem to feel optimistic that they have maneuvering room. They don't feel as fungible as their white male counterparts.

And their socialization was quite different. Although most are major, if not primary, breadwinners for themselves or their families, they are not as hung up about it. Even the most ambitious were raised to expect their lives to be multidimensional, to include some combination of family, community, and outside interests—the kind of package their fathers had in the workplace of the 1950s and 1960s.

Several therapists and counselors say that their male clients would like to make big changes and explore new careers but fear what others will think. Many tell counselors their wives won't allow it. Says Deborah Arron, a Seattle-based attorney-turned-author who now counsels lawyers on, among other things, how to leave the legal profession: "Women feel much more courageous in this area. Men feel much more tied to convention."

For female executives, there is no convention. Just as they made their own way into the corporate suites, they are now making their own way out—and confounding the com-

■ FORTUNE enlisted Yankelovich Partners to survey 300 career women, ages 35 to 49, about their thoughts at midlife. About 94% were managers or executives. Nearly half had salaries of more than $60,000.

IN THE PAST YEAR OR SO, HAVE YOU DONE OR SERIOUSLY CONSIDERED THE FOLLOWING

	TOTAL RESPONSES	RESPONSE BY AGE			HAVE KIDS?	
		35–39 years	40–44 years	45–49 years	YES	NO
Starting your own business	45%	47%	48%	40%	44%	50%
Changing job in same career	44%	45%	45%	41%	43%	43%
Going back to school	38%	38%	41%	34%	40%	32%
Taking a sabbatical	37%	46%	37%	28%	36%	39%
Changing your career	35%	42%	39%	26%	35%	38%
Making major personal change	33%	40%	40%	20%	27%	54%
Leaving job and not working	31%	37%	27%	31%	31%	32%

panies that had been grooming them for years. So many women have started their own firms that as a group they now employ about three-quarters as many workers in the U.S. as the FORTUNE 500. So many are joining the ministry that in clerical circles they've been dubbed the "midlife-crisis crowd." Increasingly, they are seeking high-level jobs at nonprofits, according to subscription rates at *CEO Job Opportunities Update,* a newsletter that lists such job openings.

They are also taking high-level jobs elsewhere in corporate America, says Mary Mattis, vice president for research and advisory services at Catalyst, A New York-based women's research group. As part of Catalyst's consulting for its corporate clients, Mattis does what she called "alumnae" interviews with women to see where they go after they leave. Contrary to widespread assumptions, "in most cases, women aren't going home to have or take care of children," she says. Sometimes women say they are because "it's a socially acceptable answer. You don't burn bridges. You don't have to explain." But much of the time, she says, "it's just not true."

The midlife exodus has taken on a life of its own. While men talk to executive recruiters when they want to make a change, women talk to other women. And for all the good fight that outfits like Catalyst are waging on behalf of women inside corporate America, outside there's an informal grapevine, an underground railroad in which women are reinforcing one another's "Who needs it?" attitude and helping one another find a better fit.

The attitude is reinforced at midlife for many high-powered women by a number of things: a sense of power about what they've accomplished; a sense of freedom from having proved themselves over and over; and increasing restlessness at having to play the game by the old male rules. "The dialogue in the press is not the same as the dialogue among ourselves," says Jeanpierre, the consultant. "This is a far richer and more diverse issue than can be classified by glass ceiling or work-family. It is an array of creative choices by people who reinvent themselves."

For many executive women, a midlife crisis is an excruciatingly painful process, a whopper of an identity crisis—like a divorce—tangled up with all sorts of other baggage. You must conceal it from your boss. If the doubts turn out to be passing fancy—as they do for many women who weather them and then continue on the same path—indiscretion could hopelessly derail you forever. You can't share them with most colleagues. Some would take advantage; others would blast you for selling out. Sometimes, after having invested so much and accomplished so much, you can't even admit a crisis to yourself.

That was the case with Janet Tiebout Hanson, one of the first women roughriders on Wall Street. Fresh out of Columbia University business school in August 1977, Hanson couldn't wait to get started. A week after graduation, she was a bond saleswoman at Goldman Sachs. It was the Wild West, spontaneous combustion, a frat house, she recalls, and she was thrilled to be part of it. Her work was her life; the firm was her family. A jock who had played everything from golf to field hockey to paddle tennis, she thrived on the competition, and it didn't take her long to make it onto the fast track. In 1986

MEN AT MIDLIFE: CRISIS? WHAT CRISIS?

Ask a bunch of prosperous, 40ish white guys from Connecticut to meet and talk about midlife crisis, and they dance around the subject as though you had inquired gently about their experiences with sexual impotence.

Midlife crisis? The men, gathered in a focus group conducted for FORTUNE by Yankelovich Partners, could be remarkably compassionate about the subject, but generally they regarded midlife crises as vaguely embarrassing things that other people—men and women—occasionally have. Says Al, a financial products wholesaler: "Midlife crisis is a label you put on other people doing bizarre behavior. But you never anticipate that you will do it."

Push them a bit, and these men admit that events—a divorce, a layoff, an ailing friend—have triggered some anxious soul-searching about what they are doing with their lives. But none of the nine concede that their midlife musings and second-guessing ever actually escalated into a crisis. And none of them report having voluntarily changed careers, spouses, or hometowns as a result of any navel-gazing.

Frankly, these men appeared stuck—trapped, in their perception, by the burden of being men, and envious of the freedom available to many professional women. "Men have responsibilities, and women have choices," says Mike, a soda company executive who admits he looks around sometimes and wonders, "Is this all there is?"

Their self-image as breadwinners, responsible for tuition and retirement, seems to have snuffed out any serious consideration of chucking everything for a new career or lifestyle. Besides, says Peter, a benefits consultant, "most men are scared to change. They're afraid of making a decision."

Professional women in the workplace have it rough in many ways, the men seemed to feel, but are freer than men to pull up stakes and try something completely different. True, they have to put up with lower wages, leering bosses, the pressure of bearing and raising children, and the isolation of being almost alone in a male world. But "a woman who is not the primary wage earner has the option of staying home," says one. That is human, not female, nature, they agree: A man happily married to a woman with a high-paying career might be pleased to stay home too.

Women, they said, were more likely to have crises because they have different "clocks" that force them to make important decisions at different times than men. "Maybe the midlife crisis for women comes in their 30s when they have to decide about having children," says John, senior vice president at an investment house. Other men in the group felt that women became very concerned about their appearance when they turned 40. When women worried that their attractiveness was ending, they worried that their career was ending too, and quit. "Women in their 40s really feel they've peaked or are about to peak, and they think they have failed," says John. "Men see themselves as having 20 more years."

"MEN HAVE RESPONSIBILITIES, AND WOMEN HAVE CHOICES," SAYS A SODA COMPANY EXECUTIVE.

When a full-fledged midlife crisis comes along, though, nearly all agreed that a woman is likely to handle it much better than a man. "Men are more drastic, more irrational," says Al. "Men buy Porsches, disappear to Florida, shack up with chippies, and come back six weeks later. Women are more responsible. They get involved socially; they join a bridge club."

How would their wives react if these men announced they were having a midlife crisis? Every reaction imaginable was predicted. "Mine would say, 'Are you out of your mind? Get back to work,' " says Andrew. Dave figures his wife would be concerned and compassionate. Al's ex-wife would have hired a private detective, figuring he was about to have an affair, he jokes.

— Brian O'Reilly

4. DEVELOPING EFFECTIVE HUMAN RESOURCES: Career and Staff Development

she got a big break: She was named co-manager of money-market sales in the New York office, becoming the first woman to be promoted to management in sales, the most macho side of the house. The move put her squarely on a partnership track.

Hanson's four-year marriage to one of her Goldman colleagues had dissolved two years before; her ex-husband now sat across from her. Although she put up a brave front, "it was too brutal for words," she recalls. While he got on with his life, she obsessed over her career, even though she was keenly aware that her long hours and lack of contact with anybody outside Goldman were boxing her in. "I was always a happy person," she recalls. "I came from a happy family; I wanted to have a happy family. That was never going to happen. I was working 100 hours a week. There was no halfway."

So the following year, flush with cash at age 34, she quit to become a triathlete. "It was a massive cover-up," she says. "I had no credible reason for leaving." The firm threw her a big going-away party and presented her with a string of Mikimoto pearls, and all the while she kept thinking to herself, "This is the dumbest thing I have ever done."

It took her five months to get over what she now figures was a major depression and also to discover that she was only a weekend athlete. She was rehired by Goldman Sachs as an outside consultant in a job that lasted about a year. In the following three years she was married, had two children, and started climbing the walls. Although she had desperately wanted a family, she couldn't stand staying at home. "For 11 years I had been like the Rambo of fixed income; then suddenly I was home. I should've gone from heroin at least to methadone," she says. She spent much of her time at home talking on the phone with her friends at Goldman—watching the game from the bleachers, she says, and crazy to get back in.

MANY WOMEN in this generation stayed in the game, postponed starting families, and looked up from their desks in their 40s only to wonder what had happened. They had felt a certain amount of control over the broad shape of their lives. First they wanted careers; then someday, somewhere along the line, they would make time for a husband; and yes, after establishing themselves in the workplace, then there would be time to consider children.

But the climb up the career ladder turned out to be time-consuming, all-consuming; and it was politically incorrect to warn that time could run out. While it became common knowledge that this generation of women could have babies well into their 40s, there

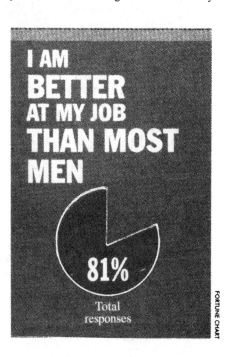

MY WORK DEFINES WHO I AM
73% Total responses

I AM BETTER AT MY JOB THAN MOST MEN
81% Total responses

was little talk of how difficult it could get after the age of 35. The dawning of that realization—right about the time a career is losing its luster—can shake the foundations at midlife. When Korn/Ferry International and UCLA's Anderson Graduate School of Management surveyed executive women in a major study three years ago, it asked how many had children. Fully 37% of the 439 women who responded did not. That compared with 5% of the executive men polled in a similar survey three years earlier. For some career women, the decision to forgo children is a definite choice; for others, it is more of an oversight.

"Probably women in such vast numbers have never had to go through this," says a 43-year-old New York banker, who for three years has been sneaking off to her infertility doctor, telling co-workers she had back problems and hoping that nobody would find out. Once a young hotshot, she feels that her career has collided with the glass ceiling, and she is considering looking for work in social service or philanthropy. "Maybe among some of the women who have not had children there is a stronger need to give back and do the nurturing in some other way," she says.

SUCH WAS THE CASE for Denise Kuhlman, a 37-year-old attorney who pointedly wanted to avoid the career path of her mother, a traditional housewife who raised six children in the small blue-collar town of Poynette, Wisconsin, about 25 miles north of Madison. Kuhlman, the youngest in the family, grew up with older sisters who scoffed at the notion of becoming a teacher or a nurse, and most certainly didn't think it necessary for any woman to snag a man. "There was such a deemphasis on family," she recalls, "I didn't think I needed it."

Many of the social activists she admired as a young woman were lawyers. So she got a law degree at the University of Michigan in 1989 and went to work for the big Seattle-based law firm Lane Powell Spears Lubersky. She worked hard and got glowing reviews despite enduring two tragedies early on. Both her mother and one of her sisters died unexpectedly after she'd been with the firm a year. As far as she knew she was up for partner; she guesses she would have made it in about two more years had she hung in there.

But she just wasn't happy. Her specialty had become bankruptcy; mostly she represented creditors. While she enjoyed the negotiations and dealmaking, the litigation and fighting left her cold. "It's a guy kind of thing. You're working by their rules," she says. There was a code of behavior, and she always felt she was bumping up against it. "The times I got the biggest pats on the back were the times I screamed the loudest," she recalls. She still remembers a meeting in which six lawyers argued for two hours over how to draft a form involving some obscure issue amounting to not much more than $7,000. They were staking out their territory, a colleague explained. "You had to play the game that way. If you didn't, it was perceived as weakness."

"It wasn't that their way is bad," she says. "It's just that it isn't my way." She realized how far she was drifting from her idealistic goals when she had to repossess an old man's house for one of her clients four years ago.

Beyond that, the deaths in her family had put her face to face with all that she had rebelled against. "I started looking at what my life was all about," she says. And she couldn't stop thinking of her sister's wake. The whole town had turned out. The doctor was crying because he felt so badly; the

142

28. Executive Women

neighbors offered to pitch in and take care of her sister's two young children. "I started to think, 'Who would come to my funeral? Would I have one that was jam-packed like hers was, or would there be nobody?'"

At the same time, it was dawning on her that she might never have a family of her own. "I love kids. I always thought I would have six kids. I figured it was just going to happen," she says. "I didn't realize the career I'd chosen would take me over and not let me do this other thing."

Without really knowing what she was going to do, Kuhlman began saving her money two years ago. "I didn't buy clothing, I didn't buy anything I didn't need, I stopped going into stores because I couldn't buy anything," she says. Then one March day last year, she took a walk around Seattle's Green Lake with a friend. By the time they had circled the lake, her mind was made up. She stood in the parking lot, knowing she had made the decision to quit. "Then I came home and called everybody up and said, 'Talk me out of it.'" When she notified the partner in charge of the bankruptcy group the next day, he didn't believe her. She finished the trial she was working on and left the firm a year ago.

Now she has accepted the realization that she might not have a family. But she is determined to have the kind of career she set out to have in the beginning. Although she is now doing free-lance law to support herself, "I have no intention of practicing law in the future. In my heart of hearts, I want to do things that are good for people," she says. She has applied to go back to graduate school to study psychology.

For some women, the thrill of the chase is enough to offset ennui. But for others the chase just gets ludicrous, especially when it leads up a male-style hierarchy they don't necessarily believe in, and further and further away from what they love best to do.

Sharon McGavin, the Red Cross executive, knew she was about to bag another promotion when she left Ogilvy & Mather as senior vice president in 1988. She knew she had a shot at the top. (Shelly Lazarus, one of her colleagues at the time, is now in the top job.) But she also knew that continuing to churn out ad campaigns was not going to sustain her. There wasn't enough newness. With the relief organization, by contrast, "at the end of the day there is a feeling that this is all very, very worthwhile," she says. Among other things, "my children are really proud of me." Taking the new job meant a huge salary cut, but her husband is a corporate attorney, and they decided they could manage after "a lot of staring at the old budget."

Simmonds, the turnaround specialist who now does a lot of her consulting for nonprofits, says her values too forced her to make a major midlife course correction. After growing, fixing, and then selling businesses, first for American Can and then for GTE, she says she began asking herself, "Was I really put here on earth to make a lot of rich white men richer?"

After a stunning career in advertising, Denise Larson, who is 40, is now deliberately trying to stay downwardly mobile. She has leapfrogged her way up Madison Avenue, advancing to ever bigger and better jobs: first becoming vice president at Young & Rubicam; then on to J. Walter Thompson, which doubled her salary; then on to Grey Advertising, which in turn made her part of a glamorous strategic planning team.

Along the way, she worked on campaigns for Kodak and Hallmark, and the Snoopy campaign for Metropolitan Life Insurance. But after 17 years, the thrill was gone. She was spending four days away from home and her 2-year-old daughter. "It wasn't the job. It was me. I was changing. I thought, 'I'm 37. I

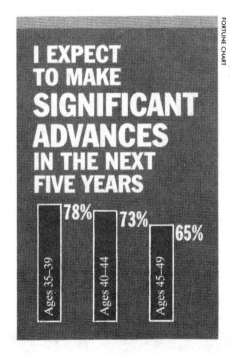

don't want to be doing this when I'm 47.'" Eventually she would make more money and maybe get another promotion. But she didn't like her role models: "I saw women whose lives I didn't want to lead—every other day at the shrink. Not that there is anything wrong with shrinks, but it is not the way I wanted to be spending my hard-earned money."

Two years ago, she joined one of her old clients, Philip Morris's Entenmann's unit (currently being sold to CPC International), where she is now market research manager. She has made it clear she doesn't want a staff or, for the time being anyway, to move up the corporate ladder. That allows her time for a life (she can drop her children off at school in the morning, for instance) and also allows her to stick to the work she loves most—talking to consumers and developing strategies for various brands.

Larson, who has two daughters and a husband who owns a veterinary practice, took a pay cut of about 20%. She says it has been something of a strain, "but it was definitely the right thing to do as a family."

Because companies are so hierarchical, she is constantly reminded of the choices she's made. "People always want to know what grade level I am," she says. But she has made peace with that. "You can view what you do as either in the box or out of the box," she says. "We need a little redefinition of work and success, and what all that means. I'm competitive, but in a different way. I want to see the brands succeed."

One reason some women weary of the game is the haphazard way they've played it. They took random walks down their career paths, following the advice of mentors rather than playing to their own strengths; taking whatever came along without necessarily taking stock of themselves. Some have reached midlife only to find they've been on the wrong path.

It was easy to do. When an opportunity knocked in the 1970s, women answered. They didn't know whether it would knock again, and they were flattered by those who took them seriously enough to take an interest in their careers. Somebody—usually male and usually senior—would suggest a direction, then volunteer to make the introductions, and then, there you were. You had a card that said Assistant Treasurer, Chase Manhattan Bank, and you could hand it out at parties, and everybody would be terribly impressed.

Carole Wright Brogdon never really stopped to consider the prevailing winds in her career until she turned 40 three years ago. She had become an accountant not so much because she reveled in spreadsheets but because she wanted to prove something. Her two older brothers were accountants; both of them were successful. "I was the girl coming up in the family. I wanted to show I could do it too," she recalls. She majored in accounting, graduating magna cum laude from the University of West Florida in 1974, and following graduation took a job at a small CPA firm in her hometown, Fort Walton Beach, Florida.

And she might have been content to stay there had it not been for her college professors, who were men. "They pushed me to work for one of the big accounting firms," she recalls. She moved to Atlanta in 1977 and, with their introductions, joined Main Lafrentz (later part of KPMG Peat Marwick). After five years she struck out for herself, first heading up accounting for one of Main's large clients, then practicing on her own, landing six years ago as director of national accounting for the Arthritis Foundation. She threw herself into the job, moving to a high-rise across the street from foundation headquarters and often working killer weeks.

4. DEVELOPING EFFECTIVE HUMAN RESOURCES: Career and Staff Development

BUT IN 1992 she hit the wall. She didn't have anything more to prove, and she says, "I just didn't want to do it anymore." She continued to work for the foundation as an outside consultant for about a year and began asking herself, "What am I going to do when I grow up?" At a dinner with friends one night, she hit on an idea. She had enjoyed renovating several of her homes; she might try her hand at homebuilding.

With some financial help from a new husband and using proceeds from the sale of her old house, she started a construction company in Richmond Hill, Georgia, outside Savannah. So far, she and a partner have sold seven of the nine houses they've built. All her houses have big porches; her nickname in local construction circles is "the Porch Lady." She mostly handles the business side, but she also gets to pick out colors and consult on designs, giving vent to a creative side that accounting had stifled. She gets to wear blue jeans and work boots. "This just doesn't compare," with her old career, she says. "It is so much better."

Alexandra Hendrickson, who is now 41, also found herself much happier once she was free to pursue what she really loved. She thought she had been on the right track. After all, she did what was fashionable for bright, ambitious women her age, getting an MBA from Wharton, working for Bankers Trust for more than five years, and then branching out into marketing at American Express. "I grew up in New York; all my family is from New York. I had a very clear idea of what life held for me there," she says.

But American Express catapulted her into midlife turmoil in January 1992 when it closed her department and eliminated her job as director of new-product development. Although she could have moved elsewhere within the company, she opted to take a severance package. She hadn't been "massively unhappy," she recalls, but she hadn't been "wildly enthusiastic," either. She decided she wanted to make a major change in her life. "I wanted to have an adventure."

SHE TOYED with starting a business. An opera buff, she thought about going into fundraising. A friend suggested she brush up on her German and go to Prague; the transition to capitalism there appealed to her interest in economics. So she flew to Frankfurt, where she spent several months studying German, and then headed off on a tour of Poland and Hungary in search of a job.

"It was terrifying," she recalls. "I got rental cars and just drove around." Nobody would take her seriously because she didn't have enough international experience. So in October 1992 she took a job as a reporter for the Budapest *Business Journal*, a little startup newspaper two of her friends were launching. It was there that she heard of an opening at the local U.S. Agency for International Development and landed a two-year job as senior privatization and banking project manager.

It has been a terrific adventure. Before, she recalls, all her energy went to figuring out how to get "one more American Express card into the hands of one more American Express member." At the agency, she occupied herself with privatization in Hungary, involving big economic and political questions that fascinate her. Her contract with the agency expired at the end of August, and she has decided to try to transfer her new expertise to a job in private industry. "What I'd like to do next is help manage a privatized or startup company to make it competitive with Western business," she says.

Zichy followed the opposite geographical path: Born in Budapest, she spent part of her childhood in Cairo and then landed in New York. But like Hendrickson, she ended up in a midlife crisis induced in part by events at American Express. At American Express Bank, she found herself immersed in a stifling corporate culture, embroiled in a lot of politics and infighting she couldn't abide. The experience left her, like many women at midlife, feeling that the male system didn't appreciate the female way: "Our fire is in different places. We have the fire, but it is not necessarily directed at power and control," she says.

She had started as a teacher, with a master's in education from Boston University and a job she loved at a high school in Greenwich, Connecticut. But some of her friends had gotten jobs paying real money in the brave new world of business, and she was jealous. "I wanted to see what it was all about," she recalls.

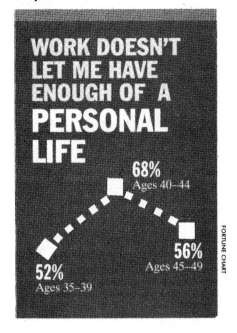

WORK DOESN'T LET ME HAVE ENOUGH OF A PERSONAL LIFE
52% Ages 35–39
68% Ages 40–44
56% Ages 45–49
FORTUNE CHART

HAS A WOMAN YOU KNOW DONE ANY OF THE FOLLOWING IN A WAY THAT WAS OUT OF CHARACTER AND SUGGESTED MIDLIFE CRISIS?

	TOTAL RESPONSES	RESPONSE BY AGE			HAVE KIDS?	
		35–39 years	40–44 years	45–49 years	YES	NO
Seeking therapy	56%	51%	59%	57%	56%	58%
Making a major career change	45%	42%	53%	39%	44%	47%
Becoming spiritual	44%	44%	40%	48%	43%	43%
Using antidepressants	41%	31%	46%	45%	42%	39%
Getting pregnant late in life	36%	44%	45%	19%	34%	44%
Getting a face-lift	32%	20%	36%	37%	35%	21%
Having an affair	30%	30%	31%	28%	32%	24%
Splurging, as on a sports car	26%	29%	27%	22%	26%	26%
Drinking and/or drug use	17%	17%	19%	15%	17%	17%
None of the above	8%	8%	7%	9%	8%	7%

FORTUNE TABLE

Her way in, through a family contact, was a job at *Institutional Investor* magazine. As she was interviewing the head of international private banking for Citibank, he offered her a job, and presto, she was an international banker. That turned out to be just the ticket for Zichy, who loves to travel. She attacked her first two international banking jobs in an adventuresome spirit, first scouring Thailand and the Philippines in search of customers for Citibank, and then jetting off to places like Abu Dhabi marketing U.S. commercial real estate investments for Merrill Lynch.

But eventually her career track carried her into management and a much more buttoned-down setting. The further she climbed up the corporate ladder and away from her customers, the more the job chafed. At American Express Bank, where she eventually became a vice president in 1988, she got some friendly advice to get rid of her red jacket, put on a blue suit, and tame down her curly blonde hair.

When the bank reorganized its international real estate division, moving Zichy's job to Joliet, Illinois, in 1988, she bailed out. She spent five years as an artist, working by day in oils, red chalks, and some pastels, and having her work critiqued at night. She read nothing but painting books and surfaced only to do occasional consulting projects to supplement her income. "The whole world of derivatives came and went," she says. "It was very strange."

She developed quite a following among her old Wall Street friends and contacts, holding four shows and selling 85 paintings through the period. Some commissioned paintings of their families. One of her old Citibank clients from Hong Kong bought six paintings right off her living room wall. Even so—and even though she had no family to support—she was finding her life "financially very scary." And, she says, "I needed more stimulation. I wanted to be connected with the business world again. I missed it."

Missing it is what happens to a lot of women. After all the twists, turns, and spills of a midlife crisis, some executive women even come full circle. George Ann Stokes, who for years has been one of the highest-ranking women, first at US West and now at Coca-Cola Foods, spent the past five years nursing herself through a bruising midlife crisis in the California wine country. Her career had been cooking along at US West; she was the vice president associate general counsel and apparently in line to succeed her boss, who was enthusiastically supporting her. Every time he would call her in to discuss the issue, she would say, "yes, yes, yes," but inside she was ambivalent.

There was "a certain dead-endedness" about the job, she recalls. In conversations with her therapist, "I was having a real inner struggle over the meaningfulness of my work—figuring out my own needs vs. what

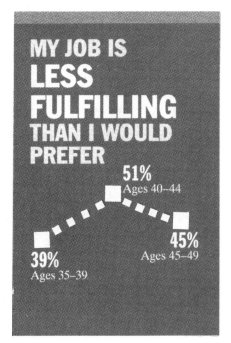

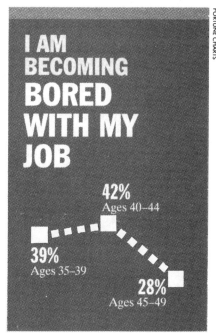

other people expected of me and how much I had let other people's expectations define my destiny," she says.

In 1990 she took herself out of the running by requesting a job in the field—general counsel of the company's marketing resources group, which published the Yellow Pages directories and developed new services. Although the new job was much more interesting to her, it was perceived as a big step down. She received phone calls from other women at the company asking how she could have let them down so.

To make matters worse, her marriage to a prominent Denver banker, Malcolm Harding, began to unravel, and she slid into a serious clinical depression. "Ours was not a bitter, angry divorce," she says, but rather "a very painful one for both sides." (The couple had no children.) At the end of 1992, during a departmental reorganization, she decided to leave the company.

Throughout this difficult period, Stokes would escape to the Sonoma County wine country, finding solace with friends. "It is enchanted there, I'm convinced of it," she says. And on a visit the following March, almost on a whim, she decided to look at property. One rainy afternoon, she walked into a little gray and white house surrounded by redwoods and red geraniums. The sun came out and streamed through its French doors. She decided on the spot to buy it and move. It is, she says, "a very soulful kind of place."

It was there, in Occidental, California, a year and a half ago, that she began to put her life back together. She read books and slept late and held soirees with friends and did something she'd always wanted to do: plant a garden. "I thought, 'I'm 55; now I can retire and live happily ever after,'" she recalls.

But after eight months or so, she began to fidget. She had spent time at a nearby Zen center trying to find solace through spirituality, but "I wasn't finding it. It just felt forced." Gardening, she found, was much harder than she thought. The herbs wouldn't grow; the deer ate the geraniums. "It was such a shock," she says, to find she didn't like it much. She hired a gardener. Eventually, she found herself browsing through the want ads, toying with the idea of becoming a wine-tasting hostess in one of the wineries.

What caught her eye instead was a job as a part-time attorney for the Council on Aging, a senior-service agency in nearby Santa Rosa. It seemed the perfect answer, since she had always been interested in helping the elderly. It turned out to be the most stressful job she'd ever had. "It was me and three paralegals and an ocean of people coming in with all manner of problems, and I was out straight," she says.

When a friend first called last November to tell her that Coca-Cola Foods was looking for a general counsel, she said: "No way. I'm happy." But in truth she was tempted. She agreed to go for the interviews and became more hooked with each one. "I felt I was on ground my experience had prepared me for," she recalls. She joined the company last April and is clearly relieved to be back in the game.

"I can't think of a time in my life when I've felt so centered. I know what's important to me. I know what I'm good at," she says. And although she can't let go of the little gray house in the redwoods, "I'm much less inclined to think when I retire I'm going to go grow herbs."

4. DEVELOPING EFFECTIVE HUMAN RESOURCES: Career and Staff Development

MORE typically, however, women don't re-emerge in big business but in small business—often their own. Janet Hanson, the Goldman Sachs dropout, discovered you can't go home again. She returned to the firm for two years only to find that she'd been shunted off the fast track. After doing a yearlong consulting project for Citibank, she started her own investment advisory firm, Milestone Capital Management, which specializes in short-term asset management for institutional investors. She hired her second husband to be her No. 2.

When she quit Goldman Sachs the first time, she had been making enough money not only to support herself but also to put a brother and sister through graduate school and set aside substantial savings. But by the time she started Milestone, she had two children and her savings were dwindling; she and her husband agreed to forgo salaries for the first two years and live off the proceeds of the sale of a house in Naples, Florida.

Milestone is in a cheery office park in Yonkers, ten minutes from her house. It clearly reflects her sunny disposition and her management style. The one-window office goes to her two employees, who keep tabs on the markets. A window office—"That's the power thing," she says. "This isn't a big power thing. This is a collaborative effort."

The way Hanson figures it, she took Goldman Sachs with her. One of her key employees is a hire from Goldman. One of her directors is a former Goldman partner; three others were Goldman vice presidents. Milestone manages more than $400 million in assets, and Hanson is clearly happy. "The way I look at it, I cut my losses 100%. I have a great husband, two great kids, a great business. I saved myself from utter destruction and ruin." Today a client has come down from Hartford to check her out, but Hanson already has done a deal with his boss, who also happens to be a woman.

"It's that chick thing," Hanson says.

That is how some experts believe women will have the most influence in business in the future—by doing things their way. It's the legacy that many in this generation of businesswomen hope to leave for the next: that they do have options; that they can make changes; that they can conduct business on their own terms. "The message of the day," says McGavin, "is that change is possible. You don't have to get it right the first time." Midlife may not ever be a day at the beach, but at least future generations of ambitious women may not have to be so badly burned.

Improving Worker Performance

Michael Barrier

Managers have many ways to accomplish it, from making sure an employee is in the right job to opening up career paths.

A small company that wants to survive, not to mention grow, has no choice but to seek ever-improving performance from its employees. "A small business's only advantage is that it gets more productivity, if it's smart, out of the limited resources it has," says Dennis G. McCarthy, president of the Paradigm Group, a training firm in Fairfield, Conn.

Of those resources, the only one that a competitor cannot readily duplicate is a company's people. But what works to motivate employees to do their best?

Money alone usually isn't a sufficient motivator. Says Robert J. Shillman, founder and CEO of Cognex Corp., a highly successful manufacturing firm based in Natick, Mass.: "People don't really work for salary or stock options or bonuses. Sure, to get the right kind of people, you have to put together a compensation package for them, but what people really work for is appreciation and the feeling that success brings to them."

Careful hiring cannot substitute for continuing efforts to help employees perform better. "You can hire the best people, but if you don't treat them right, they're not going to be the best people anymore," says Shillman, whose company makes machine-vision devices for optical detection of defects in manufactured parts.

The small-business owner who tries to bully employees into better performance is not going to get very far, either. It's true that "you can get desired behavior through fear and punishment, but it will be very short-term," says Bob Nelson, vice president of Blanchard Training & Development, in Escondido, Calif., and author of *1,001 Ways to Reward Employees*.

To help improve employee performance, a small-business owner or manager could start with questions such as these:

Do you try to make sure that there's the right fit between employee and job?
"Just because somebody has experience in a field doesn't necessarily mean that they're suited to that field," says Terri Kabachnick, a former department-store executive who is now a personnel-issues consultant in Cromwell, Conn. She cites the example of a salesman who was failing at selling high-fashion menswear, to the point that his employer had put him on probation.

"Through assessments and interviewing," she says, "we found out that he didn't have the confidence to suggest styles and colors. We moved him to an area that was his alone and that had nothing to do with fashion, or his view of himself, but had everything to do with service." That was the store's greeting-card department.

"He targeted mostly men," whom he found to be frustrated and overwhelmed by the enormous number of cards, Kabachnick says. The salesman developed a service for his customers—he took their names and all the important dates for which they would want to buy cards. Two weeks before each date, he sent his customers a selection of cards, asking them to send back any unwanted cards. Not one card was returned in that first year, Kabachnick says, and the man's card sales totaled $365,000.

ILLUSTRATION: ALBERTO PACHECO

4. DEVELOPING EFFECTIVE HUMAN RESOURCES: Appraising and Improving Performance

Do you search for ways to put your employees in direct contact with your customers?

"The companies that are doing a better job of connecting at the front line, at the point of customer contact—they're the ones that are winning today and that are going to be surviving in the long term," says Jim Harris, an Indian Rocks Beach, Fla., consultant and author of *Getting Employees to Fall in Love with Your Company*.

Employees need to be aware of how their efforts serve customers' needs. "One of the things that allows us to keep our people is that they're not just performing a task that has been outsourced, but they're actually engaged with the client, which is a much more exciting career," says Peter C. Cowie, founder and CEO of Charter Systems, a Waltham, Mass., firm that provides computer network services.

About two-thirds of Charter's 100 employees are what Cowie calls "network systems engineers." Their close involvement with customers—mostly large businesses—means that many of them get job offers, Cowie says, but "we've only lost four people we didn't want to leave the company."

Charter Systems' engineers work closely with customers in designing and supporting their computer networks, but there are many other ways to put employees in touch with customers, even when they ordinarily wouldn't see customers: by encouraging telephone contact, for example, or taking employees to trade shows.

Customer contact in itself isn't enough to guarantee improved performance, of course, as everyone who has dealt with a surly or disengaged salesperson knows all too well. "It's difficult for employees to treat customers better than they think they're being treated," Nelson says. "But if they feel they're valued, and they're excited about their jobs, it's a snap to get them to treat customers well."

Does your company's culture encourage high performance?

There's wide agreement that the tone the owner sets for the business is critical to the success of efforts to improve employee performance. Says Harris: "I know that a lot of people say that mission statements are just fancy words on a wall; and 90 percent of the time it's true. But if you really want to get at the heart of your people, you've got to give them a reason to commit. Without that, what you have is a bunch of walking dummies."

Lida Hayes-Calvert, owner of S & L Painting and Decorating, in Winston-Salem, N.C., says the decisive moment for her 45-employee firm came a few years ago when she started using a uniform service for her painters.

Providing the uniforms "was just to accomplish one goal," Hayes-Calvert says—to give her painters a more professional appearance on the job—"and it wound up accomplishing about 25" goals, including greater productivity.

Dressed in their white uniforms, each bearing the employee's name, her painters "feel good about themselves," she says. "I think that's the most important thing about motivating a person. My guys strut."

Hayes-Calvert has capitalized on the painters' enhanced self-respect by drawing them into greater involvement in the business. S & L holds safety meetings twice a month to go over problems the painters encounter on the job. "I was a junior-high teacher," Hayes-Calvert says, "and I'm always calling on [the painters to speak]. I had some little guys who wouldn't even talk, and now, you wouldn't believe it—they want to take the floor. They generate a lot of good, money-saving ideas for me"—and for S & L's profit-sharing plan.

Likewise at Cognex—if in a very different way—"the company culture is in itself a motivator," Shillman says, for most of the 300 employees at Natick. Cognex's culture is quirkier than most, complete with a company salute. On a more profound level, "you have to be willing to empower people," Shillman says. "We have a saying at Cognex: 'Don't do what you're told, do what's right.' We really mean that. There have been two instances where I specifically told senior people not to do something, they went ahead and did it, and they were right. In front of everybody, I made a big deal of this and gave them special awards."

Do you seize opportunities to offer informal rewards and recognition?

Formal awards programs can be very successful, especially if they're based on employees' opinions of one another's work.

For example, Second National Bank of Warren, Ohio, offered what it called "Tortoise Shell Awards" to honor employees who showed a positive attitude—with nominations coming from co-workers who witnessed exceptional efforts. The contest ran for a year, and the bank's 350 employees submitted almost 49,000 nomination slips.

"It was so successful that we wanted to continue that peer-recognition part of it," says Mary Roberts Henderson, who is in charge of communications and media relations for the bank. So the bank has launched two new peer-driven award programs.

But informal recognition counts for more, says Blanchard Training's Nelson. "There's a place for formal programs as well," he says, "but I think that most people overlook the informal."

Informal rewards can be both highly effective and cost-free. An effective reward "can be as simple as sincere praise," says Jack Zigon, president of Zigon Performance Group, a management consulting firm in Media, Pa. This is especially true, he says, when that praise is given with specific information about what the employee has done to merit it, so that the performance can be repeated.

> **People who are held to higher standards perform better.**
> —Dennis McCarthy, Paradigm Group

Do you try to tailor rewards and recognition to the individual?

"At the core" of successful motivation, Nelson believes, "is tapping into the things that are really important to people—taking the time to find out what those are, and developing a company culture that encourages improved performance, while Nelson's focuses more on individual techniques for rewarding such improvements.

Three books by Jack Zigon on employee performance—*How to Measure the Results of Work Teams*, *How to Measure White Collar Employee Performance*, and *Sample Employee Performance Measures*—are available from Zigon Performance Group Publications. For details and ordering information on Zigon's books, call 1-800-299-3022 and request that document No. 3500 be faxed to you; or call the order desk at 1-800-244-2892 or (610) 627-1711.

To Learn More

Several books offer additional information on employee performance.

Getting Employees to Fall in Love with Your Company, by Jim Harris (AMACOM/American Management Association, $17.95 in paperback), and *1,001 Ways to Reward Employees*, by Bob Nelson (Workman Publishing, $9.95 in paperback), offer complementary approaches to improving employee performance.

Both books are filled with specific examples. Harris' book is concerned more with

29. Improving Worker Performance

structuring your recognition around those, in the context of the job."

What is a reward to one person may be a punishment to another, Zigon points out: "You might like more responsibility; I might like less. You might like a dinner out; I'm on the road all the time, and I don't want to see another restaurant. The secret of making any reward effective is tailoring it to the individual.

"There's nothing wrong with asking" what kind of reward an employee would prefer, Zigon says. "By watching how people spend their time, listening to what they talk about, you learn about what turns them on. You can then tailor your rewards." And here, of course, is where the owner of a small business has a real advantage because it is usually so much easier for such an owner to get to know employees.

Do you realize that many of your employees may find their greatest rewards in the work itself?

It's tempting to think of "rewards" as somehow removed from the work that people do to earn them. For many employees, however, the most powerfully motivating rewards may be those that offer them greater opportunities on the job. "You've got to give people forks in the road," says Charter Systems' Cowie—that is, you must try to make different career paths available to them.

Such motivating "forks in the road" are not just for high-tech companies. At S & L, for example, Hayes-Calvert says that she now needs people who are not just painters but who can represent her in dealing with corporate CEOs on larger contracts.

On the other hand, in keeping with the idea that rewards should be tailored to the individual, business owners should recognize that not everyone is looking for a career path out of their present job. "I've worked with employees who are happy in their jobs," Zigon says. "They had a promotion, they didn't like it, and they came back."

For all small-business owners, the surest path to improved employee performance may lie in their recognition that most of their employees really do want to do a good job.

Says Paradigm Group's Dennis McCarthy: "Most people, when they get up in the morning, don't look in the mirror and say, 'How can I screw up at work today?' But, over time, they get so frustrated about not being able to do a good job that they finally say, 'I'll do what it takes to get by.'

"I don't think we expect enough out of people," he continues. "When people are held to higher standards, they not only perform better, they feel a whole lot better about it. Business owners have accepted a level of mediocrity that they don't need to accept. They've blamed it on the work force, and I think they need to look in the mirror instead."

PAINLESS PERFORMANCE EVALUATIONS

MARY MAVIS

Mary Mavis *is the director of professional development for Sibson & Company, 212 Carnegie Center, CN 5323, Princeton, NJ 08543-5323.*

Most managers shrink from their most important task—managing the performance of others. Here's how to turn a painful task into a productive one.

"Well, I think that covers it!" Sheila says, wrapping up Tom's annual performance review. "Do you have any other questions? No?... Good. I hope you don't take my criticism personally. Just make the changes we talked about, and you'll be fine."

Sheila believes that Tom leaves the meeting understanding her evaluation. But that night, Tom tells his wife that Sheila did not explain clearly her expectations for his performance or recommend specific ways that Tom can improve.

"What does she mean, I'm 'not efficient enough'? What can I do to improve?" Tom asks rhetorically. He shakes his head, feeling a familiar sense of irritation. "I just don't know what she wants from me," he says. "How can I improve when I don't know the standard for success? I really feel criticized."

Meanwhile, Sheila is telling her husband that she is relieved that the conversation with Tom went so smoothly. "I hate review time," she confides. "I never know how to talk with my people about problems, especially if the person is a 'keeper' who never forgets anything said to him. Besides, I've never even had a performance review from any of my bosses!"

Most people don't like feedback. They don't like to give it or receive it. Not surprisingly, many organizations neglect the performance-review process.

But lean organizations can't afford poor performers, and workers can't afford poor reviews. More than ever, employees need and expect useful feedback. Both supervisors and subordinates need to communicate comfortably and clearly during a review.

Because employees often perceive their supervisors as dishing out feedback but not taking it, they don't realize that giving feedback is difficult. Managers may relish a review when they can heap praise on a high performer. But when they must discuss an employee's shortcomings, the process becomes painful.

Why are even experienced managers so reluctant to conduct performance reviews? Usually for the following reasons:
▶ People avoid conflict—real and perceived.
▶ People don't want to take responsibility for their judgments.
▶ People are more certain of their judgments than of their facts.
▶ People are afraid that if they start giving clear, serious feedback, they also will receive candid feedback on their own performance.

In short, few people learn from life experience alone how to give and receive feedback well. Nevertheless, managers can't cede their responsibility to maximize employees' performance. So, most managers have to develop their feedback skills.

Managers can improve the process by learning to think differently about feedback. By focusing on the key

30. Painless Performance Evaluations

principles of effective feedback, managers can learn to
- validate feedback they offer to their employees
- observe employees' behavior and compare it to performance expectations
- attain peace of mind before, during, and after their feedback meetings.

Key principles
Effective feedback rests on three underlying principles.

Feedback takes two. Feedback takes place only during a two-way conversation in which both the parties speak openly and listen to each other's point of view. Written communication is inherently one-sided. Until we engage in conversation, we only can hope the person understands our message.

Feedback brings reality into focus. Feedback is a dynamic process that brings together two people, each with his or her own worldview, personal and professional history, and value system.

To create change, managers must understand how their employees perceive events and why they act as they do. They must remain open to employees' ideas for self-improvement. Managers who "tell" their employees how they are doing miss valuable feedback themselves. For instance, poor results that a manager attributes to an employee's carelessness might be caused by a problem with a particular process.

Good intentions matter. Managers must clarify their intentions for feedback. To evaluate others effectively, managers must genuinely want to help them. Otherwise, the exchange will run into emotional barriers and produce only rote or uninspired ideas for improvements.

Suppose an employee's poor performance has disrupted the department. The manager, sounding irritated, discusses the issue with the employee. The manager's unspoken message—"You have made me look bad, and I resent you for it"—drowns out the verbal feedback that could help the person correct the problem.

Managers can put those three principles into action by addressing four key elements when they prepare for and conduct performance reviews:
- observations—neutral facts or occurrences
- assessments—personal interpretations of a set of observed behavior
- consequences—possible or certain effects of continued behavior
- development—suggestions for improvement.

Observations
Managers must ground all feedback in discrete observations of behavior or results. For example, a manager might observe, "Sara did not deliver the report to me by the Friday noon deadline."

Observation holds the key to resolving any confusion about an employee's job performance. When employees disagree, question, or react emotionally to feedback, managers should restate the observations that initially prompted the feedback.

Observations shared by both the manager and employee form a foundation of facts on which to base assessments. ("Before we get into a general assessment, Sara, let's talk about what I've observed and what you remember about the project's execution.")

Observations make feedback "real" for employees and give them a chance to clarify their viewpoints. For example, if a manager says an employee lacks decisiveness, the manager should support the assessment with a specific instance in which the employee failed to make a timely decision. The employee then might elaborate on the circumstances. ("I could not act because purchasing could not provide the quotes to me before Monday.") The additional information might then prompt the manager to revise his or her original assessment.

Assessments
Many managers lack confidence in their assessments of employees. An assessment is a value judgment based on some standard. But, consciously or not, we often pass off our assessments as observations. ("We don't have enough work to keep the business going.")

For example, a manager might say to Sara, "You do not manage your time efficiently." This statement implies that the manager not only knows all the facts, but also knows the reason for the unacceptable results. Without explicitly linking an assessment to an observation, managers risk confusing, angering, or demoralizing employees.

The Four Elements of Feedback

Observations	Assessments	Consequences	Development
Missed the Friday deadline four times out of six.	Undependable in meeting deadlines. Standard: missing one or two deadlines might be excused, but four is a signal of a problem.	Transfer to another job if late again. Reputation for lack of dependability within any new job at the company.	Meet deadline on time. Plan: Schedule next production with manager and identify any sources of delay. Check in with manager at milestones.
Screamed at team member and team member left the room.	Unprofessional behavior with team member. Standard: Volume of voice must be within speaking level. While using an emphatic tone is acceptable, screaming is not.	Lack of employee and company respect. Reduction in bonus.	Must lower voice to acceptable volume and speak in a non-attacking manner. Plan: Coaching from manager regarding issues behind behavior.
Developed new design on time, within budget, and above industry standard.	Dependable and highly effective in program design. Standard: Program designs are expected on time. Most people meet industry standards, but few exceed them.	Opportunity for next challenging project. Recognition among peers and across department heads.	No improvement needed; however, suggest develop presentation for industry conference. Plan: Work with marketing to develop materials.

151

4. DEVELOPING EFFECTIVE HUMAN RESOURCES: Appraising and Improving Performance

Moreover, people assess the same situation very differently, depending on their outlook and experience. Suppose a technical specialist writes an internal report summarizing a major project. That specialist's manager, who has a strong background in technical writing, finds the report too formal. It doesn't "tell a story," he contends. But a manager in the finance department commends the report as easy to read; she likes the way that the specialist highlighted the project's data.

Each manager measured the same report against a different standard. Numerous factors influence managers' personal standards, such as how they were reared, where they live, and how much they earn. Managers also are influenced by their industry, professional specialty, and the organizational culture of their workplace.

Managers must gain insight into the conscious and unconscious standards they apply when they assess employees. Whether giving feedback formally or informally, managers must ask themselves, "What personal standards am I using to make this assessment?" The answer often prompts a manager to alter his or her assessment.

Managers also must consider companywide standards for behavior and performance.

Suppose an employee strongly disagrees with his or her boss in front of other managers and staff. The way the boss assesses the employee's behavior (a public challenge) will depend on the boss's personal experience and style for dealing with conflict.

But the manager also must consider whether the organization as a whole has a standard for acceptable interpersonal communication. Some organizations encourage frank and spontaneous give-and-take, regardless of the status of the parties involved or who is present. Others value a standard of "always support your boss in public," and leave challenges to the privacy of the boss's office.

Many organizational standards are implicit. Unable to articulate the standards, many managers fall back on catch phrases, such as "You didn't push the thinking far enough," or "You haven't paid your dues." Such statements are open to as many interpretations as a company has employees.

To ensure that feedback prompts desirable action, managers must make sure that employees understand the assessment. If a manager says, "I think you are overwhelmed," he or she should clearly explain what "overwhelmed" means in this context.

Consequences

All actions have consequences—some desirable, and some undesirable. For the person being assessed, some negative consequences could include termination or a job transfer. Positive consequences might include a promotion or a bonus.

Consequences vary from person to person, even if the feedback different employees receive is similar. For example, a research analyst with poor oral-communication skills might face less serious consequences for lack of improvement than a salesperson or receptionist with the same problem.

Unfortunately, during feedback, manager and employee usually forget to discuss the known or possible consequences of a given action. So each party leaves the discussion with his or her own idea of implied consequences, but with few actual facts about consequences.

Managers don't have to cite consequences for every item of feedback they offer, but they should cover important consequences. When managers make consequences clear, employees can answer the following questions after an evaluation:
▸ "Will I be fired if I don't perform an action, or will I be promoted if I do?"
▸ "Are my working relationships at risk, or are they likely to grow?"
▸ "If I develop certain skills, will I have opportunities for new assignments?"
▸ "Will I lose opportunities if I don't change certain behaviors?"

From a manager's perspective, there are three types of consequences:
▸ those they can enforce
▸ those they have seen occur in similar situations
▸ those they imagine possible.

Managers often are reluctant to state consequences when they cannot enforce them. But managers can

---

The Feedback Process
Four elements—observation, assessment, consequences, and development—make up the model for effective feedback.

- **OBSERVATION**: "Jim Has Arrived at 9:15 A.M. Three or Four Days a Week."
- **ASSESSMENT**: "Jim Lacks Disicipline or Commitment."
- **CONSEQUENCES**: "Other Employees Resent Jim's Tardiness."
- **DEVELOPMENT/IMPROVEMENT**: "Jim Must Arrive at 9 A.M. or Before, Each Day."

In real life, the process does not always flow in this orderly way. The feedback process can start or end with any of these elements. But most feedback conversations begin with an assessment and then address the other three elements as follows:
Manager: "John, your recent work has been outstanding." (Assessment)
John: "Thank you. Are you referring to any particular project or results?"
Manager: "Yes, your analysis on ACME produced four key solutions for the project." (Observation)
John: "Was there anything I could have done better?"
Manager: "There were no real problems. In the future, you might want to communicate your results sooner. (Development) I plan to recommend you for a promotion." (Consequence)

give employees useful information by explaining that the conversation will cover possible—not certain—consequences.

This approach opens the door for considering a range of possible consequences. For example, a manager might suggest that an employee cultivate a better relationship with his or her colleagues. If the employee ultimately fails to do so, the consequences might include the loss of a promotion, a tarnished reputation, loss of respect from co-workers, or simply an inability to operate efficiently.

Employees do not have to accept or agree with their managers' view of potential consequences, and managers should not try to convince them, unless of course they have the power and intent to fire or promote them outright.

Even then, a manager rarely should present a consequence as an ultimatum. ("If you don't make these changes, you will be fired!") If an employee feels threatened, he or she will resist or defend against the threat rather than focusing on improvement. The manager should consider the intent carefully and explain the consequence as a fact or a possibility. ("We need you to make these changes to fulfill your job requirements. Let's talk about whether you want to put the effort into the improvement and how we can assist you.")

Development

People need time and help to grow and develop. Helping an employee identify a goal for improvement and a solid plan for achieving the goal is an often overlooked part of the feedback process.

An improvement plan must identify a specific result, a target date for achieving the result, and steps the employee will take to achieve the goal.

If a manager can't picture a desired result, he or she has no right to give the feedback. Just as a manager must observe specifically what an employee's behavior lacks, the manager must specify the behaviors that constitute a successful performance.

From time to time, a manager might wonder exactly what he or she wants from an employee. In that case, the manager should refer to his or her observations to determine what the employee should change. For example, a manager might say, "I observed that Sara missed the deadline on Friday. I want her not only to meet the noon deadline, but also to submit her first draft to me 24 hours earlier so that I have time to add my perspective."

A manager who still cannot envision the desired performance should ask the employee for help. How might the employee work more effectively? What solution might fit her or his style? People often have the answers themselves.

This approach also reveals whether the person understood the feedback. If not, manager and employee together must clarify the assessment before focusing again on the manager's expectations for the employee's performance.

When managers offer suggestions for improvement, they should not expect people to accept their ideas wholeheartedly. With their employees, managers must explore alternatives so that the affected employee owns the solution. Managers can share remedies that have worked for them, that they have seen work for others, or that others recommend, but they can't force them on employees. People have the right to decline suggestions. If they don't have the leeway to do so in front of their managers, they certainly will follow their hearts and minds after they leave the room.

Once managers master the basics of effective feedback, they can enjoy the peace of mind that comes with saying what they mean, meaning what they say, and helping employees perform to the best of their abilities.

Implementing Compensation, Benefits, and Workplace Safety

- Managing Employee Compensation (Articles 31 and 32)
- Incentive Compensation (Articles 33 and 34)
- Executive Pay (Articles 35 and 36)
- Employee Benefits (Article 37)
- Safety and Health (Articles 38–40)

> Money makes the world go around . . . the world go around!
> —From "Money" in the musical *Cabaret*

Individuals are usually paid what others perceive their work to be worth. This situation is not necessarily morally correct. In fact, it does not even have to be logical, but it is reality. Police officers and college instructors are often underpaid. They have difficult jobs, requiring highly specialized training, but these jobs do not pay well. Other professions pay better, and many illegal activities pay better than law enforcement or college teaching.

When a company is trying to determine the salary of individuals, two markets must be considered. The first is the internal structure of the firm, including the wages that the company pays for comparable jobs. If the organization brings a new employee on board, it must be careful not to set a pay rate for that individual that is inconsistent with those of other employees who are doing the same or similar jobs. The second market is the external market for employees. Salary information is available from many sources, including professional associations and the federal government. Of course, both current and prospective employees, as well as organizations, can easily gain access to this information. To ignore this information and justify pay rates only in terms of internal structure is to tempt fate. The company's top producers are the ones in whom the competition is the most interested, and no organization can afford a mass exodus of its top talent.

One recent development in the area of compensation is a return to the concept of "pay for performance." Many firms are looking for ways to directly reward their top performers. As a result, the idea of merit pay has gained wide acceptance in both industry and government. Pay for performance has been used in industry for a long time, most commonly in the sales and marketing area, where employees have historically worked on commission plans based on their sales productivity. Theoretically, merit pay and other types of pay for performance are effective, but they can easily be abused, and they are often difficult to administer because measuring performance accurately is difficult. Sales and production have numbers that are easily obtained, but research and development is a different situation. How does a firm measure the effectiveness of research and development for a particular year when such projects can often take several years for results to be achieved?

One issue that has evolved over the past several years is the question of pay for top executives. During times of economic recession, most workers are asked to make sacrifices in the form of reduced raises, pay cuts, cuts in benefits, other compensation reductions, or layoffs. Many of these sacrifices have not been applied to top management. Indeed, the compensation for top management has increased substantially during the past several years. When former president George Bush traveled to Japan with a number of top auto industry executives, this situation was highlighted. The auto industry in the United States had been doing very poorly, while the auto industry in Japan had been very successful—especially when compared to its U.S. counterpart. A comparison of the salaries of American auto executives with those of their Japanese rivals reveals that the Japanese executives receive only a fraction of the compensation of the Americans. This might lead one to question who is worth more—senior management of a successful Japanese firm or of a less successful American firm? Are chief executives overpaid, and if so, how did they get that way, and who should set their pay? Boards of directors? Their pay is also under fire.

The fastest-growing aspect of employee compensation is benefits. Benefits are expensive to any firm, representing an ever-increasing burden to employers. As a result, many firms are reducing benefits and attempting to find more

UNIT 5

effective ways to spend their benefit dollars. Also, the needs of the employees are changing. As our society ages, there is greater interest in health benefits and pensions, and less interest in maternity benefits. Another facet of the issue is that employees are seeking greater benefits in lieu of salary increases, because the benefits, with some exceptions, are not usually taxed.

Health and safety are also major concerns of employers and employees. The workplace has become more violent as workers act out against their employers for unfairness—whether real or imagined. The history of industrialization in the United States is filled with examples of industry's abuse of the safety and health of workers. To prevent this, there is now OSHA (the Occupational Safety and Health Administration) and there are child labor laws. Today, issues concerning safety and health in the workplace include AIDS, burnout, and substance abuse. These issues reflect not only changing social conditions but also a greater awareness of the threats presented by unsafe working conditions. An attempt to address some of these issues has been to practice what is essentially preventive medicine with wellness initiatives. While there was initially some doubt about their effectiveness, the results are now in, and wellness programs do work.

All in all, salaries, wages, and benefits represent a major expense and a time-consuming management task for most firms, and health and safety requirements are a potential area of significant loss, in terms of both dollars and lost production.

Looking Ahead: Challenge Questions

Companies are involved in worldwide competition, often with foreign organizations with much lower wage rates. What should management do to meet this competition? What do workers need to do to meet this competition?

How would you implement a merit/incentive program in a staff department such as research and development or data processing? In a line department such as sales or production?

Explain why you believe some senior executives are overpaid. Do you feel some are underpaid? Cite examples and reasons for your conclusions.

What strategies should employers implement to control the rising costs of benefits while still getting the maximum value for their employees? How would you address the health care crisis for an organization?

How would you handle a situation in which an employee contracts AIDS or tests positive for HIV? or when an employee develops a substance abuse problem? or when an employee shows signs of stress and burnout, or becomes violent?

Article 31

■ Pay Cuts Remedy Financial Woes

Share the Pain to Share the Gain

Jennifer J. Laabs

Calling a layoff at the first sign of financial stress is a little like getting a paper cut and calling the paramedics. Just as minor problems shouldn't elicit drastic measures, short blips in an organization's financials shouldn't be the catalyst for a layoff.

At least that's what Reflexite, a company that produces reflective materials for various uses, thinks. While company managers concede you shouldn't just take a Band-Aid™ approach to financial problems, they do say that keeping an accurate pulse on the strength of your company's financial viability will help you avert layoffs—or at least make them a last resort—if you have the right plan, and the right resolve.

Reflexite Corp. managers came to this conclusion when they were faced with a financial downturn in 1991. Although the Avon, Connecticut-based firm that sells reflective materials used for everything from jogging shoes to highway signs wasn't losing customers or market share, the company faced declining sales as a result of the economic recession. It was cause for pause, but not yet a cause for alarm.

In fact, the company went to great lengths to avoid laying off any of the organization's 350 employees worldwide. The firm's president and CEO, Cecil Ursprung, went against the grain in suggesting that there was a better way to cut costs than cutting people out of jobs. He and his staff defied the predictable pattern of Corporate America by figuring out how to fix the problem before employee layoffs were necessary.

What resulted was a two-part plan to cut costs. It included temporarily cutting pay companywide and instituting voluntary leaves of absence. Then the company developed another innovative strategy, called the *Business Decline Contingency Plan* to get a handle on tumbling revenue.

The organization's commitment to valuing people reflects a mindset that stems from what's now seen as somewhat of a cliche for human resources professionals. But Reflexite really means it: People are its most important asset.

Valuing people is a commitment—and a tradition. In the firm's early years, the men who originally started the firm, "The Rowland Brothers"—Hugh and Bill as they're affectionately known—fell into some hard times. Rather than passing on the problems to the rest of the company, however, the founders made some personal sacrifices, such as taking out second mortgages on their homes. More than once, they were close to laying people off, but didn't. There was always another way to avert the problem.

Later, when times were good, the

CUT

PAY

Financial health is what most companies strive for. But there are times when every company has its dip into the red. Reflexite Corp. knows exactly what to cut during downturns—salaries, work schedules and raw materials. People cuts are used only as a last resort.

31. Share the Pain

Reflexite's Business Decline Contingency Plan

	DEFINITION	SYMPTOMS	ACTION TO BE TAKEN	EXPECTED RESULT
STAGE I:	Sales below budgeted sales but ahead of the same period in prior year.	1. Bookings below plan for four weeks or more. 2. Field reports confirm it. 3. Backlog levels off. 4. Large order levels fall. 5. Book-to-bill ratio falls below 1. 6. Profits below plan.	1. Defer some budgeted hires. 2. Defer some budgeted activities. 3. Heighten awareness of current situation. 4. Discuss at staff meetings. 5. Monitor overall economic conditions.	Adjust revenue and expenses to meet plan. Preserve all jobs and expected future stock value.
STAGE II:	Sales and profits below prior year for a period of one quarter or more.	1. Bookings below plan for one quarter or more. 2. Profits below prior year. 3. Backlog declines 15%. 4. Incentive pay on sales slips below plan. 5. Larger customers' businesses decline or develop credit trouble.	1. Revise Selling, General and Administrative (SG&A) expenditures. 2. Revise forecast. 3. Solicit ideas to cut costs, improve productivity and efficiency from employees. 4. Cut overtime. 5. Cut discretionary spending. 6. Redeploy sales force. 7. Increase cold calls. 8. Accelerate new product introductions.	Same as in Stage I.
STAGE III:	Business operates at break-even level or generates losses of less than $100,000 for a period of one quarter or more.	1. Backlog declines 30% from previous high. 2. Bank loans increase.	1. Solicit ideas to cut costs, etc. from employee-owners. 2 & 3. Voluntary leaves and furloughs. 4. Hiring becomes the exception. 5. More reduction of SG&A expenditures. 6. Increase management attention. 7. Monitor Stage II actions for results. 8. Defer lower-priority capital items. 9. Introduce a more aggressive revenue-generation strategy. 10. Price cuts on specification items. 11. Sales of obsolete inventory. 12. Offer extended terms for new business. 13. Accelerate new product introductions. 14. Delay refilling of vacated positions. 15. Accelerate capital work with less than one year payout. 16. Defer raises. 17. More rigorous performance reviews. 18. Defer or reduce salaries for highly compensated employees. 19. Reduce hours.	Revise plan to meet revenue expectations. Preserve jobs. Expected stock price above last year but below planned value.
STAGE IV	Business generates losses for a period of two quarters or more.	1. Lose customers. 2. Lose technological lead. 3. Core products lose market share. 4. Banks look at loans' status more carefully. 5. Suppliers don't send materials due to unpaid or late-paid invoices. 6. Stretch out payments to suppliers. 7. Lose good employees.	1. Salary deferments or reductions for balance of exempt employees. 2. Trim benefits. 3. Early retirements. 4. Voluntary resignation offering. 5. Layoffs.	Downsizing required. Some loss of jobs. Stock price falls below prior level.

Source: Reflexite Corp.

5. COMPENSATION, BENEFITS, AND WORKPLACE SAFETY: Managing Employee Compensation

Rowland Brothers had a chance to sell the company for quite a tidy little profit, but worried that doing so might result in massive layoffs of the existing staff by potential buyers, such as 3M. They also had no assurance that any of the potential buyers would keep the company—and jobs—in their native Connecticut. They felt they had been successful because of the brilliance and hard work of their employees. So, instead of selling to an outside buyer, the brothers sold the company to the employees. In 1985, Reflexite became employee-owned through an employee stock ownership plan (ESOP). Employees now own 59% of the organization.

"That's the unique part of our culture, but that's not the main reason why in '91, when things again were tough, we didn't lay people off," says Matthew J. Guyer, who's the director of operations for Reflexite North America, with responsibility for human resources matters. While disrupting people's lives and livelihoods is reason enough to think twice about laying people off, the strategy not to do so goes beyond that. "Our company president believes philosophically and ethically that laying people off is the wrong thing to do," says Guyer. "But all emotion aside, from a purely cold, calculating business opinion, it was much more expensive in the end to lay people off because no one ever forgets [a layoff]." It becomes part of corporate memory and individual motivation—or demotivation—as the case may be.

He explains that if your business is ultimately viable, it will grow back to profitability with the right nurturing. When that happens, you'll probably need to hire people back, which can be expensive in terms of recruitment, training and time it takes for new hires to overcome the initial learning curve. But in the long run, you can never buy back commitment once you lose it—at any price.

"What Ursprung believes is that as soon as you overreact by laying people off, you add this whole new atmosphere to the company in which people aren't coming to work everyday solely worried about the competition and taking care of customers," says Guyer. "They now become distracted by wondering: 'Am I expendable? Am I going to be the next one to go?'" It starts a chain reaction the likes of which few companies are prepared to deal with.

"A lot of company executives make the mistake of not counting people and their knowledge as assets the same way they do with their equipment," adds Guyer. He points out that companies don't throw out equipment when things get slow. So why throw away people? It's like throwing out the baby with the bath water. He says: "Employees are worth a lot more than their hourly rate."

Everyone takes a pay cut. So, when financial problems surfaced five years ago, instead of cutting people, one of the first actions the company took was to cut people's pay temporarily. Everyone's pay. In fact, the senior management team took a 10% cut in salary, middle managers took a 7% cut, lower-level managers took a 5% cut and all other employees took a 5% cut in the form of one day off per month without pay. On those days, the plant closed.

Because Reflexite is an employee-owned company, it's perhaps easier to align the needs of the shareholders and the employees because they're one and the same. "However, I think that also puts a little extra burden on management to do a good job because we're looking at our shareholders every day. We talk to them. We see them. We know them," explains Phil Ferrari, Reflexite's chief financial officer. "But we also believe in sharing the pain—and sharing some of that pain from the higher-end (stakeholders) down to the lower-end (stakeholders)."

The reduced-wage phase was implemented for about six months. "That helped reduce the payroll a little bit," says Guyer. Everyone's salaries immediately returned to normal after the self-imposed sanction period was over. Employees even were given a rebate on a portion of the withheld wages once profitability kicked in again. The organization continues to use a variable compensation plan based on profitability. If the company isn't profitable, nobody gets their monthly "owner's bonus"—which is figured as 3% of the company's operating profit, divvied up by shares.

Voluntary leaves of absence help reduce expenses. Another cost-cutting measure the company implemented in 1991 and again in 1995 when it began to experience another downturn was a voluntary time-off program. "The voluntary time-off program was something we coordinated with the state, having people voluntarily go on unemployment for a period of time—anywhere from one week to two months," explains Guyer. "We handled all the paperwork for them, but it was purely voluntary."

Workers who took a leave maintained full benefits, seniority and owner's bonus rights. They also had a guaranteed return date to the company.

More than 90 workers participated. Some people took the opportunity to take time off to go on vacation with their families during the summer. Others took off a week here or there just to chip in and do their part to help the organization get back on its feet.

The strategy worked. It helped the company save more than $400,000 in payroll costs during the 1991 financial downturn alone. Guyer says it worked out well because it helped occupy people's work time more fully while they were on the job. "So people weren't bumping into each other trying to find something to do," he says.

The combined strategies of pay cuts and voluntary leaves of absence produced a 17% budget savings during the 1991 downturn. But the company needed another tool to help itself through other financial and business concerns.

Plan for contingencies. Just because you want to keep people on staff, you still need a swift diagnosis and a cure for financial ills. The worse the company's problem, the more aggres-

> Our company president believes philosophically and ethically that laying people off is the wrong thing to do.

sive the approach should be to fixing it.

Reflexite managers came up with a business model they call the *Business Decline Contingency Plan* (see "Reflexite's Business Decline Contingency Plan"). It's a four-stage diagnostic tool that helps senior managers assess how bad the financial picture is and what to do about it. Laying people off is last on the list.

Business symptoms are outlined at each of the four stages, along with actions to be taken and expected results. For instance, if sales go below what the firm anticipates for a certain period of time, say, four consecutive weeks, and the salespeople confirm that sales are sluggish and their profits, in fact, come in under projections, the plan outlines what the next step should be. The more serious the symptom, the more drastic the measure.

"When we developed the plan, we wanted to make sure we'd have the right action for the right situation," says Ferrari. "Basically, the plan tries to outline what the decline is with some set of criteria. Is it a short-term problem? Is it long term? What's the duration? Is it a market concern? Is it a short-term dip? The purpose is that we make sure we match the response to the type of decline it is."

The second purpose of the plan is to serve as a good communication tool. "One of the things we believe in at Reflexite is communicating properly to employees," says Ferrari. "If they see what the conditions of the decline are and what the appropriate responses are, then they develop in their own minds what's going to happen. So it takes some of the surprises out." Some surprises everyone can do without.

"We do a layoff only as a last resort," he adds. So far, the company hasn't had to deploy that strategy. "A layoff can be a knee-jerk reaction. We try to stay away from that," says Ferrari. "We look for other areas of savings."

Communicate financials—in good times and in bad. For years, Reflexite has shared financial results with its employees, but the extent to which everyone has inspected them with fine-toothed combs has increased in recent months.

During a downturn, the first thing that senior managers do is sit down with employees and tell them—"Here's the situation." It starts getting people together to come up with some creative solutions to their problems, such as cutting back on travel, deferring new hires, running machinery more efficiently, postponing new buildings or keeping fewer raw materials in stock temporarily. While they have a corporate objective to run as lean as possible, there are always ways to trim the fat. "We've been a pretty successful company, but no matter how conscientious you are, when you're making money and stock prices are going up, there are always some things [you can cut back on]," says Guyer. You just need to look carefully at all business aspects.

Communicating the need for employees to watch the comings and goings of the business is essential. Of course, at Reflexite, employees have a vested interest. But with an objective system that helps people understand certain business conditions require certain solutions—which aren't always quick fixes—there's a good chance that any company can enjoy a healthy run for the money.

And this one has. Reflexite has been profitable every year since 1991. In 1992, sales hit $30 million; and in 1995 the company projected $50 million in revenue (actual 1995 figures aren't available). "We believe our success demonstrates what sharing ownership and decision-making can achieve," says Ursprung. He believes that if you give workers some power and some say in how the business operates, they'll repay the company a thousand times over. That's reflected by the company's financial success and the fact that in 1992, the organization won *Inc.* magazine's Entrepreneur-of-the-Year Award. And, the firm has also been featured in the U.S. Department of Labor's "Guide to Responsible Restructuring."

For Reflexite, financial problems have brought to life both the best of times and the worst of times. While the staff may have experienced the worst of times financially, the challenges have drawn the staff closer together to work out their problems as a team. That has given them renewed energy to leap forward with relentless vigor—to find remedies you can't buy in a bottle. Now that's a healthy solution to any problem.

Jennifer J. Laabs is the senior writer at PERSONNEL JOURNAL.

Nine Practical Suggestions for Streamlining Workers' Compensation Costs

Your company can do a lot to minimize its workers' compensation risks. The tips below are a good place to start.

CHARLES L. LORENZ
Director of Risk Management
Talley Industries, Inc.

Charles L. Lorenz has been a director of risk management for over 20 years and has been in the insurance and risk management field for 35 years. He is a national director of RIMS and serves on the boards of the American Management Association and the American Graduate School of International Management. He lectures extensively, and he is listed in Who's Who World Wide Registry.

There's no such thing as a "surplus" employee function today. Because companies have downsized their operations in recent years, the effects of job-related injuries on productivity are more significant than ever. And it's not only the output of the injured employee that is lost. The production of coworkers is slowed because of the loss and because, when they witness an accident, they either go to help the injured worker or stop to watch what is transpiring. Further, as every employer knows, workplace injuries can send a company's workers' compensation premiums skyrocketing.

Employers who want to reduce their injury-related costs need the commitment and dedication of upper management. The first step in achieving this commitment is for the workers' compensation risk manager to show these top managers, in real dollars, just how much a workplace injury actually costs the company. A good way of doing this is to calculate the dollar loss in production time, not only for the injured employee, but also for those employees who either assist or slow down their production to see what is going on. (A good rule of thumb is to take the injured worker's dollar loss and multiply by three.) If the injured employee must take time off from work, then calculate the time taken by other employees to fill in or the cost of hiring a temporary replacement. This produces two costs: One for the temporary employee, the other for the compensation paid to the injured worker during his or her absence.

When senior managers understand the impact of job-related injuries, they often will be much more willing to invest the time and attention needed to effectively reduce the number and cost of workplace accidents.

Below are some guidelines for companies that want to help reduce their injury-related costs.

1. ESTABLISH A SAFETY AGENDA

To control injuries, an employer must establish a safety committee, which generally will have a rotating membership of managers, supervisors, and employees. It is not necessary that a manager chair this committee, but managers should be active participants, to demonstrate that safety is *everyone's* responsibility.

The safety committee should meet a minimum of once a month (preferably twice a month) to review accidents and develop ways to prevent accidents from occurring. In addition, the members should tour company facilities, both to help them understand how accidents occur, and to reinforce to other workers how important it is that *all* employees participate in making the workplace safer.

The committee also should keep records of any corrective actions taken to alleviate on-the-job injuries. And it should be responsible for ensuring that all workers' compensation claims are made part of the review of supervisors.

It's absolutely critical for the company to hold monthly safety meetings for all employees to review the causes of previous accidents and allow employees to make suggestions for avoiding future ones. Safety meetings not only can be instrumental in creating a team approach to improving the workplace, but also, done properly, can eliminate any "we" versus "they" attitude employees may hold toward management.

2. COMMUNICATE THE WORKERS' COMPENSATION PROCESS TO EMPLOYEES

Employers must inform employees about how the state's workers' compensation process works. They should do this repeatedly, beginning with the orientation program for new employees and carrying through the monthly safety meetings for all employees. They also should inform injured employees about the system on an individual basis immediately after the injury occurs. Employees should know what they can expect from the workers' compensation system and what their rights are.

The orientation program for new employees is a very effective forum for imparting workers' compensation information. The employer should specify the carrier that is used and discuss how employees should report workplace injuries. At the time of their orientation, employees should also sign a note acknowledging that they have been advised on these issues. This acknowledgment does not take any rights away from the employee, nor does it take the place of posting workers' compensation notices as required by law. What it does do is supplement the notices and ensure that injured workers can never reasonably claim ignorance of company policies if they fail to follow procedures in reporting an injury.

The orientation also should inform employees of the doctor or doctors the company has approved for treating on-the-job injuries. Most states allow employers initially to direct injured employees to specific doctors. Research studies have indicated that, if an employee fails to go to an approved doctor, there is a strong likelihood that the claim may be fraudulent. A survey by the National Council on Compensation Insurance found that injured employees receive treatment:

• 45% of the time at industrial medical clinics preapproved by employers;

• 27% of the time at emergency rooms;

• 22% of the time from family practitioners; and

• 6% of the time from HMO doctors.

3. INITIATE MANAGED-CARE TECHNIQUES

As of 1992, 19 state have added medical cost-containment strategies to their workers' compensation systems. Many employers are using preferred provider organizations (PPOs) to treat workers' compensation injuries. These organizations help employers achieve not only medical cost savings, but also earlier return-to-work releases for injured workers. Employers also can conduct bill reviews with PPOs. A major account for a well-known workers' compensation carrier had a total of 60,000 medical bills reviewed in 1994 and estimated that its cost savings were in excess of $4.2 million.

4. FOLLOW UP WITH THE DOCTOR AND EMPLOYEE

When an employee has been injured, the supervisor should follow up with the treating doctor immediately to find out when the employee can return to work. Doctors are more likely to work actively with injured employees when the employer shows an interest in their injuries.

5. COMPENSATION, BENEFITS, AND WORKPLACE SAFETY: Managing Employee Compensation

---

EXHIBIT 1
WORKERS' COMPENSATION RELEASE FORM FOR EXITING EMPLOYEES

"I, _____ , while employed by _____ , have not had any workers' compensation claims that have not been reported to management as of this date.

Witness: _____   Employee: _____

Witness: _____   Signature: _____

Date: _____

It's also important that the supervisor and/or human resources staff keep in touch with the injured employee to ensure the employee understands what benefits he or she is entitled to and to demonstrate concern. To make these contacts, the supervisor or HR contact either can phone the employee or visit him or her at home. This "caring" approach has been proven to reduce employers' total claims costs. As the old adage goes, "If claims start correctly, they will stay that way, but if a claim starts bad, it will never get better."

To reduce lost-time cases, the supervisor or HR contact should stay in touch both with the doctor as well as the employee in order to keep track of the employee's progress and find out when they anticipate the employee can be released to return to work.

Should an employer suspect that the time lost is excessive for the injury or the claim is fraudulent, it should dispatch a rehabilitation nurse (or have the insurance carrier dispatch one) to work with the employee and doctor directly. This will help minimize the days lost.

5. TAKE STEPS TO REDUCE THE INCIDENCE OF FRAUD

Fraudulent claims have become a major problem for employers. To recognize possible fraudulent claims, employers should look for the following signs:

1. Nobody saw the injury occur.
2. The plant in which an injured worker is employed is closing or is due for a staff reduction.
3. The injured worker was on vacation or took time off immediately preceding the reported accident.
4. The injury is alleged to have happened on either a Friday afternoon or an early Monday morning.
5. The injured worker immediately retains an attorney.
6. The injured worker asks other employees how the workers' compensation coverage works before reporting his or her injury.
7. The physician the employee chooses is not on the employer's posted list.
8. A neighborhood check of the off-of-work employee finds that the employee is seldom at home, appears muscular or tan, has grease under his or her fingernails, etc.
9. The injured worker's treatment is reported to have taken place on holidays or other days when facilities would normally be closed.
10. The injured employee formerly worked for an insurance company.
11. The injured employee's salary is secondary income for the family.

Of course, these signals should be regarded as indicators, not final criteria. If three or more indicators are present, the employer should realize that the claim may very well be fraudulent.

Recently, the news media have devoted a lot of attention to fraudulent medical-provider operations known as "medical mills." These operations generally use persons known as "bird dogs" to solicit customers from unemployment offices and encourage them to file workers' compensation claims against their previous employers. They lure them into the "medical mills" with the promise of making more money than they could from unemployment benefits.

In addition a number of attorneys and medical providers who advertise directly for clients also specifically solicit employees or former employees who have questionable claims.

To help reduce the incidence of fraudulent claims by former employees, employers should consider incorporating a release document, such as the sample shown in Exhibit 1, into the exiting process.

This form has more of a psychological impact than a legal one, but it has proved very effective in reducing after-the-fact claims.

Management also should recognize that strong communications can reduce the incidence of fraudulent claims by demonstrating to employees that the process by which the employer addresses workplace injuries is both well planned and well supervised.

6. "Reengineer" the Workplace to Avoid Common Risks

Business Insurance Magazine recently reported that back injuries are the most common of workers' compensation claims, and they entail the most significant costs. The second most frequent claim, the magazine said, was carpal tunnel syndrome, and the third, repetitive motion. Since these three claims are the most prevalent and costly, it would behoove all employers to engineer them out of their facilities.

7. Design a Loss Procedural Manual

To assist in processing claims, employers should develop a workers' compensation loss procedural manual, which specifies the steps a company must take when reporting a loss to the insurance carrier or third-party administrator (TPA). It should also describe the reports the insurance carrier or TPA must send back to the employer.

The following is an example of provisions in a procedural manual:

1. *Plant Responsibilities*
   a. Mail or fax the First Report of Injury to the local Industrial Commission and send a copy to the adjuster within 48 hours of the reported occurrence.
   b. Advise the adjuster of any circumstances or conditions it should follow up on regarding how and why the injury occurred.
   c. If the claim is suspected of being fraudulent, secure a report from the supervisor as soon as possible and forward a copy to the adjuster.
2. *Adjuster Responsibilities*
   a. Within seven days, advise the employer of the reserves it has posted to pay expenses on the file.
   b. Administer the claim and make the necessary state filings other than the initial report of the claim.
   c. Work closely with the employer in investigating and paying the claim.

To assist the adjuster in its investigation, the employer should conduct an internal investigation immediately after the injury is reported. The injured worker's supervisor is the best person to handle this investigation. The purpose is to determine whether or not the claim is serious and/or questionable and to decide what preventive measures can be taken to avoid similar accidents in the future. This investigation should be discussed with the safety committee at its regular meeting.

8. Conduct Preemployment Physicals

Preemployment physicals generally help an employer detect whether a prospective employee has a condition that would affect his or her job performance. For example, if a company is looking to hire a worker to lift objects weighing up to 50 pounds, and the prospective employee has back limitations that will not allow him or her to lift objects greater than 5 pounds, the employer will be unable to hire the individual. The doctor performing the preemployment physicals should be familiar with the types of work performed at the plant and the general duties of various plant jobs. This doctor would likely be very competent to handle workers' compensation claims also.

9. Consider Alternative Workers' Compensation Mechanisms

Finally, the employer may want to consider such alternative vehicles as self-insurance or insurance with a large deductible. However, before adopting one of these mechanisms, the employer should make sure that its safety committee is functioning effectively. There must also be cooperative interaction among management, claimants, and physicians, so that the company can control costs after a claim is made.

RISKY BUSINESS: THE NEW PAY GAME

GE's pay system gets people working faster and smarter. One secret: giving workers bonuses only if they meet tough goals.

STEVEN KERR

Pay—the subject's enough to make even the most macho manager cringe. No matter how you handle this sensitive issue, you wind up making some, if not most, of your employees angry and confused. Many managers unintentionally shortchange their stars and overpay their sluggards. Or they design pay plans that send employees the wrong message or a mixed message or no message at all.

I know. I've spent two decades as a manager, a teacher, and a consultant. When it comes to pay, I've seen almost every mistake that can be made, and I've seen—and tried—a host of solutions. To find what works best, I looked at compensation practices at 75 companies. The good news is that I've found a few principles and practices that make sense. The even better news is that you can probably do most of these things at your firm without spending much money. Really.

Most of us know instinctively how to motivate and reward people. We do it with our kids or with the guy who mows our lawn or the gal who cuts our hair. When it comes to our jobs, though, we tend to get distracted by a blizzard of ideas with jargony names, offered by high-priced consultants. Does your daughter Jenny want to ride her bike with her new friend Claire? If you tell her she can, but only after she cleans her room, you've just put into place an "operationally defined, cost-neutral, performance-contingent reward system." Got it?

Where, then, to start. If your company's pay program is broken—and it probably is—don't fix it! Not yet. You've got two other issues to address before you even think about rewards: goals and measurements.

First, you need to tell people exactly what's expected of them. Not some vague mumbo jumbo about making the company or the division the best and biggest in the world, but what role you, Mr. Salesman or Ms. Engineer, are supposed to play in this great enterprise. Here's an exercise I used when I taught executive education classes at the University of Michigan. I asked all the students to write down their company's mission statements, as well as the amount of senior management time it took to develop them. I put all the notes in a shoebox, then picked one out at random. Whose finely crafted credo is this, I asked the class? Inevitably, five or six hands would go up, as managers from airlines, pharmaceutical companies, and plumbing-supply manufacturers all claimed the statement as their own.

Though it can take hundreds of hours to devise these declarations, many top managers can't distinguish their own slogans from those of their neighbors. If executives can't clearly articulate their company's reason for being, how can we expect line workers or supervisors to know their roles?

At General Electric's leadership development center in Crotonville, New York (where I work), we try to get managers to bring those lofty mission statements down to earth. Imagine you're at a party a year from now, we tell them. You're celebrating the successful completion of a big project in your division. How exactly did your leaders, peers, and subordinates change their behavior to reach this goal? We don't accept imprecise answers. What do you mean your people have become empowered? Do they participate more in meetings? Do they feel free to constructively criticize their superiors? Did they find a solution that boosted sales or improved quality or cut costs?

Once you know specifically what you want your employees to be doing in the future, then you need

ILLUSTRATIONS BY RANDALL ENOS

5. COMPENSATION, BENEFITS, AND WORKPLACE SAFETY: Incentive Compensation

to measure it. Even seemingly fuzzy stuff, like how well a manager satisfies customers or delegates authority or gets along with colleagues, can be measured through 360-degree evaluations—where an employee is rated by people above and below him in the organization—and through one-on-one interviews. The key is to ask not only the right questions but also the right people—customers, coworkers, and bosses.

People, though, aren't likely to change their behavior unless you reward them for it. Companies typically hand out bonuses or stock options as recognition for past performance. Great job landing that account, Judy, here's $2,000. But the real purpose of that award should be to induce Judy to perform even better in the future. Studies show that to truly motivate people, you have to offer them an award that's at least 10% to 12% above their base salary. In practice, companies pay out much less than that. Variable compensation—including bonuses, stock options, and profit sharing—accounts on average for only 7.5% of compensation.

So a key principle of compensation is to link more of it directly to performance. Sounds obvious, doesn't it? But consider the way we currently pay people. The two factors that usually carry the most weight are an employee's title and length of service. When you reward employees according to seniority or you give everyone on the staff the same annual percentage increase, you've turned compensation into an entitlement, not an incentive. You're giving your weakest performers a free ride. And you're encouraging your best employees to polish their résumés and look elsewhere.

Okay, so you've defined exactly what people should do to make your company flourish; you've figured out how to measure their activities; and you've committed your company to actually paying for performance. Now, you have to execute. To make things easier, keep these guidelines in mind:

RULE 1. Don't tie pay to power. In the halcyon days of the 1950s and 1960s, when companies had umpteen layers of management, it was fine to tell every subaltern with a college degree and a starched white shirt that he could aspire to fatter paychecks and juicier perks as he climbed each rung on the ladder. But in these days of downsizing, we've got a bulging cohort of baby-boomers chasing a shrinking number of slots in the hierarchy. If you continue to link rewards to rank, you're likely to create an army of malcontents. Popos is what the experts call them: "passed over and pissed off."

At GE we've tried to get away from the idea that you have to move up to make more.

STEVEN KERR, *chief learning officer at GE, runs the company's Crotonville, New York, leadership center.*

> **I**f you continue to link financial rewards with rank, you're likely to create an army of malcontents.

We cut from 29 to six the number of different salary grades—a technique known as "broad banding." This gives people more opportunities to get a raise without a promotion. We've also sharply increased the number of employees eligible for stock options, and we're experimenting with programs that reward managers for what they know, not for how many workers they supervise or how long they've been on the job.

RULE 2. Make compensation comprehensible. A Detroit auto supplier I worked with a few years ago was stunned to learn that some of its best factory workers were taking jobs at a rival company offering inferior pay packages. The competitor paid higher hourly wages, but when you added in the fringes—like health, dental, and life insurance—there was no contest between the two companies. The trouble was that the auto supplier's benefits department communicated in such abstruse actuarial double talk that workers didn't have a clue what their total compensation was worth. The company solved the problem by creating a clearly written booklet, complete with cartoon drawings, that explained all the perks.

RULE 3. Start spreading the news. When you give a deserving worker a reward, broadcast it! If you hand out a $1,000 spot bonus, but no one knows it except you and the recipient, the total number of people you've motivated is somewhere between zero and one.

Yes, paychecks are supposed to be private. That's ingrained in our corporate culture. Only the top guys disclose their comp packages, and that's only because the SEC requires them to. But when employees don't have real information, they spread rumors. And surveys invariably show that folks underestimate how well they're being paid in relation to their peers. If you posted everyone's salary and bonus on the bulletin board, the dominant reaction might well be a sigh of relief.

A couple of caveats: Don't talk about other people's money unless you're sure your measurement system works. If you aren't prepared to explain and defend your decisions—why Joe got only a $2,500 bonus while Sam in the next cubicle got $3,000—then it's better to be discreet. Also, not all workers like being singled out for praise. Some employees come from cultures like Japan that consider public commendation of an individual an affront to the harmony of the group.

RULE 4. Forget about the calendar. A reward delayed is almost as bad as a reward denied. If a rat in a cage pulls a lever and nine months later (on the anniversary of his arrival in the laboratory) you give him a cube of sugar, he's not likely to connect cause with effect. Time and again I run into companies that review people in May, then reward them the following January. Some firms require so many layers of managerial sign-offs that by the time an extra lump sum shows up in a worker's paycheck, she may be left scratching her head, trying to remember just what she did to deserve it.

At GE we invite employees to assess—and reward—their peers on the spot. A program called Quick Thanks!, used by GE Medical Systems, lets an employee nominate any colleague (even one in another department) to receive a $25 gift certificate from certain restaurants and stores in appreciation of an exemplary job done. (Over the last year GE has given out 10,000 such awards.) The employee himself often hands out the award to his deserving co-worker. And guess what? Peers are often a whole lot tougher than bosses in dishing out praise. For the recipient, it's the approbation of a colleague, not the $25, that matters most.

That's not to say instant gratification should always prevail. I once saw a chief executive give only a perfunctory "thank you" after receiving a briefing from a midlevel manager. But the next day he telephoned to say, "I really appreciated your contribution yesterday." In this instance, the theatrical pause enhanced the value of the recognition.

RULE 5. Make rewards reversible. It's no good pretending you have perfect judgment. Some of the compensation decisions you make are going to be bad ones. Also, let's face it, business conditions can change. So give yourself an out. It's virtually impossible to take back a raise. You have to deal with mountains of paperwork and endless appeals. But if you give an employee a bonus, as opposed to an increase in base pay, you don't have to live with your decision forever. He knows he'll get another bonus next year only if he keeps performing.

But be careful. For variable compensation

to work, it really has to be, well, variable. At some companies, bonuses have become so routine that employees look at them as wages by another name, as just another entitlement. And be mindful of what your competitors are doing. If your employees need to collect a bonus just to bring their compensation up to the going rate, chances are you're not paying enough base salary to begin with.

RULE 6. You can't always give what you want. But you can still, to paraphrase Mick Jagger, give what you need. I've seen companies with minuscule salary pools spend hundreds of management hours rating, ranking, and grading every single employee. But everyone gets such a small piece of the pie that virtually no one is happy. If you don't have enough cash in the kitty, try some nonfinancial incentives. Don't get me wrong. Money, when used properly, is a great motivator. But nonmonetary rewards pack potent advantages:

▶ They're reversible (see Rule 5). It's easier to cut back someone's authority or to stop giving someone opportunities to participate in plum projects than it is to reclaim a 6% raise.

▶ You can create your own supply. If you give $1,000 to Employee A, you have $1,000 less to give to Employee B. With nonmonetary awards there are fewer constraints. You can give Employee C more interesting assignments, a mention in the in-house newsletter, and a chance to make a presentation to the division head today, and then you can give the same things to Employee D tomorrow. Of course, if you create too much supply you end up debasing the currency. A nonmonetary reward quickly loses its value if it's overused.

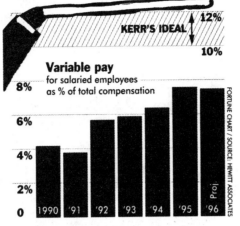

MORE CARROTS, FEWER STICKS

Variable pay for salaried employees as % of total compensation

KERR'S IDEAL 10%–12%

Variable pay like bonuses and options is on the rise but still falls short of ideal levels.

FORTUNE CHART / SOURCE: HEWITT ASSOCIATES

RULE 7. Don't be a compensation chauvinist. If you're operating overseas, be aware that some cultures are not big on the idea of incentive pay. Once, after I lectured an executive education class on the need for more performance-based pay, a Japanese manager rose in protest: "You shouldn't bribe your children to do their homework, you shouldn't bribe your wife to prepare dinner, and you shouldn't bribe your employees to work for the company." In some countries, the objections to bonuses are more fiscal than philosophical. Instead of cash, employees would rather have more leisure time, access to vacation villages, or anything the tax man can't get his hands on. I'm not suggesting that you abandon your principles, but do modify them to account for cultural differences.

RULE 8. Cheer up! If your company is breaking most of rules 1 to 7, don't despair. Your competitors' compensation practices are probably at least as messed-up as your own. You've got a wonderful opportunity to gain an edge over your rivals without necessarily having to invest more cash. In how many aspects of business is that ever the case? When it comes to rewarding employees, the key is not how much more you have to give. It's how well you give what you already have.

REPORTER ASSOCIATE *Erin Davies*

THE LONG AND WINDING ROAD

That's the direction executive compensation is taking, as companies tighten up the links between long-term profitability and their executives' net worth. Find out how they're driving the message home with new variations on the old stock-option carrot.

JOHN D. McMILLAN and STEVEN SABOW

Mr. McMillan is managing director at the Houston office of William M. Mercer Inc. Mr. Sabow is manager of the executive-compensation research group at Mercer's New York office.

Hitched your star to your company's wagon? You'd better be prepared for the long haul. Today, executive-compensation programs primarily emphasize long-term incentive programs — and that's probably where the focus should have been all along. Annual-bonus plans have been almost universal since the late 1980s, but while the average bonus levels have increased, most of the increase stems from higher profitability, not changes to the bonus plans themselves. This signifies that in the future, your compensation will probably be tied even more closely to the company's overall profitability and the shareholder value you contribute.

In general, executive pay is a function of company size. The average salary and total cash compensation (salary and bonus) for executives in industry usually depend on company revenues, and the same is true in banking and insurance. For example, CFOs in companies with revenues under $200 million earn an average base salary of $140,000, while those in companies with $200 million to $500 million receive an average of $156,700, according to our latest executive-compensation survey. CFOs working for companies with $500 million to $1 billion in revenues receive an average of $211,100. And CFOs in companies with more than $3 billion in annual revenues earn average base salaries of $313,500, more than double their compatriots in smaller companies. Pay *should* correlate with size, of course, since fewer executives are experienced at running a $10-billion company than a $10-million company. As long as we have a free market, the rarer gem will command the higher price.

Overall, executive salaries haven't been rising rapidly, headlines in recent years notwithstanding. Between 1989 and 1994, CFO salaries rose more than financial-executive salaries in other categories — by about 4.7 percent. The average salary for a treasurer and a controller rose by approximately 4.2 percent and 4.5 percent, respectively, while the average salary for a CEO increased by about 3.6 percent per year.

The average salary increase by position is less than the average salary increase budgeted for executives, which was just over 5 percent during this five-year period. One reason for the differential is that companies often replace executives who retire or leave with lower-paid executives, a phenomenon often called "turnover savings." So a company that budgets an overall salary increase of 3 percent may be able to actually give its executives 5 percent, depending on the turnover rate.

Like salaries, bonuses also vary with the size of the company. Larger companies tend to pay larger bonuses, both in dollars and as a percentage of salary, than smaller companies do. The average bonus for CEOs in companies with less than

$200 million in revenues is approximately 55 percent of salary, compared to more than 80 percent in companies with more than $3 billion in revenues. For CFOs at those companies, the numbers are 40 percent and more than 60 percent of salary, respectively. Average bonuses for CEOs have increased during the last five years by about 23 percent (or slightly more than 4.2 percent annually), while average bonuses for CFOs during the same time period increased by about 12.4 percent (2.4 percent annually).

In recent years, both the Securities and Exchange Commission pay-disclosure rules and tax laws have been modified in an effort to more strongly emphasize the pay-performance linkage. This isn't a new concept, of course. Our American sense of fairness has always demanded that pay relate to performance. Many studies have addressed this issue — with embarrassingly few indicating a close connection.

While better-performing companies often pay higher bonuses than lower-performing companies, in far too many cases they don't. However, it's exceedingly difficult to establish the exact correlation of pay and performance in the short term, since individual company goals and strategies vary widely. Virtually every company defines and measures "performance" differently.

Measuring company performance is less difficult over the longer term, especially from the shareholder viewpoint. Stock price is clearly the single most important long-term performance measure for shareholders, especially considering that institutions and pension funds own approximately half the shares in public companies, and the company's performance is measured quarterly, if not more often. More recently, the SEC has mandated showing total shareholder return (stock-price appreciation plus total dividends reinvested) in annual proxy statements, and this has become the de facto measure of long-term performance for shareholders during the last three years.

NEW STOCK ANSWERS

Companies are following this trend, too. About 30 percent of major companies with performance-share plans now use total shareholder return as an executive-performance measure, and this proportion will probably increase significantly in the future. Equally important, companies are introducing performance requirements into a wide range of stock

HITTING THE STOCK-OPTION BULL'S EYE

Company	Targets for performance-contingent stock options
Alco Standard	Long-term incentive-plan options may be exercised only with option credits, which are earned over a three-year period and which depend on the company's total shareholder return relative to the S&P 500 total shareholder return.
Charter Medical	Options vest 20 percent for each fiscal year in which the company achieves 100 percent of cumulative target earnings (before interest depreciation and taxes).
Citicorp	Options granted at $31.75 per share vest 50 percent when stock reaches $50 per share; 75 percent when stock reaches $55 per share and 100 percent when stock reaches $60 per share (and sustains each target level for 20 out of 30 consecutive trading days).
Consolidated Papers	Options granted in 1989 and 1991 vest on the company's achievement of net-income targets. The company met the goal in 1989, and the options vested. It didn't meet the goal in 1991, and the options lapsed.
Digital Equipment	Options vest 20 percent per year but may not be exercised unless the corporation's stock price averages at least $100 over 90 consecutive trading days.
Eagle-Picher	Options aren't exercisable unless the market price per share is at least 20 percent greater than the option price per share.
Newmont Mining	Options aren't exercisable unless on the day before exercise, the market price per share is at least 25 percent greater than the option price per share.
Sysco	Options aren't exercisable unless the company attains certain levels of increases in pre-tax earnings and return on shareholders' equity. If not attained within five years, the options expire, even though their term is 10 years.

Source: William M. Mercer Inc.

5. COMPENSATION, BENEFITS, AND WORKPLACE SAFETY: Incentive Compensation

plans that previously reflected stock-price growth only, creating new incentive variations.

Performance-accelerated options are one popular vehicle. Essentially, the executive receives options that will eventually vest according to a schedule, regardless of company performance. However, the vesting accelerates if the company meets certain long-term goals. For example, Avery Dennison's options vest nine years and nine months after the grant date, but they can vest as early as three years from the grant date if the company achieves specified objectives, such as increasing its return on total capital. Other companies using the performance-accelerated option approach include ITT, Mellon Bank, Monsanto, Texas Instruments, Times Mirror and Toys "R" Us.

This approach has two advantages. First, the company generally grants options at the current market price, providing the executive the benefit of future appreciation. The option-exercise price is higher for

> **Avery Dennison's options vest nine years and nine months after the grant date, but they can vest in three years if the company achieves specified objectives.**

premium or indexed options. Plus, current accounting rules don't require a charge to earnings, although the Financial Accounting Standards Board intends to require at least a footnote disclosure of the hypothetical option expense in the future for all types of options.

Performance-contingent options are quite different: They may never become exercisable unless the company achieves certain goals. For example, options granted to Citicorp executives in 1993 at $31.75 per share become exercisable based on stock-price appreciation. Fifty percent of the option becomes exercisable when the stock reaches $50 per share, 75 percent when it reaches $55 per share and 100 percent when it climbs to $60 per share. In each case, the stock must sustain the target levels for 20 out of 30 consecutive trading days. Other companies with performance-contingent stock options are Alco Standard, Charter Medical, Consolidated Papers, Digital Equipment, Eagle-Picher, Newmont Mining and Sysco (see table on previous page.)

A company using performance-contingent stock options generally must report as an expense the difference between the exercise price and the stock value on the date the contingency is satisfied. Also, since performance-contingent options may never vest, companies often grant them on a much larger number of shares than they do with regular options, and this practice can rapidly use up the available pool of reserved shares. In the future, therefore, companies may favor performance-accelerated options, which are a good way to add a performance feature to a stock-option program without an earnings charge.

Another popular compensation vehicle is the performance-accelerated restricted stock grant, which rewards long-term performance through the acceleration feature. This differs markedly from traditional and widely used restricted-stock grants, which normally vest automatically when the executive continues to work for the company. Performance-accelerated restricted stock grants will eventually vest after a certain time period, but vesting may accelerate if the company attains its performance goals. The Allen Group, Avon, Clorox and Honeywell all have made performance-accelerated grants.

Other companies have emphasized making the eventual vesting of restricted stock contingent on the company's achieving predetermined objectives. These performance-contingent grants are essentially performance shares (a long-term incentive companies have used for more than 20 years) granted in the form of restricted stock. Companies granting such awards in recent years include Ameritech, General Dynamics and Melville. Performance-contingent restricted stock is likely to become an increasingly popular form of compensation, since "regular" time-lapse restricted stock grants won't qualify as performance-based compensation for tax deductibility under the $1-million pay cap that Internal Revenue Code Section 162 (m) imposes.

BEWARE OF STICKER SHOCK

Some critics of executive pay have objected to companies granting 10-year options at the current market price, since the long-term upward trend in the market and the economy will almost certainly make the options profitable, regardless of company performance. In response, some high-profile companies have granted "premium" options, including AT&T, Colgate-Palmolive, Walt Disney, Dow Jones, Philip Morris, Procter & Gamble, Quaker Oats, Reebok, Rockwell and Time Warner.

These options differ from performance-contingent options in that executives must pay an exercise price for their premium options that's substantially higher than the current market price at the grant date. AT&T, for example, has granted options in four tiers: 25 percent at fair market value, 25 per-

> **More than 40 percent of large companies use peer-group measurement in their performance-share plans.**

cent at a price 120 percent of fair market value, 25 percent at 130 percent and the final 25 percent at 150 percent of fair market value. This approach is much less beneficial for executives than performance-accelerated or even performance-contingent options. Under either of those approaches, the executive gets the benefit of future appreciation after the grant date. With premium options, the executive gets only the benefit of appreciation over the higher, future target price. As a result, companies tend to grant premium options, like performance-contingent options, on a much higher number of shares than normal options.

On another front, the new SEC proxy disclosure rules have made three valuable contributions to evaluating executive pay over the long term: the focus on total shareholder return mentioned earlier, the requirement to include three years of pay history and, perhaps most important, the requirement that long-term performance be viewed on a relative basis over five years. The proxy rules for the last three years have required a graph showing the company's total shareholder return during the last five years in relation to both the S&P 500 (or another broad market index) and either a predetermined published industry index or a special peer or market-capital group of comparable companies selected by the company.

By requiring company total shareholder return to be compared with a broad market index and an industry index, the SEC has firmly (and, we think, appropriately) established relative performance as a comparison standard in evaluating executive compensation over the long term.

A large and growing number of companies use some form of peer-group measurement in their long-term incentive plans. More than 40 percent of large companies use it to determine long-term payout in their performance-share plans, and we expect that number to rise to more than 50 percent in the next several years.

Companies are also using relative performance in stock-option plans, in the form of indexed options. Such options have an exercise price that periodically adjusts in relation to market, industry or peer-group performance. For instance, in 1993 Dresser Industries granted options that stipulated the option-exercise price will increase in line with 30-year treasury-bond yields, less dividends paid. This assures executives benefit only beyond the "risk free" level of total return the company generates. Warner-Lambert indexed half of its 1992 option grants for senior executives to the S&P 500 for the first four years after the grant. The company must outperform the S&P 500 for these options to have any value for the first four years—a very demanding hurdle for most companies.

CONSIDER YOUR STOCK OPTIONS

Median face value (exercise cost) of options granted annually as a % of salary

Salary level*	%
$600,000	207
350,000	164
250,000	123
200,000	119
150,000	82
125,000	65
100,000	55
80,000	37
60,000	33
50,200	24

*Executives in general industry
Source: William M. Mercer Inc.

WHAT'S IT WORTH TO YOU?

Market value of senior executives' stock (100 largest U.S. industrial companies)

Percentile*	Shares owned (without options) $ millions		Shares owned (with options) $ millions	
	CEO	CFO	CEO	CFO
75th	$13.0	$2.3	$35.9	$6.0
50th	5.4	1.0	16.5	2.7
25th	2.1	0.5	9.9	1.4

Value of shares owned as a multiple of salary

Percentile*	Shares owned (without options)		Shares owned (with options)	
	CEO	CFO	CEO	CFO
75th	16.7 x salary	5.9	41.6	14.5
50th	6.6	2.7	21.7	8.4
25th	3.5	1.0	13.0	4.2

*At the 75th-percentile mark, 25 companies reported higher values (not shown). The 50th percentile is the median. At the 25th-percentile mark, 25 companies reported lower values (not shown).

Source: William M. Mercer Inc.

5. COMPENSATION, BENEFITS, AND WORKPLACE SAFETY: Incentive Compensation

The relative-performance concept is useful in evaluating long-term company and executive performance. Most companies with long-term performance plans will probably use earnings or total-shareholder-return measures relative to peer-group averages within the next several years.

By offering stock options, companies clearly are providing executives with opportunities for significant gains. Many executives receive annual stock options worth more than their salary, as shown in the table "Consider Your Stock Options." If the stock doubles in a year, many of these executives can exercise their options and realize a profit equal to their salary or more in just one year.

In most cases, companies that emphasize long-term programs give their executives enough interest in company stock growth so that their net worth will largely depend on long-term company performance. This is especially true in smaller entrepreneurial companies that don't provide pension plans but that do provide their executives with opportunities for regular stock acquisition through stock-purchase and 401(k) plans. In more and more cases, these companies are tying executive wealth to long-term total shareholder return.

KEEP IT IN THE FAMILY

Plus, companies are encouraging their executives to acquire and hold stock. That's often at the behest of a board of directors frustrated with traditional stock-option plans because so many executives exercise their options and promptly sell the stock. Approximately a quarter of the largest companies have adopted new executive stock-ownership guidelines, usually stated as a multiple of salary. Typical multiples are: CEO, four to seven times salary; COO, three to four; executive vice president, two to three; CFO, one to three; other officers, one to two; and other executives, one.

In fact, the increased emphasis on stock ownership is producing results. A recent analysis of stock ownership among CEOs of the 100 largest industrial companies indicates these executives do, in fact, company's stock (see chart "What's It Worth to You?").

In any case, the message to financial executives is clear: Put shareholder interests first, and take the long view. If the stock appreciates, for whatever reason, you'll feel it in your wallet.

AND YOU THOUGHT CEOs WERE OVERPAID

Outside directors are catching up fast

In the good old days, when shareholders rarely raised their voices, company directors would often find a crisp $100 bill tucked beneath the dinner plates in the corporate dining room. That's when the honoraria for serving on corporate boards were sparse and the perks few.

Now, as more companies heap stock-option packages onto directors, director pay is soaring to record levels. And a new analysis of pay to outside directors by executive-compensation critic Graef S. Crystal finds many companies are grossly overpaying their overseers.

Which has the dubious distinction of having the most overpaid directors in the U.S.? Dallas Semiconductor Corp. wins hands down. Thanks mainly to stock-option grants, the custom chip-maker's outside directors averaged annual pay of $195,200 from 1993 to 1995. Such compensation for a boardroom job, says Crystal, is 559% higher than it should be when taking into account Dallas's size and stock-market performance.

"INCESTUOUS." Not surprisingly, perhaps, if the CEO is deemed to be overpaid, the directors who decide what the boss gets are often mightily compensated to sit in the boardroom. "There is something incestuous going on here," says Crystal. "Is it any wonder that when a CEO is paid above competitive levels, he tends to return the favor to the people who helped him out?"

Dallas Semiconductor is a case in point, according to Crystal. Besides the overpayment to the board, CEO C. Vin Prothro, who earned an average $3.3 million in each of the past three years, or over $9.8 million total, was overpaid by 224%, according to Crystal. Prothro says it is unfair to place a value on his or the board's option grants before they are exercised. "Valuing options like that would be like going to a fortune teller to fill out your tax return," he retorts. "If I really believed what he says, I would have to call the FBI and report a theft, because I certainly don't see $9 million in my bank account."

The study examined director pay at 963 of the nation's largest public corporations. Pay includes annual retainer, meeting fees, stock-option value at the date of grant, and pensions for outside directors. Crystal looked at pay from 1993 to 1995 to smooth out the impact of a large option grant awarded in one year. The study didn't, however, tally the benefits of such perks as insurance,

DALLAS SEMICONDUCTOR
OUTSIDE DIRECTORS' AVERAGE ANNUAL PAY
$195,200
OVERPAID BY
559%

Raking It In

COMPANY	OUTSIDE DIRECTORS' AVERAGE ANNUAL PAY 1993-1995	OVERPAID BY PERCENT*
DALLAS SEMICONDUCTOR	$195,200	559
UNITED HEALTHCARE	368,000	549
CRACKER BARREL	202,900	440
WMS INDUSTRIES	163,800	422
CENTOCOR	97,300	256
NATURE'S SUNSHINE PRODUCTS	99,300	251
M. A. HANNA	141,800	247
SOUTHWESTERN ENERGY	88,900	241
ANADARKO PETROLEUM	118,000	233
LAWTER INTERNATIONAL	80,300	221

*Adjusting for company size and stock performance. Includes the value of stock options at the time they are granted.
DATA: GRAEF S. CRYSTAL

5. COMPENSATION, BENEFITS, AND WORKPLACE SAFETY: Executive Pay

one-time grants of stock options for new board members, free cars, or travel. Crystal then compared the average pay of each director to the company's average performance, measured by stock appreciation and reinvested dividends over three years.

The average annual pay for an outside director was $44,000, ranging from a high of $368,000 at Minnesota-based HMO concern United Healthcare Corp. to a low of just $550 a year for the outside directors of National Presto Industries Inc., an appliance maker in Wisconsin. The overall averages lead some boardroom observers to argue that many directors are underpaid. "A good number of companies are underpaying for the time and effort directors now have to spend on the complex issues they deal with today," says John M. Nash, president of the National Association of Corporate Directors (NACD).

That's less true, however, when companies shift more pay to stock-option grants. And almost all of the largest pay packages include hefty grants urged on companies by corporate-governance activists who say options align the interests of directors and shareholders. Indeed, a 1995 NACD task force recommended that companies pay at least 50% of director fees in equity, with an eventual goal of paying 100% in stock. Crystal found that 39% of companies now grant stock options to outside directors, up from 29% a year ago.

STINGY? Today, most companies still provide rather small option packages to directors. Bell Atlantic Corp. and Federal Express Corp. award options for just 1,000 shares annually to their directors. But some companies—especially many of those that landed on Crystal's overpaid list—are giving out much larger options.

Consider United Healthcare's outside directors. While board members there now receive an annual retainer of just $20,000 and $1,500 extra for every board meeting they attend, stock-option grants have made a huge difference. In 1993 and 1994, directors got option grants on as many as 64,000 shares, worth nearly $750,000 in total. Last year, the company became a bit stingy, handing out options on 16,000 shares worth $274,900.

That's a bit of a cutback. But it's still better than a crisp C-note under a plate.

By John A. Byrne in New York

The need for greed

It is commonly argued that to get company bosses to pursue their interests, shareholders should turn them into owners. Should they?

LAST year General Electric, an American conglomerate, earned $6.6 billion in after-tax profits by selling everything from fridges to aircraft engines. About $2.8 billion of this was paid to shareholders as dividends; the rest was reinvested in GE on their behalf. Yet America's journalists devoted far more attention to the far smaller sum, worth a mere 0.3% of that total, that was paid to one man: Jack Welch. The $22m in salary, bonus, share options and other benefits that Mr Welch received in 1995 made him America's highest-paid chief executive.

Whether Mr Welch deserved this much money is anybody's guess. The bosses of the world's biggest firms have great freedom to run them as they see fit, and it is almost impossible to compare their decisions to alternatives that were not—and never will be—taken. Nor is it easy to separate their personal contributions from plain luck.

Nevertheless, the decisions of corporate chieftains can have a huge effect on people's wealth. In total, the equity of the firms in America's Standard & Poor's 500 index is worth $4.9 trillion. To ensure that shareholders' assets are used wisely, it surely makes sense to pay their stewards handsomely. But how much is that?

For the most part, setting the amount a chief executive is paid is pretty straightforward. Shareholders have to pay him whatever sum is needed in order to lure him away from other firms in the market for talented executives. There is more to it than that, however, because one of the best ways to motivate middle managers is to make them compete with one another for promotions. To make such "tournament" schemes work, a firm must dangle fat carrots in front of managers at each stage of the competition. Thus, a board may want to pay the chief executive a wad of cash not just to encourage him to work hard, but to encourage his subordinates to do so as well.

Given the difficult climb to the top of a large firm, and the fierce competition for good leaders among the world's biggest firms, it is not surprising that many company bosses are paid enormous sums. Far more befuddling, however, is the composition of their pay.

In the 1980s, boards of directors were denounced for paying the boss a salary and short-term bonuses, rather than linking his pay to his contribution to long-term value (ie, the share price). In the 1990s, critics are levelling the opposite complaint: that chief executives are growing fat on over-generous handouts of shares and share options. According to Towers Perrin, a pay consultancy, the average chief executive in America now receives more than half of his pay in the form of performance-related bonuses, shares or other long-term incentives. How should companies design their pay packages to get the most out of the boss?

To economists, the answer to this question depends on two main factors: information and risk. Start with information. Suppose, for example, that a firm's

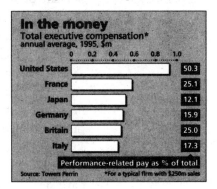

board of directors knew exactly how its boss should do his job (eg, whom to promote, which investments to make and so forth) and that they could verify whether he had done all of these things correctly. If so, deciding how to reward him would be simple: pay him if he does what he is supposed to; if not, fire him.

Be careful what you pay for

However, things are hazy at the top. It is hard to know in advance which crucial decisions a chief executive will face. And even with hindsight, those who monitor him—being not nearly as well-informed—often cannot judge whether his decisions were correct. Rather than basing the executive's pay on his actions, therefore, the company could pay him only for delivering results.

For shareholders, there is only one result that matters: a higher share price. Hence the demand by many pay gurus to give company bosses bigger stakes in their firms. It is argued that this will encourage them to act in the interests of investors, dispensing with the need for costly and imperfect monitoring.

Although this sounds simple, it bumps into the question of risk. To see why this is a problem, it helps to remember why professional managers have a function in the first place. The beauty of large, publicly traded corporations is that they allow investors to avoid taking large, illiquid, undiversified stakes in a few firms. Instead, they can pool their savings with other investors, take a small stake in each firm, and hire professionals to run them, reducing risks substantially.

However, putting too many shares in the chief executive's hands threatens to undo many of these risk-reducing gains. Consider, by way of example, a company with a market value of $10 billion. That is not a giant; it would put it in the middle of the S&P 500. Giving the boss of such a firm even an apparently trifling 0.1% stake would award him $10m of illiquid, undiversified wealth. In these circumstances, a boss faced with too many risks might avoid making investments that would create value for investors. Or he might rely too heavily on derivatives to hedge risks that are better left alone.

Awarding share options, instead of shares themselves, can mitigate this danger. Options give the manager the right to buy shares at a set price. If the share price goes above this level before the options expire, the executive can pocket the difference. By allowing the boss to reap the rewards of boosting the share price, while sheltering him from some of the pains of failure, firms can eliminate some of the problems of excess risk.

Even with options, however, the sums at stake can be staggering. To stiffen a boss's back, therefore, it is often better to base much of his pay on things over which he has lots of control, and shelter him from those over which he has little. Suppose that there is little the boss can do to prevent adverse industry-wide trends, but that there are many ways in which he can lessen their effects. It may make sense to reward him according to the performance of the firm's shares relative to those of others in the same industry.

No matter what formula a firm uses, there is no such thing as a perfect compensation scheme. There will always be an incentive to do something that is not in shareholders' interests. If they are wise, investors will not only pay their bosses handsomely. They will want to watch them closely as well.

Article 37

Balancing Work and Family Responsibilities: Flextime and Child Care in the Federal Government

Marni Ezra, American University
Melissa Deckman, American University

Do family-friendly policies make for a more satisfied federal work force? The influx of mothers into the work force has heightened the federal government's awareness of the need to help employees balance work and family responsibilities. The authors conducted ordinary least squares regression analyses using the 1991 Survey of Federal Employees to investigate how the use of family-friendly policies affects federal workers' satisfaction with their jobs and work/family balance. They found that satisfaction with work/family balance is a vital component of an employee's job satisfaction, and the use of policies such as on-site child care and flextime appear to help employees, particularly mothers, face the dual demands of work and family life better.

> *Our increasingly diverse work force struggles to manage child care, elder care, family emergencies, and other personal commitments, while working conditions become ever more important. The federal government must maintain its "model employer" status and keep the workplace a humane and healthy place (National Performance Review, 1993; 84).*

The current bipartisan concern for the changing work needs of the American family is reflected in Vice-President Gore's *National Performance Review*. In particular, the increasing presence of mothers in the work force challenges both organizations and employees to find new ways to balance work and nonwork priorities. In 1960, fewer than 19 percent of women with children under 6 years old, and 39 percent of women with children between 6 and 17 years were in the work force. By 1990, the numbers had dramatically risen to 60 percent and 75 percent, respectively (General Accounting Office, 1992; 10).

The federal government faces an especially difficult challenge in striking a balance between work and nonwork responsibilities because women's share of the federal work force increased faster than women's share of the private sector work force between 1976 and 1990 (Guy, 1993; 279). Because many women have heavy responsibilities at home once the work day is through (Hochschild, 1989), they want changes on the job that allow them an acceptable balance between work and family life. In addition, because the federal government is the largest employer in the United States, it often serves as a model for private and other public sector employers.

A growing number of employers have responded to the changing nature of the work force by offering flexible work schedules, on-site child care, more flexible leave policies, and other benefits. In the past, most employees did not need (or expect) help from employers to enable them to meet their family responsibilities. Most workers were men who could concentrate on work because "they had support systems at home, usually a wife and family" (Romzek, 1991; 228). With an increase in the number of two-career families, family responsibilities have begun to overlap with work responsibilities.

To adjust to these changes, personnel managers will need to rethink how they approach their jobs generally and how they approach recruitment and retention in particular. Personnel managers will need to change the expectations that they have about employees adjusting to the work setting and vice versa. And they will have to increase the flexibility of the organization's structure to accommodate new expectations employees have regarding work and nonwork (Romzek, 1991; 232).

This article analyzes a large survey of federal employees to assess the impact of government-provided accommodations on federal employees' satisfaction with their work/family balance and their jobs. Our study addresses the following questions. First, do the federal service's family-friendly policies, such as on-site child care and flexible work schedules, make for a happier work force? Do these policies affect some employees more than others? Second, which employees are more satisfied with their work/family balance? Third, how important is satisfaction with work/family balance to job satisfaction?

Child Care in the Federal Government

Although the federal government has more child care facilities today than ever before, "at present the U.S. has no general policy on child care" (Suntrup, 1989; 55). Before 1985, on-site child care facilities were not readily available in the federal government. In 1985, Congress passed the Trible amendment[1] which allows agencies to spend appropriated funds to provide space and services for child care facilities for federal employees (General Accounting Office, 1992; 86). While the child care situation was improved, the costs were still too high for many federal workers to afford (General Accounting Office, 1992; 87). Thus, in 1987, the Office of Personnel Management (OPM) alerted agencies to the need for affordable child and dependent care in the federal government. In 1992, only 2 percent of private and 9 percent of government organizations had on-site child care facilities (Shafritz et al., 1992; 533).

Marquart (1991) and Dawson et al. (1984) found that users of on-site child care facilities in the private sector were more likely to work overtime and were more satisfied with their jobs than those who did not use on-site care. Romzek (1991), however, argues that less complex choices, such as daycare referral services or flexible scheduling, may be a better alternative for working parents. Those with long commutes, for instance, may not want to bring their children to on-site child care facilities.

Rodgers and Rodgers (1989) found that companies that employed rigid practices regarding family responsibilities experienced greater turnover and economic losses. In addition, they found that "employees who perceived their supervisors as unsupportive on family issues reported higher levels of stress, greater absenteeism, and lower job satisfaction" (p. 123).

Although these studies provide a good frame through which to examine child care in the private sector, most do not specifically examine child care issues in the public sector. Those studies that do address the public sector fail to answer a few important questions. First, how many federal employees use on-site child care? Second, how satisfied are federal employees with their child care? Finally, do programs provided by the federal government, such as on-site child care and flexible work schedules, help parents to achieve a better balance between work and family?

Flextime in the Federal Government

Another way parents address their family needs is through flexible work schedules. According to the federal government, flextime "means a system of work scheduling which splits the work day into two distinct kinds of times—core time and flexible time. The two requirements under any flextime schedule are: (1) that the employee must be at work during core time, and (2) the employee must account for the total number of hours he or she is scheduled to work" (Merit Systems Protection Board, 1991; 33). Our study also examined other types of alternative work schedules used by federal workers such as flexiplace and compressed work weeks.

The federal government began experimenting with flextime programs in late 1972 at the Bureau of Indian Affairs in New Mexico and in 1974 at the Social Security Administration in Baltimore. Because of the success of these trial programs, Congress established a three-year, experimental program in 1979 through the Federal Employees Flexible and Compressed Work Schedules Act of 1978. Later, after a three-year continuation of this act in 1982, Congress authorized agencies to make alternative work schedules permanent in the federal government with Public Law 99-196, signed on December 23, 1985.

A substantial number of anecdotal studies concern flextime, but, like child care, most studies focus on the private sector. Researchers have found that flextime increases productivity and morale, while reducing the amount of worker absenteeism, truancy, and use of overtime (Rubin, 1979; Swart, 1985; Mellor, 1986; Dalton and Mesch, 1990; Guy, 1993). However, few empirical studies have been completed concerning flexible scheduling and even fewer address the impact of flextime on workers' family lives.

Studies of the impact of flextime on work and family have yielded mixed results. Ralston (1990) argues that women are more susceptible than men to "interrole conflict": trying to meet the dual demands of work and family, or what Hochschild (1989) calls the "second shift." Her survey of 115 women in two federal agencies showed that these women found coordinating family and job responsibilities much easier with flextime than on rigid work schedules.

Bohen and Viveros-Long (1982) surveyed employees in two federal agencies and found small but significant differences between the reported stress of parents who did and did not use flextime. They emphasized that for working mothers, more family-related benefits may be necessary to help them to address better

Table 1
Percentage of Parents and Nonparents Using Fixed, Flexible, or Compressed Work Schedules

Employee	Fixed	Flexible	Compressed
Parents (n = 10,445)	44.6	40.2	13.5
Mothers (n = 5,233)	47.2	38.6	12.6
Fathers (n = 5,212)	42.1	41.9	14.5
Nonparents (n = 17,837)	46.4	37.7	14.8
Women (n = 9,053)	47.4	35.6	15.8
Men (n = 8,784)	45.2	39.9	13.8

5. COMPENSATION, BENEFITS, AND WORKPLACE SAFETY: Employee Benefits

Methods/Hypothesis/Sample

We used data from the Survey of Federal Employees (SOFE), which was conducted by the Office of Personnel Management in November of 1991. SOFE was carried out using disproportionate random sampling of employees from all federal agencies nationwide. Individuals from the Senior Executive Service and general management were weighted in order to match their actual percentages in the federal government. The SOFE sample consisted of 30,970 employees, but we restricted our sample to full-time, permanent, white-collar employees ($n = 28,329$). We conducted ordinary least squares regression, and when appropriate, we ran separate regressions for parents and nonparents based on the assumption that children dramatically alter an individual's family responsibilities.

Three models guided our study. Our first model used satisfaction with child care as the dependent variable, which is a 5-point scale ranging from very dissatisfied to very satisfied. In this model, it was important to determine whether parents who used government programs such as flextime, compressed work schedules, and on-site child care were more satisfied with their child care arrangements than those who did not use these programs. We hypothesized that parents, especially mothers, who used these programs would be more satisfied with their child care because they might need such programs to meet their child care needs (Ralston, 1990; Presser, 1989).

In our second model, we examined more thoroughly the impact of family-friendly policies such as on-site child care, flextime, and compressed work schedules on employees' perceptions of their work/family balance. Satisfaction with work/family balance, our dependent variable, was measured on a 5-point scale ranging from strongly disagree to strongly agree with the statement, "I am satisfied with the balance I have achieved between my work and family life." We hypothesize that a work environment understanding of non-work or family responsibilities would make employees more satisfied with their work/family balance.

In the final model, we tested whether an employee's satisfaction with the work/family balance had a significant influence on their job satisfaction. We realized that work/family issues were not the only components of job satisfaction. Therefore, we have included several other measures, such as whether or not workers found that their job made use of their abilities and skills, whether their job was challenging, and if they had a clear understanding of how their work contributed to the goals of their agency. We hypothesized that these variables would comprise an important part of job satisfaction.

Sample: Our sample consisted of 28,329 federal workers of whom 37 percent were parents and 63 percent nonparents. (Parents are defined in the survey as those individuals having children living at home who are under the age of 13.) In both groups, about half were men and half were women. Approximately 46 percent of the surveyed federal employees were on a fixed schedule compared to 39 percent who used flextime and 14 percent who use compressed work schedules. Of the parents, 40 percent used flextime and 14 percent use compressed work schedules while 38 and 15 percent of the nonparents used such schedules, respectively. Among the parents, 39 percent of the mothers used flexible work schedules compared to 42 percent of the fathers (Table 1).

their work and nonwork responsibilities. Nonetheless, the survey by Bohen and Viveros-Long revealed that a third of their respondents using flextime reported that flextime allowed them more time with their families, and 96 percent of employees were pleased with their flexible schedules (p. 147).

Harriet Presser (1989) also found that flextime may make a very modest contribution to solving work/family problems but concluded that flexible hours may be of value to employees for reasons other than child care. Thus, employees in general are very satisfied with the flextime option. However, it appears to be only modestly helpful to parents, especially mothers.

Flextime research has not examined a large sector of the federal work force. Thus, various questions remain to be addressed concerning federal employees at large. For example, who is using flextime in the federal work force? Are federal workers who use flextime more likely than those who do not use it to be satisfied with their work/family balance?

Results

Child Care Satisfaction

In the first model, we looked at how satisfied federal employees were with their child care arrangements, and whether programs offered by the government such as on-site child care centers and flexible or compressed work schedules increased parents' satisfaction with their child care. Generally, parents in our sample were satisfied with their child care arrangements and married parents were more satisfied than single parents. Approximately 75 percent said they were very satisfied or satisfied, although fathers reported being more satisfied than mothers (76.9 percent compared to 72.9). In a simple cross tabulation, we found that parents who used on-site child care services were more satisfied with their child care arrangements than those who did not use them (Table 2).

However, as our regression results in Table 3 show, when separate regressions were run for mothers and fathers, we found that on-site facilities had a significant effect for mothers, making them more satisfied with their child care, but not for fathers. This finding was not surprising. Because mothers are expected to bear the majority of responsibility for child care arrangements, and it will be mothers who will be most helped by on-site care. Of the 263 parents in our sample who used on-site child care, mothers (208) used on-site child care four times more often than fathers (54).

Parents who used flexible work schedules were more likely to be satisfied with their child care although the effect was more significant for fathers than for mothers. Using compressed work schedules did not have a significant effect for either the mothers or fathers. Generally, although the results were not overwhelming, parents who used family-friendly policies provided by the federal

Table 2
Percentage of Parents Satisfied with Their Child Care

	On-Site Use	Don't Use
Satisfied	81.3	74.8
Not Satisfied	18.7	25.2

government were more satisfied with their child care than those who did not.

A separate set of questions asked parents whether they used the following work schedule options to help meet their child care needs: different shifts, flexiplace, annual leave, leave without pay, and sick leave. In almost all cases, both mothers and fathers who used these options to meet child care needs were less satisfied with their child care. Mothers and fathers who need to use these options may be unhappy with their child care arrangements and are using these options as a last resort.

Work/Family Balance

In our second model, we ran three separate regressions, two for parents (mothers and fathers) and one for nonparents. We ran separate models for mothers and fathers because we have found that family-friendly policies affect mothers and fathers very differently.[2]

We found that fathers were more satisfied with their work/family balance than were mothers (coefficient = .16 $p < .00001$), possi-

Table 3
Satisfaction with Child Care

	Satisfaction	
Characteristic	Mothers ($n = 3,965$)	Fathers ($n = 4,235$)
On-site child care	.17**	-.13
Flexible work schedule	.06*	.11***
Compressed schedule	.09	.03
Married	.11**	.73***
Spouse employed	.11**	-.28***
Other Ways to Meet Child Care Needs		
Different shifts	-.20***	-.38***
Annual leave	-.22***	-.20***
Flexiplace	.07	-.32***
Leave without pay	-.21***	-.17
Sick leave	-.20***	-.20***
Adjusted R^2	.04	.09

Notes: Numbers reported are unstandardized ordinary least squares regression coefficients.

* $p < .1$;   ** $p < .05$;   *** $p < .01$.

Variable Coding:
On-site child care: Don't use = 0; use = 1.
Flexible work schedules: Yes = 0; no = 1.
Compressed schedules: Yes = 0; no = 1.
Married: Yes = 1; no = 0.
Spouse employed: Yes = 1; no = 0.
Do you use the following (different shifts, annual leave, work at home on the clock, LWOP, and sick leave) to help take care of your child care needs?
Don't use = 0; use = 1.

37. Balancing Work and Family Responsibilities

bly because mothers were saddled with the primary responsibility for family duties (Hochschild, 1989). Men and women who had no children expressed no differences in their satisfaction with their work/family balance.

Mothers of young children (less than six years of age) were even less satisfied with their balance than mothers of older children whereas fathers with young children were no less satisfied than fathers with older children (Table 4). The existence of a highly significant relationship for mothers and no relationship for fathers signals that mothers are bearing the primary responsibility for the care of young children and that responsibility has a negative impact on their ability to balance the work and family aspects of their life. In addition, single parents were less satisfied with their balance than married parents.

Parents who used flexible work schedules were more satisfied with their work/family balance than parents who did not (coefficient = .07 $p < .001$), but when separate regressions were run for fathers and mothers, only mothers were significantly helped by having a flexible schedule. Neither mothers nor fathers were helped in their balance of work and family by having a compressed schedule.

Being satisfied with child care arrangements had a highly significant effect on the happiness of both mothers and fathers with their work/family balance although the use of on-site child care did not help parents to balance their work and family responsibilities

Table 4
Satisfaction with Work/Family Balance

Characteristic	Mothers ($n = 3,854$)	Fathers ($n = 4,156$)	Nonparents ($n = 17,003$)
Gender	-	-	-.02
On-site child care	.06	-.04	-
Satisfaction with child care	.18***	.13***	-
Children under 6 years	-.16***	.01	-
Flexible work schedule	.10***	.04	-.04***
Compressed	.09*	-.01	.06***
Married	.13**	.26***	.17***
Spouse employed	-.14***	.03	-.04*
Overtime	-.08***	-.22***	-.17***
Supervisor understanding	.02	.13***	.11***
Organization understands family duties	.11***	.20***	.22***
Adjusted R^2	.10	.18	.10

Notes: Numbers reported are unstandardized ordinary least squares regression coefficients.

* $p < .1$;   ** $p < .05$;   *** $p < .01$.

Variable Coding:
On-site child care: Don't use = 0; use = 1.
Satisfaction with child care: 1 = Very dissatisfied to 5 = very satisfied.
Children under 5 years: Yes = 1; no = 0.
Flexible work schedules: Yes = 0; no = 1.
Compressed schedules: Yes = 0; no = 1.
Married: Yes = 1; no = 0.
Spouse employed: Yes = 1; no = 0.
Overtime (in hours): 1 = rarely work; 2 = 1-5 hours; 3 = 6-10 hours; 4 = more than 10 hours.
Supervisor understanding and organization understanding: 5-point scales, 1 = strongly disagree to 5 = strongly agree.

Table 5
Job Satisfaction

	Mothers ($n = 5,057$)	Fathers ($n = 5,104$)	Nonparents ($n = 17,471$)
Satisfaction with work/family balance.	.29***	.29***	.27***
Understand how my work contributes.	.08***	.10***	.11***
Job makes use of my skills/abilities.	.26***	.28***	.28***
Job is challenging.	.22***	.21***	.23***
Adjusted R^2	.39	.42	.46

Notes: Reported numbers are unstandardized ordinary least squares regression coefficients.

***$p < .0000$.

Variable Coding:
All of the above variables are based on a 5-point scale ranging from 1 = strongly disagree to 5 = strongly agree.

better. So while it is important that workers be satisfied with their child care, on-site care may not be the best way to ensure that satisfaction. Perhaps other child care options such as referral services would be more appropriate.

Several authors have shown that if an organization supports workers in meeting their family responsibilities and fosters a family-friendly environment, the organization experiences less turnover, less absenteeism, and a happier work force (Rodgers and Rodgers, 1989; Rubin, 1979; Swart, 1985; Mellor, 1986; Dalton and Mesch, 1990; Guy, 1993). Not surprisingly, we found that federal employees who believed that their organizations understood their family duties were significantly more satisfied with their work/family balance than those who did not believe this to be true. However, Marquart (1991) notes that unless the organization and the employee's immediate supervisor are supportive of family duties, an employee may not be able to address his or her family needs adequately. We found a positive, significant relationship between supervisor understanding and satisfaction with work/family balance for fathers but not for mothers.

Job Satisfaction

Finally, in the third model, we examined whether their job satisfaction was affected by an employee's satisfaction with the work/family balance. Job satisfaction depends on more than policies concerning an employee's family responsibilities. Three independent variables in the model which did not take into account work/family balance issues (understanding how my work contributes to agency mission, job makes use of my skills and abilities, my job is challenging) were highly significant for all government employees, both parents and nonparents.[3] For parents, satisfaction with work/family balance had the most important impact on the dependent variable, job satisfaction. Clearly, the more satisfied both parents and nonparents are with their balance between work and family, the more satisfied they are with their jobs. Because satisfaction with work and family balance is a substantial part of job satisfaction, it will be important for federal personnel managers to increase their use of policies that foster a better balance between work and family (Table 5).

Conclusions

Because achieving a good balance between work and family is an integral part of job satisfaction, the federal government should encourage policies that help their workers, especially mothers, to balance their work and family responsibilities better. Because fathers were found to be significantly happier than mothers (especially mothers with young children) with their balance, finding innovative ways to help mothers balance work and family better is increasingly crucial to a contented work force. In an era when mothers constitute an expanding portion of the federal sector (Guy, 1993), employees' family responsibilities will become a more central concern to the federal government.

We found that certain family-friendly policies help mothers improve the balance between their work and family commitments. For example, the use of on-site child care and flextime had a significant impact on mothers' satisfaction with their child care arrangements. In addition, the use of flextime significantly helped mothers improve their work/family balance.

These findings lead us to suggest that the use of these types of policies should be encouraged by the federal government. Increased use of flextime should be encouraged, as it appears to help mothers significantly. While we found that approximately 2.5 percent of the sample used on-site child care, another 25 percent said that they were interested in having on-site child care where they work. If mothers who use on-site child care are more satisfied with their child care arrangements, and more employees appear to desire having on-site child care arrangements, we suggest that the federal government should consider expanding its present on-site child care facilities. Other factors such as their cost-effectiveness will simultaneously need to be considered. As Romzek (1991) has argued, not all agencies may need to install such an extensive policy as on-site child care. Instead, government agencies may want to consider establishing a referral system to help parents find affordable and convenient child care arrangements if on-site child care is not appropriate or cost-effective. Although these policies will not completely alleviate the conflicting demands placed on parents from the two sectors of their lives, they may make them easier to balance.

◆ ◆ ◆

Marni Ezra is a doctoral candidate at American University. She has published in the area of congressional elections and focuses on primary elections. Her fields of study are American government, public administration, and methodology.

Melissa Deckman is a doctoral candidate at American University. Her main areas of research include religion and politics, with her fields of study being American government and public administration.

Appendix
Questions from the SOFE Data Set

The responses to the following SOFE questions were selected from a 5-point scale: strongly disagree, disagree, neither agree nor disagree, agree, and strongly agree.

1. In general, I am satisfied with my job.
2. I am satisfied with the balance I have achieved between my work and family life.
5. My present job makes good use of my skills and abilities.
8. I have a clear understanding of how my work contributes to the mission of my agency.
18. My job is challenging.
41. When I have to take time off or change my work schedule because of family responsibilities, my supervisor has been understanding.
55. My organization understands and supports employees' family responsibilities.

The next question had the following response choices: not at all, to a little extent, to some extent, to a great extent, to a very great extent.
64. To what extent do you think your organization is effective in meeting the personal needs of employees?

Section 4 of SOFE is dedicated to work and children. We used the following questions:
3. Overall, how satisfied are you with your current child care arrangements? (see coding for responses).
7. Parents frequently adjust their work schedules to meet their child care needs. Which of the following have you used this past year to meet your child care needs?

Notes

The authors would like to thank Greg Lewis for his guidance and help with this project and to acknowledge the helpful suggestions we received from the anonymous reviewers.

1. Public Law 100-202 (1987), initially enacted as section 139, Public Law 99-190 (1985), codified at 40 U.S.C. 490b.
2. When we ran a full model for all parents, the coefficient for gender was significant at the .00001 level, showing that men and women feel significantly different about the balance they have achieved between their work and family. A single regression was run for nonparents as we did not expect that men and women without children would have different work and family responsibilities (coefficient = -.02).
3. We ran a job satisfaction model with numerous control variables including: age, race, years of service, income, gender, overtime, satisfaction with child care, flextime, and compressed schedules. When the standardized coefficients were examined, the four independent variables included in our final model each explained five times more of the variance than any other included independent variable. To have a more parsimonious model, we excluded all but four independent variables with no change in our results.

References

Bohen, Halcyone N. and Anamaria Viveros-Long, 1981. *Balancing Jobs and Family Life: Do Flexible Work Schedules Help?* Philadelphia: Temple University Press.

Dalton, Dan R. and Debra Mesch, 1990. "The Impact of Flexible Scheduling on Employee Attendance and Turnover." *Administrative Science Quarterly*, vol. 35 (June), 370-387.

Dawson, Ann G., C. S. Mikel, C. S. Lorenz, and J. King, 1984. "An Experimental Study of the Effects of Employer-Sponsored Child Care Services on Selected Employee Behaviors." Washington, DC: Department of Health and Human Services, Office of Human Development Services.

Gore, Al, 1993. *National Performance Review.* Washington, DC: Government Printing Office.

General Accounting Office, 1992. *The Changing Work Force: Comparison of Federal and Nonfederal Work/Family Programs and Approaches.* Washington, DC: Government Printing Office.

Guy, Mary Ellen, 1993. "Workplace Productivity and Gender Issues." *Public Administration Review*, vol. 53 (May/June), 279-282.

Hochschild, Arlie, 1989. *The Second Shift: Working Parents and the Revolution at Home.* New York: Viking Press.

Marquart, Jules, 1991. "How Does the Employer Benefit from Child Care." In Janet Shibley Hyde and Marilyn J. Essex, eds., *Parental Leave and Child Care.* Philadelphia: Temple University Press.

Mellor, Earl F., 1986. "Shift Work and Flexitime: How Prevalent Are They?" *Monthly Labor Review*, vol. 109 (November), 14-21.

Presser, Harriet, 1989. "Can We Make Time for Children? The Economy, Work Schedules, and Child Care." *Demography*, vol. 26 (November), 523-543.

Ralston, David A., 1990. "How Flexitime Eases Work/Family Tensions." *Personnel*, vol. 67 (August), 45-48.

Rodgers, Fran Sussner and Charles Rodgers, 1989. "Business and the Facts of Family Life." *Harvard Business Review*, vol. 67 (November/December), 121-129.

Romzek, Barbara S., 1991. "Balancing Work and Nonwork Obligations." In Carolyn Ban and Norma M. Riccucci, eds., *Public Personnel Management.* New York: Longman Publishing.

Rubin, Richard S., 1979. "Flexitime: Its Implementation in the Public Sector." *Public Administration Review*, vol. 39 (May/June), 277-282.

Shafritz, Jay M., Norma M. Riccucci, David H. Rosenbloom, and Albert C. Hyde, 1992. *Personnel Management in Government.* New York: Marcel Dekker.

Suntrup, Edward L., 1989. "Child Care Delivery Systems in the Government Sector." *Review of Public Personnel Administration*, vol. 10 (1), 48-59.

Survey of Federal Employees, 1991. Washington, DC: United States Office of Personnel Management, November.

Swart, J. Carroll, 1985. "Clerical Workers on Flexitime: A Survey of Three Industries." *Personnel*, vol. 62 (April), 40-44.

U.S. Merit Systems Protection Board, 1991. *Balancing Work Responsibilities and Family Needs: The Federal Civil Service Response.* November.

Violence in the American Workplace: Challenges to the Public Employer

Lloyd G. Nigro, Georgia State University
William L. Waugh, Jr., Georgia State University

What do we know about violent crime in the public sector workplace and what can be done to reduce it? Although public employees were only about 18 percent of the U.S. labor force, they were the victims of about 30 percent of the cases of workplace violence during the years 1987-1992. Public concern about occupational violent crime (OVC) is typically a function of media coverage, as shown by the Oklahoma City bombing, but there is great uncertainty about the level of risk that it actually poses for public workers in general and for specific occupational groups. In this article, the authors review the current state of knowledge regarding occupational violent crime in the United States and conclude that the guidance it offers to public employers is limited. It is apparent that a national database on OVC that includes information on social-psychological, organizational, and other variables is needed if current research needs are to be met. In addition to better information, public employers should approach OVC using a strategy that includes prevention methods based on careful assessments of risks, emergency management techniques and systems, appropriate human resources policies, and management training and preparation. Although needed, government regulations may be difficult to implement in the current political environment. Public employers should assume leadership in the effort to prevent OVC and to deal with its consequences.

Among the many problems confronted by public as well as private employers are injuries resulting from occupational violent crime (OVC) or workplace violence.[1] OVC injury is defined as intentional battery, rape, or homicide during the course of employment.

The available statistics on OVC in the United States reveal that it is a meaningful risk for many workers and that it may be more widespread and serious in its consequences than these data suggest. To a limited extent, the social-psychological causes of OVC are being explored, but no systematic effort has been made to identify risk factors that may be particularly relevant to the public employer.

There is reason to believe that the public sector is increasingly threatened by anti-government violence involving frustrated clients, terrorist groups with political motives, and individuals who are just plain angry at bureaucrats. The 1995 bombing of the federal building in Oklahoma City serves as the most recent and horrible example of public employees being murdered while at work. Although it is to be hoped that mass murders of government workers will continue to be rare, existing evidence suggests that the more common types of OVC may pose a growing threat to public employees, and the data on homicides reveal that some groups of government employees are at higher risk than the average worker in the United States.[2] The U.S. Department of Justice's Bureau of Justice Statistics reported that of the nation's nearly one million victims of workplace violence in 1994, 30 percent were federal, state, or local government employees (U.S. Department of Justice, 1994). Under these conditions, public policy makers and human resources managers cannot afford to ignore the potential for OVC or to assume that it may be treated as an extraordinary event that does not merit serious investment in its prevention and the mitigation of its consequences.

For the most part, public as well as private employers have resisted the idea that they should treat OVC as an *organizational* problem. Although the risk of criminal assault traditionally has been connected with certain jobs, such as law enforcement and private security, it has not been associated with many other occupations where, in fact, it does happen with some regularity. For these classes of employees, according to Janice L. Thomas, OVC "has not been considered a typical hazard that must be analyzed and acted upon by safety and risk-control professionals. In the past, when a worker was assaulted, it was considered a misfortune and a police matter" (Thomas, 1992a; 27). Pressures for change in this posture have been building, largely in response to widely publicized cases of multiple murders in public agencies as well as corporate settings and increasing public concern about violence in American society, including the workplace.

A Growing Awareness of Workplace Violence

Multiple homicides in the workplace are headline-grabbing events, and there have been more than enough bloody episodes over the last several years to keep the print and electronic media occupied (Stuart, 1992; 72-84). For sustained media attention, however, the U.S. Postal Service has had few rivals. Between August 1983 and May 1993, the Postal Service endured 10 separate episodes of murderous violence by current or former employees. A total of 29 postal workers were killed, and 16 were wounded (Barringer, 1993; A7).

Shaken by these tragic and highly publicized events, the Postal Service and Postmaster General Marvin Runyon sponsored a symposium on workplace violence on December 16, 1993. The keynote address was given by former Surgeon General M. Joycelyn Elders. In her address, she stated: "But we are not just talking about homicide here today. We are talking about a work force under siege from pressures, harassment, and non-fatal violence" (Elders, 1993). In October of that year, the National Institute of Occupational Safety and Health (NIOSH) also issued an *Alert* in which it identified workplace homicide as a "serious public health problem" that requires our attention (U.S. Department of Health and Human Services, 1993a; 5).

With interest stimulated by dramatic homicidal rampages and language such as that used by the Surgeon General and NIOSH, workplace violence has received considerable attention from the mass as well as the professional media (Marks, 1993; B1, B4). The business sections of American newspapers, *The Wall Street Journal*, and publications widely read by managers and executives, such as *Personnel Management*, *Public Management*, and the *National Underwriter* have devoted considerable space to the extent of the problem and how the prevention of violence may be made a part of the overall human resource and risk management strategies of employers (see, e.g., O'Boyle, 1992; Smith, 1993; Overman, 1993; American Management Association, 1993; Haggerty, 1993; Kurland, 1993; Miller, 1993; Manigan, 1994).

With regard to employers' obligation to protect workers from attacks by outsiders, courts in Louisiana and Delaware have ruled that "employees attacked at work are not limited to workers' comp[ensation] remedies if they show that their employer was neg-

38. Violence in the American Workplace

> Between August 1983 and May 1993, the Postal Service endured 10 separate episodes of murderous violence by current or former employees. A total of 29 postal workers were killed, and 16 were wounded.

ligent in failing to provide adequate security" (*HRMagazine*, 1992; 82). From a regulatory standpoint, although the Occupational Safety and Health Administration (OSHA) has not issued specific standards intended to protect workers from OVC, the "General Duty Clause" of the Occupational Safety and Health Act (Section 5[a][1]) requiring employers to have a workplace that is "free from recognized hazards" may be applicable (Thomas, 1992b; 61-62). The message being sent to employers by a variety of sources is clear: they should be taking steps to identify the OVC-related risks their employees face and should respond appropriately (Swoboda, 1994; E8; U.S. Department of Health and Human Services, 1993a; 5).

Empirical Studies of OVC Are Limited

NIOSH's recommendations concerning occupational homicides apply to all forms of OVC. They include the following:
1. *Prevention strategies* based on available information should be developed and implemented. Risk factors in the workplace should be identified and steps taken to minimize or remove them.
2. *Research* designed to "evaluate existing or proposed prevention strategies" should be conducted. NIOSH notes that few such studies have been done and "such evaluation research is critical to homicide prevention efforts."
3. There is a need for research into the *specific factors associated with occupational homicides*, because this information is basic to the design of prevention strategies (U.S. Department of Health and Human Services, 1993a; 5-6).

As NIOSH and other sources point out, credible empirical research on all aspects of workplace violence is sparse, and existing studies are seriously limited by inadequate reporting systems. Researchers attempting to conduct relatively large-scale aggregate studies of OVC must use data gleaned from death certificates, Uniform Crime Data maintained by the FBI, the National Crime Victimization Survey conducted by the Bureau of Crime Statistics, workers' compensation claims, and claims for compensation made by victims of crime in the 44 states where such programs exist (Kraus, 1987; Davis, 1988; Hales *et al.*, 1988). These databases were not designed to support sophisticated social science research on the extent, context, and causes of workplace violence and injuries (Thomas, 1992b; 56).

Reporting of Workplace Homicide

Although they are generally believed to underreport actual levels of OVC for reasons outlined below, NIOSH's statistics are by far the best available on a national scale, and they show that the

5. COMPENSATION, BENEFITS, AND WORKPLACE SAFETY: Safety and Health

American workplace is not insulated from its social environment. For the period from 1980 to 1989, NIOSH counted 7,603 homicides in U.S. workplaces, making murder in one form or another the third leading cause of death in the workplace, and contributing about 12 percent of all trauma fatalities (U.S. Department of Health and Human Services, 1993b; 8).

Retail trades, public administration, and transportation/communication/public utilities were highlighted as having homicide rates at least twice the overall rate (0.7 per 100,000), with taxicab establishments leading the way (26.9 per 100,000 or 21 times the national average). A relatively high rate (3.4) for justice and public order establishments (courts, police, legal counsel and prosecution, corrections, and fire protection) explained public administration's prominence in the ranking of workplace homicide rates. In addition to the elevated rate for taxicab drivers/chauffeurs, other high-risk occupations included police officers and sheriffs, hotel clerks, and security guards (U.S. Department of Health and Human Services, 1993a; 2-3).

NIOSH has interpreted its data on workplace homicides to suggest that a number of factors increase the risk to workers, the highest ranking of which is working in jobs that involve exchanging money with the public. Other prominent risk factors include working alone or in small numbers, working late night or early morning hours, working in high-crime areas, guarding valuable property, and working in exposed community settings (U.S. Department of Health and Human Services, 1993a; 4). Clearly, a number of the factors apply to public employees, such as police, social workers, guards, and those who work late night or early morning shifts.

Other Studies of Workplace Homicide

NIOSH's National Traumatic Occupational Fatality (NTOF) surveillance system uses demographic and fatal injury information from death certificates. Bell (1991) used NTOF data to investigate rates of occupational homicide for women from 1980 through 1985. Of the 950 female homicide victims, over 70 percent were employed in four occupational groups: sales, clerical, service, and supervisors. Regional homicide rates for women were consistent with the overall pattern identified by NIOSH; over 50 percent of these homicides were in the South. Likewise, older women were at higher risk, and black women were almost twice as likely to be murdered as white women.

Although the NTOF data "identified homicide as the major occupational hazard for the nation's women," Bell concluded that they significantly "underreport victimization among working women in the U.S.," because studies done on the state level suggest that death certificates will only identify somewhere between 67 and 88 percent of traumatic workplace fatalities (Bell, 1991; 730-731). There are several reasons for this wide range, including whether or not the victim's "usual occupation" is recorded, as opposed to actual employment at the time of death (Davis, 1988; 1579-1581).

Other problems include variations in state policies and practices regarding the definition of the term "injury." Bell cites the example of Louisiana, where state policy interpreted *all* injuries as accidental until 1985. Certifiers may impose their own definitions of work and, in so doing, contribute to a general under-reporting of workplace homicides (Bell, 1991; 731; Kraus, 1987; 1285-1289).

Studies of Other Forms of OVC

Because NIOSH's data are useful only for studies of workplace homicide, efforts to track other forms of OVC must rely on alternative sources. Rape and violent forms of sexual harassment are examples (Simpson and Trost, 1986). For a variety of reasons, rape is greatly underreported in the United States, and the FBI does not collect or evaluate occupational information. Other sources of data, therefore, must be used if occupational and situational risk factors are to be estimated.

In an effort to develop an estimate of the number of rapes that would fall into the OVC category, one study used workers' compensation claims (WCCs) in Ohio and computerized police reports from the city of Memphis to arrive at the conclusion that anywhere from 156 to 710 "preventable" sexual assaults in the workplace happen in this country every year. The WCCs from Ohio established that women employed in convenience food stores were at far greater risk of rape than other employed females. The Memphis data suggested that close to 1 percent of all rapes (87,340 in 1985, according to FBI statistics) "occur during the course of employment...this percentage would account for approximately 710 preventable sexual assaults occurring in the workplace nationwide each year" (Seligman *et al.*, 1987; 448). These findings suggest "that cashiers working at night in convenience stores, residential managers, and housekeepers in motels are at particularly high risk of rape" (Seligman *et al.*, 1987; 449).

Another study used workers' compensation claims in Ohio to identify occupations at high risk of OVC injuries. The results indicated that industries with the highest risk of homicide "also present the highest risk of non-fatal occupational injuries due to violence." Using WCCs also allowed the investigators to identify several other occupations at high risk of OVC injuries, most notably the hotel/motel industry, real estate, protective services, and transit workers (Hales *et al.*, 1988; 483-486). A similar study conducted in Virginia added Crime Victim's Compensation claims (CVCs) to WCC data to fill three potential gaps in workers' compensation records. First, some workers are not covered by Virginia workers' compensation, including part-time and casual workers, taxi drivers, self-employed contractors, and sole proprietors. Second, some claims are successfully challenged by employers on grounds that the death or injury did not "arise out of employment," even if it took place in the course of employment. Third, and finally, some OVC injuries are not traditionally reported or compensated. Rape is heavily underreported, and potential claims of after-the-fact psychological trauma may not be filed or compensated (Thomas, 1992b; 57-58).

In the Virginia study, WCC and CVC claims were combined for the period January 1983 through August 1990. The researchers reached conclusions not significantly different from those of other studies, including the Ohio study by Hales *et al.*, since it identified workers in convenience stores, gas stations, eating and drinking establishments, and other retail and service workplaces as being at highest risk. It did, however, suggest that the risk of OVC was higher than assumed for the construction industry

38. Violence in the American Workplace

and the nondurable goods manufacturing sector (Thomas, 1992b; 61).

The data in the Ohio and Virginia studies support the existing convention that workers are at highest risk of OVC in industries that involve the sale of goods and services in unsecured environments; the NIOSH findings have clearly established this pattern. When information available from WCCs, CVCs, and other sources, such as the National Crime Victimization Study (NCVS), is used to supplement that from death certificates, the results suggest that the actual risk of OVC, particularly nonfatal injury and rape, is more widespread and severe than commonly assumed.

Questions exist, however, about the extent to which other forms of OVC take place in a wide variety of workplaces that do not have the classic characteristics of high-risk-for-homicide environments. The available research would seem to indicate that homicide, while positively correlated with nonfatal OVC, does not necessarily provide a good picture of what is going on elsewhere; using homicide rates as surrogates for overall OVC rates is a dubious practice at best. In addition to the need to correct weaknesses in the system that exists for tracking homicides in the workplace, a national system for collecting information on other forms of OVC is required in order to identify risk factors beyond those already associated with homicides. The NCVS appears to be a promising start, since it involves annual interviews with more than 100,000 respondents who have reported a violent victimization (U.S. Department of Justice, 1994).

The Use of Case Studies to Identify Risk Factors

Beyond those few studies using combinations of available data to produce quantitative analyses, treatments of OVC in the professional management and security literature do not attempt to assess risk in any overall or aggregate sense. The data needed for such statistical analyses do not presently exist, so risk factors are identified from more or less careful searches for commonalities among individual cases of OVC. Although case studies have well-known limitations, the fine detail they provide has generated a wealth of potentially significant factors in workplace violence that are not reliably captured by death certificates, WCCs, CVCs, police reports, and other currently available criminal justice statistics.

In some cases, employers have neglected to deal with physical security problems, such as inadequate lighting and alarm systems, but many of the factors identified as contributing to OVC are social and psychological in nature, including working conditions and management policies. Smith (1993), for example, points to stress as an underlying factor in many cases of OVC involving employees. Employee feelings of loss of control in high-demand jobs, family problems, substance abuse, loss of a job, and low job satisfaction regularly surface as factors in such OVC cases.

Other contributing factors seem to be authoritarian or punishment-centered management styles, personnel policies that are indifferent to personal problems, low levels of supervisory support for workers, and cultural conflicts (Overman, 1993; 48). Smith notes that sales clerks, assembly line workers, and postal employees often feel these kinds of pressures (Smith, 1993; 31-33). For example, a 1990 survey of postal workers revealed that "most felt

> In some cases, employers have neglected to deal with physical security problems, such as inadequate lighting and alarm systems, but many of the factors identified as contributing to OVC are social and psychological in nature....

the postal service was insensitive to individual needs or concerns. Fairness of supervisors was rated substantially lower than in other service organizations..." (Smith, 1993; 32).

In general terms, discussions of OVC directed at managers and policy makers urge them to recognize conditions and situations that may expose the organization and its employees to a significant risk of violence by co-workers, customers or clients, and outsiders (Stockdale and Phillips, 1989; 214-215). The professional literature routinely identifies disciplinary and termination actions against workers as potentially high-risk situations. In many cases, as a steady stream of newspaper reports testifies, homicides and assaults on supervisors and human resources personnel take place in the context of these processes. Situations involving labor-management conflict are also potentially explosive, and plant closures and reductions-in-force are fertile grounds for OVC (Herman, 1992; 34). Substance abuse (alcohol and drugs) is often also cited as a major contributing factor (Walton, 1993; 81-84).

Available Guidance for OVC Risk Reduction

Approaches to the prevention of OVC may be divided into two general categories: (1) those based on available statistical information about risk factors and (2) those derived from patterns observed across specific cases of OVC. Public employers should be aware of both and be prepared to implement appropriate combinations. With regard to the first category, NIOSH (U.S. Department of Health and Human Services, 1993a; 4-5) and others have recommended that employers with high-risk factors for homicide take the following measures, as appropriate:

1. Make high-risk areas visible to more people,
2. Install good external lighting,
3. Use drop safes (boxes) to minimize cash on hand,
4. Carry small amounts of cash,
5. Install silent alarms,
6. Install surveillance cameras,
7. Increase the number of staff on duty,
8. Provide training in conflict resolution and nonviolent response,
9. Avoid resistance during a robbery,
10. Provide bullet-proof barriers or enclosures,
11. Have police check on workers routinely, and
12. Close establishments during high-risk hours (late at night and early in the morning).

Several of these protective measures generally follow the approach called Crime Prevention Through Environmental Design (CPTED). This method stresses dealing with the environments in which violent crimes take place, and it focuses on the direct control of behavior. CPTED seeks to establish control over the environment "through the use of four elements: (1) natural surveil-

5. COMPENSATION, BENEFITS, AND WORKPLACE SAFETY: Safety and Health

> ...training *employees to anticipate, avoid, and actually deal with violent attacks is consistent with working conditions they face on a day-to-day basis.*

lance; (2) access control; (3) territoriality; and (4) activity support" (Thomas, 1992a; 29).

Natural surveillance means designing and operating workplaces in such as manner as to maximize visibility for employees as well as law enforcement personnel. Access control involves the use of physical and psychological barriers in order to channel the flow of people in the workplace, including employee-controlled access. Territoriality means choosing location and facility designs that emphasize the employees' control over the workplace. Finally, activity support refers to work flow and other practices intended to increase the number of legitimate users available to be part of the natural surveillance strategy. The balance of NIOSH's recommendations address what Thomas calls administrative controls. These include staffing policies, training, cash management, signage, and plans for handling dangerous situations (Thomas, 1992a; 30).

OVC prevention strategies and techniques for workplaces where homicide rates are known to be relatively high and established risk factors exist emphasize the need to improve the physical security of workers. These kinds of employer investments (better lighting, surveillance equipment, protective facility layouts, bullet-proof partitions, alarms, security guards, etc.) promise relatively large and immediate payoffs. Likewise, training employees to anticipate, avoid, and actually deal with violent attacks is consistent with working conditions they face on a day-to-day basis.

The experience in dealing with the threat of terrorism in airports and public buildings may be instructive, even if they are lessons to be learned in hindsight. So-called "target hardening" through physical means such as metal detectors, limited public access, video surveillance, and armed security guards should increase the probability that "disgruntled" clients, amateur terrorists, angry parties to court proceedings, robbers, and rapists will be discouraged or foiled. It was too easy for the Oklahoma City bombers to drive their explosives-laden truck right up to the front door of the federal building and leave it there. Simply prohibiting the parking of unauthorized vehicles within a specified security zone might have discouraged the bombers.

The situation is far less clear with regard to workplaces and occupations where political or terroristic motives are not likely to pose a meaningful threat. Available data do not show relatively high homicide rates, rape and injury data are at best inconclusive, and possible risk factors are suggested by a limited number of documented cases. For the most part, the OVC prevention literature in this second category speaks to employers and human resources specialists, as opposed to public-policy makers, and it tends to concentrate on *irrational* motives for violent acts by employees and those they deal with. A rather consistent theme is management's need to implement personnel policies and management processes that improve the organization's ability to identify and neutralize potentially violent employees, customers, and clients (Manigan, 1994).

Employers are advised to evaluate their hiring procedures and to use screening procedures, such as background checks and references, to minimize the chance that a prospective employee is prone to violence under conditions that he or she may face on the job. A policy of "zero tolerance" for verbal as well as physical threats is recommended as the foundation for an organizational culture that rejects violence as a way of dealing with conflict and encourages workers to report all meaningful threats and violent acts. Mandatory drug testing is advised, as are policies banning sexual and other forms of harassment (Fitzgerald, 1993). Employee training to recognize and report potentially violent situations is an almost universal recommendation. Emphasis is also placed on policies and procedures that facilitate the identification and careful handling of workers who make threats or show potential for violence in some other manner (Walton, 1993; 82-83; Stuart, 1992; 74). Finally, employers are told to be fully aware of the range of options available to them as they seek to prevent violence, including applicable laws, administrative actions, and psychological interventions such as counseling and employee assistance programs (Cawood, 1991).

Although these prevention and mitigation strategies may be logical and intuitively attractive to some employers, they do not rest on anything resembling a credible statistical analysis of risk factors; to the contrary, they rely heavily on compilations of individual cases and a very few surveys (Seger, 1993; Society for Human Resource Management, 1993). Under these conditions, it is not surprising that OVC prevention programs, such as that of the Postal System, have come in response to one or more incidents of violence, most notably homicides that get widespread public attention, provoke legislative criticism, and result in legal actions against the employer by relatives. The great majority of employers, however, be they in the public or private sector, are in a position to argue that OVC is so rare that the occasional case (however horrible) does not require a substantial investment in CPTED, administrative measures, or "expensive" and "intrusive" government regulations.

In short, employers who have not undergone a highly visible and costly (in economic or political terms) case of OVC have little incentive to consider meaningful prevention programs. In light of the uncertainty caused by inadequate information on OVC rates and risk factors for these kinds of workplaces, NIOSH's recommendation that "a coordinated program of surveillance, epidemiology, intervention, strategy development, efficacy evaluation, and dissemination" be implemented is especially applicable (U.S. Department of Health and Human Services, 1992; 5).

An Agenda for Research on OVC

Although OVC is now receiving increasing public attention, and public as well as private employers are being urged to take steps to prevent OVC, large and crippling gaps exist in our understanding of specific employers' relative exposure, what material and nonmaterial risk factors are operating in a wide range of possible situations, and how effective current efforts at prevention and mitigation have been. A major reason for this lack of information is the limitations of the available data on OVC (U.S. Department of Health and Human Services, 1992; 2-3). In a word, reliable *intel-*

ligence is needed, and it is clear that collecting and organizing it in terms that are useful to public policy makers and employers will require a cooperative effort by a wide variety of public agencies.

An important step toward answering many questions about OVC is the construction of a database that includes those variables presently known to be at least potentially related to rates and risk factors. Although existing government statistics, if integrated, should be very useful, they must be complemented by an employer-level reporting system that captures situational, organizational, and social-psychological information. A very basic improvement would be a standardized reporting format that captures all kinds of OVC (battery, rape, and homicide) *and* the relationship of the victim to the offender. The NCVS does provide some useful information along these lines; for example, it reveals that women are more likely than men to be attacked by someone they know, including husbands and boyfriends.

Data on the primary motivations of offenders are also required. As many convenience store workers and taxi drivers already know, so-called rational economic motives dominate in certain industry and occupational categories ("Your money *or* your life" is an economic statement). The fire-bombing of an abortion clinic is an act of terrorism with political objectives. In many other cases, fear, frustration, jealousy, and revenge appear to spark "irrational" (although often explicable and perhaps predictable) acts of violence (Gold, 1986; 5-12). Simply said, strategies designed to prevent robberies, politically motivated terrorism, or other violent intrusions by outsiders may offer little or no protection against employee-on-employee assaults.

Another imperative is achieving a long-term policy commitment to preventing OVC. To the extent that this commitment would require strong regulatory interventions by federal and state agencies, such an effort may be expected to generate political controversy. With certain possible exceptions, such as convenience stores and taxicab establishments, NIOSH's statistics tell us that the nation's workplaces are not awash in a sea of blood. At least this is the case for homicides, since only about 7 out every 1 million workers were murdered while on the job during any given year during the 1980s.

It is worth noting, however, that an equivalent fatality rate for airline passengers would be considered alarming and certainly grounds for examining and probably strengthening safety regulations and inspections. And, of course, like a doomed airline passenger, a county social worker about to be murdered in her office by a client is unlikely to be comforted by the fact that this is a statistical rarity.[3]

Short-Term Implications for Public Sector Employers

Notwithstanding the violence of anti-abortion, radical environmental, anti-development, and other groups in private sector workplaces, OVC associated with public agencies has a very high media profile. The number of recent dramatic incidents, for example, has led some younger Americans to refer to angry or "disgruntled" workers as "posties," alluding to the highly publicized incidents of violence at postal facilities. Given what we know about the nature and threat of OVC overall, that perception is neither accurate nor helpful. A first step in moving beyond that perception is to develop an understanding of the practical implications of OVC for public sector employers.

An important starting point for public management is to recognize that OVC is a meaningful threat to many government workers. In large measure, the literature suggests that public and private organizations and their workers face many of the same threats from street, family, interpersonal, and even political violence. The risk factors identified by NIOSH and other agencies relating to physical security, isolation and hours, and unsecured cash and other valuables, are not restricted to either sector. The social-psychological risk factors, including increasing levels of family violence, sexual abuse, interpersonal conflict, psychiatric problems, and substance abuse that cause or encourage violence, are also shared.

The two risk factors that may differ in degree are the work-site environment itself and the influence of political motives. To some extent, public agencies may have greater long-term exposure to street crime and workplace, but not work-related, violence because of the location of many government offices. It is common practice in many larger inner cities to anchor economic development projects with government offices in hopes of stimulating economic activity. Law enforcement, public health, social services, education, and other workers are frequently located in urban settings that are relatively dangerous in terms of known risk factors, as well as rural settings that are isolated and unsecured.

The risk of OVC is also related to the condition of the organization itself. Here, too, growing numbers of public employees are finding themselves in more stressful and dangerous workplaces. Program and staffing cuts affect service delivery and the very nature of the interaction with clients. As we have noted, poor management, threats of reductions-in-force, the deterioration of salaries and benefits, shrinking opportunities for training and advancement, and other factors related to the quality of work life have been identified as risk factors (Stockdale and Philips, 1989). Indeed, the studies of the causes of recent violence in postal facilities have pointed to management problems brought on by tightened budgets and insensitive personnel policies (U.S. General Accounting Office, 1994).

Similarly, public organizations are more frequently targets of politically motivated violence. While firm data are still lacking, the anecdotal evidence strongly supports the idea that "unpopular" agencies, such as regulatory and law enforcement agencies, are frequently targets of violent attacks and threats to their workers. The journalistic literature documents increasing numbers of threats to and attacks on forest rangers, law enforcement officers, judicial officers, tax collectors, and others in similar jobs (Taylor, 1995).

What strategy should a public employer adopt then? Several approaches readily come to mind as falling within a general strategy for dealing with OVC. First, a *prevention approach* that follows the recommendations of NIOSH and other agencies concerning appropriate security precautions, training to reduce conflict among employees and between employees and clients, and environmental design to control public access to government offices more effectively is a good starting place. Second, an *emergency management approach* should provide policy structures and management processes to handle violent events. This approach should include a formal process for risk assessment, emergency plans to respond to particular kinds of violence, clearly established working relationships among the offices or agencies responsible for security and emergency response (as well as the agency's own decision makers), and simulation exercises and training programs to assure that plans for prevention and mitigation work in practice.

Third, a *human resource management approach* should focus on developing increased supervisory sensitivity to the known early warning signs of violence, and employee assistance programs (EAPs) to help workers deal with the psychological causes and results of violence; and better methods for screening job applicants. Fourth, and finally, a *management approach* should provide training that equips managers to understand the potential effects of their decisions on the safety of employees and clients. Public managers must recognize that OVC is an organizational problem that should be addressed through well-informed policies and appropriate procedures.

In the current political climate of hostility toward government regulation, especially new or expanded federal regulations, the prospects for OVC-related initiatives appear to be rather dim, with the possible exception of workplaces where homicide rates are dramatically higher than the national norm. In large measure, therefore, identifying and meeting the challenges presented by OVC is a task that will fall primarily to the nation's employers. This at least seems to be the most likely short-term situation. Levels of management concern for employees' safety and voluntary efforts to understand, anticipate, and prevent OVC may be expected to vary widely, but governments should be doing everything possible to serve as model employers in this area.

❖❖❖

Lloyd G. Nigro is a professor of public administration at Georgia State University in Atlanta. He holds the Ph.D. in public administration from the University of Southern California. Before joining the Georgia State faculty in 1979, he served on the faculties of the University of Southern California's School of Public Administration and Syracuse University's Maxwell School. He has published numerous articles on public personnel administration and administrative ethics, and he is co-author of *Modern Public Administration* and *The New Public Personnel Administration*.

William L. Waugh, Jr., is a professor of public administration and political science at Georgia State University. He is the author of *International Terrorism* and *Terrorism and Emergency Management*, co-author of *State and Local Tax Policies*, and co-editor of *Handbook of Emergency Management*, *Cities and Disaster*, and *Disaster Management in the United States and Canada*, as well as the author of numerous chapters and articles published in the United States, Canada, and Europe. His current research focuses on local government capacities, disaster policy, and geographic information systems.

Notes

1. The operational guidelines used by NIOSH to categorize an injury as having occurred at work are as follows:

On Employer Premises
- Engaged in work activity, apprentice, vocational training
- On break, in hallways, restroom, cafeteria, storage area
- In employer parking lots while working, arriving, or leaving

Off Employer Premises
- Working for pay or compensation, including at home
- Working as a volunteer EMS, fire fighter, or law enforcement officer
- Working in a family business, including family farm. Activity should be related to a profit-oriented business
- Training on business, including to and from customer/business contacts
- Engaged in work activity where vehicle is considered the work environment (e.g., taxi driver, truck driver, etc.)

2. According to the U.S. Department of Justice (1994), the average annual number of workplace victimizations from 1987 through 1992 were as follows:

Crime	Number of Victimizations	Those With Injuries
Rape	13,068	3,438
Robbery	79,109	17,904
Agg. assault	264,174	48,180
Simple assault	615,160	89,572

3. For a tragic example, see the *Los Angeles Times'* series of articles on the murder of Robbyn Panitch, a psychiatric social worker for Los Angeles County (January 27, 1990; B3; December 9, 1990; B1; and June 19, 1991; B1). She was killed by a former client who attacked her in a county building that did not have any security system. The case attracted considerable public attention when her parents attempted to sue the county, charging negligence driven by administrators' desire to save money.

References

American Management Association, 1993. "Workplace Violence: You're Not Immune." *Supervisory Management*, vol. 38 (September), 1-2.

Barringer, Felicity, 1993. "Postal Officials Examine System After Two Killings." *New York Times* (May 8), A7.

Bell, Catherine A., 1991. "Female Homicides in the United States Workplaces, 1980-1985." *American Journal of Public Health*, vol. 81 (June), 729-732.

Cawood, James S., 1991. "On the Edge: Assessing the Violent Employee." *Supervisory Management*, vol. 35 (September), 130-136.

Davis, Harold, 1988. "The Accuracy of Industry Data from Death Certificates for Workplace Homicide Victims." *American Journal of Public Health*, vol. 78 (December), 1579-1581.

Elders, M. Jocelyn, 1993. "Violence in the Workplace." Keynote Address to a symposium on workplace violence sponsored by the U.S. Postal Service. Washington, DC: U.S. Postal Service (December 16).

Fitzgerald, Louise F., 1993. "Sexual Harassment: Violence Against Women in the Workplace." *American Psychologist*, vol. 48 (October), 1070-1076.

Gold, Charlotte, 1986. "Assault on the Job." *Management Solutions*, vol. 31 (June), 5-12.

Haggerty, Alfred C., 1993. "Employers Need to Address Workplace Violence." *National Underwriter*, vol. 97 (September 27), 68.

Hales, Thomas, Paul J. Seligman, Sandy C. Newman, and Clifton L. Timbrook, 1988. "Occupational Injuries Due to Violence." *Journal of Occupational Medicine*, vol. 30 (June), 483-487.

Herman, Martin B., 1992. "Planning for the Unpredictable." *Security Management*, vol. 36 (November), 34.

Hill, Clare, 1988. "Protecting Employees from Attack." *Personnel Management*, vol. 20 (February), 34-39.

Indiana Department of Labor, 1991. "Serious Safety Order No. 1 (Amended)." Indianapolis, IN: Occupational Safety and Health Administration.

Kraus, Jess F., 1987. "Homicide While at Work: Persons, Industries, and Occupations at High Risk." *American Journal of Public Health*, vol. 77 (October), 1285-1289.

Kurland, Orin M., 1993. "Workplace Violence." *Risk Management*, vol. 40 (June), 76-77.

Manigan, Colleen, 1994. "The Graveyard Shift: Workplace Safety Is a Full-Time Job." *Public Management*, vol. 76 (April), 10-15.

Marks, Peter, 1993. "A New Worry: Going to Work Can Be Murder." *New York Times* (February 25), B1, B4.

Miller, Warren, 1993. "How to Reduce Potential for Workplace Violence." *National Underwriter*, vol. 97 (April 26), 14, 30.

National Committee for Injury Prevention and Control, 1989. *Injury Prevention: Meeting the Challenge.* New York: Oxford University Press.

O'Boyle, Thomas F., 1992. "Disgruntled Workers Intent on Revenge Increasingly Harm Colleagues and Bosses." *Wall Street Journal* (September 15), B1, B10.

Overman, Stephenie, 1993. "Be Prepared Should Be Your Motto." *HRMagazine*, vol. 38 (July), 46-49.

Seger, Karl A., 1993. "Violence in the Workplace: An Assessment of the Problem Based on Responses from 32 Large Corporations." *Security Journal*, vol. 4 (July), 139-149.

Seligman, Paul J., Sandy C. Newman, Clifton Timbrook, and William Halperin, 1987. "Sexual Assault of Women at Work." *American Journal of Industrial Medicine*, vol. 12, 445-450.

Simpson, Robert L. and Cathy Trost, 1986. "Sexual Harassment at Work Is a Cause for Growing Concern—Many Incidents Are Violent." *Wall Street Journal* (June 24), 1.

Smith, S.L., 1993. "Violence in the Workplace: A Cry for Help." *Occupational Hazards* (October), 29-33.

Society for Human Resource Management, 1993. "Workplace Violence: Business as Usual? Survey Reveals Escalating Violence." Alexandria, VA: Press Release (November 30).

Stockdale, Janet and Celia Phillips, 1989. "Physical Attack and Threatening Behaviour—New Survey Findings." *Occupational Health* (August), 212-216.

Stuart, Peggy, 1992. "Murder on the Job." *Personnel Journal* (February), 72-84.

Swoboda, Frank, 1994. "Threat of Violence Hangs Increasingly Over U.S. Workers." *Atlanta Constitution* (January 10), E8.

Taylor, Robert E., 1995. "Vitriol & Violence." *Government Executive*, vol. 27 (July), 14-15, 18, 60.

Third National Injury Control Conference, 1992. "Prevention of Violence and Injuries Due to Violence." *Journal of Safety Research*, vol. 23 (Summer), 117-118.

Thomas, Janice L., 1992a. "A Response to Occupational Violent Crime." *Professional Safety* (June), 27-31.

_____, 1992b. "Occupational Violent Crime: Research on an Emerging Issue." *Journal of Safety Research*, vol. 23 (Summer), 55-62.

U.S. Department of Health and Human Services, 1992. *Homicide in U.S. Workplaces: A Strategy for Prevention and Research.* Washington, DC: Centers for Disease Control and Prevention, NIOSH (September).

_____, 1993a. *Alert: Request for Assistance in Preventing Homicide in the Workplace.* Washington, DC: Centers for Disease Control and Prevention, NIOSH (September).

_____, 1993b. *Fatal Injuries to Workers in the United States, 1980-89: A Decade of Surveillance.* Washington, DC: Centers for Disease Control and Prevention.

U.S. Department of Justice, 1994. *Violence and Theft in the Workplace* (NCJ-148199). Annapolis Junction, MD: Bureau of Justice Statistics Clearinghouse (July).

U.S. General Accounting Office, 1994. *U.S. Postal Service: Labor-Management Problems Persist on the Workroom Floor.* Washington, DC: GAO, GAO/GGD-94-201B, Vol. II, (September).

Walton, J. Branch, 1993. "Dealing with Dangerous Employees." *Security Management*, vol. 37 (September), 81-84.

Workers Take Leave of Job Stress

To balance employees' work and personal lives and, as a result, increase productivity, some companies are providing sabbatical leave programs in addition to vacation time and leave dictated by the FMLA.

Christopher J. Bachler

Christopher J. Bachler is a freelancer based in Pennsylvania.

Mention the word sabbatical and most people think of teachers. Hailed as an opportunity for faculty members to renew their classroom-worn vigor, these leaves of absence were often used to attract people to a profession known for dubious financial rewards.

Today, what was once considered useful for teachers is reaping benefits for lawyers, consultants and techies alike as a growing number of companies experiment with workplace sabbatical programs—lengthy leaves of absence that often include full pay and benefits. Companies employ these programs as a way to deal with employee burnout and morale problems. Some even use them to ease the pain of downsizing, or to enable employees to participate in community service projects. Most often overseen by human resources departments, sabbaticals benefit both employees and employers. Workers get a break from job stress; their employers get rejuvenated employees.

"Companies are beginning to view sabbaticals as another dimension to workforce flexibility—to satisfy downsizing and redeployment objectives, and to address a need for more balance in the work and personal lives of their employees," writes Helen Axel in her special report, "Redefining Corporate Sabbaticals for the 1990's," a Conference Board publication. "Some see them as opportunities for personal growth and career development," Axel continues. "Other firms are attracted to sabbaticals because they meet social or cultural interests of the organization. To still others, they're part of a 'kit of tools' to compete in the marketplace for people with skills they need and want."

Diana Reace, manager of Hewitt Research Group, a research arm of Lincolnshire, Illinois-based Hewitt Corp., has studied workplace sabbaticals in detail. "There are many different kinds of sabbaticals," she says. "The major reasons for them are reducing job burnout, avoiding technical obsolescence, rewarding longevity on the job and use as a carrot to retain senior employees. They also make people feel better about their jobs, and help employers compete for employees."

Sabbaticals offer workers R&R.

Workplace stress is the most often cited reason for companies to adopt sabbatical programs. Disability due to stress costs the nation an estimated $75 billion annually, according to Palo Alto, California-based stress-management specialist, Sharon Kufeldt. Because few companies are immune to stress-related disabilities, many are looking at sabbaticals as an answer.

> Workplace sabbaticals in the Silicon Valley date back to the early '70s, and are seen as necessary relief from the turbulent grind of corporate high-tech.

This is particularly true among the high-tech colossi of the Silicon Valley. Workplace sabbaticals here date back to the early 1970s and are seen as necessary relief from the turbulent grind of corporate high-tech. "The intent behind our sabbatical program was to recognize that employees are more productive if they're given a chance to periodically recharge their batteries while focusing on personal priorities," says Betsy Lamb, director of compensation and benefits for Cupertino, California-based Tandem Computers Inc. "They actually come back refreshed and ready to go."

This philosophy, Lamb points out, is typical of Silicon Valley firms. "The cornerstone of Silicon Valley high-tech companies is the need to be creative. They need to offer employees a chance to focus on personal goals to stay creative."

Tandem employees are eligible for sabbaticals after four years of continuous service. The policy allows employees six weeks' leave with full pay and benefits. Even part-timers, who work 20-hour weeks, are eligible, and receive their normal part-time pay.

Another high-tech Silicon Valley company, Apple Computer Inc., also based in

Cupertino, offers its employees a similar sabbatical program. Under its terms, employees are allowed six weeks of paid leave every five years.

But the computer industry isn't alone in using sabbaticals to combat stress. Major law firms, consulting practices and other high-stress industries also offer the programs to counter the job burnout problem.

For example, Hewitt Associates, which provides management consulting services, launched an ambitious sabbatical program in 1988. "We wanted to reward the long service of our senior people," says Dave Wille, Hewitt's director of human resources. "Rather than beefing up our vacation policy, we looked at a 'vacation splash' sabbatical." Through the program, an employee is eligible for an additional three weeks of vacation after 15 years of service, and another three weeks of leave every five years after that. Principals in the firm are eligible for a five-week leave every five years. "Employees are encouraged to take the full three or five weeks at a time," Wille adds, "because the consulting business can be so draining."

Even companies such as Oak Brook, Illinois-based McDonald's Corp.—which is mostly divided into numerous regional offices and restaurants throughout the country—offer sabbaticals for key employees. McDonald's established its program in 1977.

"Our definition of a sabbatical," explains company spokesperson, Mark Walker, "is a program that offers long-term employees an opportunity to reflect on their jobs and careers, as well as the overall operation of the business, and to do it away from the daily pressures of work. We feel this time should be spent any way the employee feels will contribute to his or her personal and professional growth with McDonald's."

McDonald's offers its sabbatical program to full-time employees who have completed at least 10 years of service. Employees are then eligible for an eight-week paid leave. After 20 years of service, employees are eligible for a 16-week break. "The leave must be taken all at once," Walker says. "That's because it isn't a reward for past performance, but an investment in their futures. It isn't seen as a fringe benefit."

Sabbaticals provide time for personal pursuits and philanthropic projects. In addition to relieving stress, sabbaticals can be employed as a way to recognize employees' various personal needs. Such needs can't always be expressed in simple terms, but they may still be important to the people who have them. One person may feel a pressing need to write a book, for example, while another may wish to explore his or her family history. Still others may wish to engage in personal challenges that will help them better understand themselves.

New York City-based Time Inc.—a vast repository of "creative types"—recognized a need to provide this opportunity for its employees many years ago. Time's program, according to Axel's Conference Board report, was originally established for the benefit of its editorial employees, " ... for research and writing, with the expectation that the company would benefit from this enrichment when the employee returned. However, the leaves have long been available to employees on the business side of the company as well."

Robert Mintz, vice president of human resources for Time, says his company's sabbaticals are available to employees with 15 or more years of service. Eligible employees may take up to six months' leave, and receive 50% of their normal pay. They may also opt to break the leave into two separate three-month leaves. Employees who choose to take their leaves after 20 years of service are eligible to receive 75% of their regular pay for a three-month leave. "Given the demands on our people," Mintz reflects, "it's helpful for them to go off and explore other things. It's an opportunity for a combination of rest, relaxation and personal growth."

For these same reasons, San Francisco-based Wells Fargo & Co. provides a *Personal Growth Leave* (PGL) sabbatical for employees in good standing with more than 10 years of service. "The purpose of PGL," explains Diane Egelston, vice president of Corporate Responsibility, "is for employees with long service to take leave of up to three months, with full pay and benefits, to pursue personal interests. They must, however, demonstrate a past commitment to that interest."

Successful Sabbatical Programs Take Planning

Managers who are thinking about experimenting with their own sabbatical programs should take their time and proceed with caution. They might also consider the following suggestions:

1) Make the program available only to your best workers.
2) Restrict eligibility to top company executives.
3) Limit eligibility to senior employees who have been with the company at least 5 years (or more).
4) Experiment, first, on a limited number of employees.
5) Don't lock yourself into a permanent commitment. Make clear from the outset that your company reserves the right to cancel the program at any time (with prior notice).
6) Carefully study the results of your trial program before you decide to maintain or extend the program.
7) Consider the amount of time allowed. You should provide the employee on leave sufficient time to gain whatever benefit is desired without overextending your generosity.
8) Encourage your employees to get whatever benefit out of the program that you want them to get. The best way to accomplish that is to offer the employee some specific tips. You might even offer seminars on how to get the most from sabbaticals.
9) Before you adopt such a program, study the idea in detail. Read everything you can find on sabbaticals, consult experts, examine case studies.
10) Be sure that you have adequate backup personnel who can competently handle the work of the persons on leave, without burning themselves out.

—*CJB*

Some companies are going beyond providing sabbaticals as a way to fulfill personal needs and offering them to employees who choose to work for nonprofit groups. Stamford, Connecticut-based Xerox Corp., for example, launched its ambitious *Social Service Leave* program in 1971. Originally an experimental program, the plan was developed at the behest of socially conscious employees.

"We allow employees to take off for up to one year," explains Evelyn Shockley, program manager for Xerox Foundation, the philanthropic arm of Xerox. "We pay their full salary while they work for organizations of their own choosing."

Although employees choose their own projects, the projects must first be approved by a special committee, put together by Shockley and consisting of a cross-functional, cross-divisional group of employees. Religious or political activities are excluded from consideration. Shockley says that employees wishing to take leave must have at least three years of service with the company, must agree to submit monthly reports and adhere to site visits by public affairs personnel.

Wells Fargo was inspired by Xerox's lead. "Our *Social Service Leave* (SSL) is available to full or part-time employees who have three or more years of service," says Egelston, who's the officer in charge of the program. "The purpose of SSL is to allow employees with a demonstrated commitment to community service to work for a nonprofit service agency for up to six months, with full pay and benefits."

Egelston says that Wells Fargo supports numerous worthy projects. For example, "One of our branch managers worked for six months with the American Women's Economic Development Corp., an organization that provides training for female entrepreneurs. She developed training program components for them, and a book about obtaining loans."

Another use of sabbaticals that has emerged in recent years has come about as a result of the need to reduce the work force. Companies facing the ordeal of downsizing have eyed sabbaticals as a kinder and gentler way to ease the transition. One notable example is the colossal AT&T, which refers to its sabbatical program as a *Special Enhanced Leave of Absence* (SELOA). "We first tried Special Enhanced Leaves of Absence in 1991 as an experiment," reports Ruthanne Prange, district manager of human resources for Basking Ridge, New Jersey-based AT&T. "There were a combination of such factors as a need to reduce our work force while balancing force and load."

The AT&T program, which Prange says was tried again in 1993, was offered for periods ranging from nine to 24 months. The leaves, which were granted to 1,700 employees in 1991, were given without pay to employees who had been with the company at least five years. Prange says, however, that some benefits were offered.

The idea behind the program was to reduce the company's payroll burden, while also allowing favored employees a chance to tend to personal needs. "If people needed time to do something," Prange says, "and there were places in the business where we needed to cut back, why shouldn't we do something that allows some ventilation in the system?"

Philadelphia-based Bell Atlantic Corp. experimented with a similar sabbatical program during the late 1980s. The purpose of the program—which allowed employees to take up to two years unpaid leave—was to provide the company with a way to ease its downsizing efforts. In the short run, the absence of these employees would ease payroll expenses. It also was suspected that some workers would ultimately terminate their relationship with the company.

Bell Atlantic soon discovered, however, that using a sabbatical program as an incentive plan for work-force reduction fosters a lack of control. First, there's no control over which persons will elect to go on leave. A company could unintentionally lose some of its prize employees. Second,

Asking the Right Questions

Helen Axel, a senior research fellow at The Conference Board, offers the following key points for planning sabbaticals and related leaves:

Be clear about the objectives of the sabbatical, and make sure that they're stated in the policy. Is the interest of the policy to encourage future high performance, or is it a reward for valued service in the past? Does the policy have specific social or economic objectives? If so, are the incentives for participation consistent with these goals?

Target the right people. Are minimum service requirements appropriate for the tenure and turnover experience of the organization? Do conditions of a leave unintentionally favor certain categories of employees even though broad-based participation is desired? Is the supervisor's role in the leave application and review process clearly spelled out in the policy?

Make sure initial leave takers exemplify the policy's intent. Is the sabbatical leave expected to be used by employees at all job levels? Do employees return to their same jobs or ones very similar to those they had?

Determine the need for measuring costs and benefits. Is the sabbatical leave expected to demonstrate its cost effectiveness, or are intangible benefits sufficient justification? Should pre- and/or post-implementation surveys or employee attitudes be considered? What dollar or usage data should be collected?

Anticipate questions and be responsive to problems. Does it make sense to prepare a question-and-answer fact sheet with the announcement of the policy? How will the questions be developed? Is there a mechanism for quick responses to unanticipated problems and for fine-tuning once the program is under way?

Be prepared to adapt the policy to changes in business and/or work-force conditions. Does the policy still meet original objectives? Are those objectives still valid today? How can the policy be repositioned to reflect current business and employee needs?

Excerpt from The Conference Board Publication, Redefining Corporate Sabbaticals for the 1990's, *by Helen Axel, 1992.*

Sabbatical Programs Offer Varying Terms

Terms of sabbaticals can be as different as the people who apply for them. The following list offers a sample of that diversity.

COMPANY	TIME ALLOWED	COMPENSATION	ELIGIBILITY
McDonald's	8 weeks after 10 years, 16 weeks after 20 years	Full pay and benefits	All full-time employees
Tandem	6 weeks after 4 years	Full pay and benefits	Full- and part-time employees
Apple	6 weeks after 5 years	Full pay and benefits	Full- and part-time employees
AT&T	9 to 24 months after 5 years	No pay, most regular benefits	Full- and part-time employees
Hewitt	5 weeks after five years for partners, 3 weeks after 5 years for associates	Full pay and benefits	Full-time employees
Wells Fargo	Social Service Leave: up to 6 months after 3 years, Personal Growth Leave: up to 3 months after 10 years	Full pay and benefits	Full-time employees
Xerox	Up to 1 year after three years	Full pay and benefits	Full-time employees
Time Inc.	3 to 6 months after 15 years, 3 months after 20 years	50% pay after 15 years, 75% pay after 20 years	Regular full- and part-time employees

—CJB

there's no guarantee that leave-takers will not eventually elect to return to their jobs.

As a consequence, Bell Atlantic's sabbatical program lasted only three years, according to Joan Rasmussen, a Bell Atlantic spokesperson. "We felt that our sabbatical program wasn't effective for our company," she says. "It wasn't a permanent solution to the downsizing issue. We've since developed other incentive programs for our employees, such as early retirement programs."

HR facilitates sabbatical programs. With the exception of social service leave programs which usually are managed by agencies that take responsibility for community relations and philanthropy, most sabbatical programs are designed and administered by human resources departments. Indeed, it's often necessary for HR to assume this management role because it normally maintains records pertaining to employee eligibility. (Benefits consultants, actuaries or others who often work with HR, seem to have rarely—if ever—had a hand in the formation of sabbatical programs for any known major company.)

In addition to conceiving and administering the programs, HR people tend to assume responsibility for selling the idea to management. This is usually true of the more conventional sabbatical programs, such as those offered by Tandem, Apple, McDonald's and Hewitt.

HR rarely needs to vigorously promote the programs, however, because most employees tend to be well aware of their options to take such generous leaves. Often, companies that offer sabbatical programs will make their employees aware of them at the time of hiring, and provide references in employee handbooks.

The job of the human resources department, according to Lamb, is to smooth out any rough edges. "We try to minimize the use of temporary employees to fill in," she explains. "Rather, we use [the leave] as an opportunity for employees to 'take ownership' of their work, and to coordinate with their managers and work groups to make sure the job gets done while they're gone."

Most HR people whose companies have implemented sabbaticals haven't been overburdened by managing them. Mintz, for example, says the program at Time is fairly simple to manage. "We make sure individuals know what they need to know," he says, referring to such matters as eligibility requirements and time restrictions. "We also credit pensions, keep track of details, and make sure that the program is administered fairly and equally in all departments."

Wille also reports smooth sailing at Hewitt. "We notify associates and their managers a year in advance that they have the time coming so that they can make adequate preparations," he says.

Hewitt's HR department, according to Wille, also solicited feedback from the program's first leave-takers. "We asked our principals—during the first four or five years of our program—to provide us with a little write-up about what they did while they were away. The idea was to share this information with others who weren't sure how to use their own leave time."

Wille's department also makes an effort to obtain feedback about the effects of the program. "We want to know if, when an owner (partner) is away for five weeks, the business still runs. We also want to know if the person is refreshed and rejuvenated [upon return]."

Although HR usually manages the programs, most engage the use of special committees for approving sabbaticals. At Wells Fargo, for example, Egelston is responsible for assembling a Social Service Leave committee, and a Personal Growth Leave committee, each of which oversees one of the employee leave programs and reviews applications. Egelston chooses a chairperson for each committee who, in turn, recruits several other members, usually company vice presidents who represent various divisions of the company. Each member serves a two-year term.

Committee members meet each fall and render their decisions by early winter. "Each committee member reads through applications," Egelston explains. "They look for such things as commitment to activities, and the specificity of the plan of action. We end up selecting applicants on merit."

Egelston says each of her committees reviewed approximately 50 applications last year. Of that number, each committee selected approximately 10 candidates.

A Social Service selection committee, made up of people from different divisions and focus areas of diversity from across the nation, chooses Xerox's leave takers as well. "We bring them to corporate headquarters, where they sit for two days and review the applications," Shockley says. "The Xerox foundation staff has no vote." In a typical year the company, which employs 56,000 people nationally and nearly as many outside the country, receives between 47 and 60 applications.

Shockley says that after employees are selected for leave, her department manages the follow-up details. "We put employees through orientation and explain to them exactly what their responsibilities are to their company and organizations," she says. "We're also responsible for follow-up. We require monthly reports, and report plans for each coming month. We go out and visit leave-takers to ensure that everything is going smoothly. And, we encourage employees to keep in touch with their managers at Xerox so that their re-entry will be smoother."

Before following up, follow through. When implementing and running a sabbatical program, Hewitt Research Group's Reace emphasizes that HR people plan above all else. "Plan carefully for it," she urges. "Look carefully at goals. Is it meant to be a reward, or to help control stress? Answers to those questions will tell you who the program's for." Reace also tells interested HR people to carefully study companies that have already tried sabbaticals for their workers.

Tandem's Lamb says that companies wishing to adopt sabbatical programs should carefully consult their own internal players as well. "For HR people working on these issues, I would encourage them to have other groups explore the program, and to get a lot of feedback from employees and managers."

Adds Hewitt Associate's Wille: "First, establish up-front objectives. What are you trying to accomplish? How will you measure strict cost objectives? How will you measure morale? Also, listen to the needs of business as well as to those of your employees.

"I think companies should explore [the concept] to see if it meets some of the needs they have in terms of their relationships with their employees," he suggests. "But it depends on the company. Some may already have broad vacation policies so that additional time away from the company won't work. Others may find that their business won't allow for people to be off so long."

Poor planning is one of the major causes of problems with sabbatical programs. For example, Reace says that if a company wants to make sabbaticals available only for top people, HR must consider the effects on the morale of people who aren't eligible.

Even with planning, however, problems with sabbatical programs can occur. Through her research, Reace has identified some challenges that sabbatical planners have faced. "There has been concern about people who need them, but who don't take them," she notes. "One or two law firms have had to make their programs mandatory. The people who are susceptible to burnout are the people who think their companies can't survive without them."

Reace also suggests that timidity can be a problem. "Another element is letting people know it's OK to take leave," she points out. "One of the best ways to do that is to lead by example by having senior people be the first to use the program."

Time's Mintz claims HR's biggest problems can be self-inflicted. "We have no problems with the program," he says, "because we don't overmanage it. I advise other HR people to just follow common sense parameters, and not to make a big bureaucracy out of it."

Sometimes problems can't be avoided, however. ROLM, a Siemens company, established a pioneer sabbatical pro-

> Let people know it's OK to take leave. One of the best ways to do that is to lead by example by having senior people be the first to use the program.

gram as a way to ease the stress on its hardworking employees. "We worked long and hard hours," recalls Catherine Healy, human resources administrator for ROLM. "And the program was an opportunity to give our people time to relax and sort things out."

Under the San Francisco-based telecommunications company's sabbatical program—conceived and shaped exclusively by its HR people—full-time employees were eligible for a 12-week, fully paid leave in their seventh year. Those who desired could opt for a six-week leave at double pay.

ROLM discontinued the program in 1993. Was it because it was a failure? Not according to Healy, who even suggests that the program "may have reduced turnover." Significant changes within the organization, however, created irresistible pressures for change. "It no longer was cost-effective," Healy says, referring to the changing nature of a company that had grown dramatically over the years.

Even more than growth pressures, however, were the unique problems associated with ROLM's merger with IBM, and later with Siemens. "Sabbaticals weren't a benefit that IBM or Siemens offered," Healy explains. And because company officials desired a consistent benefits package for all employees, the ROLM division was encouraged to phase out its sabbaticals program.

(Axel's recent Conference Board report, "Redefining Corporate Sabbaticals for the 1990's," indicates that IBM does offer unpaid *Extended Personal Leaves* of up to three years for full-time employees. Workers receive full benefits during the leaves. Employees must, however, be available for part-time work during the second and third years, and are subject to annual reviews while on leave. A company spokesperson confirmed this, and explained that IBM also offers a *Flexible Work Leave of Absence,* which enables employees to work part-time for three years while receiving full benefit coverage. Full-time reinstatement after that time, however, isn't guaranteed. Approximately 90% of the average 2,500 employees on leave at any one time are women with small children.)

Sabbaticals reap benefits for workers and employers. Despite some setbacks, problems with sabbaticals seem to be few and far between. In fact, most companies insist that their sabbatical programs are little or no trouble.

Wille knows of no problems at Hewitt. "We've shown that we can work through five-week absences," he says. "Now with five years' experience, we don't have any problems. It isn't a difficult program, but it yields positive results."

The wide-spread optimism reported by administrators of sabbatical programs seems largely based on an almost intuitive sense of the programs' results, more than on any hard scientific data that validates those feelings. "We didn't spend much time looking at cost," Wille admits. "But in the consulting business, work tends to get done anyway. We find that most people are ready to cover for each other."

Lamb also acknowledges no awareness of scientific cost or benefit studies at Tandem. "We haven't undertaken any productivity studies," she says. "My suspicion is that if we did, we would see improvement because of cross-training that occurs."

Shockley offers her own positive findings, though they don't directly relate to dollars and cents either: "We feel it's a success because of the feedback we get from employees and outside organizations."

Companies that use sabbatical programs define success in many ways. Lamb explains the three major benefits of Tandem's program: "The first is rest and relaxation [for employees]," she says. "The second is our belief that we gain in productivity from employees who gain a renewed perspective. And the third is our desire to acknowledge their hard work to their own work unit."

Tandem also sees the program as a vehicle for development. "We look upon the sabbaticals as an opportunity to cross-train our employees," Lamb points out, referring to the opportunities for employees to learn other jobs while filling in for those on leave.

Walker says that McDonald's program has been a big success because, "We've found that sabbaticals bring tremendous personal satisfaction to employees and their families," he says. "The principal purpose is to enhance the quality, quantity and duration of our long-service employees' work. We believe that long-time employees are able to lend unique and valuable perspective to the business. That's why we instituted this program."

Despite all the optimism, Reace finds: "There's no overwhelming trend toward these sabbaticals." Not all organizations are equally troubled by stress problems. And some organizations—because of the nature of their business—can't spare key employees for long stretches of time.

Timidity also may be a factor. Offering generous leaves—especially during tough economic times—may seem risky, to say the least. But according to the companies that have found success from these programs, the risk is worth the price.

Surveys Document Wellness Initiatives, Link Health Risks To Higher Plan Costs

BERNICE CALDWELL

Workplace health promotion initiatives that began in the early 1980s focused on physical fitness by encouraging employees to exercise, eat balanced meals, stop smoking, and use alcohol in moderation. The objectives were to increase productivity, reduce absenteeism, and lower health care costs over the long term through reduced health care use. These early programs often failed to motivate employee participation, had no systems to measure program effectiveness, and rarely produced promised savings.

A new generation of health promotion programs have been developed that are designed to heighten an employee's awareness of healthy behaviors and/or provide opportunities for employees to become involved in healthy activities. Moreover, the new generation of programs includes systems to measure program effectiveness and to document savings.

Health promotion initiatives fall into four major categories:

1. **Behavior modification programs** that include exercise and fitness, nutrition education, smoking cessation, weight and stress management, and safety programs such as using seat belts when driving.

2. **Clinical preventive services** that include

The Cost of Unhealthy Behavior

Health Characteristic	Total Monthly Claims Cost		Hospital Inpatient Days Per 1,000		Hospital Outpatient Services Per 1,000		Physician Services Per 1,000	
	Elevated Risk	Low Risk	Elevated Risk	Low Risk	Elevated Risk	Low Risk	Elevated Risk	Low Risk
Smoking	$121.94	$93.44	388	190	1,012	949	4,652	3,736
Weight Control	125.05	90.83	420	173	1,087	914	4,449	3,671
Exercise	104.34	96.32	223	209	1,039	925	4,457	3,688
Alcohol Use	93.08	103.66	221	185	952	970	3,595	4,281
Driving Habits	103.26	94.43	213	201	1,015	930	3,697	4,039
Eating Habits	111.12	79.26	236	174	1,033	846	4,201	3,339
Stress	112.44	89.52	218	193	1,178	871	4,505	3,577
Mental Health	101.02	89.19	200	193	984	916	3,982	3,682
Cholesterol	96.13	96.29	211	195	914	988	3,720	4,003
Blood Pressure	103.46	95.62	248	200	925	968	4,192	3,765

Source: Milliman & Robertson, Inc.

coverage in employer-provided benefit plans for services such as mammograms and Pap smears, blood pressure and cholesterol screenings, well-baby/well-child programs, and immunizations.

3. *Health incentives programs* that include cash awards or premium reductions with proof that employees have obtained or maintained preset guidelines for specific health risks or that the employee has participated in preventive care or wellness programs.

4. *Education/training programs* that include medical self-care materials and patient education using books or newsletters about health care issues, health care referral hot lines offering access to nurse practitioners who review treatment programs, and education programs that encourage employees to become prudent health care purchasers.

PREVALENCE, RESULTS

The types of programs available and their effectiveness in changing unhealthy behavior and lowering overall medical care costs have been documented in numerous studies. For example, Hewitt Associates reported that more than 75% of 1,034 medium and large employers surveyed in 1993 used some type of health promotion or early intervention initiative to encourage healthy lifestyles among their employees. The graph and chart to the right illustrate the types of employer initiatives.

In another study, Milliman & Robertson, Inc., identified the relationship between health risk and behavior and the cost of medical care. Ten different health behaviors were examined from data supplied by StayWell Health Management Systems, Inc., Chrysler Corporation, and the International Union, UAW. The chart on the previous page sets out the study results.

Health Promotion Initiatives/Managed Health Provided by Major U.S. Employers in 1993 is available for $35 from Diane Schuett, Hewitt Associates LLC, 100 Half Day Road, Lincolnshire, IL 60069, (708) 295-5000.

For further information on *Health Risks and Their Impact on Medical Costs,* contact Milliman & Robertson, Inc., 15700 Bluemound Road, Suite 400, Brookfield, WI 53005, (414) 784-2250.

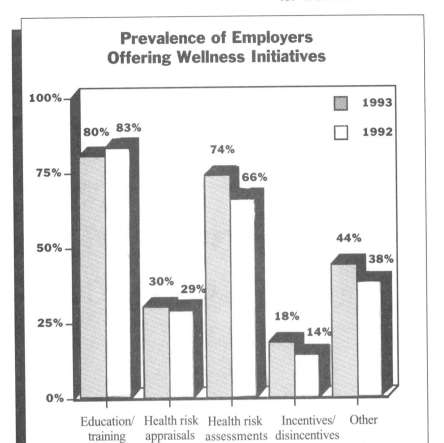

Prevalence of Employers Offering Wellness Initiatives

	1993	1992
On-site or employer-owned fitness facility	29%	31%
Subsidized health club memberships	28	27
Health-related educational materials/videos available	22	26
Physical exams	16	13
Discounts at local health clubs	7	7
Lunch-time speakers	4	4
Employer-sponsored sports teams/tournaments	1	5
Other (e.g., health information hot line)	24	17

Source: Hewitt Associates

Fostering Employee/Management Relationships

- Dynamics of Labor Relations, Collective Bargaining, and Contract Administration (Article 41)
- Disciplinary Action (Articles 42–44)
- Temporary and Part-Time Employees (Article 45)

The American labor movement has a long history dating back to the time of the Industrial Revolution. That history has been marked by turmoil and violence as workers sought to press their demands on business owners, whether represented by managers or entrepreneurs. The American labor movement exists because working conditions, pay, and benefits were very poor during the early years of the Industrial Revolution in both the United States and the rest of the world. It should be remembered that the American labor movement is only a small part of a broader, worldwide labor movement that includes most Western European societies. The working conditions under which the first American industrial workers labored would be unacceptable today. Child labor was common. There are documented instances of 6- and 7-year-old children, chained to machines for 12 hours a day, 6 days a week, who threw themselves into the machines—choosing death over life in the dehumanized and mechanized existence of the early factory. Conditions in some factories in the North prior to the Civil War were so infamous that Southern congressmen used them as a justification for the institution of slavery. Slaves sometimes lived in better conditions than the factory workers of New England and many other Northern states.

Unions exist because workers sought a better working environment and a better standard of living. Companies often took advantage of employees, and the government sided with management and the owners, frequently quelling strikes and other forms of labor protest initiated by the workers. Such incidents as the Pullman Strike, the Haymarket Square Riot, and the Homestead Strike exemplify

UNIT 6

the struggle of the American labor movement to achieve recognition and success in the attempt to improve the lives of all workers, whether unionized or not. The victories of labor have been hard fought and hard won. During the past hundred years, the fortunes of the American labor movement have varied. Today its fortunes are in decline, but the seeds of a rebirth of unionism are being sown by such unions as the American Federation of State, County, and Municipal Employees (AFSCME) and the American Federation of Teachers (AFT).

Unions have been able to achieve their gains through the mechanism of collective bargaining. The individual has very little bargaining power when compared to a company, especially huge companies such as General Motors or AT&T. Collective bargaining allows workers to pool their collective resources and power to bargain with the corporation on a more equal footing. Unfortunately for the unions, many of the industries in which they are strongest are in decline. New leadership is necessary if the American labor movement is to survive and rebound in the next century, and if it is to serve as a useful organ of society.

A union's ultimate weapon in contract negotiations, the strike, represents a complete breakdown of discipline from management's perspective. Disciplinary situations are almost always unpleasant, and today they can often lead to court cases, with all of the attendant legal questions and problems. A key to effective disciplinary action is documentation of employees' actions and the steps that were taken to correct them. Management needs to trust its employees; if it does not, the work environment becomes untenable for both labor and management.

The American labor movement has come a long way since the first strike by printers in Philadelphia in 1786. The journey, while difficult, has led to greater justice in the workplace and an increased standard of living for the nation as a whole. Unions have experienced both declines and increases in membership, but they have endured as a powerful social, political, and economic force. Whether or not they will again successfully "reinvent" themselves and adapt to a changing environment is a major question.

Looking Ahead: Challenge Questions

What trends do you see emerging from collective bargaining between organized labor and management in the next 5 to 10 years? Discuss the possibility that some concessions won by management may have to be given back to the workers.

Taking disciplinary action is often one of the most difficult and unpleasant activities that a manager must do. If you were a manager, how would you take disciplinary action? If you were the employee being disciplined, what would you do? What conflicts do you see in your responses to these two questions?

Discuss whether or not you agree with drug testing in the workplace, which is becoming a common practice in the United States.

What are some of the advantages of hiring temporary employees? How would you feel about being one? For over a year?

Putting Collective Back Into Bargaining

Using Principle-Based Negotiations

Paul Grattet

Paul Grattet is city manager of Greeley, Colorado.

Negotiating agreements with organized employees has been one of the less pleasant aspects of the local government management profession for me as a city manager. The idea that workers are on one side and management on the other always has seemed inconsistent with creating an organizational environment in which everyone is encouraged to cooperate in achieving the organization's goals.

The traditional practice whereby each side presents its demands and then spends endless hours, often beyond the expiration of the current contract, defending its position is a frustrating waste of time. The demands almost always are extremes that cannot possibly be achieved, and everyone knows it. The bargaining—anything but "collective"—goes on, often acrimoniously, with threats and personal attacks as common tactics until solutions, usually reluctant compromises, can be found. This process does not satisfy anyone because you sometimes have to give up what you previously stated was vital, which is the same as accepting a loss.

Such settlements do not foster workplace relationships that focus energy on the work. Instead, effort is spent on contract compliance issues or grievances, sometimes undermining the realization of organizational goals. Difficult contract negotiations in the public sector also do little to improve public impressions or support for the local government.

Because I have worked in two states, New York and Washington, where the process and procedures for public sector bargaining generally were mandated by the state, I know that local governments in both states have been limited in their ability to develop anything different. In 1991, I moved to Colorado and found few restraints on local government, at least when it came to collective bargaining. Although I did not expect to have to deal with this subject in my new job, the Greeley firefighters decided to petition for the right to bargain shortly after my arrival. So I had a chance to do it differently. This article relates my experience in developing an interest-focused, collective bargaining process that after three years is working well.

Environment

Greeley, which is a home-rule city, began collective bargaining with police officers several years before, authorized by a voter-approved city charter amendment. Although the experience with the police generally was good, the city council was comfortable with the status quo and did not want to approve further employee organization for the purpose of negotiating compensation and working conditions.

The firefighters already were organized and for several years had been considering a petition for recognition. Although there were no big disagreements at the time, the firefighters felt that such decisions as changes to the pension plan had been made by the council without the worker's input. They also considered a contract a safety net, should future councils seek to limit compensation or take away benefits in times of fiscal stress or competing priorities.

Soon after I arrived in Greeley, the firefighters filed a notice of their intent to petition for a vote on amending the city charter to require collective bargaining with their union. Although my experiences with collective bargaining had been less than satisfying, I did not see negotiations as something to be opposed on principle. In my judgment, however, the wording of the charter amendment had some serious problems. Consequently, I advised the firefighters that if they went forward with the amendment as drafted, I would send the council a recommendation that it be opposed.

From my study of the community political environment, it was not at all clear that opposition by the council and by me would ensure that the measure would be defeated. The firefighters had a great deal of community good will behind them, and it would be hard for the administration to argue against it because the police experience had caused no problems. Fortunately, all parties wanted to avoid a public controversy and the possible creation of long-term problems whichever way the vote went.

Setting the Stage

At this point, the firefighters were approached with the suggestion that if the proposed charter amendment could be rewritten to address some of my concerns, I would make a recommendation to the council to place the measure on the ballot, thereby eliminating the need to collect signatures on a new petition. The firefighters agreed, and a team was assembled quickly to rework the draft.

The attorney whom I hired was experienced in labor relations and shared my feelings about the traditional way of engaging in collective bargaining. A new proposal was developed that was acceptable to all parties. The council placed the measure on the ballot, and it was approved by the voters. At least, the groundwork had been laid to start a new approach.

Key Elements of the Charter Amendment

Several parts of the amendment laid the foundation for principled negotiation, a practice that is proposed by Roger Fisher and William Ury (1981) in their book *Getting to Yes: Negotiating Agreement Without Giving In*. The method prescribed by Fisher and Ury has four main elements.

First: *Separate the people from the problem.* This entails understanding each other's perceptions of the situation, recognizing the emotions involved and preparing to deal with them, and communicating effectively. Second: *Focus on interests, not positions,* the latter being solutions that may not be the best that could be accomplished. Focusing on interests requires an understanding of the difference between substantive interests and relationship interests. While the purpose of collective bargaining is to resolve substantive issues related to the workplace, the ongoing relationship is important, and each party should understand its own and each other's relationship interests.

Third: *Invent options for mutual gain.* This undertaking can be challenging until the parties get past the presumption of a "fixed pie size" or the preconception that there are no other solutions out there somewhere. Fourth: *Insist on using objective criteria* to evaluate alternative solutions that can lead to mutually satisfying solutions.

Following are charter provisions that contain these key elements.

Statement of Policy. The policy stated three important principles:

1. Public safety requires no interruption of services, that is, no work-stoppages.
2. A harmonious working relationship is a mutual goal.
3. Public services can be improved by the involvement of employees in decisions that affect them or that they would be required to implement.

This policy clearly established the paramount *shared* interests, as compared with the different or opposing interests of the parties.

Scope of Collective Bargaining. This was established in the charter to identify clearly the basic interests of the parties, to eliminate what could have been an issue in the amendment vote, and to remove a potentially difficult issue from the first contract negotiations. The charter states:

6. EMPLOYEE/MANAGEMENT RELATIONSHIPS: Dynamics of Labor Relations

Firefighters shall have the right to bargain collectively with the City respecting compensation, hours, working conditions, grievance procedure, agency fee, and other terms and conditions of employment of firefighters.

While recognizing the legitimate rights of employees to be involved in decisions which affect them, the City nevertheless recognizes that on balance, certain decisions are related more closely to questions regarding the quality or level or service to the public . . . than to conditions of employment. Accordingly, it is recognized that the employee's right to bargain collectively is limited and that the City may, but need not, negotiate over matters concerning: the direction of work of the firefighters; the decision to hire, promote, transfer, assign, or retain firefighters for cause; the decision to lay off firefighters for lack of work or funds, provided that procedures used to implement such decisions and the effects of such decisions are subject to negotiations; the maintenance of governmental efficiency; the methods and means by which firefighters are utilized to perform operations, provided . . . that minimum staffing on a piece of apparatus is negotiable; and the actions required to carry out the missions of the City.

The section on management rights was one of the most difficult to write, but we ended up with a reasonably clear statement that yet provides flexibility for the future.

Negotiation Process. The charter amendment spelled out the process of negotiation in considerable detail, from the request to initiate negotiations to the final resolution by a vote of the people should an impasse result. Important elements that affect the format or character of the negotiations process include the following:

- Initial proposals are made to identify "specific concerns or interests" on which discussion is desired. In other words, no demands, positions, or offers should be made at this point, following the Fisher/Ury suggestion to focus on interests.
- Next come discussions of concerns or interests, to assure understanding. This step is an opportunity for each party to provide background or to explain why the concern exists. For example, the employer might indicate a desire to discuss medical insurance costs due to rapidly rising claims. While taking this step helps prepare for the discussion of alternatives, it also helps develop relationships and establish communications patterns, separating the people from the problem.
- Next, the parties discuss the information that needs to be gathered to facilitate discussions, and they arrange for this to be done in a cooperative way. The purpose of this step is to prepare for inventing options and developing objective criteria for the best solution.
- Identifying options comes next. Once there is a good understanding of the concerns or interests (these might be called issues, but we try to avoid this word to discourage parties from taking sides), options or alternatives can be identified. Here, it is made clear that the suggestion of a possible solution is not binding on a party. In other words, it is not an offer, only an idea. Ideally this attitude encourages everyone to be open and to put all possibilities on the table.
- Next, the preferred options are chosen. If, after full analysis and discussion applying the agreed-upon criteria, the parties are able to find a solution that meets the needs of the parties, contract language is drafted and approved.
- If the parties are having difficulty finding a solution that meets all interests, outside parties can be called in to help achieve a voluntary resolution. This step could entail hiring an expert on a particular subject, such as on health plans, who might suggest solutions or who could provide information and aid in understanding alternatives. This also could involve retaining a facilitator or mediator.

Resolution of Impasse. If after 45 days of negotiation, unresolved issues remain, they must be submitted to a process that is called "advisory fact finding" but that amounts to nonbinding arbitration. The charter spells out the selection procedure and provides the authority and scope to be allowed the fact finder. An important requirement is that the fact finder must recommend the final offer of one of the parties. This requirement was written to encourage each party to be realistic in its final offer and to avoid the fact finder's coming up with a solution unacceptable to both parties. (In three years, this point never has been reached.)

Upon receipt of the fact finder's recommendations, the parties have 10 days for further negotiation of a resolution. If an impasse remains on any items, the city must advise the union of its accept/reject decision, then the union has five days to do likewise. Should unresolved issues still remain, the issues are submitted to a vote at the next election.

Preparing for Negotiations

After the vote on the charter, we had several months to prepare for the first contract negotiations. As some training was needed before starting negotiations, the firefighters' negotiating team was invited to participate with management in a three-day program conducted by a consultant skilled in principle-based methods. Everyone was given a copy of the book *Getting to Yes* before the training session.

The three-day session consisted of learning the principles of interest-based negotiations and practicing with role-playing sessions. The training also focused on communication because effective communication would certainly be the key needed to break out of the positional bargaining habits most of us had developed. This focus was particularly helpful to the union team because its members had no experience in collective bargaining. As management personnel learned, "Power is a product of the interpersonal relationship, not of the individual" (Hocker & Wilmot 1991).

Results

Negotiations with firefighters have gone smoothly for three years now, and contracts have been negotiated within the required time frames. Outside assistance has not been called for; nor has referral to the voters.

The first contract established a labor/management committee that has helped improve internal communications and provided an opportunity for employee input into decision making, one of the stated policy objectives. Management has learned that allowing input does not require relinquishing authority or giving up management rights.

The process has enabled us to resolve such tough issues as compensation with relative ease. It has been agreed, for example, that firefighters should be "compensated fairly," defined as being paid at the same rates paid for similar positions in the region. A methodology has been worked out for calculating the averages on which the pay rates are determined and on which the necessary data have been collected and calculations made. In the end, this process provided only one answer, and there was no need for either side to defend a position or make a compromise. There were no losers. Interestingly,

> **When the focus is on interests, it often is possible to develop win-win solutions.**

this approach has all but eliminated the parity issue between police and fire, and different percentage increases on an annual basis often have occurred.

This methodology also helps the city council fend off the persistent complaints about public sector wage levels, which average higher than some sectors of our local economy. Attention is not given to such factors as cost-of-living changes as reflected by the CPI, although our results by virtue of the methodology tend to be close to the CPI.

A Worthwhile Process

Principle-based collective bargaining is a better way to negotiate. Among the primary benefits are these:

- The long-term relationship is enhanced by encouraging cooperation and collaboration between management and firefighters.
- The focus is on common interests, rather than differences. The feeling is that "we did it together," not that one side won and the other lost.
- Employees feel empowered, which means they are likelier to share responsibility for resolving problems and achieving goals than to demand rights.
- The process has a structure with clear boundaries and steps for the resolution of an impasse (as in the final offer requirement) that motivate the parties to negotiate seriously from the beginning. I believe this is an advantage over binding arbitration, which lets someone else make the tough decisions. While the voters may make the final decision, the process is a public one that tends to make the parties more accountable. I doubt that we ever will have a vote.
- Solutions can be more satisfying than the compromises that typically result from positional bargaining. When everyone is busy defending positions, it is hard to find time to invent solutions. When the focus is on interests, it often is possible to develop win-win solutions.
- If managers can accept the idea that sharing power is a way of enhancing power, it is easier to put all the cards on the table. Also, the communication skills needed to make this process work can be learned.

Best of all, the concept of interest-based negotiation can be used in many types of dispute resolution in any organization.

References

Fisher, Roger, and William Ury. *Getting to Yes: Negotiating Agreement Without Giving In.* Boston: Houghton Mifflin Company, 1981.

Hocker, Joyce L., and William W. Wilmot. *Interpersonal Conflict,* 3rd ed. Dubuque, Iowa: Wm. C. Brown, 1991.

When the Fired Fight Back

There are better venues than court to deal with employee-discrimination suits.

David Nye

DAVID NYE, a former HR executive, is associate professor of management at Athens State College in Athens, Ala.

It's said that we're a nation of victims or potential victims. And often that potential is realized in corporate settings. When employees feel they have been done wrong, they no longer take it lying down. Instead of accepting their fate agreeably, disgruntled employees are suing corporations in record numbers.

In a study published in *Stanford Law Review*, John Donohue and Peter Siegelman found that while the number of federal civil suits rose 125 percent between 1969 and 1989, employment-discrimination suits increased 2,166 percent. That was before passage of the 1991 Civil Rights Act and the Americans with Disabilities Act (ADA).

The former law allows discrimination plaintiffs to recover compensatory and punitive damages in addition to the back pay that was allowed under the 1964 Civil Rights Act. Under ADA, those remedies are available to persons with disabilities for which employers fail to make "reasonable accommodation." One in six Americans can claim disability, as the term is defined by ADA. And both of the new statutes provide for trial by juries—folks much more likely to be peers of the accuser than peers of the accused (ever hear of a juror whose last name was Inc.?).

By 1994, more than 91,000 charges were being filed annually with the Equal Employment Opportunity Commission (EEOC); the agency's case intake was 64,000 in 1991. EEOC's case backlog in 1994 was 97,000 vs. 46,000 in 1991, and the average time to complete investigation of a charge had increased from nine to 19 months. According to Al Vreeland, partner in the Birmingham law firm of Lehr, Middlebrooks & Proctor, more than half of EEOC charges are simply mailed in by attorneys. After a complaint has languished for six months, lawyers typically exercise their right to ask the commission for a "right-to-sue" notice authorizing them to sue without waiting for EEOC to complete its investigation.

Jury Verdict Research Corp., a legal-publishing firm in Horsham, Pa., recently analyzed a sample of jury awards made to employees who sued because of discriminatory, hostile work environments, but where sexual harassment was not the issue. The median compensatory-damage award was $150,000, with a median of $160,000 in punitive damages tacked on in 43 percent of such cases. For plaintiffs demoted or denied promotion due to "unfair policies or standards," the median compensatory-damage award was

> Unfortunately, the hard-cases-make-bad-law truism may eventually render the term "binding ADR" an oxymoron—much as it has the term "employment-at-will."

$97,558; punitive damages were added in 32 percent of those verdicts, with a median award of $175,000.

Another popular tool when the fired fight back is the civil suit for unjust dismissal. In such cases, where no discrimination was alleged, the median verdict found in a Jury Verdict Research analysis was $102,000. Punitive damages were added in 26 percent of such cases, with a median of $150,000. Plaintiffs won more than 63 percent of such suits in 1993. In Montana, the only state with an unjust-dismissal statute, fired nonunion employees can seek liquidated and compensatory damages under the law. The National Conference of Commissioners of Uniform State Laws has unanimously approved a draft Model Employment Termination Act similar to the Montana statute and recommended its adoption by all the states.

Then there are the legal fees. According to Joel Kelly, partner in McKenna & Cuneo, a Los Angeles-based law firm that represents management in employment cases, a typical case that goes to trial may cost an employer from $75,000 to $100,000 in legal fees. And an atypical case? Rockwell International Corp. won a lawsuit filed against it by a senior executive, but the "victory" cost the company more than $1 million in expenses, according to Marc Kartman, Rockwell's assistant general counsel. And when it loses a discrimination case, an employer may have to pay the plaintiff's legal fees as well; attorney Kelly notes that California courts have approved recovery of attorneys' fees as high as $400 per hour.

The Alternative: More Head than Heart

In contrast to litigation, says Kelly, "A garden-variety wrongful-termination arbitration can be concluded in less than six months, does not entail expensive, time-consuming discovery, and will cost a fraction of what it takes to carry a case through trial." He notes that employment arbitrators, professionals familiar with workplace issues, are "far less likely to decide a case on the basis of emotion or confusion, as is often the case with a jury, and more likely to base their decisions on the evidence and governing law." Arbitration outcomes are thus more predictable and cases far less susceptible to runaway damage awards, he concludes.

Not surprisingly, 48 of 110 respondents to a 1994 survey by Organization Resources Counselors Inc., a New York-based HR and management consulting firm, used alternative dispute resolution (ADR) for nonunion employees. The procedures employed typically took one or more of the following forms:

- *An ombudsman.* Definitions vary, but this is usually a trained employee or consultant available for confidential discussion early in the dispute-resolution process. Often an influential person, the ombudsman also summarizes upward feedback for managers and recommends changes to management to correct problem areas.
- *Neutral fact-finding*, in which an independent third party investigates the facts surrounding the grievance and presents those facts to the decision makers.
- *Panel review*, in which an employee's grievance is heard by other employees; the employees may be peers of the grievant, members of management, or some combination thereof.
- *Mediation*, in which a trained individual from inside or outside the organization recommends, but cannot dictate, a solution to the dispute.
- *Arbitration*, under which a neutral, third-party professional hears the dispute and makes an award that is usually final and binding on both parties.
- *In-house counselors or advocates* who assist grievants in preparing and presenting their cases.

Of respondents with ADR programs in the ORC study, 47 percent used an internal ombudsman; 42 percent, peer review; 28 percent, neutral fact-finding; 25 percent, mediation; 25 percent, outside arbitration; and 4 percent, other methods. The following summary of three ADR programs shows how these techniques may be used in combination.

Polaroid's Five Steps

Edwin Land established Polaroid Corp.'s ADR system in 1949. The system's nucleus was a powerful, 32-member employees' committee that served as an employee advocate. The committee was dissolved in 1992 after the U.S. Department of Labor determined it was not in compliance with the Landrum-Griffin Act. Other advocates handled grievances until 1994, when Polaroid piloted a new program. The new approach was developed by a task force that studied the ADR practices of 22 other companies, including Federal Express Corp., IBM Corp., Control Data Corp., and Bank of America. The task-force proposal for the program was then critiqued by managers and employees at various Polaroid plants.

Polaroid's is a five-step process. An employee with a grievance first discusses it with the department manager. If the grievance is not resolved, it goes to the division manager. If still dissatisfied, the grievant may appeal to a panel of three company officers or five randomly selected, trained peers. The peer panel has the same authority to decide a grievance as does the officer panel. If still not satisfied, the grievant may appeal to Polaroid's president, and finally to binding, third-party arbitration.

According to Polaroid legal administrator Bonnie Low Frankel, the ADR process is instructive for all concerned: "It helps hold management accountable for their decisions while affording employees a mechanism to voice disagreement as well as positive ideas," she says. "The peer panels also give employees an idea of the difficulty that management faces in making termination decisions. And while our process can't make everyone happy, it does tend to deflect the tendency of disgruntled employees to seek legal recourse, something that's expensive for the employee and generally not constructive."

Over the past 10 years or so, about 25 cases each year have been settled at the panel level; three or four go to arbitration. Along with discharges, internal-selection issues are the most frequent subject of grievances at Polaroid. Frankel notes that any Polaroid employee can bid on open job postings, and with a highly experienced and skilled work force, differences in individual qualifications can be hard to discern.

At Rockwell, Binding Arbitration

In addition to the whopping legal expenses involved, Kartman says, the earlier-mentioned lawsuit sensitized top management to the amount of time such activity can take. Rockwell senior executives, including the CEO, had to give depositions in the case, and the top HR executive gave testimony at a five-day trial. As a result, Rockwell revived and implemented a proposal for a grievance procedure that provides for binding arbitration at the last step. The first step of the process calls for the employee to discuss the problem with his supervisor; if the dispute is not then settled, the HR staff investigates and recommends a solution; the third step involves a peer review similar to Polaroid's process. But unlike the Polaroid approach, the Rockwell plan may oblige a grievant to seek binding arbitration if he wants to press on.

Rockwell initiated its arbitration procedures in 1992 by requiring 970 executives to sign a mutual agreement to arbitrate employment disputes— including disputes covered by statute—as a condition of participation in an executive stock plan. The ADR program was later extended to cover all nonunion employees at some locations. New hires at Rockwell must sign the mutual agreement to arbitrate as a condition of employment. For current employees, requiring the agreement is limited to cases in which special consideration can be offered, e.g., promotion or transfer. "We didn't adopt the program as a way of winning," Kartman notes. "If anything, given that a company often has the power to out-lawyer an employee in litigation, employees probably prevail more in arbitration. We simply see arbitration as a fairer and more cost-effective way."

6. EMPLOYEE/MANAGEMENT RELATIONSHIPS: Disciplinary Action

Brown & Root's Wide Open Door

This Houston-based construction company has a core work force of 28,000 in 40 states. Building on an open-door policy that permitted employees to take complaints to any level of management, Brown & Root Inc. implemented a comprehensive ADR program in 1993 after study by a task force, input from employees, and guidance from a consulting firm. In its first year, some 500 employees used the program. Of the 383 cases resolved, 300 were settled in-house—43 percent in a week or less and 75 percent in four weeks or less. (Forty-five of the open cases represent persons who contacted the program and were not heard from again. The company explains that it hires thousands of construction workers each year, and turnover may be as high as 500 percent.) In addition to the open-door policy, Brown & Root personnel have several ADR options:

- Calling an employee hotline and talking to an adviser who performs much the same function as Polaroid's counselors;
- Requesting consultation with an attorney of their choice. After a $25 deductible, the employee pays 10 percent of the attorney's fees; Brown & Root pays the other 90 percent, with a maximum annual benefit of $2,500 per employee. So far, some 50 employees have used the legal consultation plan at a cost to the company of about $50,000;
- In-house mediation; or
- Outside mediation or arbitration (limited to disputes involving legally protected rights). Twenty-five cases have gone to mediation, seven to arbitration.

How the Courts See It

The interest in employment ADR has not been lost on the American Arbitration Association (AAA), a private organization that provides mediators and arbitrators for both commercial and labor disputes. In 1993, AAA established special rules for grievance arbitration in which no union is involved. The rules require, for example, that the grievant and management have equal voice in selecting the arbitrator. In 1994, 278 cases were heard by AAA arbitrators under those rules, vs. 168 in 1993. During 1994, AAA assisted employers in setting up arbitration plans covering about 800,000 nonunion workers. Robert Meade, the association's vice president for program development, notes that the big surge of interest in employer-initiated ADR came in mid- to late 1994 and is increasing at a faster pace in 1995. "Litigation costs are the main reason," he explains.

If litigation costs pushed development of ADR, the 1991 Supreme Court case of *Gilmer v. Interstate/Johnson Lane Corp.* provided an irresistible pull for many companies. The high court had earlier held in *Alexander v. Gardner-Denver* (1974) that a fired employee could ignore an unfavorable arbitrator's ruling rendered under a union contract and sue the employer under the same claim of illegal discrimination.

After stockbroker Robert D. Gilmer was fired, he sued in federal court under the Age Act. The employer argued that Gilmer had waived his right to sue when, as part of a required registration with the New York Stock Exchange, he agreed to submit to arbitration any controversy stemming from termination of employment. The Supreme Court ruled that the SEC agreement to arbitrate was enforceable under the 1925 Federal Arbitration Act, which makes private arbitration agreements enforceable. (Most states have similar laws, and 15 states expressly permit arbitration of employment claims.)

In *Gilmer*, the Supreme Court cited its ruling in a 1985 Sherman Antitrust Act case. There, the court held that in agreeing to arbitrate a statutory claim, a party does not give up legal rights "but only submits to their resolution in an arbitral, rather than judicial forum." The court majority also declared that times had changed and earlier courts' mistrust of arbitration as a valid substitute for litigation (e.g., as expressed in *Gardner-Denver*) was no longer valid.

Attorney Kelly points out that *Gilmer* did not involve an employment contract and thus skirted a key issue. The FAA does not apply to contracts of employment of seamen, railroad employees, or "any other class of workers engaged in foreign or interstate commerce." The federal circuits are split as to whether that exclusion applies only to transportation workers or to all workers in interstate commerce.

However, given *Gilmer*, other federal court rulings, and congressional recognition of ADR, legal experts generally agree that the Supreme Court will rule that employment contracts containing agreements to arbitrate statutory claims are enforceable under the FAA. The court would also likely rule that the FAA's exclusion of certain contracts applies only to the transportation industry. "*Gilmer* all but eviscerated *Alexander v. Gardner-Denver*," says Kelly.

But legal experts also raise an important caveat: The courts will continue to refuse to enforce arbitration awards and agreements where the arbitration process lacks basic fairness. Paul W. Cane Jr., a partner with Paul, Hastings, Janofsky & Walker, another Los Angeles-based firm that represents management in employment-law matters, advises clients who are considering ADR: "Don't be greedy; don't stack the deck by having a management-selected arbitrator or by denying the grievant prehearing discovery or legal counsel." He also recommends using a reputable referral source such as AAA and a mutual arbitrator-selection process such as striking names from a submitted list. Some corporate practitioners agree.

William L. Bedman, associate general counsel for Brown & Root, comments: "We tried to make our program as legally transparent as possible; whatever rights employees have under state or federal law they have under our program. The arbitrator is expected to apply the applicable law as a judge would."

But a host of other legal and administrative issues remain in setting up arbitration plans for nonunion staff. For example, who pays the arbitrator's and referral agency's fees? A typical bill for an arbitrator's fees and expenses for a case requiring a one-day hearing may range from $1,500 to $2,000. AAA charges filing fees from $500 to $5,000, depending on the amount of the claim. If the claim exceeds $50,000, there may be an additional administrative fee of $150 for each hearing day. Some firms require grievants to pay half of such costs to discourage frivolous complaints pursued under a "What-have-I-got-to-lose?" theory. Other companies, like Polaroid, pay all arbitration expenses. Does this create an inference that the arbitrator might favor the party who foots his or her bill? "We have yet to have an employee insist on paying half," Frankel replies.

Uncover Conflicts and Resolve Them

Another issue is whether the requirement to arbitrate should be mutual—lawyers say this makes the agreement more binding, but attorney Cane points out that management may nonetheless wish to exclude from arbitration claims for which a judicial forum is preferred, such as injunctive suits against a former employee for intellectual property violations. As noted by Polaroid labor counsel Ann Leibowitz, "If the ADR process is intended to provide for arbitration of certain matters but not others, it must be drafted with exquisite precision."

Clearly, management needs the advice of counsel in fashioning ADR procedures. But ADR will not likely succeed unless management's view extends beyond defensive legalisms. ORC offers a perspective: "Organizational conflict is a three-part continuum: suppressed [invisible] conflict, constructive differences, and differences that have evolved into troublesome disputes. . . . HR and law professionals are focusing on the third to the exclusion of the other parts. An organization's conflict-management strategy ought to be to expand the middle and shrink the two ends."

Some ADR systems are indeed built around programs designed to uncover conflicts and resolve them at the lowest possible level. Such programs typically feature training for supervisors, grievance advisers, and peer panelists in listening skills, fact-gathering, and nonconfrontational approaches to resolving conflicts. Brown & Root's advisers, for example, undergo up to 20 hours of refresher training annually in dispute-resolution techniques; Polaroid has a structured training regimen for grievance-panel members that includes such subjects as evaluating evidence and decision making.

It is also important that an ADR program be compatible with the organization's culture. For example, Polaroid has long-service employee-owners (average age is 47) who are concentrated in a small geographic area. A company with a less cohesive culture might be less apt to cede grievance-settlement power to employee peer panels. And even though Brown & Root's new, multioption system encourages employees to air disputes at lower levels, the company has maintained the open-door policy—a longstanding tradition.

Unfortunately, the hard-cases-make-bad-law truism may eventually render the term "binding ADR" an oxymoron—much as it has the term "employment-at-will." Rockwell's Kartman makes the point:

"My concern is that there will always be those outfits that do what we have tried not to do and set up arbitration agreements and procedures that will be seen as, and will be in fact, unfair. These will then be held up as an example of what is going on generally, and Congress will see a need to step in and protect everybody."

PRIVACY

Background checks, drug tests, workplace monitoring—how far can an employer go? Recent court cases provide some answers.

Ellen Alderman and Caroline Kennedy

ELLEN ALDERMAN and CAROLINE KENNEDY *are attorneys and co-authors of* In Our Defense.

Employers argue that in today's increasingly competitive economy, they have a right to choose the workers who best fit the job, and in order to make informed choices, they need information—information that can be acquired only through such procedures as background checks, credit checks, and drug tests. Once workers have been hired, the argument goes, monitoring is then essential to maintain and often improve productivity.

Driving much of the expanded need for information are the expanded responsibilities of the employer in two important and costly areas: health insurance and liability. Health-insurance costs have been eating into corporate profits at an exponential rate. Insuring high-risk workers, like smokers or skydivers, further drives up the cost of insuring everyone else. But to know which workers are high-risk requires still more information, whether from medical tests or personal questions and surveillance. A second justification for workplace monitoring is that employers face liability for the actions of their employees. Also, under the fast-growing tort of "negligent hiring" an employer can be sued for its failure to adequately check the past histories of its workers. Indeed, in some workplaces, such as day-care centers, employers are required to check the background of their job applicants.

There is nothing new about corporate control over people's lives. Articles on the subject invariably refer to stories of Henry Ford's investigative team, which went door to door checking on the hygiene and morals of the first assembly-line workers. Nineteenth-century company housing evolved into the 20th-century company town, where, directly or indirectly, the boss knew about every aspect—personal and professional—of the workers' lives.

Today, a host of new privacy issues are coming over the horizon. We have tried to highlight some of them in the stories that follow. Does an employer's need to ensure a safe workplace justify asking intrusive questions? Can an employee's personal life or sexual orientation be grounds for dismissal? And what happens when privacy can be invaded by new technology and no law exists to cover a perceived injury?

A robust economy is obviously in everyone's interest. Improving efficiency and performance contributes to that end. Careful selection and monitoring of workers are important management tools that entail some intrusion into personal lives. But might we reach a point at which the workplace has become so dehumanized that any increase in profit is not worth the sacrifice of privacy?

Drug Testing

The hottest workplace privacy issue of the 1980s was drug testing. As a central weapon in the Reagan administration's "war on drugs," government agencies led the way in instituting drug-testing programs for their work forces. These were challenged as a violation of the Fourth Amendment's prohibition against unreasonable search and seizure. In 1989, the Supreme Court upheld post-accident drug testing of railroad workers, and testing of Customs Service personnel involved in drug-interdiction efforts. Since then, drug-testing programs affecting government workers in public-safety jobs, like pilots, train engineers, or police officers, have generally been upheld, whereas blanket testing of administrative or clerical workers has not.

In the private sector, where workers are not

protected by the Fourth Amendment, drug testing has become widely accepted, particularly in the pre-employment context. According to the American Management Association, an estimated 91 percent of large companies now test their workers for drugs.

In 1990, a woman who worked for the Ford Meter Box Co. in Wabash, Ind., was fired for flunking a drug test. But what she tested positive for was nicotine. Ford Meter Box forbade its employees to smoke, even on their own time at home. Although the woman did not get her job back, her case led the Indiana legislature to pass a law prohibiting companies from firing employees for smoking. The legislation does, however, permit employers to charge additional health-insurance premiums for employees who smoke. *Bone v. Ford Meter Box*, Indiana 1991.

> A federal judge ruled that cohabitation is in fact a "recreational activity" protected by New York law and is not usually grounds for firing.

In April 1989, a benefits clerk at the Conagra Poultry Co. in Denver was notified that her employer planned to institute a drug-testing program. In addition, Conagra required employees to disclose all prescription medications they were taking. The clerk refused to sign the disclosure form and was fired. She sued for invasion of privacy, among other claims. The court dismissed her case. *Mares v. Conagra Poultry Co. Inc.*, Colorado 1991.

In 1982, an employee of a New Hampshire Papa Gino's for nearly 10 years was confronted by a supervisor with rumors that he had been seen using drugs outside work. The employee took a polygraph test and answered questions relating to his alleged drug use. When the examiner reported his belief that the man was lying about using drugs, the man was fired. He later claimed that he had been forced to take the test under the threat of losing his job and had been asked numerous non-job-related questions about private matters. A jury found Papa Gino's investigative techniques "highly offensive to a reasonable person" and awarded the employee $398,200. In 1986, the U.S. Court of Appeals for the First Circuit upheld the verdict. *O'Brien v. Papa Gino's of America Inc.* New Hampshire 1986

In 1988, Congress passed the Employee Polygraph Protection Act (EPPA) of 1988, which essentially bans the use of polygraphs, voice-stress analyzers, and other physiological tests as job-screening devices by private employers. Exceptions were made for the pharmaceutical industry, security-guard companies, and government. Testing of employees suspected of specific incidents of theft is still permitted under the EPPA.

Off-Duty Behavior

In October 1990, Sue Everett, manager of corporate training and development at Rohr Industries, was fired after nine years of "above standard" performance. Rohr had conducted a clandestine investigation into her personal life to confirm rumors that she was dating Ken Bingham, the unmarried director of human resources, to whom she did not report. He was also fired. The couple sued Rohr for invasion of privacy, among other claims. In November 1992, after a seven-week trial, a jury awarded Bingham $3,265,568 and Everett $1,035,693.

Rohr appealed the verdict. Meanwhile, Bingham has not been able to find another job. Though Everett was employed at an eyeglass-lens company at the time of trial (which accounted for the lesser amount of her damages), she has since been laid off. The couple is still together. Neither has received any money. *Bingham and Everett v. Rohr Industries Inc.*, California 1992

Laural Allen and Samuel Johnson met while working as sales associates at the Wal-Mart store in Johnstown, N.Y. Allen was separated and Johnson was single at the time they began seeing each other. When Allen's estranged husband served divorce papers on her at work, both Allen and Johnson were fired. It turned out that their relationship was in violation of company policy on fraternization set out in an employee handbook: "Wal-Mart strongly believes in and supports the 'family unit.' A dating relationship between a married associate and another associate . . . is prohibited."

In July 1993, the attorney general of New York filed suit against Wal-Mart for violating a brand-new state law prohibiting employers from firing workers who engage in lawful recreational activities off-duty and off-premises. In January 1995, a New York court held that "dating" was not a "recreational activity" protected by the statute, and issued a decision in favor of Wal-Mart.

The company has, however, altered the fraternization policy. The new version requires evidence of improper conduct at work (including "open displays of affection" and "making the work environment uncomfortable") before an employee can be fired. *State v. Wal-Mart Stores*, New York 1995.

6. EMPLOYEE/MANAGEMENT RELATIONSHIPS: Disciplinary Action

In February 1993, Katz Media, a company that sells radio and television advertising time, fired the man who was its vice president and New York sales manager. Two days later his girlfriend, who had worked at Katz for 11 years as an administrative assistant, was demoted to an entry-level position. She resigned in June 1993 and sued the company, claiming she was discriminated against because she lived with the vice president.

Katz argued that under *Wal-Mart*, the case should be dismissed. However, in August 1995, a federal judge refused, ruling that cohabitation is in fact a "recreational activity" protected by New York law and is not usually grounds for firing. *Pasch v. Katz Media Corp.*, New York 1995

In Indiana, it would be wise to adopt a healthy lifestyle if one wants to keep a job. A man went to work for the Best Lock Co. in 1984. Best Lock had a TAD rule, which prohibited the use of tobacco, alcohol, or drugs at any time—whether on or off the job. In 1989, the man admitted he had been drinking off-duty in a bar on a few occasions between December 1985 and February 1986. He was fired. He sued for unemployment compensation, claiming that the TAD rule was unreasonable. He won. *Best Lock v. Review Board*, Indiana 1991

Electronic Surveillance

In December 1994, voice mail entered the fray. In what appears to be the first voice-mail privacy case, a McDonald's manager in Elmira, N.Y., sued the franchise owner.

The manager had been a McDonald's employee for nearly 20 years when, in 1993, he began having an affair with an assistant manager at the McDonald's in nearby Binghamton. The couple often left romantic messages in each other's voice-mail boxes, which belonged to a voice-mail system linking a dozen McDonald's outlets. Though the manager claims he was told that only he knew the code to retrieve his messages, he believes that at some point another employee began retrieving the messages—and passing them on to the owner. According to the manager, in late 1993 the owner ordered the other employee to play the messages for the manager's wife.

The manager filed the suit against the owner for $2 million. The suit is pending. "$2 M Suit in Sweet Nuthin' Eavesdrop," *New York Newsday*, Jan. 20, 1995

In 1990, an inspector with the U.S. Postal Service received two anonymous letters alleging that gambling was taking place in the downtown post office in Lahaina, Hawaii. The letters were turned over to the police, who installed four video cameras in the ceiling and smoke detectors of the break room at the post office. A switcher and recorder were hidden in a yellow box on top of a vending machine. No warrant was obtained.

The images from the cameras were transmitted to a van parked outside the post office. Two police officers watched the activity in the break room during work hours for an entire year. When new tapes were required, the police officer on the case changed them at 3 a.m. to preserve secrecy. The police accumulated 50 videotapes containing 1,200 hours of footage. The officers testified that only a minute fraction reflected any gambling.

The Supreme Court of Hawaii found that the employees had a reasonable expectation of privacy in their break room and that their employer could not "consent" to a search on their behalf. The court found that the search violated the Hawaii state constitution and said the tapes could not be used against the postal workers. *State v. Bonnell*, Hawaii, 1993

In 1989, workers at telephone equipment manufacturer Northern Telecom Inc.'s Nashville plant discovered that their employer had been eavesdropping on them. For 13 years, the company had secretly intercepted and recorded personal telephone calls made by employees from the cafeteria, conference room, and guard station. Eight hundred and thirty-four employees sued the company for violating federal and state law, including invasion of privacy. The judge ordered all original tape recordings of private conversations filed with the court, and prohibited disclosure of their contents except for those involved in the litigation.

The case was settled in June 1992. Northern Telecom agreed to pay $200,000 into a fund. The eight plaintiffs whose voices could be identified on tapes of outgoing calls made from the cafeteria telephones each received $901.92. The 47 plaintiffs whose voices could be positively identified on tapes of other phone calls each received $450.96. The 761 remaining plaintiffs who could present adequate evidence that they had used the telephones each received $225.48. *Parish et al. v. Northern Telecom*, Tennessee 1992

Terminating Problem Employees

Consistent Procedures Should Be Emphasized

Bettye Springer

While an employer's best defense against a wrongful discharge claim often is established through careful employee selection and consistent disciplinary procedures, the manner in which the employee is terminated also is important in protecting against liability. The best methods of minimizing claims associated with termination coincide with those methods dictated by good business judgment and common sense. Be professional and courteous, and treat the employee with dignity and respect during the termination process. Try to be fair. If a lawsuit does result from a termination, a judge and jury will be influenced most favorably by an employer who took safeguards to avoid an unfair decision.

Deciding to Terminate

Terminations have the potential to turn into million-dollar decisions and should be treated accordingly. No single supervisor should be authorized to terminate an employee. Where immediate action is required, a supervisor's power should be limited to suspension, to allow for a complete review of an employee's performance. If a supervisor, acting alone, terminates an employee, too often management either must accept a marginal decision (with the accompanying risk) or must severely undercut the supervisor's authority and ability to manage by reversing his or her decision.

In reviewing an employee's performance to determine whether termination is appropriate, the employer should

6. EMPLOYEE/MANAGEMENT RELATIONSHIPS: Disciplinary Action

consider its own past practice. Specifically, the employer should consider:

- What incidents have resulted in termination in the past? And do these examples indicate that discharge is appropriate in this situation?
- If past practice indicates that termination is inappropriate, is the current situation *clearly* distinguishable from past incidents?
- If past practice indicates that discharge is inappropriate, have new policies or procedures been announced (well in advance of the current situation) that fairly alerted the affected employee to the employer's new approach?
- Did the employee to be terminated have a fair chance to learn of the new policies or procedures?
- What will the termination do to the employer's EEO-1 report?

Terminating the Employee

The manner in which termination decisions are communicated to the employee is important. Many times, it is the way a termination has been handled, rather than the termination itself, that has led to litigation. Even individuals who cannot function as satisfactory employees deserve to be treated with respect.

Unceremonious dismissals, with accompanying public embarrassment, are no longer just insensitive: they are now invitations to litigation. The most difficult cases that employment lawyers must defend are those in which an employee has been fired in a callous manner. Juries are more sympathetic and awards are higher when terminated employees have not been treated with honesty and dignity.

The following are guidelines for the termination process:

- Have the supervisor meet face to face with the employee.
- Have a witness present at the termination meeting.
- Avoid scheduling a termination meeting before a holiday.
- Give the employee both oral and written—in that order—notices of termination.
- Inform the employee in the oral and written notices of any policies regarding return of property, such as keys.
- Schedule an exit interview, and include the time and place of the interview in the oral and written notices.
- Ensure the employee's presence at the exit interview by notifying him or her that the final paycheck will be given then.
- Notify managers affected by the discharge that the employee has been terminated. Do not inform coworkers or associates who do not have a business "need to know."

Consistency

The importance of consistency in applying disciplinary policies and termination procedures cannot be overemphasized. If, for example, one employee is terminated for a particular type of misconduct after a second offense, and another is terminated for the same type of misconduct after four offenses, the inconsistent application of disciplinary procedures can have a devastating effect on the employer's case in litigation. To ensure consistency, all disciplinary actions, particularly terminations, should be discussed with personnel officials. Written documentation of all facts leading to prior disciplinary actions and terminations must be prepared and maintained in the employee's personnel file.

Bettye Springer is a partner at Haynes & Boone, Fort Worth, Texas, where she counsels public employers in the areas of management labor and employment law. The source of this article is HR Report, *published by ICMA.*

■ Give Them a Piece of the Pie

Are Your Temps Doing Their Best?

If temps aren't motivated to do top work, your company will suffer. Luckily, getting the most from your temps often is a matter of applying techniques you already use for permanent employees—such as giving them a stake in the company's success.

Shari Caudron

When Bill Hardgrove, 45, started his tenure as a temporary worker about a year ago, his first assignment was in the accounting office of a large moving company. His job? To decide whether to extend credit to clients, to follow up on overdue accounts and to reconcile account balances. Problem was, he was given all this responsibility but had no authority to act on his own recommendations. "I had to ask the Controller for everything," he says, "including gaining computer access to do account entry and adjustment."

With more than 23 years of experience in the financial-services industry, including managing a credit union and owning a collections firm, Hardgrove considered this a slap in the face. "I felt like I was shrinking professionally," he says. When the moving company offered him a regular job after four months, he declined.

His next two temporary assignments were no better. His supervisors never asked about his skills and expertise, even though he gave each of them a resume on his first day. They didn't give him challenging or creative work. They never asked him to lunch. Feeling ignored and unimportant, Hardgrove did just what he was told—and not a bit more. "I wasn't about to leave an extra nickel on the table when I left," he says.

Hardgrove's experience is pretty typical of today's temporary worker. Most temps, forced into the temporary employment market by necessity, are eager to perform well—because what they really want is a full-time job offer or, at the very least, a good reference. More than three-fourths of temps on the market today became temporary employees with the hope of finding full-time jobs, according to the National Association of Temporary and Staffing Services (NATSS) located in Alexandria, Virginia. Many also seek temporary work to widen their breadth of skills.

Yet, according to Helen Axel, author of a 1995 Conference Board report on contingent employment, managers tend to overlook the need to motivate temporary employees because their view of temps is stuck in the old school—that is, when temps were used primarily as replacements for sick and vacationing clerical workers. "In those days, temps were warm bodies you bought for a short amount of time," she says. "You hoped you got someone good."

But that attitude no longer will work. In the last 10 years, the temporary work force has increased from 400,000 people to more than 2 million workers, or 1.5% of the work force. Furthermore, they're staying on the job longer. A recent study by the NATSS shows that 56% of all temporary assignments last more than 11 weeks, and 11% last longer than a year. Not only that, companies are using temps in more highly skilled positions and in more strategic ways, such as helping with work overload and completing special projects. All of these changes point to a greater need for developing motivational techniques.

If you've invested money to train temporary workers for special assignments, for example, you want them to be motivated to remain on the job long enough for you to recoup the cost of that training. But even if you haven't invested valuable training dollars, the mere fact that temps are on the job longer means that any lack of motivation—and thus, productivity—is more easily noticed.

Unfortunately, too many employers behave in ways that sap the motivation right out of temps. They still treat temps like second-class citizens, even though they're using more of them, for longer periods of time and in increasingly responsible positions.

If you want to get the best work from your temporary employees, you must get over the notion that temps are somehow different or difficult to motivate. In reality, it's not that hard to get good work out of them. Give temps adequate training and orientation, provide meaningful work, pay them what they're worth, push them to use their talents and stand back.

Recruit and welcome temps as you would any other worker. The first rule of thumb in motivating workers is to hire those who appear to have a good degree of self-motivation. How? Instead of accepting whomever the staff-

6. EMPLOYEE/MANAGEMENT RELATIONSHIPS: Temporary and Part-Time Employees

ing agency sends you—if you use an agency—ask the company to send its best candidates for an onsite interview so you can provide some input on the selection.

At Harris Bank in Chicago, temporary employees are used in the credit-services operation for data entry. The bank would like these employees to stay for about a year—until technology that's now being developed has been completed and installed, making those positions obsolete. Unfortunately, extensive turnover has been a problem. That is, it was a problem until hiring managers got involved in the recruitment process.

"Our leasing company now arranges interviews with three candidates for each position," says Kassie Matos, assistant vice president. "It sends them to us and we have a chance to assess how prepared they are and how eager they are to work for the bank on a long-term temporary basis." Because of stringent laws regarding employer status, the bank can't directly extend a job offer to an agency employee. But, after interviewing candidates, it does provide input that's usually followed by the agency.

Taking time to interview the temps not only helps the bank spot motivated employees, it also indicates to the temps that the bank is concerned about finding the right people for the job. Once candidates realize the bank cares about hiring individuals who will give a little extra, they subconsciously try harder to become that individual. And temps who buy in to the job through this process tend to remain on assignments longer. In fact, Matos says being able to spot motivated employees in the interview process has helped the bank avoid hiring the kind of temp who only stays for a couple of days or a week. "It's very time consuming and costly to terminate an employee lease and start over again," she explains.

But even self-motivated people can quickly sour to the situation if they're not integrated into the workplace. Thomas Kohn, president of Reflex Services, a staffing agency based in Pittsburgh, believes the biggest mistake companies make when it comes to managing temporary workers is failing to provide an adequate orientation. "It's very demotivating not to know even basic things, such as where the cafeteria and restrooms are, when breaks are scheduled and what the general policies and procedures are," he says.

Matos agrees and says all temporary employees brought in to Harris Bank are given such an orientation. They're handed an employee manual, the policies are reviewed, they're walked through the department, and then another employee takes them to lunch to answer any questions they might have. It gives new employees a great sense of security to meet a co-worker right away and have a contact to go to with questions, she says.

Finally, during the orientation, take time to learn about temps' specific goals and talk about how the company might help meet them. If the possibility of regular employment exists, for example, tell them. If not, tell them you'd be willing to provide a good reference assuming that they adequately perform the duties asked of them. Individuals who see longer-term personal gain are among the most motivated temporaries on the market.

Money motivates. It's a fact. Temps who feel adequately compensated will spend less mental energy thinking about their compensation and more on the tasks at hand. For this reason, the first step in offering financial motivators to temporaries is to make sure they're compensated at competitive market rates. While there's no blanket pay rate for all temps in all industries, the Bureau of Labor Statistics recently published a useful report: the average hourly earnings of temporary workers in 50 occupational categories, broken down by 2,100 metropolitan areas. The report, titled "Occupational Compensation Survey—Temporary Help Services," is available at no cost by calling 202/606-6220.

Once you've determined the appropriate market rate for your group of temps, consider offering merit pay or bonuses to outstanding temporary workers or to those who have been on the job a certain amount of time. (If you don't have an internal means of hiring temporary employees, you can negotiate for wage incentives through your staffing agency.) The idea is to encourage temps to stick around as long as possible because experienced employees are more productive.

At Olin Corporation in Detroit, a maker of swimming-pool chemicals, seasonal temps are hired each year to help with the pre-summer upswings in production and shipping. The company encourages temps to come back year after year by paying returning temps higher wages than new temps.

The financial incentives at Harris Bank are a little different. After two months, agency temps who show great potential are invited to take the skills-assessment test offered by HR to all potential new hires. If they pass, they have the opportunity to become a bank employee and join the other 118 members of the *Reserve Force*, the bank's internal temporary pool. Upon receiving membership into the Reserve Force, temps get an automatic wage increase of 80 cents an hour, and they have the opportunity to apply for any open position at the bank after being a Reserve Force member for six months.

Share information, increase challenges, elicit input. To keep temps motivated, you've got to keep them in the loop. Communicating with temporaries about their jobs and how their jobs fit into the overall goals of the department, division or company not only helps them understand their roles, it helps them feel valued, necessary and part of the team.

At Ford Motor Co. in Detroit, temporary engineering employees worked for two and a half years to complete an automotive oil study at the company's certification testing laboratory. The project—analyzing exhaust gases produced by differing blends of oil—met its goals and was completed on schedule. "There was absolutely no difference in the level of productivity between the temporary workers and the regular employees of the testing lab," says Joe O'Hagan, principal engineer.

He believes it was because the company gave temporary workers the same memos, newsletters and bulletins about the company and the testing lab as it gave regular employees, even though their project had very little to do with the rest of the lab. "We treated them as if they were an integral part of our team," he says. "And to be part of our team, they had to know what everybody else knows. We worked to make sure they understood the big picture."

It's also important to keep temps interested. For starters, give them challenging work commensurate with their skill levels. Let them show you what they can do. As Max Messmer, chairman and CEO of Robert Half International, a staffing firm based in Menlo Park, California, says: "The single most demotivating thing for temporaries is when companies don't realize and/or take advantage of their full range of experience." Barbara A. Poindexter, employee representative and personnel officer for Pittsburgh-based PNC Bank, N.A., couldn't agree more.

"If the temporary is a professional worker being required to do professional work, give him or her work that is compatible with and takes advantage of his or her skills and experience," she says. "It's very demotivating to work beneath your capabilities."

At PNC Bank, Poindexter recently brought in four temporary HR recruiters to hire 325 employees within four months for a new loan center. She interviewed all the candidates recommended by the staffing agency, looking for the professionals who were uniquely qualified to take on this challenge. Once they were hired, she explained the parameters of the job and told the recruiters exactly what they'd be required to achieve. Then, she let them have at it.

"Regardless of whether they're temporaries, professionals want to be challenged," she says, adding that the first step in matching a skilled temporary worker with a job is knowing exactly what you're hiring for. "Don't build the job around the person's skills. Match the person to the job. A mismatch can be very demotivating."

Another key point in motivating temps is asking for their input. Along with being recognized for their skills and experience, temporaries also want to be recognized for their opinions and good ideas. But many companies overlook temps as a valuable source of information, Messmer says. They're missing an excellent opportunity. "Temps are objective, they don't have an ax to grind and most of them don't understand the politics of an organization," he says. "Most of them are dying to give you their opinion, and they feel flattered when you ask."

Nancy Camarata, director of WRAP accounts at Lord, Abbett & Company, an investment-management firm in New York City, uses accounting temps to reconcile monthly balance statements. Her receptiveness to their comments pays off. For example, it was the temps who recently pinpointed a bug in the software program that incorrectly recorded information on recent transactions. "I rely heavily on temps to spot patterns in the accounts and for input on technology being developed that will eventually reconcile accounts automatically," she says. "It makes temps feel valued to contribute their opinions."

In the end, perhaps the best advice about how to manage temps comes from the workers themselves who've experienced all the insecurity, isolation and ostracism that the word "temporary" can carry with it. Bill Hardgrove, who survived three demotivating temporary assignments before landing a very rewarding long-term assignment with Pepsi-Cola Co. in Denver, suggests all companies treat their temps like Pepsi treats him.

"I was hired to monitor accounts receivable and manage collections on accounts worth several million dollars of business," he says. "From the beginning, the company knew what I was capable of. Managers read my resume, asked good questions, and they've given me increasing levels of responsibility. I have my own phone number and voicemail. I can take advantage of flexible scheduling if I have to go to an interview or doctor's appointment. I track my own time. And I go to meetings just like any other employee. In fact, the second day I was here I was invited to attend a companywide celebration that lasted all afternoon."

What does Hardgrove have to say to other companies struggling to motivate their cadre of temporary workers? "A temp isn't a chimpanzee," he says. "Many arrive with specialized skills they're eager to use." The trick is in learning what those skills are and how to create an environment in which temps want to put them to work for you.

Shari Caudron is a contributing editor at PERSONNEL JOURNAL.

Whatever You Do, Don't Treat a Temp Like a Temp

For the most part, temporary employees feel just like regular employees. They park in the same lot, report to the same supervisors, eat in the same lunchroom and have similar professional goals and capabilities as many other workers. For this reason, everything you do to motivate temps should be designed around not treating them like temps.

Tecora Rogers is a computer-support services manager at Frankel & Co., a Chicago-based promotions and marketing firm that, among other things, produces all the graphics used in McDonald's promotions. She uses agency temps on a daily basis in her department to put together a wide range of documents, from overhead slides to newsletters.

"From day one, I do everything I can to make sure they feel as though they belong and don't feel any less important than any other employees," she says. The list of things she does neatly sums up what all companies should be doing when it comes to motivating temporary workers. She:

1. Sends temps to the same company orientation as other employees.
2. Gives them the same autonomy as regular workers. "I tell them it doesn't matter how they get a job done, as long as it's done timely and well."
3. Asks them to participate in department meetings and shares all company memos with them. "I expect the same quality from them. To do that, they must have the same knowledge base. The more they know about the company, the better they perform."
4. Identifies high-potential people, and keeps them motivated by giving them higher levels of responsibility.
5. Demonstrates her level of trust by giving temps keys to the internal offices. (Only regular employees have keys to the outside doors, however.)
6. Invites temps to all company social functions.
7. Never, ever, refers to a temporary worker as *the temp*. Instead, she introduces the worker by his or her name. "In every sense of the word, temps are part of this department. I don't want to do anything to make them feel like they don't belong."

—SC

International Human Resource Management

The world is changing and getting smaller all the time. At the beginning of this century, the Wright brothers flew at Kitty Hawk, and some 25 years later, Charles Lindbergh flew from New York to Paris, alone, nonstop. In 1956 the first transoceanic telephone cable was laid, linking Europe and North America. And in 1969 the spacecraft *Eagle One* landed on the moon, and Neil Armstrong said, "One small step for man, one giant leap for mankind."

Indeed, the giant leaps have become smaller. The world has shrunk due to transportation and communication. Communication is virtually instantaneous—not as it was during the early part of the 1800s, when the Battle of New Orleans was fought several weeks after the peace treaty for the War of 1812 had been signed. For centuries, travel was limited to the speed of a horse or a ship. During the nineteenth century, however, speeds of 60 or even 100 miles an hour were achieved by railroad trains. Before the twentieth century was half over, the speed of sound had been exceeded, and in the 15 years that followed, humans circled the globe in 90 minutes. Less than 10 years later, human beings broke free from Earth's gravity and walked on the Moon. The exotic became common-

UNIT 7

place. Societies and cultures that had been remote from each other are now close, and people must now live with a diversity unknown in the past.

A shrinking world also means an expanding economy, a global economy, because producers and their raw materials and markets are now much closer to each other than they once were. People, and the organizations they represent, often do business all over the world, and their representatives are often members of foreign societies and cultures. Human resource management in just the domestic arena is an extremely difficult task; when the rest of the world is added to the effort, it becomes a monumental undertaking.

Workers in the United States are competing directly with workers in other parts of the world. Companies often hold out for the lowest bidder in a competition for wage rates. This often forces the wage rates down for higher-paying countries, while only marginally bringing up the wages of the lower-paying societies—a development that is bound to have a direct impact on the standard of living in all of the developed countries of the world.

As more firms become involved in world trade, they must begin to hire foreign workers. Some of these people are going to stay with the firm and become members of the corporate cadre. In the global economy, it is not uncommon for Indian employees to find themselves working for American or European multinational corporations in, say, Saudi Arabia. This presents the human resource professional with a problem of blending the three cultures into a successful mix. In this example, the ingredients are a well-educated Asian, working in a highly traditional Middle-Eastern society, for a representative of Western technology and culture. The situation involves three different sets of values, three different points of view, and three different sets of expectations on how people should act and be treated.

American industry does not have a monopoly on new ideas in human resources. Other societies have successfully dealt with many of the same problems. While U.S. firms certainly will not adopt every idea (lifetime employment as practiced in Japan seems the most obvious non-candidate), they can learn much from organizations outside the United States.

Once an employee has been assigned to a foreign post, he or she must learn how to interact with the local economy, culture, and customs. Because of the great diversity of the human race, it is, of course, impossible to know all cultures and languages. As a result, many firms have begun training the people they are sending abroad in the cultural and social practices of their destinations. Such training is useful not only for Americans interacting with foreign societies, but also for the non-U.S. nationals interacting with American culture.

Faster and better communication and transportation are leading to a more closely knit social, cultural, and economic world, where people's global abilities can make the difference between the success or failure of an organization.

Looking Ahead: Challenge Questions

How does the smaller world affect the practice of human resource management?

What are some considerations of transnational firms in the human resource area?

How would you expect organizations in the future to view the market for potential employees?

What can U.S. organizations do to help foreign employees and their families moving into the United States? Into another country?

JOBS FOR LIFE
WHY JAPAN WON'T GIVE THEM UP

When recession struck, Western doomsayers started writing obits for lifetime employment. But the system is stronger than ever. Here's why.

Eamonn Fingleton

NO ASPECT of Japan's remarkable economy has been so consistently underestimated as its employment system. Because the system's three main principles—lifetime employment, company unions, and seniority pay—flout free-market ideals, Westerners consider it self-evidently incapable in the long run of withstanding global competition from the "more efficient" hire-and-fire labor system of the U.S. and Europe. Thus, every time Japan's economy slows down, influential foreign observers can be counted on to write the system's obituary. Such reports reached a peak during the recession of the early 1990s, when Western publications, led by the *Wall Street Journal* and the *Economist*, vied with one another in printing comments from anonymous sources suggesting that lifetime employment was doomed.

The truth is precisely the opposite. Lifetime employment makes more sense now than ever, and the system's continuing strength is a key reason why Japan, with an unemployment rate of just 3% at its peak during the last recession, has been the one major industrial country to buck the global trend of ever-rising rates of structural unemployment.

Why have Western observers constantly been blind-sided on this point? In part, because they misunderstand a not-quite-what-it-seems system that contains several hidden elements of flexibility, as we shall see later. More important, though, is the widely held and mistaken belief that lifetime employment is deeply rooted in Japanese culture. This is pure myth. In fact, in the early days of Japan's industrialization, employers generally operated by hire-and-fire rules, and as a result suffered many of the same labor problems that we think of as peculiarly Western.

Although absenteeism is virtually unknown in Japan today, a century ago it was so common after payday that employers paid different workers on different days to stagger the disruption of output. In the 1920s, Japan suffered a series of bitter strikes in steel, shipbuilding, and mining, and labor turnover in some industries was as high as 100% a year. As recently as the late 1940s Japanese labor relations were notable for widespread confrontation, chaos, even violence.

The employment system in its present form has existed only since World War II. It was consciously invented as Japan's answer to a Western labor regime that Japanese business leaders and bureaucrats concluded was inappropriate for an advanced economy. One vital element was the formation of informal employment cartels in many industries. These restrict competition for labor by requiring rival employers to refrain from hiring from each other. This practice immediately explains one of the most puzzling aspects of the present-day system, Japanese workers' apparent lack of interest in changing jobs. The key reason is not loyalty, as Westerners often imagine, but lack of opportunities.

VIA THE Employment Security Law of 1947, government officials also won case-by-case powers to block employers from advertising for labor and from hiring any worker whose job change required a change of residence. While these comprehensive curbs strengthened the hand of employers in resisting demands for wage increases, they were balanced by a regulation making it illegal for employers to fire workers. Here stands revealed the reason why Japanese employers persistently refuse to break with the lifetime employment system: They provide job security not because they want to but because they have to.

Despite such legal coercion, however, Japan's employment system offers a host of advantages, many of which are not widely recognized in the West, and only one clear disadvantage—the fact that employers cannot cut labor costs as fast as their Western counterparts when demand turns down.

Consider Japanese corporations' well-deserved reputation for the speed with which they introduce productivity-enhancing new technologies. A big reason is that since Japanese workers enjoy lifetime job guarantees, they see no downside risk in helping employers improve productivity. In fact, they embrace new technology because they know it will enhance their company's future and their own jobs.

One notable example: automation. Japanese workers are delighted for robots to take over dirty, dangerous, and repetitive jobs such as pressing and painting. These machines are often treated as part of the corporate family, to the point where they are named after favorite female singers and movie stars. By contrast, American workers are naturally suspicious of such new labor-saving technology because they know from experience that U.S. employers often use it to cut jobs. It is not surprising, then, that with only half America's work force, Japan has three times as many robots in operation.

If a corporation is to innovate, it must also train its workers to handle ever more sophisticated tasks. Here again the Japanese labor system provides a vital advantage because companies can undertake expensive training programs confident that their enterprise will reap the rewards. By contrast, American employers increasingly consider training a dubious investment, since in the U.S. system trained workers are free to take their skills to rival employers. A recent survey found that U.S. corporations are only one-seventh as likely as their Japanese counterparts to provide new recruits with formal training.

Another major strength of Japan's labor system is the way it encourages corporations to invest in research and development. The key factor here is that thanks to the no-poaching rule, Japanese companies know that their expensively acquired R&D secrets will not leak to competitors via the job market. Such losses are a major problem for American corporations, particularly in the case of innovative new production techniques that are hard to patent but easy for a rival employer to acquire by headhunting a key employee. And since Japanese corporations can expect to keep more of the rewards from R&D than their American competitors, they naturally do more of it. As of the early 1990s, Japan's commercial R&D spending was running at about 3% of GDP, vs. just 2.2% for the U.S.

Now consider the high quality of Japanese management, which is rightly considered a major source of Japan's success. Why are Japanese managers so good? The answer lies mainly in the long-term accountability built into the lifetime employment system. A Japanese executive knows that the decisions he makes today will remain permanently on his record, and he may be asked to account for them many years from now. He cannot simply sweep problems under the carpet.

Japan's employment system also reinforces the labor peace that has generally prevailed in that country in the postwar era, despite the bizarre (at least to Westerners) ritual of the annual wage negotiation. Each year, in many Japanese industries, demonstrating workers fill the sky with red Marxist banners. Labor leaders use language so fiery they would risk arrest in many countries. Sometimes a mob of slogan-chanting workers will corner a top executive in his office and hold him hostage for hours.

If management still has not gotten the message, a union will have no hesitation in resorting to the ultimate weapon—the strike. But at this point things take a distinctly Japanese turn. A Japanese union's idea of a strike is a one-hour work stoppage timed for the lunch break: Workers indignantly put down their tools at noon and don't report back for work until one! If the union has planned things right, the "strike" will not have cost the company a single unit of lost production.

UNDERNEATH this theater of the absurd lies a great deal of uncommon common sense. Because the Japanese corporate system has been deliberately arranged to align workers' interests with their employers', a striking Japanese employee generally feels he's striking against his own long-term future. He knows the company will be left weakened and may not have the capital to stay the course in the technology race, which in turn means lower pay raises and less in the kitty for retirement benefits.

What has helped reinforce Japan's latter-day labor peace is that by the late 1950s workers began to recognize that the old them-and-us divide between management and workers had truly begun to disappear. Because workers had been given lifetime job security, they, more than shareholders, had become the real beneficiaries from an enterprise's existence.

Indeed, that stock enemy of American labor, the grasping chief executive officer who is "incentivized" by huge stock options, is unknown in Japan. Top Japanese executives are generally salaried employees like everyone else and do not have stock options—a fact that probably reflects an informal prohibition imposed by the Finance Ministry. Thus, they are under no pressure to make penny-wise, pound-foolish cuts in staffing to manipulate short-term profits. And when they call for pay restraint from the work force, as they do in bad times, they act in the role of the workers' leaders, not the workers' opponents.

> Japanese robots are treated as part of the corporate family, to the point where they are named after female singers.

Top executives in Japan are also modestly compensated by international standards. On an after-tax basis, a typical Japanese CEO is paid only about ten times the earnings of the most junior staff member and just four times the salary of middle-aged workers. The norm in corporate America is close to 100 times, a gap that Fujitsu Chairman Takuma Yamamoto has characterized as "absurd."

It is sometimes assumed that Japan's low executive compensation is simply a manifestation of the strong egalitarianism that runs through East Asian culture. In fact, this policy of keeping a tight lid on top salaries is the linchpin of a highly systematized salary structure in which managers and workers are generally paid and promoted according to seniority rather than competence. In the Japanese promotion race, merit becomes a decisive factor only in the case of senior positions that become available toward the middle or end of a manager's career.

This systemization extends beyond individual corporations. Major companies in the same industry typically pay nearly identical salary scales. In the auto industry, for example, the starting salary for graduates recruited in 1993 was $1,700 a month at all five of the biggest companies—Toyota, Honda, Nissan, Mitsubishi, and Mazda. Every Japanese corporation discloses its starting pay rate in public financial reference books, providing a useful signaling system for young graduates as they size up prospective employers.

All this saves Japanese companies the enormous transaction-cost burden of setting salaries on a person-by-person basis. And given the no-poaching rule of Japanese cartels, Japan's egalitarian salary system is easy to maintain.

The primary rationale of the salary system is to foster teamwork among managers and to eliminate a possible source of friction and jealousy between close colleagues. The system also makes it easy for top management to win workers' cooperation for postings in different departments, a factor that explains not only the speed with which Japanese companies can restructure themselves in a crisis but also the generally high level of communication and cooperation that exists between different departments.

Promotion by seniority rather than competence is to Western eyes one of the strangest aspects of the Japanese employment system. But it has its advantages. One is that it provides a powerful force for cooperation between the generations. Although Westerners argue that competent young people are blocked from realizing their potential in such a system, the truth is generally the opposite. Because senior managers are fully protected against being leapfrogged in the promotion race, they are much more likely than senior managers in the West to mentor their staff.

7. INTERNATIONAL HUMAN RESOURCE MANAGEMENT

PERHAPS the biggest misconception about Japanese labor economics in the West is that it gives workers a free ride for life. Nothing could be further from the truth. Since seniority pay is, in effect, a form of deferred pay, one of the most persuasive disciplinary tools in the Japanese system is early retirement. Generally, the poorer a person's long-run performance has been, the more likely he is to be asked to take retirement in his 50s or perhaps even in his late 40s. This is a much feared penalty because it means that he misses out on the best earning years of his life.

Officially, early retirees leave voluntarily, but in reality, most do so under threat of coercion. They know that if they resist, their employer has ways of making things uncomfortable. But if they go quietly, they can expect to get a significant termination payment and, more important, vital help in establishing a second career elsewhere. In most cases, large corporations find jobs for their early retirees in closely associated, if less prestigious, companies.

Peer pressure also serves to enforce labor discipline. Workers in a Japanese corporation generally function as part of a clearly identified team, and assignments are given to the team rather than to individuals. Persistent offenders of the team ethic risk ostracism by their peers. This pressure helps explain the apparently irrational behavior of Japanese workers in, say, not claiming their vacation entitlements: An individual worker feels obligated not to claim his rights if this would impair the group's chance of gaining a large salary bonus.

For the worst cases, companies find ways to harass a habitual shirker into resigning. Typically offenders are assigned to the *mado giwa zoku*—the tribe by the window. This denotes a special dunce's corner in which Japanese companies place certified pariahs. The term's significance derives from the fact that in Japan's huge open-plan offices, the further away one is from the center of the floor, the less important one's position or section.

The Japanese labor system contains several other hidden checks and balances without which it would not be an effective tool for employers. Corporate Japan's system of paying large twice-yearly salary bonuses, for instance, is an important shock absorber. In bad times these can be cut or even eliminated, allowing corporations to reduce annual pay levels by as much as 40%.

Another hidden element of flexibility: If a company can convince the authorities that without layoffs its whole future will be jeopardized, it can usually gain exemption from the no-layoff law. Ordinarily this loophole is available only to small employers, which means that companies lower down in the *keiretsu* system operate with employment practices closer to American-style hire-and-fire. Thus, big employers at the top of the *keiretsu* can count on their suppliers' labor flexibility as a swing factor in maintaining their group's viability in tough times.

> **Firing is rare and expensive: Staffers at Japan Airlines were paid as much as $600,000 each to leave.**

A final nuance of the system is that many corporations maintain a large pool of low-grade, mainly white-collar workers who are specifically denied employment security under a legal loophole providing for "temporary" employment. Although in practice such workers are rarely fired, the fact that they can be affords corporate planners a further insurance policy against bad economic conditions.

Such safety valves apart, Japan's labor system aims to provide stable long-term employment for virtually all higher-grade workers. It is backed by tough laws requiring employers to pay significant compensation to any permanent staff member who is involuntarily terminated. The strength of these laws can be gauged from the fact that some staffers at Japan Airlines recently were paid as much as $600,000 each to leave.

Perhaps the most ingenious aspect of Japanese labor economics is the extent to which the main elements of it are mutually reinforcing. The lifetime employment system, for instance, bolsters the company union system. Because employees don't expect to be fired, they have no need for industrywide unions and are content to entrust their negotiating power to company unions.

Similarly, the employment cartels' requirement that companies not hire from each other is a hidden support for the lifetime employment system: It protects employers against the loss of their most talented and productive workers. By contrast, in the modern American employment system, where aggressive employers are allowed to hire away their rivals' best people, any company that offers career-long employment security finds its payroll gradually silts up with subpar performers.

The most profound self-reinforcing effect of the Japanese labor system is the way that lifetime employment helps stabilize the economy in times of recession. To an individual employer, the no-firing rule may seem undesirable but, from the nation's point of view, the rule pays off in damping the downswing in the business cycle. In the Western system, by contrast, workers fired in a recession necessarily cut back their consumption, which throws other workers out of a job and thus further burdens the national welfare system. Japanese planners believe, not unreasonably, that workers contribute more to national output if they are in jobs rather than in dole queues.

When we add up all the fine print, a picture emerges of a highly organized and quite self-sustaining employment system—a system that is the antithesis of the cultural hangover it has long been portrayed as in the West. Jobs for life may be on the way out elsewhere in the industrialized world. But in Japan, at least, they are a central part of a labor system with a bright and stable future.

Managing Human Resources in Mexico: A Cultural Understanding

Randall S. Schuler, Susan E. Jackson, Ellen Jackofsky, and John W. Slocum, Jr.

Already, the North American Free Trade Agreement (NAFTA) appears to be a big hit. Exports are surging and U.S. job loss appears to be minimal. NAFTA's proponents indicate that the agreement should ease U.S. world trade deficits by making American goods more attractive. And as Mexico strives to modernize its businesses, U.S. investments will keep pouring into the country to help with the process. A survey of more than 1,000 senior executives by KPMG Peat Marwick found that 25 percent have formed alliances with Mexican companies, while 40 percent plan to recruit or have already hired people fluent in Spanish to help them enter the Mexican market.

As U.S. firms set up operations in Mexico, they are confronted with the same challenge as in the United States: How can they most effectively manage their human resources—the people upon whom they depend for success? They realize that being competitive takes more than low cost; it also requires high quality. Because a key ingredient in producing high-quality goods is a company's human resources, mismanaging these resources could result in: (1) a loss of skilled workers; (2) an increase in wages; (3) a reluctance to train new workers; (4) a consequential decline in quality; and (5) an eventual loss of competitive position.

All this can be avoided by an informed approach to managing human resources in Mexico. Such an approach is based on an understanding of the cultural differences between Mexico and the United States. Although it does not provide all the answers, it can maximize the potential benefits resulting from an understanding between the two countries. It can also offer an explanation for what exists in Mexico today and for what may or may not work as the competition for skilled human resources heats up.

CULTURAL VALUES

The differences between Mexican and American human resource management practices can be traced partly to the underlying differences in values between the two countries. In his seminal work on cultural values, Geert Hofstede proposed a framework to study the impact of societal culture on employees. This framework, widely accepted and used by managers to understand differences between cultures, consists of four cultural dimensions along which societies can be classified:

Power Distance: the degree to which unequal distribution of power is accepted (such as between manager and workers).

Individualism: the degree to which individual decision making is valued.

Uncertainty Avoidance: the degree to which uncertainty is tolerated (such as regarding job security or work role behaviors).

Masculinity: the degree to which society values assertiveness, performance, ambition, achievement, and material possessions.

More than 50 countries have been classified as being low, medium, or high along these four cultural dimensions. Descriptions of these extremes are provided in **Figure 1**. The results

> *Close neighbors that they are, Mexico and the United States must still appreciate their cultural differences when it comes to managing workers.*

7. INTERNATIONAL HUMAN RESOURCE MANAGEMENT

Figure 1
Characteristic Extremes of the Four Cultural Dimensions

POWER DISTANCE	
High	*Low*
• Focus on order	• Focus on equity, fairness
• Well-defined, stable hierarchies	• Flat organizations
• Managers are gods, but paternal	• Democratic managers, use of exchange relations
• Centralized decision making	

INDIVIDUALISM	
High	*Low*
• Emphasis on the person	• Emphasis on the group
• Creative person valued	• Creative person disruptive
• Initiative valued	• Conformity valued

UNCERTAINTY AVOIDANCE	
High	*Low*
• Focus on security	• Open to the unknown
• Uncomfortable with risk	• Risk equals opportunity
• Defined roles	• Flexible roles
• Focus on information sharing	• Often quick decisions
• Focus on trust	
• Focus on rules (often informal)	

MASCULINITY	
High	*Low*
• Clear sex roles: men dominant	• Flexible sex roles: "fuzzy"
• Survival requires aggressiveness	• Focus on quality of life, nurturing, the environment
• High performers receive high monetary rewards	• High performers receive recognition

Source: Geert Hofstede, "Cultural Constraints in Management Theories," *Academy of Management Executive,* 7 (1993): 81-94.

Figure 2
Importance of Human Resource Practices: United States versus Mexico

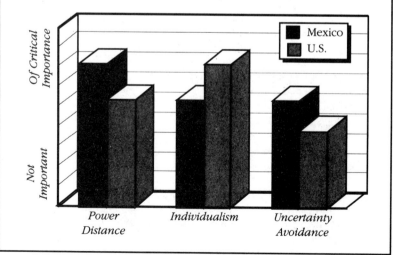

comparing the United States and Mexico show minimal differences in masculinity, but significant differences in power distance, individualism, and uncertainty avoidance:

	U.S.	Mexico
Power Distance	40	81
Individualism	91	30
Uncertainty Avoidance	46	82
Masculinity	62	69

Thus, in comparison with the U.S., Mexico's culture is more group- or family-oriented, places more importance on well-defined power and authority structures in organizations, and prefers more certainty and predictability. An analysis of managerial practices in the U.S. and Mexico implies substantial differences in these three cultural dimensions. Applying these differences to managing human resources can be instrumental for U.S. firms desiring to operate in Mexico as effectively as possible with both expatriates and local country nationals on the payroll.

Because our focus is on aiding U.S. firms that do business in Mexico and employ Mexican workers, the general descriptions provided below are based on the results of several case studies of large U.S. firms operating in Mexico. The studies are supplemented by a recent survey of human resource managers in the two countries. These managers were asked to describe specific practices in their organizations, such as benefits, career planning, decision-making, and socialization tactics, and relate which practices would be most applicable and important for a firm to be competitive as it moves forward. Not surprisingly, their comments are rather consistent with the details of the four dimensions shown in Figure 1. As seen in **Figure 2**, the evaluation of these human resource practices are in line with Hofstede's findings. Details of the study are provided in **Figure 3**.

POWER DISTANCE

The degree to which the unequal distribution of power is accepted, such as that between manager and workers, is considerably higher in Mexico than in the United States. It can be measured in terms of hierarchical structures, formal or informal relations between them, and the personalization of rules and regulations.

Hierarchy

Mexican organizations reflect the hierarchical structures of church and government. That is, most firms have a bureaucratic structure with power vested at the top. The director general or the *presidente* of the firm has often achieved that position through favors and friendships nurtured over years. Senior managers reporting to the director general are expected to show him proper respect, and usually have the authority to make decisions pertaining to their division.

Employees below these levels have little authority. Because of this, most employees desire that the authority over them be wielded in a kind and sensitive manner. Mexican employees appreciate managers who show a true personal interest and communicate respect for them. If they are told what to do, they try hard to do it. Power is based on trust between worker and supervisor that flows from the top down. Through this paternalistic management system, good labor and community relations are established. In Mexico, workers are rewarded for being loyal and following directions from the person in charge.

Formality

Mexicans tend to prefer a more distant relationship between workers and managers than what is typically found in a society that ranks low on power distance, such as the United States. In low-power-distance societies, status differences between workers and managers are minimized. In walking through Mexican manufacturing plants and construction sites, one rarely sees a Mexican manager getting his hands dirty. Instead, supervisors are told what to do, then pass along these instructions to workers. In contrast, American managers can often be seen walking through the plant, informally chatting with workers and getting their hands dirty when appropriate. Similarly, Mexican managers are typically attired in business suits that reflect their status in the organization, whereas in many U.S. plants managers wear jeans and sport shirts and "look" like workers.

Mexican workers expect managers to keep their distance rather than to be close, and to be formal rather than informal. Calling workers by their first names is not common in Mexico because it would violate status differences between managers and workers. Elderly or eminent people in Mexican organizations are usually referred to as Don and Doña. Nevertheless, despite this need for distance and formality, Mexicans value working conditions in which supervisors are understanding. They look up to bosses who treat them in a warm but dignified manner. Managers who occasionally appear in the company cafeteria, walk through the shop floor, and mingle with them on May Day (Mexican Labor Day) are respected by the workers.

Personalization

In contrast to the people in the U.S., people in Mexico take a more casual approach to rules and regulations. Rules tend to be a loosely applied set of guidelines that indicate what ought to be done, but not what necessarily *is* done. For example, stop signs and no-parking signs are routinely ignored, and one-way streets have traffic in both directions. Few Mexican drivers, it seems, feel obliged to follow "normal" traffic laws. Likewise, Mexican workers may permit themselves to be guided by their own "inner clock" rather than the "clock on the wall." Consequently, many U.S. firms provide buses to pick up workers at various locations so as to avoid uncertain arrival times as well as complications due to traffic problems.

In Mexican organizations, formal rules and regulations are not adhered to unless someone of authority is present. Managers are more likely to be obeyed than a rule because of who they are and the authority they exercise. Without a strong emotional bond between people, rules tend to be ignored. On the other hand, U.S. managers believe that rules establish a system of justice that emphasizes fairness, and thus should be applied impersonally.

Figure 3
HR Survey

To explore the differences between U.S. and Mexican firms, we conducted secondary analyses on data obtained as part of a larger international survey conducted in 1991. This was a worldwide study of human resource policies and practices conducted by IBM and Towers Perrin. The survey data that form the basis of the analysis in this article have been published in *Priorities for Competitive Advantage: A Worldwide Human Resources Study* (IBM/Towers Perrin, 1992). In developing the survey questionnaire, some of the authors of this article were invited to incorporate policies and practices and then write survey items that represented the academic and practitioner research and literature through 1990. These items were reviewed for representation and agreement by a series of other academics and practitioners identified by the IBM Corporation.

A major topic addressed in one section of the questionnaire was "human resource concepts and practices for gaining competitive advantage." In this section, respondents were asked to indicate the degree of importance they attached to each time in their firm's attempt to gain competitive advantage through human resource policies and practices. They indicated this for the current year (1991) and for the year 2000. For the purposes of this study, we have analyzed the data for the year 2000. This allows us to consider the extent to which future plans and expectations within the firms surveyed are likely to converge.

The specific firms included were those identified jointly by IBM and Towers Perrin as being the most effective in highly competitive environments in each of several countries. Details of the sample, though the names of firms are anonymous, are provided by Towers Perrin (1992). The respondents included the chief operating officers and the senior human resource officers. In total, there were 67 respondents from Mexico and 1,174 from the United States. The several case studies were conducted by Gillian Flynn. The companies used in those case studies are cited in this article. The original study is found in "HR in Mexico: What You Should Know," *Personnel Journal*, August 1994, pp. 34–44.

Suggestions for Managers

Results of our study corroborated the reality of status differences in managing human resources. We found that tactics promoting equality, employee involvement in decision making, open communication channels, and employee ownership were generally not regarded as necessary or desirable for gaining a competitive advantage in Mexico. Thus, given that Mexican society is high in power distance, we suggest that U.S. firms that use such practices should modify them in working with the Mexican culture. In other words, it is probably unnecessary for senior Mexican managers to involve employees in decision making. A manager should rarely explain why something is to be done, lest workers perceive this as a sign of weakness. Communication channels should follow the hierarchical structure of the organization.

We also found that as firms seek to manage the most out of workers, they are turning their attentions to developing employees with multiple skills that cross functional departments. In cultures with high power distance, such as Mexico, employees rely on a strong hierarchical structure, with those in power demonstrating care and concern for their subordinates. Power flows from the top down, so whatever a supervisor tells a worker to do has been authorized by his boss. Mexican employees expect management to be paternalistic and watch out for them, rather than being dictatorial. Again, unless there is a strong emotional force or bond, employees in Mexican plants tend not to obey rules and regulations. The manager's ability to create such bonding is instrumental in motivating and directing the career paths of subordinates.

> "In cultures with high power distance, such as Mexico, employees rely on a strong hierarchical structure, with those in power demonstrating care and concern for their subordinates."

INDIVIDUALISM

Individualism has come to be seen as practically the defining characteristic of American society. Not so in Mexico; the degree to which individual decision making is valued is much lower. This can be seen in terms of caring for workers and their families, establishing workplace harmony, and exhibiting paternalism toward employees.

Family and Responsibility to Care

Workers generally do not place high priority on organizations in which self-determination is encouraged. Employers have significant responsibility for the conduct and improvement of workers' lives in the Mexican organization. Having a job is viewed as a social right. In other words, Mexicans grow up assuming that society owes them a job. Consequently, having a job is far more than just an exchange of money for labor.

Mexican law and history reflect the Mexican view that the employer has a moral and family responsibility for all employees, even when there is a union. The Mexican employee is not just working for a paycheck. Workers tend to expect to be treated as the "extended family" of the boss, and to receive a wider range of services and benefits than what is provided north of the border. Examples of these benefits include food baskets and medical attention for themselves and their families (apart from social security). Medical benefits are not considered "an extra" or discretionary; to the Mexican worker, they simply fulfill the employer's role and responsibilities.

Because the cost of newspapers makes help wanted advertisements useless, recruitment is done primarily by approaching people and asking them to apply. So it is common to find many family members working at the same plant. Another significant aspect of employee retention and recruitment involves the need for workers to feel they are part of the operation. The plant will be populated by people oriented to traditional Mexican values and social structure. To achieve this, employers make certain to celebrate numerous holidays, and it is common for companies to throw parties for a variety of events.

Corresponding to this practice is the Mexican view that employees have a reciprocal obligation to be loyal, work hard, and be willing to do whatever is requested of them. American managers who accept the Mexican sense that a job is more than a paycheck and who try to fulfill their part of the "bargain" can reap the benefits of employee loyalty, including a willingness to come to work every day and to work conscientiously.

Harmony

Just like a family that encourages its members to work together by doing their share according to their roles, the Mexican organization encourages and values harmony, rather than conflict. Compared to the United States, there is a low tolerance for adversarial relations in Mexican organizations. This even permeates union/management relations. Under Mexican labor law, union and management both strive to maintain a posture whereby the union is accountable to the workers while management directs the day-to-day business affairs of the firm. Management that directly addresses the workers is welcomed by the unions as a way to foster good relations and minimize grievances. The union disciplines workers who violate the rules; managers are expected to discipline supervisors.

Mexican employees value peaceful relations between union and management. Though such relations could cause American workers to feel they are being coopted by management, in the case of Mexico harmonious relations are seen as normal. Employees are selected because they have demonstrated an ability to get along with others and work cooperatively with those in authority. Obedience and respect are in contrast to the value American workers place on independence and confrontation. Meetings are forums for people to receive orders, not for discussion and debate.

This characteristic of harmony affects the compensation system as well. Mexican workers prefer to receive compensation as soon as possible after work is completed. Therefore, *daily* incentive systems with automatic payouts for exceeding production quotas, as well as monthly attendance quotas, can be used effectively to motivate workers to higher levels of production.

These incentive pay programs, however, need to be used with care because they may ruffle a few feathers in Mexico, especially among workers. Why? Workers receiving more pay could be viewed as having connections to the higher echelons. Variable pay-for-performance creates social distance among employees. "It's much more important for a Mexican person to have a congenial working environment than it is to make more money," says Alejandro Palma, intercultural business specialist for Clarke Consulting Group. "There have been cases where very good workers, ones who have performed well and received [monetary] recognition for that, have left the company because they felt ostracized by their co-workers."

Instead, Palma suggests other reward strategies, such as making the outstanding worker a team leader. This plays into their desire for respect without isolating individual workers. Says Palma, "Employees-of-the-month programs—where it's on a rotating basis, not permanent like salary compensation—seem to be OK, because everyone has a chance." Other incentives include family days or other activities that include workers' relatives.

The need to keep wages low to maintain a competitive edge leads many employers to add small benefits, such as food baskets, free bus service, and free meals for the workers. These benefits, which are not considered wages, are given personally to the worker. One reason for this system is that under Mexican labor law, a worker's salary cannot be reduced when his job is downgraded. Because these bonuses are paid based on performance, they do not fall under the law and may be withdrawn when the worker's performance suffers. Benefits such as offices, cars, and the like are offered only to managers and accentuate the differences between levels in the managerial hierarchy.

Paternalism

In the United States and other individualistic cultures, people are expected to take care of themselves, and are rewarded for being masters of their own fate. People frequently change jobs and organizations in an effort to improve themselves. Most employees believe that their corporation is no longer responsible for their welfare and that they must manage their career as best they can. Similarly, organizations often downsize or reorganize in an attempt to improve their cost position with little or no regard for the human consequences. There is a sense of independence between the worker and the organization. At times, this leads to adversarial relations.

> "Mexican companies have a significant responsibility under Mexican labor law for the life, health, and dignity of their workers."

In contrast, as mentioned earlier, Mexican companies have a significant responsibility under Mexican labor law for the life, health, and dignity of their workers. Organizations take on a paternalistic obligation to their workers. Managers tend to ignore workers who criticize others or who take their complaints to the union because these workers do not exhibit the spirit of cooperation that Mexican society rewards. Mexican workers rally around emotionally charged management speeches that extol them to improve their group's performance rather than management programs that stress competition with others.

Paternalism also influences the labor relations system. The Mexican Federal Labor Law governs all labor matters, and the state labor boards, made up of representatives from the government, unions, and management, oversee the enforcement of the law. After hiring, an employer has 28 days to evaluate the employee's work ethics. After that period, the employer is expected to assume responsibility for the worker; job security is granted and termination becomes expensive. For example, an employer that decides to fire a worker who has been with the company for six months could be charged for an additional six weeks, plus vacation pay and bonuses. Workers may be dismissed only for causes specifically set out in the Mexican Federal Labor Law. These include falsifying employment documents and committing dishonest or violent acts during working hours. Therefore, it is important to screen employees before hiring.

UNCERTAINTY AVOIDANCE

The third cultural value to be considered here, uncertainty avoidance, refers to the extent to which people of a society feel threatened by unstable and ambiguous situations and try to avoid them. In Mexico, a high uncertainty avoidance society, workers typically desire close supervision rather than being left alone. They try hard to follow directions and do what they are being asked to do.

Compensation systems emphasize consistency and certainty, and they are based on rules and regulations. Thus, companies attempting to use incentive pay need to be careful. Arturo Fisher, a consultant for Hewitt Associates who specializes in Latin America, knows of pay plans that have worked, but he expresses concern at their use. "[Mexicans] are more oriented to guaranteed situations, guaranteed pay," says Fisher. "So, pay at risk is OK, but you have to communicate it a little bit more." Workers have assigned roles and are rewarded for following them efficiently. Job security is also highly valued. In low uncertainty avoidance cultures, such as the U.S., managers' and workers' tasks are less structured. Employees are encouraged to take risks and tend to rely more heavily on their own initiative and ingenuity to get things done.

In our study, we found that staffing practices are ways in which companies can influence the amount of uncertainty in the organization. Managers in Mexico tend to follow consistent, though not necessarily equitable, recruiting and training practices. Employees who have long tenure in the system are prized because they have embraced the values of the organization and have demonstrated that they can uphold its traditions.

Success in managing people across the Mexican border is a matter of being able to translate an understanding of relevant cultural differences into action. The job of the human resource manager is not only to understand these differences, but to adjust the relationship between the organization and its workers to be in line with the cultural values of Mexico. It should then be more naturally possible for managerial actions to be in line with the beliefs of that society. From this report, the context of work in Mexico versus common U.S. managerial practices should take into account the differences in the strengths of hierarchical relationships and risk avoidance as well as the collective nature of Mexican society.

Certainly Mexico will continue to become a more important trading partner for the United States in the twenty-first century. Most assuredly it will also continue to be a key location for U.S. companies setting up shop. But as in the United States, doing business effectively involves using all resources wisely. And the most important of these resources is the people—the human assets.

In managing human assets effectively, it pays to "think globally, but act locally." U.S. firms operating abroad have mostly paid attention to local conditions, particularly laws and regulations. These tend to be more obvious, explicit features of doing business in another country. Less obvious and less explicit are the social customs and patterns of behavior that are acceptable to the population. The experiences of many firms, such as Motorola, Nabisco, Ford, General Electric, and General Motors, in selecting, motivating, training, and retaining employees in Mexico indicates that these less obvious and less explicit aspects of a country are neither unimportant in doing business effectively nor the same as in the United States. Their experiences are certainly consistent with the researchers who have argued for years that it is important to heed the admonition, "When in Rome, do as the Romans do."

It might be tempting to suggest that differences between Mexico and the United States are due more to legal and economic factors than to culture. But those studying cultures might suggest that legal and economic differences are preceded by cultural differences. Economics surely have an impact on the management of human resources, particularly through compensation levels, but this is also true when one compares compensation levels in Kentucky versus New York. Many managers are already factoring in some aspects of country characteristics when managing human resource assets. What we are suggesting is that companies extend this factoring to include aspects of national culture. We hope that some of our review has shed light on exactly how the cultural differences of Mexico and the United States affect the management of human resources in these two important countries.

This article, however, is by no means exhaustive. Considering all the topics and activities in human resource practices, such as staffing, appraising, training/leadership, and work design, the existing data and that from our study permitted us to review and describe only some of them. Using Hofstede's cultural classification, however, we could offer some further suggestions and propositions that the manager could consider in crafting a package of human resource management practices to use in setting up operations in Mexico.

By way of review, Mexico is high on power distance, low on individualism, high on uncertainty avoidance, and high on masculinity; and the United States is low on power distance, high on individualism, low on uncertainty avoidance, and high on masculinity. The reader, however, is justified in saying that things could—indeed do—change. The reader is also justified in saying that even within the United States there are cultural differences that also affect how human resources are managed. This of course confirms our major premise: that a systematic understanding of the relationship between dimensions of culture and consistent ways of managing human resources can be used to one's advantage in crafting a set of human resource practices.

Randall S. Schuler and **Susan E. Jackson** are professors of management at the Stern School of Business, New York University, in New York City. **Ellen Jackofsky** is an associate professor of organizational behavior and an associate provost of academic affairs at the Cox School of Business at Southern Methodist University, Dallas, Texas, where **John W. Slocum, Jr.** is the O'Paul Corley Professor of Management.

Dealing with Diversity: The Coming Challenge to American Business

Kenneth J. Doka

In 1965, the basis for a profound demographic change occurred in the United States, largely unrecognized and unheralded at the time. The Immigration Act of 1965 was President Johnson's attempt to fulfill a campaign pledge of John F. Kennedy in the critical Midwest belt: to eliminate the quota system for immigration that had favored Northern and Western Europeans. In the first stage of the act, from 1965 to 1967, the unfilled quotas of these Western European nations were used to augment the quotas of Eastern European nations. After 1968, however, quotas were abolished with the proviso that no one country should exceed 10 percent of the total immigration to the United States.

The impact of this change in immigration law was profound. Challenging 200 years of immigration trends, a significant number of migrants began to come, not from Europe, but from Asia, South America, the Caribbean, and Africa. Leading to an unparalleled diversity in American life, this immigration shift is affecting our society deeply as we enter the next century. The nonwhite population has surged to one-fifth of all Americans. And even within these racial groupings, there is far greater differentiation. For example, African-Americans may include American-born blacks, those from diverse Caribbean cultures, and more recent migrants from Africa.

Recent years have seen increasing recognition that traits of cultural groups persist for generations. Social scientists have long recognized that the United States is much more than a melting pot in which all ethnic groups eventually mix their characteristics and traits into one. Rather, it is better described as a "salad bowl" or a "grand mosaic," in which each group maintains significant aspects of identity.

This increasing diversity will continue to affect and shape all institutions within the United States. Already, educational institutions—from elementary schools to universities—are struggling with the issue of how to accommodate an increasingly culturally diverse student body and staff. But American business will also be drastically affected. First, this increasing diversity will open new domestic markets for a wide variety of goods and services. Second, it will create new challenges for businesses in managing a diverse work force and effectively seeking diverse consumers. Third, it can provide American corporations with a special edge in competing in the global marketplace—a marketplace that provides unique challenges and vast opportunities to U.S. businesses.

> *Tending to the cultural differences in one's own back yard will help bear fruit in the competitive global marketplace.*

EMERGING MULTICULTURAL MARKETS

Although pasta was made in the United States even before the American Revolution, it became far more common in the 1880s as the rate of Italian immigration increased. Originally marketed as an ethnic food in distinct Italian markets by such immigrants as Ronzoni, pasta became a food that transcended its ethnic roots. Now the average American consumes more than ten pounds of pasta per year. In some surveys, Americans are more likely to eat pasta at any given meal than any other food.

48. Dealing with Diversity

The popularity of pasta illustrates how ethnic foods become assimilated into American cuisine. Originally developed and produced for a distinctly ethnic market, they are gradually introduced into the mainstream, sometimes changing culinary accents to adapt to more general tastes. Once the market broadens, a wide variety of competitors may produce the product. Naturally, a critical mass within the ethnic group is necessary before a product can be marketed.

Pasta is only one of the foods—albeit one of the most popular—that have managed that shift from an ethnic specialty to a cultural universal. Potatoes, pita bread, and frankfurters, to name a few, have all crossed the invisible ethnic barrier to become standard American fare. Other ethnic foods, such as bulgar wheat, sesame seed paste, and chick peas, have migrated from their original Middle Eastern specialty stores to the shelves of health food stores and the health sections—at least—of supermarkets. In a similar way, ethnic restaurants, again often begun by serving within their own cultural groups, have also developed wide appeal for their cuisines. Italian and Chinese restaurants are ubiquitous presences in towns and shopping malls throughout the country.

> "Ethnic entrepreneurs are well advised to recognize the emerging opportunities sustained by a critical mass within their ethnic group."

As the nation becomes even more diverse and a wider array of ethnic groups are able to support their own cultural specialties, more and more Americans are being exposed to a wider variety of food, cuisines, products, styles, and activities. Some of these will cross that barrier from being simply an ethnic product or activity and will reach a wider market, perhaps as a brief fad or fashion, perhaps in a more sustained way.

This may alter the U.S. in many ways, not just in cuisine. For example, soccer was once a sport limited to newer European immigrants, not yet assimilated into "American" mainstream sports. Now it is being played throughout the nation. Quite possibly, as more and more young Americans play soccer and are exposed to international competition, professional soccer will one day be the equal of professional football, basketball, or baseball.

Similarly, as Mexican and Central American migration increases, a number of markets are emerging. First, there is a growing market for the products used by these ethnic groups. For example, tortillas, a staple of the Mexican diet, are becoming increasingly popular throughout the United States. Second, these tastes are also influencing the American palate. Tacos and salsa are rapidly gaining in popularity as a classic party snack. Third, as millions of Americans gain broad exposure to such Mexican-influenced food, a market begins to grow for more authentic cuisine. And as immigrants become more established and create that critical ethnic mass in a given community, they are positioned to take advantage of that market. Mexican food is now joining Chinese and Italian food as a common popular choice throughout the country.

As a diverse America creates new demands for a wide variety of products, ethnic entrepreneurs are well advised to recognize the emerging opportunities sustained by a critical mass within their ethnic group. There may be increased opportunities as their products become recognized and assimilated into the larger population. If and when that happens, these entrepreneurs may face four challenges:

1. Their product may need to be modified to cross over into a larger market, with the resulting risk of the product losing part of its original customer base.

2. There may be temptations to expand prematurely. Whereas Italian foods have shown a consistent and stable growth, other products have been more temporary—a fad or fashion that experienced only a moment of popularity. Nehru jackets, for example, loosely based on an East Indian style, had only a brief moment of glory in the 1960s.

3. If the market does prove stable and profitable, it is likely to attract a wide range of corporate competitors. For example, Mission Foods, a Mexican company based in Los Angeles, has edged out other ethnic-based companies to sell the largest amount of tortillas in America—more than 230 million in 1991. Yet as the market has grown, it has attracted other competition. The second largest tortilla maker is now Tyson Foods.

4. If ethnic entrepreneurs are too slow to recognize their potential, others will. Although Emanuele Ronzoni and Giovanni Buitoni parlayed ethnic businesses into major enterprises, it was another Italian, Francesco Paolucci, who founded Chun King, the first mass producer of Chinese food.

SERVING AND MANAGING DIVERSITY

In 1990, an altercation began in a Korean-owned grocery store in Brooklyn, New York that precipitated a neighborhood boycott of that store and resounded a few years later as an issue in the 1993 New York City mayoral campaign. Though the details of the encounter between a Korean-born grocer and his Caribbean-born customers are still in dispute, it is clear that the conflict was culturally based.

7. INTERNATIONAL HUMAN RESOURCE MANAGEMENT

To Koreans, it is polite to avert one's eyes from a customer. A customer must never be physically touched, even in making change. And there is no bargaining over prices. But to Caribbeans, storekeepers are expected to barter and banter, and relationships are warm and personal. So the Korean storekeeper in Brooklyn perceived the Caribbean customers as loud and threatening, while the customers saw the storekeeper's behavior as cold, condescending, and arrogant.

This incident illustrates how difficult it can be to serve customers from different cultures. Communication is based on a common set of shared verbal symbols that constitute language, para-verbal actions (tone, volume) and nonverbal behaviors (body language). When individuals have different understandings of these behaviors, along with different norms about the conduct of business, it is easy to misperceive another's message.

It is often said that culture hides from those who know it best. One can often accept one's own cultural construction of reality as *the* reality. The fact that others have different norms and behaviors is not even considered, especially in the common transactions of everyday business.

Sometimes this inability to understand other cultural norms can lead to open conflict. In the 1992 riots following the Rodney King case, Korean-owned stores were the primary targets. Two factors seem to have exacerbated the conflict. First, different cultural norms about treating customers, discussed earlier, generated resentment. Second, there is a strong norm in the African-American community that local businesses ought to support their community. The Koreans' family-centered norms meant that Korean merchants tended to hire family members and rarely contributed to local charities.

Such resentment occurs not only between customers, but in competition and with other merchants. When I was growing up in Astoria, New York, many of the local merchants resented the new Greek store owners, complaining that they lacked community spirit because they failed to join local merchant associations or contribute to common causes such as seasonal displays. The newer Greek merchants simply did not understand these norms. As they assimilated into the community, however, they began to take active roles in local associations. It is now these second-generation merchants that level similar complaints against more recent Asian immigrant merchants.

These conflicts can also become serious. Many merchants may deeply resent cultures that have a strong family work ethic, because it gives those families a strong competitive edge. If family employees work for less than minimum wage and for extended hours, the competitive playing field is no longer level.

The difficulties of intercultural communication and the disparity of norms about work also affect the corporate level. Managing a diverse work force has become a critical management skill. Corporations that can maintain such a work force in a supportive environment can be spared the trauma and costs of bias and discrimination lawsuits. But there is an even more important incentive. Corporations that encourage and nurture diversity among their employees are far better positioned in both differentiated domestic and global markets. These firms will gain two critical advantages. First, they will have an inside track on understanding the needs and opportunities presented by other cultural groups. Second, they will have cultivated sensitivities that will more successfully market to other groups.

Managing a diverse work force means that managers need to understand the culture(s) and perspectives of their employees and consumers. For example, in many cultures, it is inappropriate for people to herald their own attributes or advance their own interests. Career ladders that expect employees to apply for advancement may mean that members of such a culture are under-represented in management and supervisory positions. In other cultures, members may be subservient to authority, finding it difficult to ask for help. Or a person may be reluctant to take on additional authority or initiative without specific direction. Knowing the attributes of another culture—attitudes toward authority and responsibility, communicative styles, and so on—can facilitate effective interaction.

> "Corporations that encourage and nurture diversity among their employees are far better positioned in both differentiated domestic and global markets."

Of course, this knowledge must always be balanced by a strong sense of the individual. People are always different. Culture itself is a continuum. Some people strongly reflect cultural values, while others are more assimilated. Diverse traditions can exist within a larger culture. Thus, rather than simply perpetuating stereotypes, cultural understanding should instill a sensitivity that underlies dialogue. This is the second critical attribute of the effective multicultural manager: becoming an effective and sensitive communicator able to understand and transcend employees' cultural background. Effective managers can interpret their own and their employees' cultures to motivate and direct workers in fulfilling organizational and personal goals.

Marketing strategies must also be adapted to increasingly diverse consumers. Major corporations, such as Procter & Gamble, have already recognized the advantage in addressing specific ethnic groups, such as Latinos or Asians, in their own media and their own language. This in turn has opened windows of opportunity for ethnic-oriented marketing and advertising agencies that can help manufacturers or mainstream advertising agencies avoid language gaffes and craft ads in culturally appropriate ways. At the same time, it has helped fulfill two other functions: (1) providing additional channels of opportunity and mobility for members of ethnic minorities, and (2) honing a corporation's sensitivities and cultural skills for competing in the global marketplace.

The ability of companies to transcend these cultural differences will be critical to maintaining not just profits, but social unity. As the Korean grocery boycott in Brooklyn showed, incidences that flare can have wide repercussions that damage intergroup relationships. In addition, perceptions that economic opportunity exists for all members of society can ease feelings of discrimination and hopelessness and encourage minority entrepreneurs.

CULTURAL SENSITIVITY IN THE INTERNATIONAL MARKET

There has been—and in many places still is—a persistent myth of the "ugly American" that emphasizes the cultural insensitivity of U.S. business people. American businesses may have considerable work to do as they compete in the global marketplace. Fewer Americans have considerable facility with foreign languages compared to other industrial nations. Training is always necessary in the nuances of other cultures. In some cases, American business laws and practices, such as laws forbidding bribes, may place American firms at a competitive disadvantage in some countries. U.S. resistance to metric measurement also limits competitiveness.

For the United States to compete effectively in the expanding global marketplace, American firms will need to learn much about the foreign people and places they will be dealing with. Culture will affect all business functions, from production to marketing to human resource management. Advertising will be affected by a culture's sense of aesthetics. Picturing a man and woman in a gentle embrace, for example, may be totally unacceptable in certain cultures. Nonverbal and paraverbal behaviors will also differ. In *The Silent Language* (1959), Edward Hall pointed out how American attitudes toward time are not consistently held in other cultures. Whereas Americans value promptness and read disrespect in lateness, other cultures may not give time the same meaning. Each culture will have different attitudes toward work and varied concepts of motivation. Varied ideas of prestige, women's roles, kinship, and mobility can complicate business relationships between members of different cultures. In some countries, such as Saudi Arabia, the very ability of a woman to do business would be severely compromised. As Morrison, Conaway, and Bordens (1994) point out, each country has its unique overtones, behavioral styles, business practices, negotiating techniques, and protocol.

Different languages are especially problematic. Most languages have varieties of dialects reflecting regions or class distinctions. And languages are always in process. This makes translation a careful art, complicated by idioms and terms often having no cultural equivalents in another language. Many American job titles may not translate into other cultures. For example, Filipinos have no word to express "florist" because their cultural equivalent would be a young girl who sells flowers in a marketplace. It becomes essential, then, to have at least two people review a translation. Such a system could have prevented one card company that made Spanish language cards from creating a "get well" card for people who were already dead!

Though cultural and linguistic complications make international business complex, the United States does have many advantages. English is as close to a universal language as exists. American cultural images predominate in the media and styles throughout the world. Despite anti-Americanism, the antipathy that some nations generate in certain countries is far more hostile. For example, Japan's legacy from its imperial past makes it a far less acceptable partner to many Asian nations than the United States. The traditional U.S. receptiveness, however ambivalent, toward immigrants has placed it on the receiving end of a "brain drain," with inventors and entrepreneurs from many cultures emigrating to it. Finally, a U.S. corporation's own domestic experience in marketing and managing in a diverse culture can allow its background of experience, skills, and ethnically related personnel to position itself well into the world market.

For the United States to position itself in the multicultural marketplace, it will need a work force experienced and comfortable in dealing with cultural diversity. This means training. Part of that responsibility will lie in education. Schools that provide inclusive curricula, foreign language instruction, and cultural sensitivity can prepare students to function more effectively in a multicultural environment. Even more important, schools can provide a model for diversity. Students who are exposed to an environment in which they interact with people of many cultures, including teachers and administrators, will be better able to function in the multicultural marketplace.

But while schools may prepare students to take their place in a multicultural society, U.S. businesses and corporations also have to look to themselves. In some cases, training sessions on cultural sensitivity and managing cultural diversity can be effective ways to begin. They may also need to consider other innovative programs. For example, Korean merchants in Chicago have hired an African-American woman to serve as a mediator. Among her duties is going undercover to shop, and then sharing her experiences with the merchants.

Such programs are effective ways to sensitize, yet they are only beginnings. Businesses need to really examine their own environments. Is diversity reflected in their own management at all levels? Do people from other cultures seem to have equal access to career ladders? Do organizational rewards recognize effectiveness and sensitivity in managing a diverse work force? Do policies promote and support diversity? Is one group always being written up for disciplinary procedures? Does Personnel treat all groups similarly? If there is a company cafeteria, how culturally diverse is the menu? Companies may wish to review these questions in a regulated organizational process. Reviewing disciplinary actions can sometimes uncover discrimination or cultural miscommunication. Reviewing promotion records can reveal similar results. One organization noticed that although many of its engineers were Asian-Americans, few applied to be supervisors. In a review, they realized that in many customs, it was considered inappropriately brass to apply for a promotion. The policy was then changed to allow nominations of both oneself and others. This widened the applicant pool considerably.

The growing diversity of our nation presents a challenge not only to business but to society as well. If we can manage diversity well, we can maintain unity and vitality and position ourselves well in the world marketplace. If we cannot, our own sense of national pride and purpose may be threatened. Economic institutions will be critical to this effort. If U.S. businesses can surmount this challenge, they will not only contribute to national unity and policy, but they can better achieve their own goals and become important players in the multicultural marketplace.

References

Edward Hall, *The Silent Language* (New York: Doubleday & Co., 1959).

Terri Morrison, Wayne Conaway, and George Bordens, *Kiss, Bow or Shake Hands: How to Do Business in Sixty Countries* (Holbrook, MA: Bob Adams, 1994).

Kenneth J. Doka is a professor of gerontology and multicultural education at the Graduate School of the College of New Rochelle in New York, and a longtime member of the World Future Society.

Building a Global Workforce Starts With Recruitment

Your company will never be truly global until every employee has a global mindset. If you recruit with this in mind, you'll have global-thinkers—and doers—worldwide.

Shannon Peters Talbott

If you're an HR professional in an international corporation, which members of your workforce are global employees? U.S. citizens living abroad? Japanese employees working in the United States? Swedish managers who are helping to set up operations in Portugal? Or every single member of your workforce?

Without hesitation, most HR professionals would include the first three categories of employees in their answer. Expatriates, usually defined as those living and working outside their home countries, are obviously global: They're key to the success or failure of international business, whether they remain abroad long term or work short stints while operations are being established. Selecting the right people for these assignments is a matter of great concern, as early return or failure is costly and can be damaging to business relations with international partners or customers.

But, where do you find these expats? Do you go out and hire them for the job, or do you select them from among your workforce? Most often, expatriates are selected from within the corporation. Why? Current employees usually are more in sync with a company's organizational culture, and they also have the skills necessary to do the job.

As many HR professionals are learning, however, employees need more than technical expertise to succeed. And, unless every member of an organization is looked upon as a global employee, it may be difficult to find people who have the skills necessary to perform well in the international environment. By keeping long-term goals in sight during recruitment efforts, multinational firms can build a globally aware workforce—one composed of talented members who support the company's global philosophy, have expat potential and can propel the business into the 21st century.

Make every hire a global effort.
Every year, hundreds of companies expand their operations into the global marketplace. At the same time, corporations that are established in the international sphere redefine their business to maintain a competitive edge. For organizations in both categories, recruitment and international assignment are key determinants of long-term success.

For many corporations, international recruitment is synonymous with expatriate selection. Within this area, significant progress has been made to ensure candidates are screened for global competency, which—according to most experts—includes such qualities as flexibility, open-mindedness, technical expertise, multiple language proficiency and the willingness to take risks. Says Shirley Gaufin, vice president of HR for Bechtel Group Inc. in San Francisco: "Global awareness is a subtle characteristic, but it's absolutely essential for ex-

7. INTERNATIONAL HUMAN RESOURCE MANAGEMENT

patriate success. It's part of someone being a good leader, part of someone being flexible and adaptable."

Today, HR professionals in progressive global companies are discovering that it isn't enough just to look for these skills among members of the expatriate community. Rather, every employee needs to have a certain level of global awareness, and many companies are finding that screening must begin at recruitment. Take, for example, Tetra Pak Inc., a multinational corporation based in Lund, Sweden. At the company's U.S. headquarters in Chicago, personnel manager Barbara Shimkus looks for expat potential every time she makes a hire. "We don't often go out and search for someone to go abroad next year. Expatriates are selected from within the company," Shimkus says. "But when we recruit, we always look for candidates who have global potential. We're interested in people who eventually could relocate internationally and handle that adjustment well."

Overall, Shimkus says candidates with international backgrounds are best suited for careers with the company. She says: "Business is changing, and companies can no longer seek out employees who have limited themselves to a domestic view of the world. Employees who will lead us into the future are those who understand business in the international arena."

Gaufin agrees. At Bechtel, she works with approximately 25,000 people who are handling diverse projects in more than 70 countries worldwide. Recently, Bechtel went through a major restructuring, giving its international regions more autonomy. Instead of ruling from above, the company is focusing on multinational awareness and cultivation of its global talent. Gaufin explains: "In the past, we were more of a U.S. firm doing business internationally. We are now becoming more 'global.' As part of that, we're working to develop a stronger global workforce." What does this mean for recruitment? Bechtel is placing more emphasis than ever before on global competencies, assuring that every member can contribute to future multinational growth.

As Gaufin and Shimkus note, it's to every company's best advantage to consider the future and hire those who can support upcoming needs. But in addition to recruiting for expatriate potential, HR professionals are finding that employees who have international experience and language proficiency help the company function on a day-to-day basis. To see why this is true, just look at the operations of an average global company. Managers must understand differing cultural norms to perform well on business trips and short-term assignments in other parts of the world. HR professionals need to be aware of legal differences surrounding benefits and compensation, as well as local norms regarding vacation and child care. Receptionists and other staff members must answer daily phone calls and correspondence from overseas.

At Tetra Pak, global interaction is common, and employees with multiple-language skills are in high demand. "It seems like every day we're searching the office for someone who speaks Swedish or German or Spanish to translate a fax or interpret a phone call," says Shimkus. Bechtel's internal communications staff are regularly reminded that their employee newsletter reaches an international audience: "We're very careful to avoid mention of the seasons, for example, because they differ with the hemispheres," Gaufin says. This type of awareness is needed by every employee. "Every day, our employees have to consider the fact that they're working within a global framework. There are time changes, cultural variations—small differences that matter."

Gaufin says the more capable employees are at understanding these everyday differences, the more successful the business will be on a global level. "Every employee needs to have a global state of mind, whether it's someone who works overseas or in the United States," Gaufin says. "Employees have to be able to look at the company—and our business—in a global way."

Realign your recruitment strategies. Identifying the need for these employees is just one-half of the battle: Finding them is the other. Not all applicants have the flexible personalities needed to perform well in a global environment—and even fewer have any sort of international training. In fact, according to the American Institute for Foreign Study, just 5% of college graduates are proficient in a foreign language, and less than half of all students studying business take a course that's internationally focused. Without a recruitment effort that's designed to attract those with global competencies, HR professionals are unlikely to find top talent.

John Amato, former manager of global assignments for St. Louis-based Monsanto Corporation, says that small changes to recruitment advertising can help companies identify global potential. "In writing job descriptions, get away from focusing only on the job's technical skills," Amato says. "Of course, technical expertise is important. But recruitment advertising can tell the applicants a lot more about future potential of the position when you describe behavioral traits needed for the job."

Changes of this type can help companies get a more globally qualified pool of applicants for every hire. This is especially true when recruiters combine the new job criteria with expanded international networking efforts and targeted recruitment campaigns. As Amato recommends: "Network among the global community. Attend conferences where you can meet other specialists. This can help you expand your global applicant pool." Amato also says to look among the college ranks, especially at schools that specialize in international education. Shimkus agrees. "When we recruit from these colleges, it gives us confidence we're identifying people who have a global foundation and a wider understanding of the world," she says.

Identification of global talent is essential to Mary Scelba's recruitment efforts. As assistant vice president of strategic staffing and planning for Warren, New Jersey-based Chubb & Son Inc., she looks for international competency during every recruitment effort. With more than 15% of the company's employees outside of the United States—and rapid overseas growth—Chubb & Son considers global awareness a must-have criterion for every new hire. "An ideal employee is one who is open to other cultures, someone who has multiple-language skills, someone who's flexible and adaptable to meet our changing business needs," Scelba explains.

No positions are less vital to Chubb's global development than the company's international branch managers. To be assured of the highest quality employees in these positions, Chubb recruits globally minded people to participate in the company's international trainee program. After an extensive training in Chubb's practices and standards, these employees move into management slots.

Recruitment efforts for trainees are initially conducted locally, using traditional methods—local campus recruiting, newspaper advertisements and employee referrals. However, Scelba frequently supplements the branches' efforts by identifying potential within the United States. She says that universities offer a concentration of qualified applicants: "We attend international career consortiums that are held specifically for international students. The attendees are ideal applicants." Why? Chubb is looking for people who have just completed master's degrees and who also have three to five years experience working in their home countries. Because the attendees have studied in the United States, they offer additional benefits to the U.S.-based company: "Most are fluent in English and understand U.S. culture. They're bilingual, globally minded and already have international experience to build upon," Scelba says. "But many of them are planning to return to their home countries to work. We source them here, interview them, then refer them to our overseas branches for potential hire."

Make recruitment a first step.
Whatever your methods for identifying talent, efforts to build your company's international potential must continue long term. Recruitment is just a first step in developing a global workforce, a first stage in cultivating global leadership and supporting your international business. For employees who are already on board, multicultural training and international exposure can strengthen global competencies that already exist. Career planning and internal networking can help top-potential employees excel. And, when overseas assignments are necessary, expats can perform most successfully with a comprehensive expatriation and repatriation program. But, the whole process begins with early identification of potential. "Employees who have strong global skills are a requirement—not only for expatriate positions, but to support immediate needs," says Amato. "Selection of the right people is crucial to the success of international business."

The global business environment is growing so rapidly, you can't afford not to recruit people with global mindsets. If it isn't crucial to your company today—it probably will be tomorrow.

Article 50

■ Prepare To Walk a Moral Tightrope

Put Your Ethics To A Global Test

What seems a cut-and-dried matter of ethics in the United States, may not translate to your operations overseas. As companies struggle to determine what's right and what's wrong, HR is helping them define global ethics and communicate this to workers across the globe.

Charlene Marmer Solomon

Charlene Marmer Solomon is a contributing editor at PERSONNEL JOURNAL.

Global scandals make headlines daily. There was the Daiwa Bank trading scandal, in which billions of dollars were lost from improper bond trading—and hidden by high banking officials. There was the 1995 U.S. Department of Labor report documenting child labor abuse in 56 countries where children are used to mine gold, among other things. Then there was the Exxon Valdez disaster, the BCCI (Bank of Credit and Commerce International) debacle, and the Bhopal catastrophe. And there were other events that never made the newspapers: piracy of intellectual property, payments to third parties so companies could do business, nepotism and conflict of interest.

All these incidents have one thing in common: they're a matter of ethics—or a lack thereof. The issue of global business ethics is the ultimate dilemma for many U.S. businesses. As companies do more and more business around the globe, their assumptions about ethical codes of conduct are put to the test. Corporate executives may face simple questions regarding the appropriate amount of money

50. Put Your Ethics to a Global Test

to spend on a business gift, or the legitimacy of payments to liaisons to "expedite" business. Or they may encounter out-and-out bribery, child-labor disputes, environmental abuse and unscrupulous business practices. As organizations expand globally, HR managers must play a role in helping to define and achieve ethical behavior from employees throughout the world.

> "One of the myths about global business ethics is that when you do business in other cultures, they will have a whole set of different ethical values and mores...."

To accomplish this, many international businesses are creating codes of conduct, like the ones such companies as IBM, Xerox and Shell Oil have had for years. These three companies, and others, including Levi Strauss, Honeywell, Digital Equipment and H.B. Fuller, are taking their efforts even further—by incorporating their messages into everyday business practices and making them living documents.

What are global ethics and how do they impact business? Defining ethical behavior in a domestic setting is tricky enough. Not only do people respond differently to moral questions, but individuals—even in the same culture—interpret morality differently. When you add the cultural overlay, business ethics can become a quagmire of moral questions. Some even say the term "global ethics" is an oxymoron. Is it?

"One of the myths about global business ethics is that when you do business in other cultures, they will have a whole set of different ethical values and mores. That simply is blown out of proportion," says W. Michael Hoffman, executive director of the Center for Business Ethics at Bentley College in Waltham, Massachusetts, and co-author of "Emerging Global Business Ethics."

"When you dig deeply enough and scrape away all the trappings, the real ethical solid building blocks or principles of most cultures are the same."

For example, most people agree mistreating children is wrong, but they sometimes disagree about what constitutes mistreatment. For instance, most Americans consider child labor mistreatment. But in countries in which economic conditions warrant child labor, and laws and definitions of the family unit support it, it isn't regarded as cruel, but rather as a fact of life. "You have to understand the full context of the ethical decision-making of each culture. Once you understand it, you might say it's ethically incorrect without believing it's immoral," says Hoffman.

He says it's important for Americans—who sometimes get too moralistic—to walk a moral tightrope between the two extremes of ethical fanaticism and ethical relativism as we venture into other societies. "Ethical fanaticism is the position that says my ethical position is right, and I have the absolute answers. It doesn't recognize legitimate ethical disagreement and has no tolerance or appreciation of different perspectives, including cultural perspectives," Hoffman explains. "Ethical relativism is an equally bad extreme because it's saying there are no absolute values, which eventually leads to a state in which there's nothing right absolutely or wrong absolutely. It's a philosophical position that says I have no way of telling you you're morally wrong if you go out and kill or eat people because there are no absolute values."

Walking the middle road isn't always easy, however. Some global actions clearly lack ethics, such as the actions of Nazi Germany, for example. But there are others that are gray, such as the use of DDT in countries where there are no substitutes and without which the crops would be consumed by insects. Even the use of bribes can be debated on moral grounds. Bribes of hundreds of thousands of dollars to line a military general's pocket, most would agree is wrong, but what about payments to people who take goods off the docks to expedite service? That isn't considered unethical under many circumstances.

Ethics are a matter of business. In response to these questions, some groups are taking a leadership role. The Caux Round Table is one such organization. Created in 1986 by Frederik Philips (former president of Philips Electronics) and Olivier Giscard d'Estaing (vice chairman of INSEAD), the Round Table brings together leaders from Europe, Japan and the United States. Their mission: To focus attention on global corporate responsibility, in the belief that the world business community plays a role in improving economic and social conditions.

Including such giants as Siemens AG, The Chase Manhattan Corp., ITT Corp., World Bank (France), Minnesota Mining & Manufacturing Co., Canon Inc. and Matsushita Electric Industrial Co. Ltd., the group has developed world standards to measure ethical behavior. The standards are based on two principles: the concept of human dignity, and the Japanese doctrine of *kyosei*—the idea of living and working together for the common good to enable mutual prosperity. The Round Table is proactive in its commitment to global responsibility. Founders believe business can be a powerful force for good because it's essential to provide employ-

---

Contemplating Global Ethics: Where Do You Start?

1. Think about your company's mission statement and values.

2. Clearly articulate those values. Define a code of ethical behavior.

3. Remember that cultural differences dictate flexibility and sensitivity.

4. Develop training in which employees learn—and apply—the company's values.

5. Create appraisal systems that reinforce the ethical behavior the company demands.

6. Communicate company ethics wherever and whenever possible.
—*CMS*

ment and products and—more importantly—because it has the capacity to improve the lives of its customers and employees.

The Round Table lays out seven general principles that range from the general edict to protect (and where possible, improve) the environment, to more specific ideas, such as supporting the multilateral trade systems of the world. Underlying these ideals is the assumption that respect for cultural differences requires sensitivity and some flexibility. One of the most astounding aspects of the document is that it's values-driven but steeped in business acumen.

Indeed, Robert MacGregor, president of the Minnesota Center for Corporate Responsibility—the group largely responsible for the language of the *Caux Round Table's Principles for Business*—sees ethical behavior as a business imperative. "The world has shrunk and is so interconnected that behaviors everywhere affect behavior everywhere else."

For example, although a company can save money by laying off expensive American workers and hiring cheap child labor in Bangladesh, these types of actions will backfire financially for a company in the end. "We want companies to move their jobs and capital around the world while making money, [and still] following responsible standards."

H. B. Fuller Company, makers of adhesives and other specialty chemicals, agrees that honesty and trustworthiness—themselves important—translate into dollars and cents. Case in point: The St. Paul, Minnesota-based company pursued buying a subsidiary from a European adhesive manufacturer. It was the only American firm out of a dozen companies interested in the purchase. The European company was interested in H. B. Fuller's bid. but looked a little nervously at the U.S. company because the subsidiary wasn't making money and had too many people in the business. "Their perception of U.S. companies is that they don't think twice about having massive layoffs regardless of what it does to people," says Tony Andersen, chair of H. B. Fuller's board of directors. "We showed them through oral histories—examples within our company—that our corporate culture values people. That really counted to this large European company, which helped us finance the acquisition."

Clearly stating company values is the first step. H.B. Fuller's situation demonstrates how ethics stem from corporate values. "You've got to think through very clearly what your company's values are—what you stand for wherever you do business," says John Buckley, ethics officer for Maynard, Massachusetts-based Digital Equipment Corp., which has more than 50% of its employees outside the United States. Digital's *Code of Business Conduct* clearly defines practices the company expects its employees to use in their daily activities. This substantial 27-page booklet, which addresses such ethical issues as managing company information and gift giving, provides the wisdom in a specific manner that requires employees to think about their behavior. For instance, in the section on gifts and entertainment, employees are given the following scenarios to think about: "You receive an unsolicited holiday gift from a supplier; you're invited to an annual trade show at a resort by a supplier who offers to pay your airfare and hotel bills; customers are visiting a Digital site for the day and you would like to take them to lunch. Do you know the proper business use of gifts and entertainment?" it asks.

The rest of the chapter details the company's position on gift giving and receiving, its implications and possible misinterpretations. It's straightforward and unambiguous, and offers the chance to question one's own actions.

"Wherever we do business, it's highly dependent on personal relationships between the people conducting the business. By basing our code of conduct on the company's core values, we believe it's more transferrable and adaptable internationally," says Buckley.

Step two: Communicate. Clear principles are one thing, but they're useless unless they're communicated to employees. Digital communicates its values through company newsletters, electronic transmissions and in training programs. Everyone receives a code of conduct booklet, and the company requires all managers to discuss the code with their employees at least once a year.

Honeywell Inc., based in Minneapolis, recently has translated its formal code of ethics into six foreign languages. Senior

> **An important part of the ethics training is to help people learn a decision-making tool—a process for making ethical decisions called the *Principled Reasoning Approach* that relies on thoughtful evaluation and rational process to figure out how ethical principles translate into behavior.**

management regularly communicates the importance of ethics and compliance in newsletters, ethics presentations and other periodic communications. For example, a recent newsletter for the Asia Pacific region included a letter from the president talking about bribery. He reiterated that bribery will not be tolerated at all, and that the company will walk away from business rather than engage in bribery.

Levi Strauss & Co., a recognized leader in corporate social responsibility, encapsulates its values in the company's mission statement, and reiterates them in an *Aspirations* statement and in a printed code of ethics. The San Francisco-based company clearly defines business ethics and commitment to employee respect and fair treatment. Its statements clarify what's important, and what's expected in behavior.

But Levi Strauss doesn't leave the translation of its statement to chance. Since 1988, the company's HR department has conducted global training on different aspects of the aspiration statement. Managers and employees from around the world participate in three- to five-day courses on various aspects of leadership—one of which is ethics. The three-day ethics course gives people the opportunity to understand the company's expectations and definitions,

50. Put Your Ethics to a Global Test

and also gives them the chance to identify their own moral principles to see where they overlap with the company's.

"When people are clear about their own values and can identify the principles that make up ethical behavior, they have the tools for looking at potential decisions and the possible impact on different stakeholders, and whether or not the decision is an ethical one based on these principles," says Richard Woo, currently senior manager for global communications and previously regional manager for community affairs for Asia-Pacific.

An important part of the ethics training is to help people learn a decision-making tool—a process for making ethical decisions—called the *Principled Reasoning Approach*. The Principled Reasoning Approach isn't simply a name; it relies on thoughtful evaluation and a rational process to figure out how ethical principles translate into behavior.

Here's an example: The company went through the process when it considered whether or not to enter the South African marketplace. Levi Strauss convened a cross-functional task force, called the South Africa Policy Group, made up of Levi Strauss' managers worldwide and included people from marketing, operations, finance and community affairs.

The group met over several months for one or two days at a time, and in between, members researched specific issues and reported back to the group. It researched the history of apartheid and the movement of businesses in the country—who decided to leave and who decided to stay. It identified the principle interests and who the different stakeholders were, including the anti-apartheid community that would be affected by Levi Strauss' decision. The task force sent several key members to South Africa to conduct site visits and interviewed the ANC, members of the current government and members of community organizations. Finally, it talked with other multinational corporations already doing business in the country.

All of this took place as South Africa was going through the changes that eventually led to its free elections. The task force was able to make a recommendation to the company: that when certain conditions changed—including free elections—it would be the appropriate time for Levi Strauss to enter South Africa.

Such an inclusive information-gathering process allowed the company to make an informed decision that was based on its principles. It was able to create milestones so the company could judge the most appropriate time.

Since free elections were held, Levi Strauss South Africa opened both marketing and production facilities, including a multiracial, multicultural management team. The business also maintains an active corporate social investment program, which includes charitable contributions to the community—so it can be part of helping the country grow through the transition.

Apprise your business partners of your standards. Levi Strauss also has global sourcing and operating guidelines that address workplace issues. The company uses these guidelines to select business partners who will manufacture its products. Established in 1992, its guidelines were the first created by a multinational company for its business partners. The terms of engagement detail everything from environmental requirements to health and safety issues. Among them: wages, discrimination, child labor and forced- or prison-labor issues. To create these guidelines, the company used the Principled Reasoning Approach. And to launch them, it conducted audits of contractors it was using worldwide.

Implementing the guidelines, Levi Strauss discovered that in Bangladesh, it had two contractors using workers in the factories who appeared to be underage. International standards have set a reasonable working age at 14. When the company brought it to the attention of the factory owners, the owners asked the company what it wanted the factory to do. There were no birth certificates so there was no way to know exactly how old these children were. Also, even if the children were younger than 14, they would very likely be a significant contributor to the family income and probably would be forced into other ways of making a living that would be more inhumane than working in a factory—such as prostitution or begging.

"So, we were faced on the one hand with a set of principles that were very clear, and on the other with the reality of underage workers and severely impacting their family incomes," says Woo. The solution? "The contractor agreed not to hire any more underage workers," he says. They also hired a physician to examine children who seemed to be less than 14 years old using growth charts identified by the World Health Organization. Although not hiring young workers may force them to find work elsewhere, Levi Strauss' position is to be ethically responsible for business issues it can control—such as responsible child labor conditions—as opposed to social conditions in a country that it has no control over.

Levi Strauss also negotiated for the contractors to remove the under-14 workers they already had from the production line and continue to pay them wages as if they were still working. In exchange, Levi Strauss covered the cost of the children's uniforms, tuition and books so they could go to school. When the underage workers reach the age of 14, they will be offered back their original factory jobs. The contractors complied with all this, "to maintain the contracts with us," says Woo.

> **We were faced on the one hand with principles that were clear, and on the other with the reality of underage workers and impacting their family incomes.**

As a result of the company's guidelines, the organization has made an impact on suppliers around the globe. It has brought about shorter work hours, seen infrastructures reinforced for better health and safety, seen fire extinguishers and fire exits put into workplaces, and seen contractors install equipment to meet environmental guidelines.

Translate ethical behavior into performance. Once guidelines such as Levi Strauss' are in place, it's crucial to reinforce principles and ethical actions. Honeywell encourages its business units to use its code as part of their performance evaluations. Levi Strauss includes ethical practices as part of its professional evaluation. In other words, it ties compensation to performance, which includes ethics. Employee's annual performance review includes questions about ethical dilemmas.

Accountability for the company's code of ethics counts at H.B. Fuller, also. The organization identifies people within the business who are in positions that could be subjected to difficult moral decisions. In addition to being sure these employees understand the code of conduct, they receive an "audit" in which they're asked about anyone who has done something that in their view might be questionable. "We communicate that it's really number one in importance," Andersen explains.

Despite its importance, ethics often fall by the wayside because companies aren't clear on what they consider right and wrong. "It's a difficult thing—to understand what's the bedrock that defines your company and the way you operate, while keeping an open mind and trying to learn business practices in other countries," says Buckley. "How do you make the trade off?"

You have to really think about it. Be open-minded. Learn. And be prepared to take the hard stand. "At some point you're going to come up with the decision of not pursuing a piece of business because it violates your values. It could be labor practices or environmental concerns or corrupt payments. It could be that you realize you can't do business while maintaining a diverse work force and that violates your principles."

Hoffman calls it the *child test*. "If the action gives you any pause—and you can't imagine explaining it to your child—then it's probably a good thing to stop, look and listen before crossing the track."

In any case, managers in multinational companies who are confronted with these situations have to think through their own ethics. It's more than a delicate balance; it's a critical balancing act.

Index

absenteeism, 20, 87
acquisitions, 32, 139
affirmative action, 35-42
Age Act, 206
age discrimination, mature workers and, 84-91
AIDS (acquired immune deficiency syndrome), Americans with Disabilities Act and, 51-56
Alco Standard, 169, 170
Alexander v. Gardner-Denver, 206
alternative dispute resolution, 205, 206, 207
America Online, 82, 96, 97
American Association of Retired Persons, 84, 85, 86, 88, 90, 91
Americans with Disabilities Act, 45, 47, 48, 68, 204; AIDS and, 51-56; learning disabilities and, 57-61
Amoco Corp., 27, 66, 67
appearance, personal, employment discrimination and, 43-51
Apple Computer Inc., 190-191, 193
arbitration, 205, 206
artificial intelligence, 106
assessment, feedback and, 151, 152
AT&T (American Telephone and Telegraph), 85, 97, 170-171
attention span, in learning-disabled workers, 59
Axel, Helen, 190, 192, 194, 213

baby boom, 119-120
back injuries, 163
background checks, employee privacy and, 208
battery, and occupational violent crime against public employees, 182-189
Bechtel Group Inc., 233-234
behavior modification, wellness initiatives and, 196
Bell Atlantic Corp., 192-193
Bencini, Hillary M., 81-83
benefits systems, interactive, 104-107
bps (bits per second), 97, 101
broad banding, 166
Brown & Root Inc., 206, 207
Brown v. Board of Education, 35
bulletin board systems, 100, 101
burnout: of executive women, 139-147; of older workers, 88

carpal tunnel syndrome, 163
casual dress policies, 47
Caux Round Table's Principles for Business, 238
centralized databases, for human resource departments, 106-107
Change Agent, role of, in total quality management, 14
Charter Medical, 169, 170
Charter Systems, 148, 149
Chevron USA, staff redeployment at, 134-136
child care, and flextime in the federal government, 176-181
Chili's Grill and Bar, 60, 61
Chubb & Son Inc., 234-235
Citicorp, 169, 170
Civil Rights Act of 1964, 35, 48, 62, 68, 204

clinical preventive services, wellness initiatives and, 196-197
Clinton administration, economic policies of, 7, 10
Cognex Corp., 147, 148
Colgate-Palmolive Co., 110, 112, 170
collective bargaining, unions and, 200-203
Colley, Sandra, 58, 59-60, 61
commitment, employee, loyalty and, 20-22, 23
communication: handling problems with, 122-124; social IQ and, 118-121
compensation: executive, 168-172, 173-174, 175; at General Electric, 165-167; pay cuts and, 156-159; workers', 160-165
CompuServe, 82, 96, 97
conceptual workers, 160
conflict of interest, 236
consequences, feedback and, 151, 152-153
Consolidated Paper, 169, 170
contingent employees. *See* temporary workers
Continental Airlines Inc., 48-49
contract labor, 32
control, employee empowerment and, 115
Corning Inc., 30, 94; leadership qualities at, 125-128
Council of Economic Advisors, 7, 8
crime, occupational violent, 182-189
cross-training, 79
cultural relativism, sexual harassment and, 66
culture, corporate, 10, 21, 32, 148, 158; recruitment and, 92, 93, 95

defined contribution retirement plans, 105-106
Deloitte & Touche, 94-95, 139
development, feedback and, 151, 152, 153
Digital Equipment Corp., 28-29, 169, 170, 237, 238
directors, stock options for company, 173-174
disabled workers. *See* Americans with Disabilities Act
discrimination: age, 84-91; firings and, 204-207; personal appearance and, 43-51
diversity: and cultural differences of Mexican workers, 221-228; and employment discrimination based on personal appearance, 43-51; as global issue, 228-232
Dlott, Jo Anne, 49, 50
downsizing, 6-12, 19, 23, 92, 95, 160, 166; sabbaticals and, 190, 192-193
dress codes, corporate, 47
Dresser Industries, 28, 29-30
drug testing, employee privacy and, 208-209
Dworkin, Terry Morehead, 62, 63, 64
dyslexia, 58

Eagle-Picher, 169, 170
education, and staff development programs at local universities, 132-133
E. I. DuPont de Nemours, 66, 79
electronic surveillance, employee privacy and, 210
e-mail, 32, 81, 96, 101, 106

emergency management approach, to occupational violent crime, 187-188
emotional intelligence, communication and, 118-121
employee stock ownership plan (ESOP), 158
employee-practices liability insurance, 64
empowerment, employee, 23, 114-117, 165, 203
Enron Corp., 27, 110
Equal Opportunity Employment Commission (EEOC), 45, 48, 62, 204
E-Span, 99-100
ethics, business, as global issue, 236-240
European Free Trade Association (EFTA), 17
European Union, 17
e-World, 82, 96, 97
executive information systems, 106
executives: compensation for, 168-172, 173-174, 175; women, 139-146
exit interview, 212
extended personal leave, 194-195

Facilitator, role of, in total quality management, 14
Family and Medical Leave Act, 78
family issues: and flextime and child care in the federal government, 176-181; individualism and, 224; work priorities and, 78-80
Federal Express Corp., 205
federal government, flextime and child care in, 176-181
feedback: motivation and, 111; performance evaluations and, 150-153
firings: employee-discrimination suits and, 204-207; of problem employees, 211-212
flexible work leave of absence, 195
flextime, and child care in the federal government, 176-181
Ford Motor Company, 97, 214
formality, power distance and, 222-223
401(k) retirement plans, 105-106
Fourth Amendment, to the U.S. Constitution, 208
fraud, workers' compensation and, 162-163
Friendship, Commerce and Navigation Treaty, 68
FTP (file-transfer protocol), 98, 101, 102

Gellerman, Saul, 111, 112
General Electric, 165-167, 175
GEnie, 82, 96, 97
Gilmer v. Interstate/Johnson Lane Corp., 206
glass ceiling, 137, 142
global issues: and cultural differences of Mexican workers, 221-227; diversity as, 228-232; ethics as, 236-240; leadership as, 125; and lifetime employment in Japan, 218-220; recruitment as, 233-235; sexual harassment as, 65-69
Goleman, Daniel, 118, 119
grooming, employment discrimination and, 43-51
groupware, 32
Guest, David, 13, 15

harmony, individualism and, 224-225
Harris v. Forklift Systems, Inc., 62

H. B. Fuller Company, 237, 238, 240
health issues, wellness initiatives and, 196–197
height, employment discrimination and, 43–51
Hidden Persuader, role of, in total quality management, 14
hierarchy, power distance and, 222–223
hiring practices, affirmative action and, 35–42
HIV (human immunodeficiency virus). *See* AIDS
Home Shopping Network, 85, 86, 89
homepage, 98, 101
homicide, and occupational violent crime against public employees, 182–189
Honeywell, 97, 170, 237, 239
hostile takeovers, 23
hostile work environment, sexual harassment and, 62–64, 204
HTML (hypertext markup language), 100, 101
human resource management approach, to occupational violent crime, 188
Hydro Quebec, 100–101
hypertext, 96, 101

IBM (International Business Machines), 27, 28, 97, 194, 195, 205, 237
Immigration Act of 1965, 228
impulsivity, in learning-disabled workers, 59, 60
individualism, as cultural value, 221, 224–226
inflation, 6, 11
Information Age, 125
information gathering, online services and, 96–103
information, motivation and, 111
Ingersoll-Rand Company, 29–30
injuries, job-related, workers' compensation and, 160–165
insurance, employee-practices liability, 64
interactive benefits systems, 104–107
Internal Contractor, role of, in total quality management, 14
international business, sexual harassment and, 65–69
Internet, as recruitment tool, 81–83, 96–103
ITT (International Telephone and Telegraph) Corp., 170, 237

Japan, lifetime employment in, 218–220
J. B. Hunt Transport Services, 27, 28, 29
job analysis, two approaches to, 72–77
job sharing, 32, 79
John Hancock Mutual Life Insurance Co., 58–61
joint ventures, 32
judgment, in learning-disabled workers, 59, 60

keiretsu, Japanese, 220
kiosks, 32, 33, 104
knowledge workers, 60
Koch, William, 30–31

Landrum-Griffin Act, 205
Lau Technologies, 28–29
layoffs, vs. pay cuts, 156–159
leadership, qualities of, 125–128, 129
learning disabilities, managing employees with, 57–61
legal issues: and employees' right to privacy, 208–210; and employment discrimination based on personal appearance, 48–49; firings and, 204–207; sexual harassment and, 62–64, 68–69
Levi Strauss, 237, 238–239
lifetime employment, in Japan, 218–220
Linville, Jan, 57, 61
loss procedure manual, for workers' compensation, 163
loyalty, and social contract between worker and corporation, 19–26

Madsen, Dave, 81–83
mailing lists, e-mail and, 98, 101
Malcolm Baldrige Quality Award, 112
managed health care, 161
management approach, to occupational violent crime, 188
management, human resource, 13–19
marketing strategies, diversity and, 230–231
Martindale, Lee, 44–45
masculinity, as cultural value, 221, 222
mature employees, recruitment of, 84–91
McDonald's, 85, 87, 88–89, 191, 193, 195, 210
mediation, 205; in sexual harassment suits, 63–64
memory, in learning-disabled workers, 59
men, midlife crisis of, 141
mergers, 32, 139
Mexico, cultural differences in managing workers of, 221–228
Microsoft Corp., 27, 97
midlife crisis, of executive women, 139–146
minimum wage, 12
modeling/forecasting software systems, 106
modem, 96, 101
Monsanto Corp., 16, 170, 234
Morem, Susan, 49–50
motivation, 110–113; improving, 147–149; of older employees, 87
multiculturalism. *See* diversity
multinational corporations (MNCs), 13, 234; sexual harassment and, 65–69

NAFTA (North American Free Trade Agreement), 221
National Health Service, Britain's, 14–15
National Institute of Occupational Safety and Health (NIOSH), 183, 184, 186, 187
negligent hiring, 208
nepotism, 236
networking, online services and, 96–103
Newmont Mining, 169, 170
newsgroups, 96, 101
nonverbal cues, communication and, 118, 119

observation, feedback and, 151, 152
obsolescence, career, 88
Occupational Safety and Health Administration (OSHA), 102
occupational violent crime, 182–189
off-duty behavior, employee privacy and, 209–210
older workers, recruitment of, 84–91
ombudsman, 205
online services, as recruitment resource, 81–83, 96–103
organization man, 20
outsourcing, 32, 34

part-time employment, 32

paternalism: individualism and, 225–226; in relationship between worker and corporation, 19–20, 25
pay cuts, vs. layoffs, 156–159. *See also* compensation
performance evaluations, feedback and, 150–153
performance-based compensation systems, 23
performance-based management, 112
performance-share stock options, executive compensation and, 168–172
perseveration, in learning-disabled workers, 59, 60
persistent generalized lymphadenopathy, 53, 54
personal appearance, employment discrimination and, 43–51
personal growth leave, 191, 193
personalization, power distance and, 223–224
phased retirement, 91
plateauing, career, 88
Polaroid Corp., 205, 207
polygraph testing, 209
position classification questionnaire, as job analysis method, 72–77
power distance, as cultural value, 221, 222–224
PPG Industries Inc., 66, 68
preemployment physicals, workers' compensation and, 163–164
preferred provider organizations, health, 161
prevention approach, to occupational violent crime, 187
principle-based negotiations, collective bargaining and, 200–203
principled reasoning approach, to business ethics, 239
privacy, employees' right to, 208–210
public employees, workplace violence against, 182–189
Public Law 99-196, 177

Quality Manager, role of, in total quality management, 14

racial issues, affirmative action and, 35–42
rape, and occupational violent crime against public employees, 182–189
Reace, Diana, 190, 194
reasonable accommodation, of disabled workers, 54, 59–60
reciprocity, employee loyalty and, 21
recognition, motivation and, 148–149
recruitment, 92–95; as global issue, 235–237; Internet and, 81–83, 96–103; of older workers, 84–91
Reflexite Corp., Business Decline Contingency Plan of, 156–159
Rehabilitation Act of 1973, 45
Reich, Robert, interview with, 6–12
Reisman, Elaine, 58, 59, 60, 61
repetitive motion injuries, 163
retirement, phased, 91
rewards: compensation and, 166–167; motivation and, 148–149
Rexor Corp., 30–31
Rockwell International Corp., 170, 204, 205–206, 207

safety, workplace, 160–161
search and seizure, unreasonable, employee drug testing and, 208–209

Securities and Exchange Commission, 169, 171, 206
self-esteem, in learning disabled workers, 59
service delivery model, of human resources, 32–34
sexism, 140; executive women and, 137–138
sexual harassment, 62–64, 65–69, 184, 201
Sherman Antitrust Act, 206
Simons, George, 49, 50
SmithKline Beecham, 66, 67
snail mail, 101, 103
social contract, breaking of, between workers and management, 10, 19–26
social IQ, communication and, 118–121
Social Security, 88, 104, 177
social service leave, 192, 193, 194
special enhanced leave of absence, 192
spin-offs, 32
staff development, at local universities, 132–133
Staples, 98, 103
stock options, executive compensation and, 168–172, 173–174, 175
strategic alliances, 27–31
stress, workplace, 54; sabbatical leave and, 190–195
Supreme Court, 61, 208. *See also* individual cases
Sysco, 169, 170
Systems West Computer Resources, 81

Tandem Computers Inc., 190, 193, 194
target hardening, terrorism and, 186
task inventory, as job analysis method, 72–77
telecommuting, 32, 78–79
Telnet, 98, 101
temporary personnel, 79, 193, 213–215
termination. *See* firings
terrorism, 186, 187
Texas Instruments, 92–93, 170
Texas Refinery Corp., 85, 89
Thurow, Lester, 125–126
Time Inc., 191, 193
total quality management, 14
training: of older workers, 88–89; staff redeployment and, 134–136
Trible Amendment, 177
trust, downsizing and, 9
turnover, employee, 20, 87

uncertainty avoidance, as cultural value, 221, 226–227
unemployment, 6, 7
unions, trade, 10; collective bargaining and, 200–203; HR management and, 15–17
United Healthcare Corp., 173, 174
universities, staff development programs at, 132–133
Usenet, 98, 101
utilitarianism, 19, 21, 22, 25

value added, human resources services and, 32–34
violence, workplace, against public employees, 182–189

Wal-Mart, 209–210
Walt Disney Co., 49, 170
weight, employment discrimination and, 43–51
wellness programs, 196–197
Wells Fargo & Co., 191, 192, 193–194
women: executive, 137–138, 139–146; and flextime and childcare in the federal government, 176–181
workers' compensation 160–164; occupational violent crime and, 184–185
Workplace Industrial Relations Survey (WIRS), 13
workplace violence, against public employees, 182–189
World Wide Web, 96, 101
wrongful termination, 211
Wymer, John F., 62, 63, 64

Xerox Corp., 79, 192, 193, 237

Zivolich, Steve, 58, 60, 61

Credits/Acknowledgments

Cover design by Charles Vitelli

1. Human Resource Management in Perspective
Facing overview—Dushkin Publishing Group illustration by Mike Eagle. 44—Capital Cities/ABC Inc. photo by George Lange.

2. Meeting Human Resource Requirements
Facing overview—TRW Incorporated photo.

3. Creating a Productive Work Environment
Facing overview—Buick Motor Division photo.

4. Developing Effective Human Resources
Facing overview—TRW Incorporated photo.

5. Implementing Compensation and Security
Facing overview—TRW Incorporated photo.

6. Fostering Employee/Management Relationships
Facing overview—TRW Incorporated photo.

7. International Human Resource Management
Facing overview—TRW Incorporated photo.

PHOTOCOPY THIS PAGE!!!

ANNUAL EDITIONS ARTICLE REVIEW FORM

■ NAME: _____ DATE: _____

■ TITLE AND NUMBER OF ARTICLE: _____

■ BRIEFLY STATE THE MAIN IDEA OF THIS ARTICLE: _____
_____

■ LIST THREE IMPORTANT FACTS THAT THE AUTHOR USES TO SUPPORT THE MAIN IDEA:
_____
_____
_____
_____

■ WHAT INFORMATION OR IDEAS DISCUSSED IN THIS ARTICLE ARE ALSO DISCUSSED IN YOUR TEXTBOOK OR OTHER READINGS THAT YOU HAVE DONE? LIST THE TEXTBOOK CHAPTERS AND PAGE NUMBERS:
_____
_____
_____
_____
_____

■ LIST ANY EXAMPLES OF BIAS OR FAULTY REASONING THAT YOU FOUND IN THE ARTICLE:
_____
_____
_____
_____

■ LIST ANY NEW TERMS/CONCEPTS THAT WERE DISCUSSED IN THE ARTICLE, AND WRITE A SHORT DEFINITION:
_____
_____
_____
_____

*Your instructor may require you to use this ANNUAL EDITIONS Article Review Form in any number of ways: for articles that are assigned, for extra credit, as a tool to assist in developing assigned papers, or simply for your own reference. Even if it is not required, we encourage you to photocopy and use this page; you will find that reflecting on the articles will greatly enhance the information from your text.

We Want Your Advice

ANNUAL EDITIONS revisions depend on two major opinion sources: one is our Advisory Board, listed in the front of this volume, which works with us in scanning the thousands of articles published in the public press each year; the other is you—the person actually using the book. Please help us and the users of the next edition by completing the prepaid article rating form on this page and returning it to us. Thank you for your help!

ANNUAL EDITIONS: HUMAN RESOURCES 97/98
Article Rating Form

Here is an opportunity for you to have direct input into the next revision of this volume. We would like you to rate each of the 48 articles listed below, using the following scale:

1. **Excellent: should definitely be retained**
2. **Above average: should probably be retained**
3. **Below average: should probably be deleted**
4. **Poor: should definitely be deleted**

Your ratings will play a vital part in the next revision. So please mail this prepaid form to us just as soon as you complete it.
Thanks for your help!

Rating	Article	Rating	Article
	1. Has Downsizing Gone Too Far?		25. Send Managers Back to School at the Local University
	2. Does Human Resource Management Make a Difference?		26. New Skills Equal New Opportunities
	3. People and Their Organizations: Rethinking the Assumptions		27. Women in American Boardrooms: Through a Glass, Darkly
	4. Wedding HR to Strategic Alliances		28. Executive Women Confront Midlife Crisis
	5. Do Your Human Resources Add Value?		29. Improving Worker Performance
	6. Moment of Truth for the Class of '70		30. Painless Performance Evaluations
	7. Does Image Matter?		31. Share the Pain to Share the Gain
	8. The Americans with Disabilities Act and the Workplace: Management's Responsibilities in AIDS-Related Situations		32. Nine Practical Suggestions for Streamlining Workers' Compensation Costs
			33. Risky Business: The New Pay Game
			34. The Long and Winding Road
	9. Get the Best from Employees with Learning Disabilities		35. And You Thought CEOs Were Overpaid
			36. The Need for Greed
	10. Sexual Harassment: Reducing the Risks		37. Balancing Work and Family Responsibilities: Flextime and Child Care in the Federal Government
	11. When Sexual Harassment Is a Foreign Affair		
	12. Manage Work Better to Better Manage Human Resources: A Comparative Study of Two Approaches to Job Analysis		38. Violence in the American Workplace: Challenges to the Public Employer
			39. Workers Take Leave of Job Stress
	13. Family or Work? A Matter of Priorities		40. Surveys Document Wellness Initiatives, Link Health Risks to Higher Plan Costs
	14. How to Recruit Online		
	15. Unlock the Potential of Older Workers		41. Putting Collective Back into Bargaining
	16. Attracting the Right Employees—and Keeping Them		42. When the Fired Fight Back
	17. Catch the Wave as HR Goes Online		43. Privacy
	18. Interactive Benefits Systems Save Time and Dollars for Employers, Employees		44. Terminating Problem Employees
			45. Are Your Temps Doing Their Best?
	19. The Top 20 Ways to Motivate Employees		46. Jobs for Life: Why Japan Won't Give Them Up
	20. Empowerment		47. Managing Human Resources in Mexico: A Cultural Understanding
	21. Social IQ and MBAs		
	22. Handling Communication Problems		48. Dealing with Diversity: The Coming Challenge to American Business
	23. Leadership		
	24. Not Enough Generals Were Killed!		49. Building a Global Workforce Starts with Recruitment

(Continued on next page)

ABOUT YOU

Name _____ Date _____

Are you a teacher? ❏ Or a student? ❏

Your school name _____

Department _____

Address _____

City _____ State _____ Zip _____

School telephone # _____

YOUR COMMENTS ARE IMPORTANT TO US!

Please fill in the following information:
For which course did you use this book? _____
Did you use a text with this ANNUAL EDITION? ❏ yes ❏ no
What was the title of the text? _____
What are your general reactions to the Annual Editions concept?

Have you read any particular articles recently that you think should be included in the next edition?

Are there any articles you feel should be replaced in the next edition? Why?

Are there other areas of study that you feel would utilize an ANNUAL EDITION?

May we contact you for editorial input?

May we quote your comments?

ANNUAL EDITIONS: HUMAN RESOURCES 97/98

| BUSINESS REPLY MAIL |
| First Class   Permit No. 84   Guilford, CT |

Postage will be paid by addressee

Dushkin/McGraw·Hill
Sluice Dock
Guilford, Connecticut 06437

No Postage
Necessary
if Mailed
in the
United States